THE SPIRIT OF FRENCH CAPITALISM

CURRENCIES

New Thinking for Financial Times
STEFAN EICH AND MARTIJN KONINGS, EDITORS

The Spirit of French Capitalism

Economic Theology in the Age of Enlightenment

CHARLY COLEMAN

STANFORD UNIVERSITY PRESS
Stanford, California

STANFORD UNIVERSITY PRESS
Stanford, California

© 2021 by the Board of Trustees of the Leland Stanford Junior University.
All rights reserved.

No part of this book may be reproduced or transmitted in any form or by any means, electronic or mechanical, including photocopying and recording, or in any information storage or retrieval system without the prior written permission of Stanford University Press.

Printed in the United States of America on acid-free, archival-quality paper

Library of Congress Cataloging-in-Publication Data
Names: Coleman, Charly, author.
Title: The spirit of French capitalism : economic theology in the age of
  Enlightenment / Charly Coleman.
Other titles: Currencies (Series)
Description: Stanford, California : Stanford University Press, 2021. |
  Series: Currencies : new thinking for financial times |
  Includes bibliographical references and index.
Identifiers: LCCN 2020020357 (print) | LCCN 2020020358 (ebook) |
  ISBN 9781503608436 (cloth) | ISBN 9781503614826 (paperback) |
  ISBN 9781503614833 (epub)
Subjects: LCSH: Capitalism—Religious aspects—Catholic Church. |
  Economics—Religious aspects—Catholic Church. | Capitalism—France—
  History—18th century. | France—Church history—18th century.
Classification: LCC BX1795.C35 C65 2021 (print) |
  LCC BX1795.C35 (ebook) | DDC 261.8/508828244—dc23
LC record available at https://lccn.loc.gov/2020020357
LC ebook record available at https://lccn.loc.gov/2020020358

Cover design: Rob Ehle

Cover image: Saint Sacrement, Houilles (Yvelines), Église paroissiale Saint-Nicolas, Confrérie du Saint Sacrement, 1836. Bibliothèque de l'Institut national d'histoire de l'art, Collections Jacques Doucet, OB 2 (54).

Typeset by Kevin Barrett Kane in 10/15 Janson Text

Contents

List of Figures   vii

Acknowledgments   ix

INTRODUCTION   1

1 **THE ECONOMY OF THE MYSTERIES**   29
2 **PERPETUAL PENANCE AND FREQUENT COMMUNION**   69
3 **THE SPIRIT OF SPECULATION**   101
4 **USURY REDEEMED**   139
5 **THE CULT OF CONSUMPTION**   175
6 **LUXURY AND THE ORIGINS OF THE FETISH**   211
   EPILOGUE: ENCOUNTERS WITH ECONOMIC THEOLOGY   253

Notes   273

Bibliography   315

Index   357

Figures

0.1 Bernard Picart, *Les vertus de l'Agnus Dei* (1723)   2

1.1 Nicolas Henri Tardieu and F. Desbrulins, *Loüé soit le très saint sacrement de l'autel* (1731)   30

1.2 Tardieu and Desbrulins, *Loüé soit le très saint sacrement de l'autel* (detail)   31

2.1 *Custos unitatis schismatis ultrix* (1752)   70

3.1 *Arlequyn actionist* (ca. 1720)   102

3.2 *Arlequyn actionist* (detail)   103

3.3 Workshop of Bartolomeus Zeitblom, panel representing a mystic mill (n.d., ca. 1455–1522)   104

4.1 *Les ordres du roy exécutez par sa chambre de justice pour punir le vice, abolir l'usure et faire regner l'abondance et la paix dans ses états* (1717)   140

5.1 *Le moine secularisé* (1678)   176

5.2 Rosary (eighteenth century)   191

5.3 Rosary, consisting of ten beads (eighteenth century)   192

5.4 Bernard Picart, *Religieux en noir avec un chapelet à la façon des catholiques* (1728)   205

6.1 Hyacinthe Rigaud, *Charles de Saint-Albin, Archbishop of Cambrai* (1723)   212

7.1 House of Chanel, ensemble (ca. 1927)   269

7.2 House of Dior, wedding ensemble (1968–69)   270

Acknowledgments

Since grace figures as a major theme in this book, it seems especially fitting to recognize those to whom I owe its existence. A Chamberlain Fellowship for Junior Faculty from Columbia University funded the initial research. The School of Social Science at the Institute for Advanced Study in Princeton offered the ideal environment for writing the first draft. Didier Fassin set a rigorous tone in our weekly seminars. Joan Scott inspired me every single day; I am honored to call her a friend. IAS fosters new and often lasting partnerships with scholars from around the world. I am lucky to have met Johanna Bockman, Peter Coviello, Sara Farris, John Modern, Peter Thomas, and Andrew Zimmerman—fellow travelers, intellectual and otherwise. The Heyman Center for the Humanities at Columbia gave me the space to see the work to completion. I especially thank the Center's executive director, Eileen Gillooly, and the seminar conveners, Eugenia Lean and Dorothea von Mücke. A Lenfest Junior Faculty Development Grant from Columbia has allowed me to meet final production costs.

Colleagues offered assistance at every turn. From Paris to Palo Alto, my fellow *dix-huitièmistes* Keith Baker, David Bell, Dan Edelstein, Jan Goldstein, Gary Kates, Anthony LaVopa, Arnaud Orain, and William Sewell led by the example of their own work while making decisive interventions in mine. At Columbia, Matthew Jones, Camille Robcis, and Emmanuelle

Saada championed the project in word and in deed. I am no less grateful for the camaraderie of Manan Ahmed, Casey Blake, Christopher Brown, Elisheva Carlebach, Victoria de Grazia, Catherine Evtuhov, Pierre Force, Hilary Hallett, Adam Kosto, Gregory Mann, Małgorzata Mazurek, Franck Polleux, Pamela Smith, Michael Stanislawski, and Carl Wennerlind. Susan Pedersen deserves a special note of thanks. She was and is my mentor in the best sense.

The chapters first took shape during lectures, conference presentations, and article submissions. Peter Gordon kindly gave me the chance to articulate the first findings of my research during a conference co-organized with Sarah Shortall at Harvard. I later had the honor of speaking at the Stanford Enlightenment and Revolution Seminar, the University Seminar in Early Modern France at Columbia, the Social Science Seminar at the Institute for Advanced Study, the Princeton Eighteenth-Century Seminar, the Columbia Heyman Center Seminar, the Eisenberg Institute at the University of Michigan, and the Triangle Intellectual History Seminar at the National Humanities Center. In New York, the Consortium for Intellectual and Cultural History and the Eighteenth-Century France Working Group have provided forums in which I could share ideas with scholars who inspire me: Andrew Clark, Madeleine Dobie, Jeffrey Freedman, Stefanos Geroulanos, Jeff Horn, Lucien Nouis, Thierry Rigogne, Joanna Stalnaker, and David Troyansky. My dear friend Andrew Jainchill read and commented on the penultimate draft of the manuscript. His erudition and expertise prompted me to think more carefully and saved me from numerous errors. Material from the introduction was previously published as "The Vagaries of Disenchantment: God, Matter, and Mammon in the Eighteenth Century," *Modern Intellectual History* 14, no. 3 (Nov. 2017): 869–81. An early version of Chapter 3 first appeared as "The Spirit of Speculation: John Law and Economic Theology in the Age of Lights," *French Historical Studies* 42, no. 2 (April 2019): 203–38, and is reproduced by permission of Duke University Press.

Stanford University Press is a beacon of scholarly publishing. Emily Jane Cohen and Kate Wahl deftly guided the book through the review stage. The anonymous readers approached their task in an ideal fashion, offering candid yet sympathetic advice. Erica Wetter took on the project with aplomb. She and Faith Wilson Stein offered excellent advice on every matter under the sun, from the first page to the last. Joe Abbott's light yet thoughtful touch gave me the latitude to make the most of his copy edits. Heath Rojas prepared an early version of the bibliography with great care. It is impossible to overstate the efforts of Jessica Ling, who moved heaven and earth during the production phase. David Luljak left no stone unturned in compiling the index.

Words could never express, much less repay, my debts to friends and family. They are grace incarnate. Adam Przeworski and Joanne Fox-Przeworski opened their home to me in Paris and are no less generous with their wisdom and wit. It is my greatest fortune to count Molly Przeworski as a friend. Lili Sella is a never-ending source of joy and inspiration. Ali, Minoo, and Azadeh Rashidi; Sophie, Shane, and Jack Johnson; and Iris St. John have taken me in as one of their own. My mother and stepfather, Cindy and Tommy Hammonds; my brother, Nowlin Coleman, and his wife, Leslie; and my nephew and niece Atticus and Jolene sustain me, even from afar. I wrote much of the manuscript alongside Judith Surkis, who parsed each word with beauty and brilliance. Bahareh has remained with me through everything. This book is dedicated to her as a testament to the life we have made and recreate in our own way.

THE SPIRIT OF FRENCH CAPITALISM

INTRODUCTION

AT THE DAWN OF THE FRENCH ENLIGHTENMENT, Jean-Frédéric Bernard and Bernard Picart published a seminal work of comparative religion. Both were Huguenot refugees who had fled France for the Dutch Republic. Bernard oversaw the composition of more than 3,000 pages of text; Picart produced some 250 plates.[1] The seven folio volumes of *Cérémonies et coutumes religieuses de tous les peuples du monde* (1723) ran the gamut from the ancient Greek polytheists to contemporary debates over Quietism and Jansenism. Fulsome exposés detailed the rituals of Jews, Muslims, Buddhists, Shintoists, and the "idolaters of the two Indies."[2] But another faith stood foremost in the authors' minds as at once strange and familiar. Part of the first volume and the entirety of the second scrutinized the Catholic obsession with material objects like the Agnus Dei, which Bernard illustrated in finely grained detail (fig. 0.1). The pope himself blessed the medallions, made of unused wax from Easter candles and stamped with the image of Christ as paschal lamb, which were cast by the millions to satisfy global demand.[3] Picart's composition is a *trompe-l'œil*, with the Agnus Dei featured in the reproduction of an actual handbill from 1662 advertising the "great profit" that the devotional object bestowed on believers. Among other marvels, it "wipes away sin," "confers graces," and protects from illness, shipwrecks, and other misfortunes. Prayer beads, a prayer ring, and a scapular surround the notice as if on display in

Figure 0.1 Bernard Picart. *Les vertus de l'Agnus Dei*, 1723. In Jean-Frédéric Bernard and Bernard Picart, *Cérémonies et coutumes religieuses de tous les peuples du monde*. Bibliothèque nationale de France.

a boutique.⁴ Bernard and Picart's message was clear: the Roman Catholic Church harbored inveterate fetishists whose ostentatious rituals contributed to the wanton economization of spiritual life.

The decidedly Protestant stance adopted in *Cérémonies et coutumes religieuses* foreshadowed things to come: a supersessionist account of intellectual and material progress. Karl Marx hailed Adam Smith, born a Scottish Calvinist, as the "*Luther of Political Economy*" and the progenitor of an "enlightened" science of production. Catholics were, like mercantilists, outmoded "*fetishists*" who mistook the "*subjective essence* of wealth" for an "*objective* substance confronting men."⁵ Max Weber followed suit with his contentious claim that Puritan anxieties for signs of salvation inspired compulsive profit-seeking among once and future capitalists.⁶ Scholars committed to divergent ideological and disciplinary positions have remained beholden to grand narratives along Marxian and Weberian lines, with rationality—whether financial, political, scientific, or religious—serving as the coin of the realm.

Picart's image and Marx's metaphor signal this book's chief problematic: the convergence of spiritual and material wealth under the auspices of *economic theology*, a term of art denoting the economic dimensions of theology and the theological dimensions of the economy. As a historical corpus, economic theology refers to the economic writings of theologians themselves, a surprisingly rich and varied literature that remains neglected despite its prominence during the period. As an interpretive framework, economic theology points to (1) a belief in the economy as a means of redemption and fulfillment and (2) an economy of belief by which persons and objects were designated as sources of value. From an economic-theological perspective, Catholicism did not merely approximate Puritan ideals of industry and austerity in a French religious context; rather, it posed forceful alternatives and additives of its own. Nonetheless, historians and sociologists seeking confessional antecedents to economic modernity have long held the British case as paradigmatic. Weber's thesis on the Protestant ethic buttresses the foundational myth of Anglo-American exceptionalism while marginalizing not only France, the most powerful kingdom in eighteenth-century Europe, but also much of the globe.⁷

This study argues for the vital influence of Catholic economic theology as the spiritual ground in which the master-ideas of French political economy took root. It makes the case that the early modern economic sphere encompassed a range of activities aimed at stewarding wealth broadly conceived, from the celestial treasures embodied in communion and indulgences to stylized projections of royal power in painted portraits and on minted coins. A set of reproducible practices instantiated value both in its earthbound and otherworldly forms. Receiving a pardon, partaking in the Eucharist, or purchasing a rosary entailed a transaction with the "divine merchant [*Marchand Dieu*] of paradise," to cite the seventeenth-century religious writer François Arnoulx.[8] Each exchange deepened relations with an infinitely superior party who stored up every good imaginable yet was equally willing to disburse them without limit.

Under the Old Regime, the clergy were both practically and theoretically entangled in a host of economic affairs. The French or Gallican church performed functions associated with a state bank, regularly transferring massive sums to the monarchy as the lender of first and last resort. Beyond providing financial services to the crown, ecclesiastics administered a vast spiritual economy, redeeming the debt of sin and distributing the bounty of grace through the sacraments, the denial of which condemned souls to eternal suffering. The potential for metamorphosis, which extended from the transubstantiation of the Eucharist to banknotes and fashionable goods, underwrote faith in the material economy as a realm of mysterious forces endowed with procreative agency. Astute yet ambivalent participants in the eighteenth-century consumer revolution, theologians laid bare the spiritual and psychic mechanisms by which new wants crystallized into new needs. Anticipating Marx's critique of fetishism, they denounced the blasphemous rage for commodities as symptomatic of idolatry. At the same time, they recommended mass-produced instruments of piety to assuage suffering in this life and to assure salvation in the next. These ideas and practices demonstrate that, from its inception, the modern economy has reached far beyond rational action and disenchanted designs in ways that scholars of religion and capitalism, and of the European Enlightenment and the French Revolution, have yet to apprehend.

Only by engaging with economic theology can we begin to understand how the quintessential capitalist fantasy of unbridled consumption first coalesced—in, as the following chapters will show, ruminations on the mystery of the Eucharist, the generative faculties of money, the legality of usury, the allure of commodities, and the limits of luxury. Even during the Enlightenment, a sense of the miraculous did not wither away in the cold gaze of calculation. Rather, it emerged anew as a belief invested in the perpetual, endlessly creative expansion of the economic domain. In contrast to Weber, I reveal the existence of a distinctly *Catholic ethic* that animated the French spirit of capitalism. This imperative privileged the marvelous over the mundane, consumption over production, and the pleasures of enjoyment over the rigors of delayed gratification. Although the modern economic system may be said to contain both sets of impulses, the latter continues to dominate in narratives of its religious origins.

The Spirit of French Capitalism

For generations, scholars regarded the French economy as bound to traditional hierarchical strictures that limited growth, from the demands of an absolutist monarch and feudal lords to monopolistic trade corporations. Their findings echoed the pessimism of eighteenth-century observers who regarded debt and depopulation as omens of France's commercial decline and its seeming powerlessness to forestall England's rise to prominence.[9] More recent literature emphasizes dynamism over stagnation and the possibility of change within existing institutions.[10] Real wages for Parisian workers began vying with those of Londoners, especially in the late eighteenth century, although not at a rate sufficient to compensate for rising prices. The return on rents, however, grew by a third, and as the population increased, so did total economic productivity.[11] Excepting periodic short-term crises in the 1760s and 1770s, French trade flourished as never before, with Paris, Bordeaux, and Lyon emerging as financial centers led by major banking houses as well as a network of more modest notaries.[12] The nobility blazed a trail toward protoindustrialization in funding the use of steam engines for shipping, cotton spinning, mining, and iron casting.[13] The sugar islands of Saint-Domingue and Martinique brought unprecedented wealth to planters and merchants, and with generally higher profits than their British competitors, despite restrictions imposed by royal trading companies. Foreign trade quintupled between 1716 and 1788, from 215 million livres per year to 1.62 billion. The state's revenues likewise rose with each passing decade, approaching 500 million livres by the eve of the Revolution.[14] The ever-shifting sands of fashion in wardrobes, jewelry, household furnishings, and personal consumption reached new heights of quantity and quality—or, for some commentators, sunk to new depths of depravity.[15] As Louis-Sébastien Mercier ruefully noted in the 1780s, "the mania for overabundance has impoverished everyone. . . . No century has ever been as profligate as ours. One spends his entire income, displays a scandalous excess, and wishes to outshine his neighbor."[16]

Whatever Mercier's misgivings, France stood at the apex of early modern capitalist development by multiple metrics—credit and consumption, self-interested ambition and patriotic motives, metal and paper money, metropolitan and transoceanic circuits of trade.[17] Its economy, although overwhelmingly agrarian, loomed over Europe as a center of luxury production with colonies across the world. The French government manipulated the fiscal apparatus in an effort to generate revenue and service debt. It even experimented with liberalizing the most precious commodity of all, grain, in the 1760s and 1770s.[18] Ultimately, the kingdom oscillated between two competing impulses. One privileged the corporatist order, the stability of rents, and economic paternalism alongside age-old laws against immoderate wealth creation and display. The other embraced financial speculation and commercialization despite their depersonalizing effects.[19]

The Gallican church, fiercely Catholic yet jealous of its temporal prerogatives, contributed morally and materially to these undertakings both as a bulwark of tradition and agent of change. The First Estate collected the tithe (a tax on agricultural produce that was intended to fund religious services), which by 1789 raised the staggering sum of 180 million livres, equivalent to 80 percent of the total raised by all royal levies.[20] The Assembly of the Clergy imposed charges on holders of benefices and venal offices. It committed to investing in perpetual and lifetime annuities [*rentes perpétuelles* and *viagères*]. The church formed a "state within the State"; its various sources of income yielded two times the amount of the *taille*, or basic land tax.[21] Ecclesiastical institutions owned thousands of properties with associated seigneurial dues and privileges. Despite prohibitions against charging interest, members of the clergy amassed debt contributing to the royal purse, whether in the form of rents, loans assumed on the king's behalf, or officially voluntary payments known as the *don gratuit*, which during the eighteenth century averaged more than 3.6 million livres per annum.[22] By virtue of their social standing and moral vocation, priests served regularly not only as chaplains but also as legal arbiters in merchant courts.[23] Preachers gave financial advice from the pulpit. Religious orders operated poorhouses, hospitals, and other charities. As individuals and as a corporate body, the clergy could scarcely afford to neglect economic matters.

The eighteenth century, long seen as a beacon of Enlightenment, offers a unique perspective from which to gauge the connections between secularization and capitalism. The church remained a preeminent authority in spiritual, political, and fiscal affairs; its clergy advised the government in various enterprises from foreign policy to plans for agricultural improvement. Economic theologians participated in diverse systems of production, consumption, and distribution that influenced classical political economy yet have gone largely unrecognized by historians. This book explores their activities in concert with two major trends in recent scholarship on Old Regime and Revolutionary France that the academic division of labor has set apart: the revival of religion and the resurgence of economic history.

The revisionist literature on the French Revolution denied that class interests mechanistically determine the intellective dimensions of social life. From the ruins of the Marxist paradigm arose a new religious history of the long eighteenth century, a period once synonymous with virulent anticlericalism, ascendant skepticism, and declining belief.[24] Scholars have identified the role of religion in the emergence of what were once regarded as unambiguously secular ideas and institutions. The specter of a hidden God compelled theologians and philosophers to conceive of society—a "divinity . . . on earth," according to the *Encyclopédie*—as an enclosed domain populated by creative, knowledge-generating human subjects.[25] This view in turn precipitated the coalescence of intersecting spheres of activity, each with its own dynamics. For instance, according to David Bell, the modern idea of the French nation sprang from a need to "discern and maintain terrestrial order in the face of God's absence." Political leaders during the Revolution adapted clerical strategies for promoting civic devotion through theater and festivals in latter-day crusades to regenerate the body politic.[26]

Despite fears to the contrary, revisionism did not sound the death knell of economic history. A new wave of scholars, armed with insights gleaned from intellectual and cultural approaches, has returned the field to prominence. Political economy is now understood not as the discovery of eternal laws of development but rather as the product of intense contestation in the face of urgent conceptual and practical problems.[27] The menace of public debt haunted French writers, who warned of the existential wager behind modern finance: states seeking military supremacy would be tempted to borrow funds to the point of ruin.[28] Government officials and merchants struggled to reconcile geopolitical exigencies with traditional virtues. Their labors met with only partial success. Grievances of middling elites occasioned by the liberalization of the grain markets, the commercialization of the nobility, and the expansion of plantation slavery depleted the crown's political capital and moral credibility.[29] The vertiginous growth in transatlantic trade incited thinkers across the ideological spectrum to scrutinize the regime's inability to meet the demands of globalization, setting the stage for its eventual collapse.[30]

Whereas historians of economic thought reflect the sense of dread in their sources, cultural and social historians of consumption find glimmers of progress. Shaking off dogmas regarding the productive base, scholars have paid renewed attention to the role played by modes of expenditure in the crystallization of capitalism as an economic and cultural system.[31] The expansion of global trade and financial markets, the plethora of money and credit instruments, a growing taste for colonial products like sugar, coffee, and chocolate, and the vogue for French fashions in clothing and interior design augured a new dispensation. In 1695 Pierre Le Pesant de Boisguilbert proclaimed that "all wealth in the world, for the prince and his subjects alike, consists only of consumption."[32] The following century witnessed a rise in the purchase of market goods that fundamentally altered how persons related to things and shifted the locus of political power.

The consumer revolution is bourgeois revolution for a postindustrial age. According to William Sewell, Marxian economic critique should de-emphasize the "wage-labor relationship" in favor of "the conversion of use value into exchange value."[33] The eighteenth-century fashion industry acted as a catalyst for turning a hierarchical society into one based on the abstract interchangeability of persons and things. Even if aristocratic taste stood in the cultural vanguard, the possibilities for emulation by the middling and working classes meant that economic and civic equality gradually, if paradoxically, reinforced each other.[34] This transformation did not occur in a seamless manner. French economic operations assumed myriad forms, from sprawling royal manufactories and the guild system to independent entrepreneurs in the clothing trades and rural subcontractors in the putting-out system.[35] The tendency of capital to occlude the labor that produced it did not wish away the work of artisans, domestic servants, or the hundreds of thousands of enslaved persons who toiled on Caribbean plantations. Although Voltaire remained stalwart in his defense of enlightened luxury, a chapter from *Candide* featured the account of an African slave, who, after relating the horrors of dangerous working conditions and brutal punishments under inhumane masters (he himself had lost a limb for attempting escape), quipped that "it is the price we pay for the sugar you eat in Europe."[36]

Even money, the ultimate capitalist totem, remained mortgaged to the past and tied to the conditions of its production. In the eighteenth century, metal currency coexisted with land, rents, and venal offices. These equally attractive stores of value required common effort and mutual commitment. Given the scarcity of coin, financial, moral, and religious credit subtended while also altering economic relations. Artisans were required to possess technical acumen as well as personal honor to attract a clientele that in turn sought to project a reputation for cultural discernment. Completing the cycle of production and consumption, a merchant's financial survival depended on the customer's willingness to pay for goods; however, the timeliness of remuneration could vary depending on the status of the buyer. As Rebecca Spang argues, the history of monetary objects belies the tendency to segregate the economy from other spheres and to distinguish the seemingly "solid reality" of gold and silver "from intangible faith."[37] The multivalent nature of social bonds implicated the clergy, not only given their use of financial instruments and role as advisers to merchant courts but also in accordance with the rituals they performed to keep material and spiritual capital in circulation. After all, the terms *credit* and *creed* share a common derivation in the Latin verb *crēdere*—that is, to believe.

Priests and pastors elaborated an economic theology that plumbed the depths of human desire. Although the church rebuked luxury pursued in the name of vulgar self-glorification, popes and bishops surrounded themselves with pomp. They also dispensed heavenly riches, promising physical as well as spiritual redemption from the wages of sin. The faithful believed that bodies could be healed, worldly ventures made successful, and souls rescued from purgatory through the surfeit of merit acquired by Christ, the Virgin Mary, and the saints. A fashionable means for obtaining these blessings involved the acquisition and use of devotional objects of the kind illustrated by Bernard and Picart. Produced for a mass market, these "populuxe" commodities doubled as repositories of immense spiritual wealth accessible to all comers.[38]

By situating theology and economy within a single interpretative frame, this book reveals the spirit of French capitalism, understood in Sewell's terms, following Marx, as the rule of the commodity form. Early modern theologians frequently remarked that manufactured objects appeared to take on a life of their own. Mere trinkets organized human existence in beguiling ways that obscured human labor and forged a community of buyers.[39] My study historicizes the insights found in *Capital* as a successor to eighteenth-century economic theology without accepting Marxian claims as pure dogma. In so doing, it contributes to the emerging field of heterodox economics, which calls into question the fixity of laws governing market relations and remains open to an array of alternatives, both past and future, for which the classical liberal and socialist traditions cannot fully account.[40]

French trade during the eighteenth century underwent rapid expansion—at once on a global scale and within the constraints imposed by an absolutist monarchy that ruled over a hierarchical society of orders.[41] What concerns me are the ways in which the anticipation of rising material quantities led to perceptible qualitative changes in how economic desire was experienced and how it found concrete expression. Against the dour prognoses of Thomas Malthus and David Ricardo, Marx and Friedrich Engels contended that the forces unleashed by capitalism held the possibility of ending "all the old filthy business" of ruthless, zero-sum struggles over scarce resources.[42] *Philosophes* and abbés foretold this revelation a century earlier. Belief in limitless accumulation did not arrive as a mathematical certainty. It required faith and psychic investment in freedom from want, which political economists modeled in part on the mind-altering magnificence of sacramental signs.

The Catholic Ethic

This book analyzes the formative effects of economic theology in France during the age of Enlightenment. By necessity, however, it also traces lines of inquiry that extend beyond a single period or national context. Debt and redemption were perennial concerns for a church founded by an act of expenditure—that is, Christ's sacrifice. Nonetheless, the spiritual economy varied in relation to its terrestrial forms over time. Turning from the medieval preoccupation with voluntary poverty, early modern Catholicism upheld the fecundity of the sacraments against Protestant invectives. In the seventeenth and eighteenth centuries, French thinkers applied this fortified doctrine to shore up their kingdom's distinctive alliance of ecclesiastical and financial power and to articulate a religious response to expanding possibilities for consumption. The enrichment of the mundane world, then, need not entail the looting of the heavens; rather, faith in celestial opulence could affirm the prospect of accumulation in the here and now.

Accounting for this state of affairs requires a brief excursus on the twin histories of Christian theology and philosophy—one that attends to the deep religious past as well as to persisting debates over the nature of the secularization process. Indeed, economic theology has its own fraught but telling genealogy. The term alludes to Carl Schmitt's understanding of political theology—a body of secularized religious concepts that structure modern categories of sovereignty and the state.[43] My approach departs from Schmitt to align with what Hans Blumenberg has called the "*reoccupation*" of classic theological problems by the subject matter of human history. The apparent continuities between spiritual and temporal power indicate "a mortgage of prescribed questions," the "answer positions" to which have been filled with an unrelated content that performs a function similar to its theological predecessor.[44] To adopt elements of Blumenberg's method, although not his normative stance, the capitalist ideal of limitless material profusion owes its existence not to the inevitable transposition of originally religious values into an economic register but to the unforeseen convergence of theological and material determinants.[45] As I will show, the Catholic ethic evolved out of contingent interactions between the doctrine of sacramental plenitude and the consumer revolution of the eighteenth century.

Since economic theology refers both to a discrete canon of sources and a framework for interpreting them, it has drawn the attention of scholars of religion. According to Giorgio Agamben, theology has always contained within itself seminal economic logics and categories. His claims for the existence of a Christian *oikonomia* from the second and third centuries seemingly obviates the need to chart its subsequent migration to the material realm. For Agamben, following Michel Foucault, the "economy" originated in the early history of pastoral governmentality—or the conditioning of the community of believers as a population—rather than in the science of wealth creation and resource allocation codified in the Enlightenment. As such, Agamben looks to the church fathers, who organized the three persons of the Trinity on the model of the classical *oikos*. God reigned from on high and left the stewardship of the ecclesiastical order to surrogates. Out of this arrangement emerged the distinctively Christian demarcation of sovereignty and administration that structured Nicolas Malebranche's occasionalist rendering of providence and Adam Smith's vision of a self-organizing economic sphere.[46]

The work inspired by Foucault and Agamben argues along chronological and theoretical lines extending from the political theology of late antiquity to the neoliberal financial order.[47] By enveloping the present in an eternally recurring past, this approach neglects questions of change over time that historians must necessarily confront. If Christian theology was already structured by economic relations in the patristic period, the effects of these relations only became fully apparent once human forces of production seemed to resemble God's creative power. Despite claims to universal naturalism, nascent economic science revealed its religious origins in moments of speculative crisis compounded by confessional violence, financial experimentation, consumer revolution, and intellectual tumult.

As Walter Benjamin noted, capitalism thus assumes the form of a "pure religious cult, perhaps the most extreme there ever was."[48] The obverse holds equally true. Catholic theology was shot through with economic significance—not only in the terms of the Trinity or the Incarnation but also in relation to material wealth. The system was general rather than restricted, concerned not with preservation of scarce resources but the dissipation of superabundance.[49]

This rendering of the theological economy breaks with Weber's thesis in *The Protestant Ethic and the Spirit of Capitalism* (1904–5), which argued that the "worldly asceticism" of English Calvinists, Pietists, Quakers, and Anabaptists gave powerful impetus to "rational bourgeois economic life." The soul's election was settled from the moment of birth. No human act could sway the determined course of events, a predicament that led to anxiety as well as coping mechanisms for alleviating spiritual doubt. Although meritorious deeds could not assure entry into heaven, the faithful might discern in their "calling" a sign of their fate. Believing that fidelity to God-given vocations presaged salvation, Puritans glorified unrelenting diligence. Their equally fervent commitment to austerity led them to save the returns on their labor, thereby facilitating investment. Ironically, then, the Puritan disdain for wealth established conditions for its accumulation.[50]

It is well known that Weber's work met with immediate controversy.[51] As Felix Rachfahl noted in an early review, Paris, Antwerp, and Amsterdam had emerged as centers of commerce and industry well before the Protestant Reformation.[52] Werner Sombart posited Judaism as the antecedent to Weber's Protestant ethic in a manner that the historian Yuri Slezkine describes with characteristic aplomb as "Puritanism without pork."[53] Weber sounded an equivocal tone that further complicated his case. The essay's first edition identified Calvinism as "the cradle of modern economic man"; a subsequent introduction to the text stipulated that it furnished "only one side of the causal chain" linking religion and capitalism.[54]

Historians have found these pronouncements sufficiently expansive to discover the values associated most strongly with Calvinists in other times and places. Giacomo Todeschini's groundbreaking work on the economic doctrines of the medieval church preserves the paradoxical mode of the original Weberian claim but shifts its chronological and geographical scope to the thirteenth-century Mediterranean. The Franciscan ideals of voluntary poverty and "'rational' asceticism" had the unanticipated effect of stoking interest in the functioning of markets. Monastic self-denial produced surpluses to be invested in campaigns championing personal salvation and the good of all. Given the order's aversion to handling money, friars delegated their financial affairs to merchants, whom they also charged with overseeing from a Christian perspective the profitable circulation of wealth throughout the community.[55]

In a tour de force of economic-theological analysis that ranges from the medieval period to the present, Eugene McCarraher, like Todeschini, breaks with the Weberian theme of the "disenchantment of the world" while upholding the essential narrative of *The Protestant Ethic*.[56] English Puritans and their American progeny make up the religious forebears of capitalism, which in McCarraher's view "has been a regime of enchantment," if not "a *mis*enchantment, a parody or perversion of our longing for a sacramental way of being in the world." The modern corporation acts like a vulgarized church, with economic science as its dogma and money as its holy ghost. The fetish-character of commodities mimics the means of transcendence without reaching the loftier orders of spiritual fulfillment, which McCarraher identifies first with the Catholic tradition and then with "Romantic sacramentalism." Market forces have perverted the desire for communion. The critical task, then, is to resurrect faith in the "grandeur of God" as manifest in the wonders of nature and in fellowship with all beings.[57]

The difficulty with such noble aspirations lies with their presumption of the return to a culture of belief that, like Jean-Jacques Rousseau's state of nature, no longer exists and may never exist again. If theology has always posited an economy, albeit in a highly contingent manner, then one must face the disquieting prospect that the past cannot be merely lived anew.[58] Religious tradition is no refuge from the economic system that has come to dominate it. In the beginning, there was no Word, but rather a void, and in the end there will be no salvation. The routinization and banalization of commodity fetishism have left humans not so much desensitized to quotidian miracles as dependent on their presence. This book does not view economic theology as a tragic deviation from a higher calling but as what that calling has unexpectedly made possible.

For much of Christian history, the convergence of the theological and the economic fields remained latent or confined to monastic communities before becoming fully explicit in clashes between Protestants and Catholics over the nature of the sacraments.[59] France was the first battleground of the Reformation outside the German-speaking lands. The Wars of Religion (1562–98) altered the spiritual as well as political and economic terrains of the kingdom. The Reformers' doubts compelled the Gallican church to hone its doctrines and redouble its efforts at evangelization. Prelates avowed the Eucharist as the body and blood of Christ, a priceless artifact worthy of unending devotion. Bishops authorized the founding of confraternities in which the clergy and laity engaged in frequent communion and the perpetual adoration of the host while amassing rosaries, medals, and other objects. The papacy endorsed such practices by issuing countless indulgences. Drawn from the spiritual capital of the saints, these pardons quantified the advantages of religious observance in this life and hastened the acquisition of eternal riches in the next.

At the same time, the French crown continued the singular policy of allowing "baptized Jews" to settle in the kingdom even as it moved against the Protestant minority with renewed vigor after the revocation of the Edict of Nantes in 1685. This decision coincided with attempts to systematize maritime law and commercial practice. As Francesca Trivellato argues, the debate over interest-bearing contracts played out against the backdrop of intentionally ambiguous religious and economic policies. In Bordeaux, Jewish merchants remained under the watchful eye of church and state but were allowed to live in relative peace. Nonetheless, French commentators inherited a potent myth from the devoutly Catholic lawyer Étienne Cleirac: that Jews were responsible for inventing bills of exchange. Perpetuated by the major economic thinkers of the Enlightenment, Cleirac's account introduced a "crisis of legibility" in the heart of commercial discourse, problematizing the acceptance of financial instruments that had long circulated among Christians and Jews alike.[60] This ambivalence belonged to the wider legacy of Catholic reform, which oscillated between attraction and revulsion in its treatment of wealth.[61]

The church had frequent recourse to the language of terrestrial riches in describing the splendors of heaven. Although such rhetoric had patristic and medieval precedents, it took on new meaning as the possibilities for consumption proliferated in the seventeenth and eighteenth centuries.[62] In reaction to Protestant asceticism and iconoclasm, Catholic economic theology elevated manifestations of opulence. Over time, it also conferred credibility on the idea of abolishing physical as well as spiritual deprivation through the employment of capital. The Eucharist, a ritual that made thinkable the everlasting circulation of otherworldly treasures, established a template for such ambitions. The host furnished a visible, reproducible sign of Christ's embodiment that drew divinity back into the mundane world with each act of consecration. In an analogous manner, the material economy came to be resacralized—understood as an immanent force with all-encompassing creative power, the prime mover of human history.[63]

As these manifold applications indicate, economic theology coalesced in an array of sources. Successive pontiffs and bishops issued thousands of indulgences to French confraternities, with figures for the dioceses of Tournai and Cambrai remaining nearly as robust between 1720 and 1760 as they were in the mid-seventeenth century, after a period of decline around 1700.[64] A new genre of spiritual manuals directed members in their devotions and the management of their assets. The monarchy, the parlements (sovereign law courts), and the theological faculty of the Sorbonne found it necessary to adjudicate recurring doctrinal controversies—most notably over frequent communion in the 1640s and the refusal of sacraments in the 1750s. The Scotsman John Law's experiments in public finance during the regency of Philippe d'Orléans (1715–23) triggered a rush of speculative activity among traders, who made and lost fortunes overnight. Political tracts, newspaper accounts, personal correspondence, memoirs, and stage plays represented the seemingly incredible scene. In 1720 alone, 48.2 percent of all satirical works made reference to Law, among them popular prints and ditties that likened the issuing of banknotes to transmutation and transubstantiation.[65] The collapse of what became known as Law's "System" locked church and crown into structural indebtedness. A staggering number of treatises were published on the question of usury—more than two hundred volumes, amounting to sixty thousand printed pages—the lion's share penned by ecclesiastics.⁶⁶ Theologians set the terms of the early modern luxury debate with their injunctions against avarice and immodest display. The polemics touched nearly every work of moral and political philosophy from the period, spawning forty-seven devoted studies between 1762 and 1791.⁶⁷

The intellectual, religious, and economic history of the eighteenth century changes in substance and form when viewed through the prism of the Catholic ethic. To be sure, names such as Bernard Mandeville, John Law, Voltaire, and Anne Robert Jacques Turgot will strike an immediate chord with specialists. Nonetheless, historiographical conventions have unduly cloistered the sacred from the profane, obscuring how the Gallican church affected French finances and how civil law remained bound to canon law. A publicist for Law's bank, the abbé Jean Terrasson, justified the productive potential of paper currency in terms of transubstantiation. Contributors to the *Encyclopédie* gave credence to articles of faith regarding usury and luxury. The Physiocratic movement led by François Quesnay embedded its quantification of the net product in a natural order derived from Malebranche's understanding of divine providence. Taking cues from Archbishop François de Fénelon's *Télémaque*, Rousseau advocated the subordination of property rights to an omnipotent force, the general will, that altered the moral bearing of individual citizens.

Although philosophical doubt was on the rise in the eighteenth century, religious observance stood firm throughout the kingdom, albeit with considerable local variation. Likewise, recent work in historical epistemology bears out Ernst Cassirer's claim that the Enlightenment itself heralded a "new form of faith."⁶⁸ Dan Edelstein has sketched the contours of a so-called Super-Enlightenment, an "epistemological no-man's-land between *Lumières* and *illuminisme*," where speculation was rife, myth structured narrative, and nature had not ceased to amaze.⁶⁹ The mainstream Enlightenment coexisted with occult practices—not only, as scholars have demonstrated, among Freemasons, Mesmerists, and other marginal figures but also among the clergy who presided over French spiritual life.⁷⁰ The Bourbon monarchy conferred theologico-political legitimacy on a sacrament that exalted bread and wine as the body and blood of Christ. Crowned heads solicited the advice of alchemists who claimed that the philosopher's stone turned lead into gold. *Philosophes* discovered the secret of perpetual generation in various channels, whether money, land, or manufactured commodities. Rather than the triumph of intellectual and financial skepticism, economic theology exposes the proliferation of beliefs vested in multiple sources of value, from the treasury of saintly merit to the capacity of banknotes to produce wealth through circulation.

A Visible Hand

Historians of Enlightenment-era religion and economics have tended to follow three central plotlines, either in isolation or in tandem. Functionalist narratives characterize earlier generations of scholarship, which portrayed the eighteenth-century Gallican church as adopting mercantile language in an appeal to bourgeois sensibilities.[71] Support for Catholicism declined not under assault from the *philosophes* but because the church itself proved receptive to ideas that showed the inadequacy of traditional doctrines for a world bent on economic and scientific progress.[72] These scholars do not consider the possibility that theologians themselves made significant contributions to financial practices. Furthermore, their methodological assumptions require revision in light of the work of contemporary economists who emphasize the ways in which the dismal science depends on vagaries of faith and states of mind as much as on verifiable models.[73]

A second narrative strategy, writ large in the scholarship on Jansenism, offers Catholic variations on Weber's Protestant ethic. As Bernard Groethuysen described the enlightened yet faithful bourgeois, "Everything about him exuded regularity; he worked out of a spirit of order, not out of ambition; his advancement was regulated beforehand, leaving no room for those extravagant hopes so dangerous to the Christian soul."[74] According to historians of economic thought, the prominent Jansenist writer Pierre Nicole formulated a doctrine of enlightened self-interest to explain why sinful humans were not predestined for vengeful conflict. Mandeville later translated the anthropological pessimism of Port-Royal's moral philosophy into an apologia for greed.[75] It is no coincidence that such accounts portray Jansenists in terms reminiscent of the Puritan ideal type: embattled, hypervigilant, self-disciplined, and spiritually driven but resigned to living in a fallen world.

A third, related approach privileges narratives of supersession, whereby Catholicism, Calvinism, Jansenism, or Judaism, having transmitted an entrepreneurial imperative, recede into the shadows of economic life. For Weber, Puritan rigors silently capitulated to the "temptations of wealth" and "utilitarian worldliness" that structure an "iron cage" of rationality.[76] Albert Hirschman sought to rehabilitate Weber's thesis in a celebrated work on how material gain became a dignified calling. Augustine introduced the potent idea of the "countervailing passion," with glory moderating avarice. In the eighteenth century, moral philosophers turned from biblical prohibitions to a more thoroughgoing account of the human mind. Rather than the substitution of bourgeois for aristocratic ideals, a new order entrusted society with engendering a felicitous balance between them. Mandeville, Montesquieu, Smith, and David Hume articulated the theory of *doux commerce*, according to which self-interest restrained more domineering, potentially antisocial, impulses in a chain of psychological actions and reactions.[77]

Jonathan Sheehan and Dror Wahrman offer a marvelous elaboration of similar themes. Enlightenment-era expositors of the economy spoke a common "language of self-organization" that first emerged in theological notions of providence before being applied to the natural and the social worlds. It gradually became apparent that "unseen and powerful forces" produced coherence out of apparent chaos, "immanently, without external direction." Sheehan and Wahrman explain this realization as an outcome awaiting its cause, which they associate with the financial and consumer revolutions of the eighteenth century. Fashion, sex, and easy credit came to be seen as the means by which egoistic desire led inadvertently to the common good.[78]

One recognizes the same dynamic in historical works tracing the theological origins of the modern economic regime. Dan Edelstein credits the seventeenth-century jurist Jean Domat with formulating a theory of "social naturalism" that adapted Jansenist doctrines "to envision the economy as a natural, self-organizing system guided by the 'invisible hand' of God."[79] Like Sheehan and Wahrman, Edelstein introduces welcome nuance into the paradigm of secularization, drawing attention to the remnants of divinity that persist as an absent cause. Nonetheless, their histories culminate in the ineluctable occlusion of religion. After promulgating abstract laws of the natural and civil domains, the supreme being effectively wrote himself out of human affairs. Sheehan and Wahrman cite Turgot, the farseeing *philosophe* and controller-general of finances during the early reign of Louis XVI, as emblematic of this development.[80] Turgot will also feature among my dramatis personae, albeit from a different perspective. His interventions in debates over the frequency of taking the sacraments, the nature of money, and lending at interest show him to be an economic theologian par excellence.

While this book underscores a Catholic ethic of expenditure as a point of contrast to Calvinist asceticism, it also aims to avoid the impasses to which work inspired by Weber has led. Religion and capital do not stand as transhistorical givens; their relationship must be accounted for rather than assumed from one period to the next. In seventeenth- and eighteenth-century France, the tendency of post-Tridentine spirituality to mobilize economic metaphors in justifying celestial and material wealth necessitated continual refinement and elaboration. Whereas the Weberian tradition tends to operate in an ironic mode predicated on unintended consequences, the Gallican church harbored few illusions regarding the intellectual, cultural, and practical dilemmas it faced. Intramural struggles among the clergy over frequent communion, penance, usury, and luxury expressed their conscious, at times anguished, efforts to reconcile divine dictates and worldly preoccupations in keeping with the taxonomy of riches cascading from the heavens down to earth.

Ecclesiastics took the lead in depicting and analyzing economic endeavors, from public finance to the brisk trade in devotional objects. Yet historians have largely passed over their reflections. Tellingly, the rare forays into the economic thought of theologians reserve pride of place for Jansenism, a doctrinal current denounced by early modern detractors as crypto-Calvinist. According to Fredric Jameson, religious doctrine functioned in Weber's thesis as a "vanishing mediator" of the elective affinities between Protestantism and capitalism that disappeared once the economic system no longer required religious legitimation.[81] In place of accounts featuring God's imperceptible surrender to Mammon, the chapters that follow take up the conspicuously visible hand of theologians in financial affairs throughout the period, from managing the debt of sin to raising the titanic sums regularly demanded by the French crown.

Sacred Semiotics

Each chapter of this book takes an image as its point of departure. The engagement with visual culture follows early modern practices and preoccupations. Emblems and devices were indispensable to religious pedagogy, interior decoration, royal rituals, and the self-fashioning of aristocratic and literary personas.[82] During the Protestant Reformation, theologians debated the potency of images, icons, and relics. At issue was whether graphic and textual elements had the power to summon persons, places, and things. Faith in this capacity had economic- and political-theological repercussions. Divine-right absolutism regarded the king as the sacred embodiment of God's majesty, a fount of privilege with spiritual as well as social and financial effects.

The intellectual and religious history of the period was bound up in the semiotic problem of representation. Protestant iconoclasts claimed that the host reflected its signifier in a merely passive sense. Catholic apologists responded by expounding on the veracity of transubstantiation. In Paul Friedland's useful account of the distinction, Catholic ceremonies entailed "re-presentation," or "the act by which an intangible body is literally made present in concrete form."[83] The church demanded that the faithful consume the sacraments owing to their potential to redeem sin, which the Catechism of the Council of Trent cast in terms of a debt to be paid. Within this system of material signs, re-presentation implied not only moral transformation but also the proliferation of grace.

The most fecund of the sacraments was the Eucharist. The host appeared on thousands of altars at once, each retaining its status even if left unused. Remarkably, then, it shared with money the ability to be replicated and stored, an attribute expressed in theory as well as practice. Wafers were stamped in the same way as coinage. From the first centuries of church history, the theological luminaries Gregory of Nyssa and John of Damascus referred to divine and human souls in numismatic terms.[84] During the medieval and early modern periods, clerics were presented with tokens for attending Mass. These medals, also known as *méreaux*, functioned as a kind of currency for purchasing actual foodstuffs.[85] If Christ could assume the outward appearance of a unit of exchange, it was because his body and blood served as the measure of all value.

The utility of minted coin derived not only from the rarity of precious metals but also from the enactment of monarchical glory. Like the species of communion, re-presentations of the king were seen not as static replicas but as active mediations between various dimensions of his body: political, religious, fiscal, and bureaucratic. "Majesty," declared Jacques Bénigne Bossuet in a work from 1709, "is the image of the grandeur of God in the prince." Given that "God is infinite," it followed that his earthly lieutenant "cannot be regarded as an individual man. He is a public person, all the state is in him, and the will of the entire people is contained within his own."[86] It was only as a projection—on a portrait, a medal, or a coin—that the monarch could attain the absolute status he claimed for himself. These signs constituted his real presence.[87] *Hoc est corpus meum* found its analogue in the formula *l'État, c'est moi*. Material signs instantiated authority through the performance of rituals such as coronations, processions, the healing of illness, and even the issuing of currency.

Protestant critics not only subjected these analogues to ridicule in polemical writings and sensationalist prints; they also expressed their outrage in physical acts of desecration against relics, shrines, altars, and even consecrated hosts.[88] Their actions should not be taken at face value alone. Parody presumed the existence of beliefs it sought to discredit. For instance, when Bernard and Picart made cutting remarks about the Catholic veneration of relics and devotional instruments, or when Dutch commentators on Law's System mocked its resemblance to alchemy, they admitted that their opponents sincerely held the very convictions they were deriding. Satire created a distance from the object of scorn while also reaffirming its fascination for religious devotees and financial investors, who at times were one and the same.

The semiotics of sacramental power structured the imbrication of theology and economy. There was an empirical relationship of identity insofar as ecclesiastics acted as economists when assessing the value transmitted through the bodies of Christ and king or addressing issues related to lending at interest and conspicuous consumption. Metaphor gave expression to a second register of the relationship. Theologians alluded to treasure in describing celestial riches; likewise, political economists appropriated theological schemas of providential order and limitless abundance in formulating a science of commerce. Perhaps most crucially, the spiritual economy furnished a model for the resacralization of its material counterpart. Guided by the desideratum of inexhaustibility, *philosophes* and Physiocrats established the threshold between salutary and ruinous forms of consumption in an experimental, even improvisational, fashion. Having first codified this ideal, economic theologians refused to abdicate their position as arbiters in debates over money, usury, and luxury. Their most enduring contribution was to legitimize the material realm as a field in which ever greater quantities of goods circulated via the medium of financial instruments—not only currency but also bills of exchange and other forms of credit.

Circuits of Economic Theology

Taking up the forms and functions of such emblems, this book traces the circuits of economic theology from the European Reformations to the intellectual ferment of the Enlightenment. Chapter 1 examines the doctrinal settlements reached during the Council of Trent (1545–63). In response to Protestant challenges, the Tridentine catechism upheld the productive character of the sacraments by avowing that the Eucharist operated as a sign that brought the body and blood it signified into being. Yet the prelates at Trent did not merely reiterate ancient teachings; rather, their deliberations marked a shift in emphasis from the visceral or fleshly aspect of the rite to its economic valence. Reverence for the host surged among the thousands of men and women who enlisted in religious and lay confraternities. Members incurred devotional as well as financial obligations, the fulfillment of which made one eligible to receive indulgences granted by the pope. Their liturgies articulated a new Christian variant of materialism, with the Eucharist as its venerable base. Professional theologians defended transubstantiation in Thomistic terms, while justifying the doctrine as a means of spiritual enrichment that assured consolation in this life and eternal beatitude in the next. Before Adam Smith, pastors such as Esprit Fléchier and François-Léon Réguis made explicit references to what the latter termed an "economy of providence" and the "invisible and all-powerful hand that blesses the commerce and enterprises" of believers who engage in alms-giving.[89] In their view, prosperous souls who emulated divine largesse through the exercise of charity stored up riches on earth as well as in heaven.

The Tridentine directive to commune as often as spiritually feasible provoked anxieties over the potential for the abuse and debasement of the means of salvation. The ensuing controversies form the subject of Chapter 2. In the 1640s, the Jansenist Antoine Arnauld challenged the continual use of communion, drawing the lines of a protracted theological battle between the militants of Port-Royal and the Society of Jesus. A century later, the Jesuit Jean Pichon's defense of frequent communion elicited a response no less violent than had Arnauld's criticism of the practice. During the same decade, it fell to the French crown to adjudicate between the Parlement of Paris and the Gallican episcopate in cases involving the refusal of the sacraments to Jansenists. This dispute carried sweeping implications for the limits of royal as well as clerical authority and even compelled ruminations over whether subjects had a right to communion akin to that of property. Set apart by the Council of Trent for its semiotic power, the Eucharist symbolized the economic logic pervading spiritual as well as temporal governance.

Chapter 3 traces the surprising influence of sacramental theology on the reception of John Law's System. Allusions to the mysteries of transubstantiation and transmutation abounded in cultural productions of the period, which depicted banknotes and company shares as yielding previously unfathomable riches. A Eucharistic-alchemical complex lent itself to describing these instruments and their myriad effects. Priests-cum-alchemists cast the hermetic arts in explicitly Catholic terms, likening the philosopher's stone to the consecrated host. Cartesians such as Robert Desgabets and Jean Terrasson justified the infinite extension of matter with direct references to the sacrament. Terrasson went so far as to convert his metaphysical doctrines into an economic theology of money. His defense of the System held that, like the Eucharist, paper's efficacy followed from its dual nature as both visible and transparent—that is, as a means of exchange that not only passively reflected but also brought into being the very existence of wealth. The spiritual ideal of boundlessness drove participation in the System, emboldening investors to place their faith in accumulation without limit.

Law's fall from fiscal grace in 1720 left the Gallican church to play a prominent role in public finance during a time of chronic indebtedness. Chapter 4 examines eighteenth-century answers to the seemingly intractable question of usury. Pope Benedict XIV's 1745 encyclical on the legitimacy of interest-bearing contracts prompted soul-searching among clergy and laity alike. The archbishop of Paris commissioned lengthy compendia on how priests and parishioners should conduct themselves in commercial transactions. Theologians who favored interest—including Turgot, an ex-seminarian—highlighted the peculiar character of money as a substance that could maintain and even augment itself. Defenders of tradition denied that financial instruments could share in the re-presentational productivity of the sacraments, thereby implicitly confirming the association. Even as credit relations grew more impersonal, the French economy could not subsist without faith in money's capacity to breathe life and value into matter.

Belief in spiritual as well as financial currencies extended to what these means procured, thus completing the logical circuit of structural indebtedness and material excess. Chapter 5 approaches devotional objects, the market for which escalated after Trent, as an incitement to spending for pleasure. Instruments of piety possessed value not only as productions of artisanal labor authorized by church and state but also as keys unlocking spiritual treasures. Like the Eucharist, the Rosary attracted mass devotion on the part of the laity. Once established as a remunerative observance, the demand for prayer beads set an entire economy in motion. Confraternities were founded with the ideal of saying the Rosary in perpetuity. Trade corporations and religious orders sold the necklaces in shops and along pilgrimage routes. Successive popes actively encouraged the market by issuing indulgences for little more than carrying an accessory. Huguenot skeptics such as Bernard and Picart took note of the church's permissiveness as proof of its spiritual venality. Through both celebration and critique, the Catholic valorization of *jouissance*—literally, according to the *Dictionnaire de l'Académie française* (1762), the "full and complete enjoyment of the possession of one's goods"—sustained the consumer revolution in an overdetermined manner rather than as a singular cause with fixed effects.[90]

Chapter 6 and the epilogue reinterpret the luxury debate from the standpoint of economic theology. Clerical polemicists—Jean Pipet, Pierre de Gourdan, and Jean du Pradel among them—condemned luxury as the symptom of a deep-seated spiritual illness, with women as its most dangerous vector. Those afflicted fell prey to a delusion that worldly idols could bring the fulfillment that only celestial riches promised. Theological appraisals of feminized luxury acquired new force in the middle decades of the eighteenth century, as French subjects immersed themselves in a glittering market for goods. *Philosophes* sought to distinguish legitimate sources of wealth from wasteful profligacy. Rousseau joined the Physiocrats not only in elevating agriculture as a nation's material base but also in avowing *jouissance* as the guiding virtue of economic activity. Turgot supplemented the landed theory of value with his observation that proprietors were motivated less by pastoral virtue than by the pleasures that money could buy. Georges-Marie Butel-Dumont expanded the purview of respectable enjoyment to include every imaginable good. His faith in superfluity presaged Marx's critique of commodity fetishism, which itself drew on the anthropological research of the eighteenth-century polymath and *Encyclopédiste* Charles de Brosses.

Theology and the Fetish

Enlightenment-era struggles for the soul of the economy turned on the contested boundary separating licit channels of generation from the deification of spiritless things. Although the commodity fetish is closely identified with Marx, ecclesiastics had long denounced luxury as idolatrous while, at the same time, inscribing profusion in the very materials of the sacrament. According to the tenets of transubstantiation, the species of communion contained the entirety of Christ's existence, body and soul. This attribute found powerful scriptural confirmation. In the Gospels Jesus fed five thousand followers with only five loaves of bread and two fishes at his disposal.[91] Sacerdotal assistance was necessary but not sufficient to consecrate the commodities of bread and wine. Christ supplemented human labor through a dual intervention—at once from on high and through his real yet spectral presence at the altar—giving rise to boundless wealth.

Marx grasped that the commodity was "a very queer thing, abounding in metaphysical subtleties and theological niceties." He identified the market's allure with fetishism, an impulse that called to mind "the mist-enveloped regions of the religious world." After the introduction of money as the universal equivalent for the products of labor, "circulation becomes the great social retort into which everything is thrown, to come out again as a gold-crystal." No object, not even "the bones of saints," could hope to "withstand this alchemy."[92] We have seen Marx refer to Smith as the Luther of economic thought. In a late work he returned to post-Reformation confessional distinctions to code the quintessence of the modern economy as Catholic. Interest-bearing capital seemed to transcend the limits of human labor by generating itself. The formula M-C-M', whereby the sale of commodities yielded a greater quantity of money, gave way to the fantasy of M-M'. Here one encountered "the religious *quid pro quo*, the pure form of capital.... The transubstantiation, the fetishism, is complete."[93]

Classical political economy could not account for capitalist production because it confused social effects with natural causes. Marx's response employed religious metaphor to defamiliarize the economic sphere; however, he passed in relative silence over the vibrant traditions to which his critique alluded. As we will see, early modern theologians and alchemists frequently referred to the language of eternal riches in describing heavenly as well as earthly abundance. Adopting the boundless productivity of the Eucharist as an exemplar, the Catholic ethic established a law of surplus with moral and material inflections. The overwhelming debt of human sinfulness was not only negated by Christ's death on the cross; it was also converted into the grounds for the proliferation of grace. Salvation called for the labor of the faithful while still requiring divine largesse. Catholic economic theology operated through a mode of semiotics that vigorously enacted what it signified. This active form of representation, or re-presentation, lived on as a signature, or a literal sign that passed between the sacred and the profane without loss of meaning.[94]

The religious served not only to mystify the economic but also to demystify it. Enchantment at once clarified and obscured. Men and women devoted themselves with abandon to new forms of wealth—from the paper notes of Law's Banque royale to the agricultural profits heralded by the Physiocrats, from objects of piety promoted by the clergy to cutting-edge fashions in furnishings and dress. Commodified talismans imbued seemingly banal substances with spectacular fecundity. Like sacramental wealth, the exalted matter of money and land enabled spontaneous, limitless productivity. Luxury presumed and even redeemed inequality: the rich were implored to give to the less fortunate without calculating the costs. Freed from the bonds of subsistence, *homo economicus* placed his faith in *jouissance*, preaching the virtues of enjoyment over the tribulations of bare life. According to the Catholic ethic, all-consuming desire became its own eternal reward.

CHAPTER 1

The Economy of the Mysteries

IN 1710 THE PARISIAN PARISH of Saint-Benoît celebrated the establishment of a confraternity venerating the Eucharist. A commemorative print (fig. 1.1) publicized the order's spiritual riches. A rendering of Christ as sacrificial lamb signifies the profitable loss of life crystallized in the sacrament itself. A monstrance containing the host attracts the gaze of attending cherubs along with the devotions of Saints Benedict and Denis. The engraving's lower half is given over to Pope Urban VIII's brief of 1641 stipulating plenary indulgences to members on entry into the association and at their deaths, as well as partial indulgences for visiting its church on feast days. The decree is reproduced in full (fig. 1.2), its contents poised to overwhelm the space allotted. As an iconographic ensemble, the image translates the glories of the pictorial representation into the brief's quantifiable terms and points to an apparent equivalence between these registers of meaning. Christ's simultaneous existence along various axes of the composition further reinforces his ubiquity, and indeed multiplicity, as Logos, sacrifice, sacrament, and indulgence. Each manifestation generated rewards through a miraculous act of mercy.

As a doctrinal performance, the image turns on a series of transubstantiations: the Word made Flesh and back again, bread and wine consecrated as Christ's body and blood, pious deeds into exemptions from temporal

Figure 1.1 Nicolas Henri Tardieu and F. Desbrulins. *Loüé soit le très saint sacrement de l'autel*, 1731. Bibliothèque de l'Institut national d'histoire de l'art, Collections Jacques Doucet, OB 2 (44).

penalties for sin. This chapter aims to make sense of these exchanges in all their polyvalent splendor. It argues that the sacraments wielded economic as well as theological power during the seventeenth and eighteenth centuries. With the Eucharist and penance in particular, the economic dimensions of spiritual life came spectacularly to the fore. The host and the chalice symbolized and projected a vast bounty offered to fallen souls. Communion conveyed a form of wealth that was infinite and everlasting, on earth as in heaven.

The Last Supper originated in the Gospels. Jesus likened his sacrifice for humankind to acts of consumption—breaking bread and sharing wine. He further charged his disciples with continuing the practices "in remembrance of me."[1] The ritual underwent profound shifts over time.[2] In ecclesiological terms, the so-called papal revolution launched by Gregory VII (r. 1075–85), which established the supremacy of the church over spiritual matters and precipitated the codification of canon law, also upheld the preeminence of the Eucharist among the sacraments. Before this period the *corpus verum* stood for the community of believers; henceforth, it referred to the Eucharist

Figure 1.2 Tardieu and Desbrulins. *Loüé soit le très saint sacrement de l'autel* (detail). Bibliothèque de l'Institut national d'histoire de l'art, Collections Jacques Doucet, OB 2 (44).

itself, while the church was associated with the *corpus mysticum*, or, in Michel de Certeau's phrase, "the body to be constructed" through sacramental means.[3] By positing the church as a truth that remained hidden, the irrefutable presence of Christ himself in the consecrated host became not only a devotional aspiration but also a practical necessity. Theologians such as Gregory of Nyssa and John Chrysostom employed a range of metaphors to describe this manner of incorporation: transmutation, translation, commingling, and consumption.[4]

The reordering of the existential status of the *corpus verum* and the *corpus mysticum* attended the gradual consolidation of the sacramental system. Opposing Berengar of Tours (ca. 990–1088), who held that wafers retained their physical form while also symbolizing the savior, Lanfranc of Bec (ca. 1005–89) defended the emerging doctrine of transubstantiation: bread and wine became the actual body and blood of Christ. This arrangement meant squaring the circle between Jesus's material being and the spiritual nature of communion.[5] In eleventh- and twelfth-century debates over theological realism, Thomas Aquinas and Duns Scotus embraced an Aristotelian understanding of matter, according to which God miraculously intervened to convert bread into the divine body and soul so that only the accidents or purely contingent physical appearances of the former remained. Such explanations left unresolved difficulties. In particular, theologians realized the need to defend transubstantiation against the charge that it contravened the Ten Commandments, which prohibited the worship of any corporeal thing.[6] Sacred matter contained a fraught but productive paradox. To cite Caroline Walker Bynum's expression, the divine manifested itself through sensible forms as "the changeable stuff of not-God and the locus of a God revealed."[7]

Nonetheless, the Eucharist retained its associations with nourishment, the archetypical economic function. Believers approached the host as the most precious substance imaginable to the exclusion of other foods, taking care to save the least crumb of the wafer and spending lavishly on tabernacles in which to store it.[8] The Feast of Corpus Christi was instituted during the thirteenth century, celebrated in public processions and embellished with an extensive iconography. Popular religiosity and clerical power clashed over the occasions when the use of the sacrament was deemed appropriate. For instance, theologians debated whether the Eucharist should be used in juridical ordeals and considered whether one could subsist on the host alone. Ecclesiastical authorities struggled to verify or refute Eucharistic miracles such as wafers tinged with blood or attempts by the laity to employ the host for personal ends.[9]

The Council of Trent signaled a totalizing effort to impose greater intellectual precision and liturgical order on the church's most sacred rite. Martin Luther exploited medieval disputes in buttressing his view of consubstantiation, which held that bread and wine existed alongside Christ's body and blood.[10] The church responded with an unequivocal statement of the veracity of transubstantiation. In so doing, the prelates who gathered at Trent espoused an avowedly economic understanding of the Eucharist, which stressed the profits to be gleaned from its celebration.[11] This reappraisal of doctrine subjected the material aspects of devotion to priestly oversight. It enshrined the consecrated host as a tangible artifact in a sacramental system oriented toward the accumulation of grace rather than purely mundane advantages, while declaring that the celestial and terrestrial spheres converged in the miracle of the Incarnation.

Although the Eucharist held pride of place in medieval devotion, Trent codified church teaching by justifying transubstantiation not merely through Thomistic categories but also in reference to scripture, especially Christ's miracle of turning water into wine at the wedding at Cana, the mention of daily bread in the Lord's Prayer, and the Last Supper.[12] Equally significant, the council affirmed that the change could occur without destroying the appearance of bread and wine. Such a model turned from an emphasis on Christ's wounded flesh to the appearance of his resurrected body under seemingly commonplace guises.[13] Likewise, theological metaphor came increasingly to rely on allusions to terrestrial wealth and debt in accounting for the host's power together with supernatural occurrences involving Christ's blood, the Virgin's milk, and other visceral manifestations of holy presence. In contrast to these purely physical signs, which posed the persistent problem of either explaining or denying decay, the treasure encompassed by the sacrament was deemed inexhaustible—both because priests could consecrate hosts at will and because each particle contained Christ's body and soul in its entirety.[14] Ultimately, the source of change emanated less from doctrinal innovation per se than in reinterpreting church teaching as warranting an expanded economy at once salvational and material.

Emboldened by Tridentine affirmations, the Gallican church celebrated the host as the supreme conduit of value in a fallen world. The Eucharist figured as a sign, but one that summoned the faithful to consume the body and blood of Christ as holy matter. The seventeenth and eighteenth centuries offered regular opportunities to partake in the sacrament, both through mass adoration and in the practice of frequent communion. Members of religious and lay confraternities honored this quotidian miracle in activities ranging from silent prayer to public processions, for which they received the spiritual currency of pardons authorized by the pope and ratified by local bishops. Theologians honed an elaborate rhetoric venerating transubstantiation as the means of conjuring celestial wealth. Sermons echoed a gospel of marvels, according to which plenitude overcame scarcity, motive was liberated from the strictures of self-interest, and the verities of sacramental re-presentation were aligned with alms-giving.

This chapter follows the fundamental truth conveyed in the iconography of the devotees of Saint-Benoît: theology was always already economistic in an expansive rather than narrow sense. Both historically and logically, an economic theology operated alongside the material economy. The doctrinal system constituted a science of determining and distributing value by way of the boundless riches contained in the sacraments. Human desires found realization not in instrumental employments but in gratuitous acts of sacrifice to God. The duality of bottomless debt and miraculous expenditure concretized the longing for *jouissance*, or enjoyment via possession without limit.

Catholic economic theology transcended the axioms of classical political economy, with its fixation on maximizing production in a world of scarce resources.[15] The Eucharist could be produced ad infinitum and worshipped without end through collective effort, binding creator and created in prolific charity. Such activities would appear anathema to economic rationality as typically imagined. Yet this was not the case for the spirituality of Catholic revival in France, a kingdom that embraced devotional fervor at the same time that the monarchy institutionalized its financial reliance on the clergy. The Gallican church sought to formalize the Tridentine valorization of the sacraments against Protestant stipulations of lack. Likewise, theologians and *curés* struggled to ground the ways of the world, with its hardships and demands, in the inescapable reality of transubstantiation.

The Re-presentational Logic of Sacramental Theology

The Council of Trent galvanized a church determined to preserve unity in the face of impending fragmentation.[16] The assembly was caught in a power struggle between the imperial court, the papal curia, and the episcopate. Military rivalry further threatened the proceedings. Keen to exploit religious warfare in the German-speaking lands as a means of foiling Habsburg supremacy, and anxious to preserve royal authority over the French church, King François I (r. 1515–47) advised deferring convocation of the council. Pope Paul III (r. 1534–49) envisioned a doctrinal bulwark against the heretical implications of *sola gratia*, *sola fide*, and *sola scriptura*. Emperor Charles V (r. 1519–56) favored more comprehensive institutional reform in the hope of reaching a settlement with the Lutherans. Lengthy delays eroded the possibilities for rapprochement. The sessions thus turned to fortifying Catholic orthodoxy against Protestant resistance, above all in matters related to the administration of grace. The thrust of Luther's objections and the church's hesitant parries thus delimited the spiritual economy as the field of conflict on which the European Reformations would unfold.

Theological as well as geopolitical considerations led the council to dwell on cardinal differences with the Reformers on the nature and function of the sacraments. According to Luther, baptism, penance, and the Eucharist passively attested to the status granted by God to the individual soul.[17] For Catholics, in contrast, the sacraments possessed active symbolic power. As a compendium of positive theology drawn up to fend off Lutheran heresy, the Tridentine catechism (1566) exalted the sacraments owing to their economic-theological potential to forgive the debt incurred when mere mortals trespassed against divine commandments. Each served as a "visible sign of an invisible grace, instituted for our justification," empowered to "represent by virtue of outward appearance in their administration what God by his omnipotent virtue ... affects within the interior of the soul." Despite Protestant skepticism, the sacraments "have been established not only to represent but also to produce and bring about that which they represent." The manual further distinguished the sacraments' capacity to transmit "sanctity and justice" from that of other images such as the icons of saints. Unlike merely human works of art, the Eucharist actualized the body and blood of Christ on the altar while also inducing "the grace received by those who participate in it with purity of conscience."[18]

If Protestants augured the modern regime of representation, fixed but also freed by the inertia of the sign, Catholicism retained the long-standing ideal of semiotic efficacy. In France this desideratum was reinforced by the political theology of the Old Regime, which drew deeply on sacramental doctrine. Like the bread and wine of the Eucharist, the image of the king was viewed as embodying what Louis Marin termed the "mysteries of royal substance."[19] Re-presentation called forth, projected, and augmented that which was signified while also mediating between its various dimensions—visible and invisible, material and spiritual. Like the king's ceremonial, immortal body, the consecrated host could appear anywhere at any time. Communion operated as a discreet ritual and as the instantiation and mobilization of an entire apparatus of grace, glory, and authority.

The Tridentine catechism elaborated its sacramental theory within a general economy predicated on the church's "power to redeem sins," with God as a charitable "creditor."[20] Pastors of souls should encourage parishioners "to consider the infinite goods that follow resurrection and that are the recompense of good works." Everlasting life promised a "beatitude so complete, so perfect, and so fulfilling in all manner of goods that we propose it to ourselves as the end of all our thoughts and all our desires." The church classified "all imaginable pleasures" as either "essential" or "accidental" goods. The first pertained to the "vision and possession of God," defying comprehension as the "source of every perfection and every good." Yet humans had no choice but to seek knowledge through the senses. Souls consumed by the "love of God" were likened to irons in the fire, rendered, as if in a partial transubstantiation, "different from themselves, without changing their nature."[21]

The sacraments affected metamorphosis by virtue of their constitution. Each ritual had its "matter" or "element" and appropriate liturgy or "form." As the catechism explained, "it was necessary that words be joined to matter" since the former are "the most revealing [*significatifs*] of all the signs." The seven sacraments corresponded to the stages of human life. Baptism washed away the stain of original sin. Confirmation in childhood marked one's passage into the community of believers. Penance offered absolution for sins committed after baptism. The Eucharist staged Christ's sacrifice on the altar and consummated the fallen soul's reconciliation with the divine. Marriage governed sexual life, joining husbands and wives for the sake of procreation. Holy orders sealed a celibate union between the church and those taking religious vows. Extreme unction, or last rites, prepared the soul for death. These ceremonies featured myriad components—water at baptism, consecrated bread and wine at the Eucharist—but all "imprint[ed] on the soul" their indelible "character," which was "forever attached to it" and had the effect of "rendering us capable of receiving saintly things," thus "distinguishing us from other men."[22]

Even the etymology of the term *sacrement* signaled generative potential. Linguistic genealogy and the history of religions reinforced over centuries the articulation of theological and economic power. Each compounded the other with supplemental meaning—that is to say, with semiotic as well as spiritual value. According to Nicolas de Blairye, whose *Thrésor des grandes richesses de l'Église* (1618) refuted Protestant efforts to strip the Catholic Church of its monopoly over celestial wealth, *sacrement* derived from the Latin *sacrum*, or "the wage or money that petitioners placed in the hands of the pontiff" in ancient Rome.[23] The Christian papacy subsequently assumed the title Pontifex Maximus along with its financial prerogatives. Prior to the Romans, the Greeks had monetized receipts given in exchange for animal sacrifices.[24] The Thirteenth Session of the council likewise designated the Eucharist as the "pledge of our future glory and everlasting happiness."[25] The Cordelier monk and vehement anti-Jansenist Jacques du Bosc rendered this passage as the "guarantee [*gage*] and foretaste of future glory," a "germ of eternal felicity."[26] In so doing, he underscored the pecuniary nature of the rite (as a *gage*, guarantee, pledge, collateral, or wage), the dividends of which followed from the sacrament's productive nature.

Echoing the catechism, Bosc hailed the Eucharist for its unique re-presentational prowess. For instance, baptismal water retained its power only for the duration of the ritual; its value was consumed entirely by use. In contrast, the host exhibited its "perfection" as soon as the "matter is consecrated," which suggested that, like currency, the wealth it enacted needed not be spent all at once.[27] Yet the bishops and ambassadors of Trent did not settle for a simple financial analogue or the reduction of the host to the minted coin. It was less that money fixed the meaning of the Eucharist than that the Eucharist was the most potent means of circulating value, an instrument that money merely resembled in function. Hence the catechism left no doubt that, even among the sacraments, communion "greatly surpasses the others in holiness and in the number and profundity of the mysteries that it encompasses."[28]

Reverence for bread and wine encoded the Eucharist as sustenance, albeit one governed by profusion rather than dearth. Grain, the most pervasive foodstuff, became in transubstantiated form the redemptive flesh and blood of Christ. As the catechism and its latter-day expositors made clear, communion converted the basis of "ordinary nourishment" into the "spiritual nourishment of the soul."[29] This association amplified the social estimation of bread, which had long been the object of superstitious attachments. It was customary to carve the sign of the cross into the crusts of ordinary loaves and to bless those that had fallen to the ground with a kiss.[30] As for the wafers themselves, the dough was treated like minted metal, pressed into a circular shape and frequently stamped with a monogram. This work was forbidden to bakers. Until the French Revolution, it remained the privilege of master artisans, known as *oublieurs* or *oublayeurs*. Flour destined for the production of hosts was required to be unleavened. Moreover, legal statute dictated that the finest grain available be reserved for the Mass.[31]

The Eucharist was characterized by its capacity not only to be preserved but also to transform otherwise banal matter into sublime substance. Its primacy issued from both its particular quantities and qualities. All sacramental rites had the power to alter their participants. Eucharistic consecration did so even more fundamentally in that it affected the human soul along with the materials employed in the ritual. When the priest commemorated Christ's sacrifice at the Last Supper, declaring "Take this and eat it, for this is my body," the Incarnation occurred anew.[32] The miracle disseminated a "grace" that served "to nourish and to conserve spiritual life" while also promising "a thing to come of which it is the collateral [*gage*]—that is, the eternal glory we will possess in heaven."[33]

The Council of Trent avowed transubstantiation, a doctrine long contested among Catholic theologians and that Lutherans and other Protestants sought to attenuate if not eliminate altogether. The impossibility of reconciling these positions precluded an eventual settlement, despite Charles V's overtures to set aside the matter.[34] *Pace* Luther, the catechism stated that Jesus's self-identification in the pronouncement, "This is my body," carried a literal meaning. Consumption functioned on an economic as well as spiritual level, given that it led not to a dwindling of resources but to gains through the discharge of debt. This reality could be ascertained through sense experience in the metabolizing of bread as nourishment. The church thus oscillated between allusions to the physical world and theological explanations that deployed the Scholastic terminology prevalent during the period. The real presence marked a regularly occurring wonder. It signified the existence in the host of the same Christ who had been "born of the Virgin" and was forever "seated at the right hand of the eternal father," so that "there remains nothing of the substance of the bread and wine." Down to its least particle, the consecrated wafer contained a "true body" with actual "bones and nerves" that was joined to "human nature" and the essence of "divinity." Yet Christ's appearance defied physical laws as commonly understood. His body did not exist in a single point of space but rather infused the entirety of each and every host. What is more, the real "accidents" or sensible qualities of the bread and wine persisted without adhering to any "substance" of their own.[35]

Beyond the marvel of transubstantiation itself, there remained the impossibility of adequately itemizing its "fruits" except by stressing the "abundance of goods encompassed in these august mysteries." The Eucharist forged a social bond among individual believers as "living members" of a single body who shared an acute attraction to the "pleasure" gleaned from "divine things" and a concomitant disdain for human objects fashioned in their defective image. The soul could be cured of the "mortal venom of the passions" aroused by worldly goods through recourse to a "heavenly antidote." The catechism employed such medical metaphors in the service of a more fundamental truth: that the Eucharist offered "an extraordinary means of procuring eternal glory."[36] Spiritual health and wealth followed one from the other.

The council dictated how believers should consume the sacrament. On whether the laity had the right to commune in both species, the assembly declared that this privilege belonged to the clergy alone. In so doing, it reversed a previous decision by Pope Pius IV (r. 1559–65), although exceptions were made for the kingdoms of Hungary and Bohemia until the early seventeenth century.[37] There was no advantage to taking one, the other, or both species, since the bread and the wine each contained the whole of Christ's being. The profusion of grace suspended the effects of difference—social, spiritual, or material. Believers were expected to approach the altar in all cases with "reverence and holiness." Although the exact dispositions for communion remained a source of debate, it was generally agreed that one could not be in a state of mortal sin.[38] The catechism further specified that believers should reflect on the miracle of transubstantiation so as to "discern the body of the Lord." This scrutiny extended to inspecting one's conscience for offenses requiring absolution. Communicants fasted the preceding night; couples were instructed to abstain from sex for several days. Even the most pious participants remained "unworthy" of enjoying "this divine gift" by virtue of their own merit. Nonetheless, they were encouraged to commune regularly—or, in the words of Augustine, "to live in a manner that you can receive Holy Communion each day."[39]

Through the Eucharist, believers reflected on the Logos in all its economic-theological glory. The rite embodied "a treasure that includes all the riches of heaven."[40] The meanings attributed to this speech act depended on faith in the life everlasting but also conveyed a sense of opulence in the present.[41] The Gallican church loomed as a repository of great wealth. The accumulation of edifices, relics, lands, and financial holdings gave its pronouncements illocutionary force and social power. The key to the economy of grace could not be material without also being semiotic—or, more precisely, the semiotic announced a new material reality through supernatural means. Protestantism challenged the church's monopolization of celestial as well as terrestrial goods. The Catholic response, gradually formulated at Trent, upheld the conviction that the sacraments produced what they symbolized and in turn symbolized what they produced.

Although France equivocated in ratifying the dictates of Trent as law, its clergy contributed decisively if belatedly to the council's work. Charles de

Guise, cardinal of Lorraine, orchestrated his kingdom's efforts to save Trent from infighting among Catholic rulers. On his initiative the council settled on a flurry of articles in 1563 regarding the sacramental character of holy orders, priestly oversight of marriage, the responsibilities of bishops, and ecclesiastical immunity from civil sanctions. Racked by religious unrest and concerned with maintaining independence from Rome, the French Crown did not endorse the program directly. Even so, the Paris Faculty of Theology immediately assented to the council's pronouncements. The Ordinance of Blois (1579) and the Edict of Melun (1580) assimilated Tridentine decrees under the auspices of the French church's right to self-legislate in consultation with the king. Despite the Parlement's charge that Trent posed an intolerable affront to Gallican liberties, the Assembly of the Clergy at last confirmed its acceptance in 1615.[42]

This measure signaled not the successful conclusion of ecclesiastical reform but rather a new phase in its political, religious, and financial implementation. Faced with the prospect of massive seizures of property, the clergy had already pledged to discharge the king's debts in acknowledgment of his defense of Catholicism during the Wars of Religion. The so-called contract of Poissy (1561) involved first servicing and then redeeming annuities or *rentes* on the Hôtel de Ville. The monarchy failed to meet its obligations, necessitating new terms. Accordingly, the laws issued at Blois and Melun dealt with not only matters of clerical governance but also the fiscal relations between the church and crown.[43] Unofficial assent to the Tridentine program came at the price of the priesthood's agreement to regularize formerly extraordinary contributions to the public purse. It was at this conjuncture that economic theology took a distinctly Gallican form—at once national and Catholic, temporal and spiritual, fiscal and metaphysical.

The Council of Trent bequeathed to France "a mortgage of prescribed questions" in a double sense.[44] Debates over the function of grace as a spiritual currency occurred within the same framework as efforts to strike an appropriate balance between claims to property and the exercise of sovereignty, whether temporal or ecclesiastical. Theologians embraced the logic of the sacramental economy even as they clashed over questions of its administration. To cite a notable case, the Jansenist Antoine Arnauld analyzed the scriptural utterance "This is my body." As he reasoned, the demonstrative pronoun implied not equivalence but metamorphosis via signification. Christ effectively announced that he had "seen the bread as bread until the last moment of its being bread" and then "his body in place of the bread in the first moment of its existence." Arnauld likened the gesture to an alchemist's declaration on discovering the philosopher's stone: "This lead is gold." Lead was not "the figure" of precious metals; rather, transmuted lead became gold, a shift denoted by the relationship between the subject and predicate of the sentence. A simple statement could "indicate transubstantiation," a process in which change occurred beyond the purview of the senses.[45] Luc Vauban, a member of the Society of Jesus, discovered similar wonders in the "mysteries of religion," which he depicted as "rich and abundant mines that are never exhausted." The Eucharist "always produces in well-disposed souls some new degree of sanctifying grace." The "incalculable treasures" included "every supernatural gift," among them "greatness, joy, wealth," and "sublime dignity."[46] For Jansenist and Jesuit alike, despite (or more likely, as we will see, owing to) their pitched battles over frequent communion, re-presentation occurred within a set of economic relations understood in sacramental terms. It connoted activity and productivity grounded by substance but always poised to redefine its metaphysical base.

The French delegation at Trent championed the new catechism, expressing what Alain Tallon has called a "Gallican sensibility." Rejecting the anthropological pessimism of Luther and especially Calvin, the compendium imagined the faithful in a struggle for justification, with the Eucharist as their most valuable asset.[47] Long before the absolutist state perfected the art of manipulating financial obligations, the Catholic Church had carefully honed spiritual practices associated with maximizing redemption. The council bolstered these economic-theological techniques. Communion circulated the power it engendered between divine sovereigns, human monarchs, and their subjects. If sin was understood in terms of debt, God was a creditor no less than a creator. The supreme being no less than the kings of France set the church the task of converting the obligations owed by debased souls into monuments of eternal glory.

Thesaurus Meritorum: The Economy of Penance

Penance is as old as Christianity, a faith founded on human fallibility, culpability, and indebtedness. As Paul explained in the Epistle to the Romans, "for if the many died through the one man's trespass, much more surely have the grace of God and the free gift of grace of the one man, Jesus Christ, abounded for the many."[48] Exceeding the mere equilibrium demanded by justice, the economy of grace promised plenitude. This economic-theological dictum validated penance in word and deed. The very etymology of the term—rooted in the Latin verb *paenitet*, itself derived from *paene*, or "almost"—reflected its origins in the desire to overcome scarcity.[49]

Theologians classified penance among the sacraments as early as the eleventh century. Thomas Aquinas and his fellow Scholastics clarified its doctrine with an eye to the moral disposition of the penitent. Forgiveness advanced in stages, from attrition, or a base dread of punishment, to the true repentance of contrition as avowed to the priest. Sentiment and action thus followed one from the other: fear and loathing prompted confession, and confession accompanied the transfer of redeeming grace via sacramental intervention. The Fourth Lateran Council dictated that all believers confess and commune at least once a year, at Eastertime.[50]

During its session of November 25, 1551, the Council of Trent affirmed the necessity of formal penance with ecclesiastical oversight as "a laborious kind of baptism." It required the fulfillment of three component tasks: contrition, confession, and atonement. To affect true spiritual change, penitents should admit a "sorrow of mind and detestation for sin" privately before the clergy, who were authorized to "impose salutary and suitable satisfactions" like prayer and fasting. As the catechism explained, these acts "mark that which occurs internally in the soul."[51] Yet penance, like the Eucharist, far surpassed the believer's efforts, since the treasure of the church served as an inexhaustible endowment from which to redeem sin.

The clergy further offered valuable dispensations in the form of indulgences, which reduced the temporal penalty for sin and thus the period that a soul would spend in purgatory. Although the practice had long associations with unscrupulous behavior that drew heavy criticism, including Luther's first public break with the Catholic Church, pardons survived the

Protestant Reformation.[52] The Council of Trent declared that "all evil traffic in them, which has been a most prolific source of abuses among the Christian people, be absolutely abolished." Henceforth, the church would grant indulgences "piously, holily, and without corruption."[53] Despite calls for restraint, the post-Tridentine period witnessed a surge in the number of pardons, as we will see in the case of remissions granted to Eucharistic confraternities.

The French church epitomized the trend toward proliferation. After a momentary decline, conferrals of pardons rose under the auspices of the Catholic League during the Wars of Religion and with the encouragement of a reform-minded clergy. Spiritual directors produced hundreds of guides instructing their use in penance. The publications often coincided with Jubilee years, enthusiasm for which continued until the end of the Old Regime.[54] Bossuet clarified that the value of indulgences followed from "the efficacy of the blood," which was "of so great a price that it conveys its value to . . . the suffering of the saints." His prayer affirmed the "infinite intercession" of Christ on behalf of humanity, underscoring the economic relationship between penance and grace. "I acknowledge your plenitude," he wrote, "which extends over me by itself, and by the graces that it pours for me over all the members of the holy society." Through saintly ministrations and divine charity, he continued, "I enrich myself" and "associate myself with your treasures, the immense wealth of your blood."[55]

A magnanimous spirit characterized the Jubilee, a state of exception that nonetheless occurred at regular intervals. Every fiftieth year, the ancient Israelites had observed a period of general restoration—agricultural land was laid fallow, slaves were freed, property reverted to its former owners. The church adapted biblical precedent, holding Jubilees every twenty-five years in the eighteenth century. When Pope Innocent XIII (r. 1721–24) announced the Jubilee of 1725, he proclaimed his intention to "distribute the treasures of heavenly goods." The faithful made pilgrimages to the Roman basilicas of Saint John Lateran, Santa Maria Maggiore, and Saint Peter, all venerable monuments to the church's spiritual authority and worldly splendor.[56] Celebrants could also visit more proximate sanctuaries as authorized by their bishops. Provisions were even made for those at sea to fulfill obligations on their return. Worshippers who undertook ecclesiastical visitations, along with fasting, confession, communion, and alms-giving, were entitled to "plenary indulgence and the remission of all their sins."[57]

Prelates modified the requirements for their respective dioceses and devoted substantial resources to observing the Jubilee—adorning cathedrals and ministering to the physical as well as spiritual needs of pilgrims.[58] The bishop of Châlons reiterated the pope's pronouncement that "the treasures of the Church" were opened for the forgiveness of sin, stipulating that indulgences applied only to the "remission of temporal penalties." Contrition remained essential. "To earn this Jubilee," it was necessary to confess, fast, and venture to at least one of several designated churches in the span of two weeks. The bishop also noted that "the faithful are exhorted to give alms as liberally as possible," a gesture that reinforced the convergence of economic and theological elements in the instruments of penance.[59] Following the canons of Trent, the correct spiritual disposition manifested itself in concrete acts of piety and charity, not as total indemnification for sin but as a means of preparing the soul to receive divine aid.

The instructions of the bishop of Châlons resonated with more general statements on the part of theologians, who found in the Jubilee a reason to explicate the means by which the debt of sin passed over to the marvels of redemption.[60] Claude Joly, who served as bishop of Saint-Pol-de-Léon and of Agen, composed a classic of the genre, *Doctrine des indulgences et du jubilé* (1671), which appeared in several editions throughout the eighteenth century.[61] He echoed his fellow pastors in advising that indulgences operated in tandem with the believer's state of mind. The sacrament "remits the offense of and penalty for sin," provided that petitioners "receive it with great contrition." Even priestly absolution did not negate God's order of restitution, which changed from an "eternal" to "a temporal penalty." These punishments offered a double advantage. Not only did they pale in magnitude to the "infinite malice of sin," but they also provided occasions to share in "the fruit of the sufferings of Jesus Christ."[62]

These glorious concessions drew on the merit accumulated by Christ, the Virgin, the apostles, and those who died as martyrs. Taken together, their virtuous acts amounted to an "infinite" and "inexhaustible" bounty.[63] Responding to potential objections, Joly accounted for how such a state of affairs came to be. Mary, being without sin, had no need for reparation; thus, the merit of her works entered without loss into the "spiritual treasure of the Church." The superfluity of her virtue, then, found its use in "fulfilling the payment of our debts." Lest one fear that the arrangement implied the exploitation of the righteous, Joly considered whether the Virgin and the saints had failed to receive "all the recompense that their good works merited." Although they had "suffered more than God demanded of them for their sins," a just reward awaited them in heaven. The balance of their "superabundant satisfactions" redounded to lesser souls on earth.[64] The sheer fecundity of the church's limitless capital, then, overwhelmed the possibility of the penitents' want.

Joly elaborated the "dispositions" necessary to acquire the grace of indulgences. Believers recognized with a "firm and lively faith" the church's authority over sin and its "utmost generosity [bonté]" in exercising it. Their gratitude prompted "a sincere and veritable conversion of our heart to God" and thus a rejection of "all moral and venial sin."[65] Failure to realize these lofty aims followed from the "little esteem we have for so great a treasure and for the spiritual good that we receive from it." As a corrective, one could ponder the immense "value of all the sufferings of Our Lord, the least of which is of an infinite price." Reasonable souls would embrace virtue after a moment's comparison of this sacrifice to the "horrible torments" of hell or purgatory. The soul grasped its true interest through simple spiritual arithmetic. Joly diagnosed the tendency for miscalculation as an effect of the "excessive love that we have of the pleasures of the body and the mind," including "earthly possessions." Penance deepened a preference for "eternal goods" with "all our heart," relegating the pursuit of temporal belongings to those deemed strictly "necessary."[66]

Joly's contemporaries debated the relative facility with which one might benefit from spiritual pleasures. For instance, the Benedictine Gabriel Gerberon railed against perceived abuses, such as the belief that merely carrying a medallion, or "some blessed speck," entitled one to indulgences without concerted effort. Indulgences did not obviate punishment but rather affected the "change of one penance into another."[67] Simon Michel Treuvé, the canon of Meaux under Bossuet and a fervent Jansenist, issued an even sterner warning against misappropriation of the sacraments. He reminded readers of their "appalling" unworthiness before God, which recommended the deferment of absolution. Indulgences served less to exculpate guilt than to provide "an aid and a supplement" for those who "work seriously and without flattering themselves." Treuvé specifically equated the Jubilee to "a treasure of money." The confessor should approach this wealth as a wise "administrator" who stewarded resources "without passing for a spendthrift" or bowing to "so imprudent and poorly regulated a disbursement."[68]

The Jesuit Louis Bourdaloue proved relatively lenient in bestowing the surplus of "general grace" during the Jubilee, noting that it was "in our own interest and for the sanctification of our souls" to "make the use of it as God desires." Bourdaloue surveyed the practice from the Old Testament to the New, from the forgiveness of worldly debt to its spiritual analogue in "goods to come." These shifts facilitated the increase of riches beyond what was possible in the material realm so that fallen souls would have the "perfect enjoyment [*jouissance*] of true possessions by recovering the merits that they had acquired before God and that sin had caused them to lose." In contrast to Gerberon and Treuvé, Bourdaloue stressed that the Jubilee promised universal rather than merely personal redemption in "a precious outpouring [*écoulement*]" of "divine sources of the Savior." Echoing Cartesian arguments made famous by Bernard Le Bovier de Fontenelle in *Entretiens sur la pluralité des mondes* (1686), he imagined the possibilities of multiple planets in need of salvation. The Jubilee heralded the "excess of the efficacy and the virtue" contained in Jesus's blood, a single drop of which "would suffice to redeem a thousand worlds." Communion with such exquisite flesh required emulation of its sacrifice through the "absolute renunciation" of sin, along with fasting and the giving of alms, "in order to spread among the living members of Christ the tributes that penance imposes on charity."[69]

Whereas Saint Paul had depicted the faithful as "slaves to righteousness," for Bourdaloue the church was the "dispenser of the infinite treasure of the satisfactions of Jesus Christ."[70] The shift from *oikos* to general economy entailed intense scrutiny of the believer's conscience. Whereas Gerberon and Treuvé took care to qualify allusions to spiritual wealth with reminders of human debasement, Bourdaloue offered consolation. Joly, for his part, grasped the quandary of indulgences even while extoling them as "so easy a means to satisfy justice." Pastors sought to legitimize their power to redeem sin without lulling the laity into complacent "self-love [*amour-propre*]."[71] One strove for virtue while recognizing that human effort counted for little more than a pittance in comparison to the treasury of merit. Despite their differences, rigorist and permissive theologians of penance found comfort in the magnanimous terms on which sinners repaid their debts to a divine creditor whose bottomless wealth obviated the need for an exact accounting.

Transubstantiation in Perpetuity: Confraternities and the Spirituality of the Catholic Reformation

Trent valorized the abundance of communion and penance against the Protestant Reformers who aimed to diminish the sacraments in quantity and quality. For Luther, only baptism and the Eucharist could be said to warrant the designation fully; penance did so in a partial sense.[72] Calvin's liturgical criteria were characteristically more severe, allowing for baptism and the Last Supper alone.[73] Neither believed that these rites conferred grace in and of themselves. Rome reacted by affirming the full complement of seven sacraments, entrenching confession and communion ever more deeply in the lives of the clergy and laity alike.[74] The *bon curé*, called to meet exacting standards of residence, intellectual formation, and pastoral care, demanded that individual believers examine their consciences with greater regularity and rigor.[75] Likewise, the consecrated host became a fixture in both interior and exterior manifestations of piety. The greater emphasis placed on mental prayer induced more frequent participation in the Eucharist, which necessitated consultation with spiritual directors because one could not commune if found to be in a state of mortal sin.[76]

The French king served as an exemplar for his realm, attending services daily. The number of subjects emulating him rose throughout the seventeenth century and well into the eighteenth.[77] In 1645 the Assembly of the Clergy ordered Catholics to attend Mass at least once a month; among the middling and lower reaches of society, the majority did so every Sunday. The priesthood elucidated the significance of Mass to the faithful—for instance, through the catechism, translations of the Missal into the vernacular, and religious instruction at *maisons d'éducation*.[78] In practice adherence varied by region and was concentrated in the northern and eastern provinces, from Brittany to Franche-Comté. But abstention did not necessarily signal indifference. Rather, worshippers could demur from a sense of reverence or a wish to cultivate the proper disposition through prayer and penance. The ideal remained perpetual reflection and celebration. This spirit infused the ritual of the Forty Hours, during which the host received veneration for a designated period, quantified by the biblical number associated with times of trial as well as renewal.[79]

Church and state enlisted French subjects in a campaign to elevate the Eucharist in social and religious life. Institutions and private individuals established foundations for Mass and every conceivable embellishment of the host. On July 2, 1650, a merchant named Claude Sonnius, from the rue Saint-Jacques in Paris, donated eleven livres, five sols in rent to the Confrérie du Saint-Sacrement, attached to the now defunct Church of Saint-Benoît-le-Bétourné, for the maintenance of a lamp to shine without interruption on the altar.[80] In Argentan, members of a confraternity reported expenditures of 15,000 to 20,000 livres on "vases in gold and silver," the "decoration of the tabernacle" used in displaying communion wafers, the building of a new sacristy, and other "magnificent ornaments."[81] An association in the Parisian parish of Saint-Sulpice collected contributions from dozens of benefactors in the second half of the century for masses, processions, and acts of restitution in cases where the host had been stolen by malevolent parties.[82]

Confraternities played an indispensable role in advancing the cult of Eucharistic devotion. The members' fervor held fast even in an age of purported "laicization," John McManners's term for the self-fulfilling prophecy by which the people retreated from demonstrations of religious commitment while the church gradually abandoned popular devotional practices. Nonetheless, these brotherhoods and sisterhoods found new adherents.[83] In 1621 there were 363 *confréries de dévotion* open to all, as well as associations linked to a particular guild.[84] Sixty-one new establishments were made in Bordeaux alone between 1680 and 1728, and another forty-one between 1729 and 1769.[85] At the turn of the eighteenth century, a total of 1.5 million French subjects belonged to one or more of fifteen thousand religious societies.[86] The Parisian Filles du Saint-Sacrement claimed thirty thousand to forty thousand members.[87]

Tellingly, these voluntary associations had long served a dual economic and spiritual function.[88] In *confréries du métier*, artisans organized themselves in the service of religious and professional organizations. Each occupied its own chapel in the parish church, which its members furnished and maintained. They secured material provisions to aid the living and to fund burial masses for the dead. They were also notorious for debauched socializing, especially on feast days. Yet by most accounts confraternities founded independently of the guilds—and promoted by Dominicans, Ursulines, and Jesuits—discharged their duties with care. Associates tended to church buildings and other ecclesiastical matters, collected and distributed charity, and ministered to the bodies and the souls of the infirm. The clergy attempted to turn such diligence to their advantage by founding or reviving pious orders with the support of bishops and their agents during visitations.

In keeping with Tridentine sensibilities, the Eucharist became a conspicuous object of veneration. Although associations boasted of their lineages, many could trace their founding or the confirmation of their privileges only to the sixteenth and seventeenth centuries—that is, after Pope Paul III's approval of an archconfraternity in honor of the Blessed Sacrament at the Roman Church of Santa Maria Sopra Minerva.[89] The French confraternity at the Church of Saint-Eustache was established in 1421. Pope Urban VIII (r. 1623–44) granted "several indulgences" in 1636; four years later, the archbishop of Paris ordered that a procession with the host be held the first Thursday of each month (in honor of the day of the biblical Last Supper). Charles VI (r. 1380–1422) and Louis XIV (r. 1643–1715) issued letters patent attesting to the decree, which Louis XV (r. 1715–74) had formally registered by the Paris Parlement.[90] Sodalities of the Holy Sacrament thus emerged as a quintessential institution of Catholic reform.[91] Devotees engaged in public processions, prayerful vigilance over the host, and the transport of the viaticum to the dying. They sought to nullify the sacrilege committed by Protestants who denied the miracle of transubstantiation, as well as by Catholics who demeaned it through malign neglect. Their acts of virtue earned fulsome recognition from Rome. Between 1650 and 1799, 9 percent of all indulgences were granted to Eucharistic confraternities.[92]

Excepting the Compagnie du Saint-Sacrement, an order founded by *dévots* at court, Eucharistic associations attracted members across the social spectrum.⁹³ Brothers and sisters committed themselves to the stewardship, display, and circulation of the host as a source of spiritual and physical redemption. The order founded in the Burgundian town of Noyers in 1623 typified this sense of purpose.⁹⁴ All Catholics were explicitly welcome, "even the poor," provided they resided in the city and were capable of performing duties. Members attended Mass each Thursday as well as a procession and vespers the first Thursday of the month. They were obliged to commune far beyond the minimum stipulated by the Councils of the Lateran and Trent—at Easter, Pentecost, All Saints' Day, and the Feast of Corpus Christi. In keeping with the new orientation of Catholic reform, their prayers emphasized the productive and transformative aspects of the sacrament. "O bread of life!" according to one invocation, "you enliven my spirit and fortify by heart." In a reversal of purely corporeal metabolization, the devotee proclaimed that "I will not change you into myself." Rather, "you will change me into yourself." The liturgy concluded with paeans in rapid succession: "O precious blood! O price of my redemption! O infinite treasure, dear Jesus!"⁹⁵

The confraternity of the Saint-Barthélemy parish—located opposite the Palais de la Cité in the capital—upheld especially strict standards for individual and collective self-governance. Women and men could join regardless of rank, provided they espoused "equally ardent and respectful affection" for the "great mystery that is the archetype of all the others." The parish priest assumed the role of perpetual director, thus assuring clerical oversight; in addition, members elected two "masters and administrators" on a biannual basis to manage social and liturgical activities. A council of local notables served as advisers. The masters guaranteed that the sanctuary did not lack candles—six for the altar and twelve for the chandelier above the choir. They also arranged for a verger and two children to accompany the viaticum and for men to carry the dais in mandatory processions held the first Sunday of the month. Deceased members were entitled to a Requiem Mass. The association would freely lend "necessary things," but the bereaved would incur unspecified "customary expenses" if they wished to employ "fine trappings [parements]."⁹⁶

Unsurprisingly, the regulations addressed financial matters in detail. Dues were set at thirty sols upon entry and fifteen sols per year thereafter; falling into arrears resulted in relinquishing the right to a funeral service.

Masters were prohibited from spending more than fifty livres without the approval of their colleague and the parish priest. If a charge exceeded 100 livres, it required the entire council's assent. While in office, masters were to keep scrupulous records and submit to an audit. Their purview extended to the entirety of the association's capital, both spiritual and material, from papal bulls to the "cross and holy relics" left in the masters' care.[97]

The religious if not financial obligations in the town of Faverney, east of Noyers, were more formidable still. The order sought to justify its rigor with reference to local history. The only qualification for entry was the payment of a fee, considerably lower than that imposed by the Saint-Barthélemy associates. The expense was cast in the nomenclature of a "*cens*" paid in kind. The amount depended on income but could be no less than six deniers (a modest but typical sum for a feudal due). Brothers and sisters attended Mass daily. They recited prayers on rising each morning and retiring each night, devoting Fridays to the "mystery of our redemption." They were to avoid drunkenness and violent disputes. Attendance at monthly assemblies and confessing and communing monthly gained members plenary indulgences. The privilege was deliberately gratuitous to honor the "incredible flurry of miracles" occasioned by the sacrament during a disaster that befell the sanctuary in 1608.[98] Flames from a chandelier had engulfed the altar, the adornments of which were related in luxurious detail. There was a marble tabernacle festooned with silk. It sheltered a reliquary made of gilded silver "exceeding the weight of a *marc*" within which was a crystal flute containing a bone from Saint Agatha. A communion wafer was encased in glass, ringed by silver. All these treasures were destroyed in the fire, save for the host.[99]

According to the Faverney statutes, God authorized the miracle to "prove to our eyes the validity of the indulgences that attracted so many to his blessed temple." The papal brief proved equally "incombustible" next to the object of veneration, prompting worshippers to declare, "O gracious God! What consolation it is to know that we have forever in hand the title of our assurance, to draw from the treasures of the Church, and to remit in full what your justice demands for the temporal punishments of our sins!" The host rightly conveyed the "richest present," the "epitome of your every marvel," and the "gift par excellence of your inordinate charity."[100] The sodality's rule thus oriented members in a spiritual economy of abundance.

The debt incurred from their sins knew no limit, nor did Christ's generosity. The Eucharist mediated between these infinite quantities as a store of value surpassing the effects that embellished it.

Successive popes opened the *thesaurus meritorum sanctorum* to confraternities. In Noyers Gregory VI (r. 1621–23) offered new members "plenary indulgences and remission of all their sins." Pardons of "seven years, and as many quarantines" (corresponding to forty days' worth of penance), were issued to those who fulfilled one of several possible devotions, such as visiting the parish church on the feast days of Peter, Paul, Ascension, and Assumption, praying for the end of heresy, lodging the poor, settling quarrels, attending the burials of brothers and sisters, joining processions of the sacrament, or carrying the viaticum to the sick and dying. Sixty days accrued for engaging in religious instruction and similarly benevolent acts.[101]

According to this general framework, the issuing of pardons accompanied induction into the confraternity, participation in ceremonies featuring the host, and the performance of charitable works. Exact qualities and quantities varied depending on time and place.[102] The system would seem arbitrary outside the theological-economic rationale of the penitential regime. As the Council of Trent declared, "It is absolutely false and contrary to the word of God that guilt is never remitted by the Lord without the entire punishment being remitted also." Otherwise, one might fall prey to "*treasuring up to ourselves wrath against the day of wrath.*" The soul's moral edification required that the church impose punishment for sin. Should the clergy prove lax, "they might become partakers in the sins of others." The reprobate could not claim that salvation followed immediately from personal labors. Rather, sinners remained as if indebted even once the obligation had been discharged. Punishment allowed them to join their forces to those of Christ, whose sacrifice gave human undertakings their efficacy in matters of grace.[103]

The sense of inexhaustibility of guilt and mercy stoked the desire for perpetual adoration. Fallen souls could emulate divine largesse through the exercise of charity, inspired by the love of God and of one other. According to the *Instructions* issued by a confraternity in Rouen, theirs was to be a "society of several persons of every condition." Christ called the rich and poor without distinction to take part in the "commerce of piety." Heeding his call, the first Christians reportedly met in worship regardless of the hour. In the centuries that followed, a division of labor had been instituted owing to the "needs of families" and the sheer "number of worshippers."[104] The recognition of physical and social limitations compelled believers to find ways of translating the boundlessness of divine love into suitable observances.

Pope Paul III established the principles of perpetual adoration in 1539, which were adapted for France in the 1640s by Gaston Jean Baptiste de Renty, the lay director of the Compagnie du Saint-Sacrement, who urged the devout in the parish of Saint-Paul to pray before the sacrament each evening for an hour.[105] The practice soon found adherents in Dijon; indulgences granted by Pope Clement X lent further encouragement. New orders were founded throughout the second half of the seventeenth century: in Brittany in 1651, Lyon in 1667, Dreux in 1698, then Amiens, Beauvais, Lisieux, and elsewhere. Participants strove "to render to Jesus Christ, present in the Most Blessed Sacrament at the altar, all the honor it is possible to give him, in attempting to fulfill every obligation toward him," from "homage," "gratitude," and "love" to "satisfaction or restitution."[106]

Despite professing selflessness, the Rouen instructions stated unrepentantly that "there is a great deal of profit to be hoped for in this devotion." Members believed that their efforts yielded spiritual, material, and social gains. Veneration of the host facilitated "a great number of good works," among them "the adornment of churches, the respectability of altars, [and] the maintenance of eternal flames [*lampes ardentes*]." The general "renewal of good morals, religion, and piety" secured the tranquility of the community. Given the transitive property of grace, each member benefited from the toil of his brethren on account of belonging to the same body. Those who frequented the sacraments should expect that "Jesus Christ will commit himself to lavishing a singular glory on you for all eternity" out of proportion with the humble aid rendered by his servants. Indulgences spurred members to more strenuous effort in order to "enrich with particular graces" the "assiduous worship" of the "most precious wage of our salvation."[107]

To this end, the *curé* drew up an agenda for the constant adoration of the host. Members fixed appointments for a specific hour, or hours, depending on their number as well as their station; substitutions were permitted but only with prior approval. In parishes lacking clocks, groups of worshippers would take longer shifts—for instance, from noon until dusk—obviating the need for exact punctuality. If a particular hour was oversubscribed, two or more members were allowed to worship in tandem. The period allotted was to be given over to mental or vocal meditation, at the conclusion of which one recited the Lord's Prayer and the Angelic Salutation five times. One then arranged to confess and to take communion within the week. Acknowledging inevitable difficulties, the manual's authors affirmed that perpetual attendance was sustainable, noting that the practice had endured without interruption for more than sixty years.[108]

The confraternity offered guidance on how to approach the sacrament with due reverence. One was expected to arrive in a timely fashion, as if attending an audience with the king. Taking Mary and John the Baptist as models, brothers and sisters rhapsodized over the marvels of the real presence with saintly ardor. The host recalled Christ's venerable duties as savior, judge, sovereign, and spouse. When taught verbally, prepared scripts allowed those who could not read to participate in the order. If minds wandered, one might say the Rosary or seek reparation for crimes of "divine *lèse-Majesté*" committed against the sacrament—stabbing it with knives, feeding it to dogs, or defacing the altar on which it rested.[109] These injunctions reminded members that the their exertions were made out of an indebtedness that could never be overcome through purely human faculties.

At the same time, the Rouen manual implored the confraternity to receive the fullness of divine benevolence. The seemingly infinite insolvency of sin necessitated the mobilization of spiritual wealth on a monumental scale. The faithful were invited to the table of the "holy banquet" of the Eucharist, which anticipated "the wage of eternal glory" in the life to come. Prayers lingered over the pleasures of communion as a "magnificent feast" where "one tastes spiritual delights as from their source"—that is, from Christ's own body. Although this rhetoric recalled a certain hedonism, the author maintained that devotees should cultivate "a most ardent love," with God as its "sole object."[110] Their professed desire reflected the seemingly paradoxical attributes of the Eucharistic rite. Communion took place in time; even so, it necessitated worship that transcended time. The miracle of transubstantiation called forth Christ immediately, immanently, but also promised fulfillment in the future. The consecrated host stood as the perfect artifact—wondrously whole, body and blood—yet it also represented Jesus's physical suffering on the cross. The sacrifice it commemorated was reserved for sacred moments yet was conducive to frequent observance.

As for the benefits that accrued, the guide answered unequivocally: "You can ask for your every spiritual need, and even your temporal needs, according to God's inclination." Celestial riches did not exclude the possession of material goods; rather, the former and the latter fell along a single continuum. Yet the imperative of exalting Christ reigned supreme. Brothers and sisters were to strive for the "augmentation of his glory in this mystery, the conversion of his enemies, and the multiplication of his true worshippers."[111] Reflections on the Eucharist mirrored the effects of the sacrament itself. Both acts called forth a body, whether that of Christ or of his assembled church.

The order followed its qualifications of spiritual self-interest with a digression on indulgences. Associates were reminded that such a "grace" was "too significant" to ignore. Those "who neglect this spiritual treasure" acted as "poor stewards [*ménagers*] in the business [*affaire*] of their salvation." Even so, the question remained of whether the pursuit of indulgences could serve as a "principal motive" for adoring the host. Although Christ's offer of "recompense" served "to attract his children to this devotion," it should not be taken as "the end" in itself. Only "mercenaries" comported themselves in such a vicious manner. The desire for pardons promoted spiritual toil in the form of prayers and receiving "communion with fervor." The love of God ultimately transcended egoism to embrace an ethic of service. "Perfect worshippers" resembled "courtiers" who obeyed the commands of their divine "sovereign" without hesitation. Their code depended on a rejection of instrumentality, a breach in the correspondence between means and ends. Given the pricelessness of Christ's sacrifice, disengagement posed the sole manner of veneration "worthy of him" and "proportionate to his nature." As the Gospel declared, one must "honor God" with all one's heart and soul "without distraction [*partage*], without interest, and without hypocrisy."[112]

The Eucharist traversed multiple divides—not only between sin and redemption and means and ends but also between death and life. According to the statutes for the confraternity at Menin, Christ had "paid our debts" through "an excess of incomprehensible love" and by "enduring torments of which the human mind has never truly conceived the price." Communion, the "invaluable wage" of this sacrifice, rewarded those willing to "diligently work" toward their moral regeneration. The pain of illness was the mirror image of the "abundance of goods" guaranteed by the sacrament. Quoting the Psalms, a "torrent of your [God's] pleasures" billowed through heaven; by drinking its waters, the elect would fall "intoxicated." Human souls could not hope to contribute "the least thing for so powerful and generous a master" and should thus proceed "without ever thinking of the advantages that one finds in fulfilling these holy obligations." The eye trained not only on "*the goods* [biens] *of the Lord* but also on the Lord himself," the possession of whom "all other goods are merely the consequence."[113] By subsuming the physical and the pecuniary, the spiritual economy mitigated a purely venal understanding of wealth. Divine subsistence surpassed but also furnished the template for the enjoyment of lesser things.

The confraternity of the Saint-Hilaire parish in Reims—the city where French kings were anointed and crowned—based its liturgy on a variant of the Christian materialism endorsed by its counterpart in Rouen. Jesus was ever-present in the host, an emblem of recurring loss that necessitated constant adoration in turn. No individual possessed the wherewithal to fulfill the demand, necessitating the sharing of labor. By the same token, Pope Innocent XI (r. 1676–88) capitalized on the boundless merits of the saints by granting perpetual indulgences. In exchange, associates declared their allegiance to Catholic Reformation teachings, especially transubstantiation, even if "reason" and the "senses" obscured its certitude. In the spirit of Trent, they regarded their personal and collective indebtedness as a spur to heightened devotion. A "prayer to Jesus Christ" instructed worshippers to state that "I adore you with all my heart, . . . and with the joy of depending on you as your creature and your slave, redeemed by the infinite price of your blood and your death." No compensatory act sufficed for "the contempt and humiliations" Christ endured on behalf of humankind. According to the logic of mutual sacrifice, the prayer continued: "I wish to debase myself" and "pronounce that I am nothing but a void [*qu'un néant*]." The petition concluded on a note of longing: "O Jesus, when will I be everything to you, and when will you be all things to me?"[114] These exuberant sentiments convey in word and deed a thoroughly economic system of relations between

God and the soul, plenitude and lack, the whole and its parts. Christ's unfathomably painful death on the cross heaped the sins of creation onto his broken body and miraculously redeemed them. His mortal followers were justifiably implored to emulate him in full cognizance that their every effort, up to self-annihilation, fell short of perfection.

The only recourse in an economy where the parts could never equal the whole, and the debt of sin never repaid by those who had incurred it, was a paradoxical surrender to superfluity. The Reims statues offered commentary on the Litanies of the Sacrament—the original text of which enumerated a succession of riches, each followed by the rejoinder to God, "*Miserere nobis* [Have mercy on us]." The Eucharist encompassed "all the mysteries of your glorious and mortified life." The passages on "Panis supersubstantiales [Supersubstantiated Bread]" clarified further that the "celestial" nourishment found in the host reigned "above every created substance." During communion, flawed beings made contact with this transformative agent, which existed "above nature" and thus evaded comprehension by sense experience.[115]

The section "Donum transcendens omnem plenitudinem [Gift transcending all abundance]" imposed coherence on the potentially contradictory elements of sacramental yearning. The devotee addressed the Eucharist as Christ, and Christ as the Eucharist, declaring "you comprise all the gifts that God has ever given us, and you infinitely surpass them." The "miserable sinner" and "ungrateful creature" amounted to nothing before such an "incomprehensible gift." Given the absolute inequality between the human and the divine, hope for reconciliation lay in conversion through sacrificial expenditure. The host, which replicated the miracle of the Incarnation, affected a radical change in those who consumed it. "Transform me into you, Lord," the worshipper entreated, "so that nothing of the former man remains in me." In contrast to "the pleasures of the world," only the "bread of the Eucharist" offered a sustenance that "never disgusts" its recipient.[116]

Confraternities participated in an elaborate economic theology. Their writings, which emphasized liturgical and administrative matters rather than theological explication, nonetheless presumed a sophisticated model of exchange between the divine and human spheres. Members mobilized spiritual capital drawn from Christ and the saints, authorized by ecumenical councils, and upheld by successive popes. Brothers and sisters also served as stewards for a range of financial assets. Their rules demanded substantial if intermittent labor, guided by a standard of perpetual adoration befitting its object. Believers undertook their devotions both out of a sense of overwhelming debt and in anticipation of a wondrous surplus. As the cases of Rouen and Reims indicate, the Eucharist elicited a Catholic rendering of utility in value production and distribution. Associates could infer no direct relationship between effort and outcome when the minimal threshold of observance called for continual worship. Foreknowledge of celestial bliss served as a motive detached from the immediate pursuit of personal interest. Devotees worked for nothing yet gained everything.

Toward a General Economy of Salvation

The circulation of spiritual wealth met with resistance throughout the century, above all in the fierce polemics between Jesuits and Jansenists. These debates form the subject of the next chapter. Yet the Eucharist retained its prestige despite its highly contested status; indeed, it attracted controversy owing to its pricelessness. From the 1680s to the 1780s, the sacraments figured not only as bearers of value in its purest sense but also as the archetype for marshaling and distributing worldly riches. To grasp the enduring continuities between the sacramental and material economies requires plumbing the depths of the former and acknowledging the religious contingencies that gave shape and substance to the latter.

The tract *La merchandise spirituelle* (1529) offers a glimpse into the pre-Tridentine past and omens of the future. As the title implies, a transactional *modus operandi* distinguished the work from later guides to Eucharistic devotion. The unnamed author addressed himself to fellow merchants with a "profitable [*salutaire*] thing for our social condition [*état*]." His work sought to reorient aspirations away from mundane trifles to "the true and principal merchandise." It was worth enduring "great difficulties" to "acquire spiritual and heavenly riches," alongside which gold and silver paled in comparison.[117] Nonetheless, the faithful were expected to strive for profit through labor in both the spiritual and material realms.

On the authority of the Dominican friar and former archbishop Antonio of Florence, the trader of souls justified his approach with reference to a great chain of commodities. "Worldly and terrestrial" merchandise occupied the lowliest rung and brought no satisfaction to God. Next came merchandise considered "licit and permitted for human life," the use of which was governed by laws established in the Old Testament. In founding the new law, Christ had enshrined the third and most esteemed merchandise, which was thoroughly "spiritual" in nature. "Hoard up [*thésaurisez*] the treasures of heaven," Jesus urged his followers. To this end, God distributed "talents," or "his gifts and the graces," with the expectation that beneficiaries "multiply and profit from them through truly bargaining in a spiritual manner [*spirituellement marchander*] during our lifetimes."[118] Tellingly, the reference to talents had a dual meaning. It could imply either a personal aptitude or the ancient Greco-Roman unit of currency that featured in the Gospel parable of the good steward (or, in French, *économe*).[119] However demanding the toils of this life, created beings were ultimately destined for "eternal beatitude." Christ himself desired that "we enter and do spiritual business [*marchandions spirituellement*] in this region," following his pronouncement during the Sermon on the Mount that "where your treasure is, there will your heart be also."[120]

The Council of Trent affirmed the re-presentational character of the sacraments—and, in so doing, introduced a more nuanced understanding of the relations governing means and ends. The shift from corporeal imagery to more abstract symbols of value occurred in a halting fashion, with the two registers often overlapping. Consider, for instance, the work of François Arnoulx, canon of the cathedral of Riez. His literal-minded guide, *Merveilles de l'autre monde*, first published in 1614, depicted heaven and hell in the most dramatic terms he could muster, alternatively glorious or noxious. The damned suffered from "tears in their eyes, cries of demons in their ears, stench in their nostrils," as well as "a fear-stricken heart, hunger in the belly, pain in the kidneys, aches in their sides, weariness in their limbs, and nervous tremors." Eternally rotting corpses were fruitful even in their putrefaction, sufficient to disseminate "the plague throughout the world."[121]

In *Du paradis et de ses merveilles* (1638), Arnoulx taught readers that the City of God offered weary pilgrims "the presence of every good and the absence of every evil—in a word, all that one could desire." If hell descended into bottomless depths of deprivation, the "heavenly empire" rose up as "this marvel of the world," one "so excessive in its dimensions" that all the angels laid claim to a "perpetual heritage" greater than the globe. In this "mighty kingdom," no one or nothing was excluded. God reigned on high from a "throne of immutability," with Mary as his queen, Christ as the "sovereign judge," and the apostles as his "notaries." Following the Psalms, "glory and riches abound throughout and overflow in his house." The divine king held court among his "innumerable" angels, each "more beautiful than this entire visible world." The "contentment and joy" of a single celestial subject "surpasses all the pleasures" to be found on earth.[122]

Arnoulx continued his description of blameless superabundance in a similar vein. The celestial city was composed of "nothing but gold." It was also a realm of "exquisite pleasure [*volupté*]," perfectly sensual yet also "chaste and holy." He assured future denizens that heaven "will beckon until you are drunk on the finest wines that fall and flow from heavy torrents in every kind of delight." Ecstasy resolved into the stillest peace, perfect knowledge, absolute beauty, and life without end.[123] The rationales for striving, for pride itself, fell away before the supreme being: "Each will love him more than oneself, and he will love all the blessed thousands upon thousands of times more than they love themselves." The absence of self-regard won a still greater devotion, that of and in "God himself." The dictates of charity extended to one's fellows, among whom there would be no *meum* or *tuum*. As with the children of Job, "each shared in the goods and wealth of the other as if his own," and "the riches of each were held in common by all."[124]

Arnoulx later turned his attention to the "money" that circulated in the City of God. He demanded that his readers banish from their thoughts "the treasures of this world" and "all its storehouses filled with silver" to dwell on the unfathomable nature of Christ's sacrifice. Of heaven's graces, Arnoulx stipulated, "the savior of the world has bought them most dearly wholesale [*en gros*]" only to "sell them, equally dearly, in retail [*en détail*] to his greatest friends" among the martyrs and the saints. Yet this commercial deity neither sought his own profit nor our own in the transaction, given the "high value and excellence" of heaven. Numbers failed to quantify a glory regarded "so great that it exceeds as many pleasures as have ever been" and thus "cannot be measured." It defied description altogether; every language spoken lacked the words necessary to portray it. Such was the magnificence of "the salary [*salaire*] and the recompense of the blessed."[125]

In a manual entitled *Le chrestien heureux* (1686), the Jesuit Pierre de Gourdan deepened and refined elements of Arnoulx's economic theology, relating it to the expenditure of the Mass. Following the church father Saint John Chrysostom, he defined the Eucharist as "the treasure of all the riches of God" both on earth and in heaven. By participating in the faith, the believer shared with the "Redeemer" in "an entire infinity of perfections and happiness." This abundance assumed an occult quality but also made itself manifest in celebrations across the "inhabited world."[126] For Gourdan, communion wielded the power to transform "our most onerous labors into the tenderness of his [God's] love" and "criminal pleasures" into "adoration."[127] As a source of spiritual capital and moral conversion, its productivity had no limit.

The Mass would make happiness our "incontestable and perfect possession" but only "if we were strongly persuaded that we would receive ... the graces we demand." The appropriate frame of mind recalled that of "when you see your money being counted"; in such moments "you have no other desire than being paid." The "secret" of Christian duty, then, was "to be enflamed with a most ardent desire." Gourdan implored believers to reflect on Christ's largesse, which "changes our vices into his virtues, our misery into his bliss, our unhappy life into his divine life."[128] In a similar manner, the miracle of transubstantiation turned bread into flesh, rendering it the source of "all the treasures of his wisdom and of God's science hidden there." Consecrated wine surged in a "flood that carries divine life and the price of the redemption of the world." These transformations made possible a series of exchanges, among them the union of the "eternal Word" with a human soul, of created beings with their creator, and of all believers in a universal church. Frequent communion could precipitate these effects, whether one received it formally from a priest or mentally in the course of one's daily life.[129]

Gourdan railed against those who defiled the Mass by attending services in flamboyant dress. The task of ridding churches of such pretentious displays was critical for lavishing on "God all the glory that he desires." If Christ's crucifixion gave rise to a profusion of goods, so would "the sacrifice of luxury" in clothing. The death of the savior was the act of a god in human form. We must follow his example by toppling the "idolatry that *amour-propre* wants to establish in our hearts." Casting off the sordid robes of venality, the fulfilled Christian realized Saint Paul's dictum: "Clothe yourself with Jesus Christ." To do otherwise amounted to a "double idolatry, active and passive," depending on whether one exulted in oneself or sought adoration from others.[130]

The fetishization of commodities and of other bodies has a Christian history that long precedes the Enlightenment.[131] Theologians such as Gourdan struggled to distinguish idolatry from the worship of the real presence. Yet he could not fail to account for the banal medium in which Christ appeared on the altar. The slippage became apparent in his recommendation to engage frequently in the "communion of the mind," during which worshippers recalled the "divine Word" not only at Mass but also each time they encountered bread in its profane iterations.[132] Fetishism, then, remained in the eye of the beholder. Diligent observance oriented the soul toward everlasting goods and promoted a sense of fulfillment in their consumption. At the apex of this taxonomy Gourdan placed the Eucharist, the preparations for which reflected its immeasurable value. On the eve of communing, the faithful meditated on the mysteries of the Last Supper. "*I have desired with an infinite desire,*" read one such homage, "*to eat this paschal feast with you, O my Lord,* and to make this passage from my life to my death." The soul's moral existence met a fitting end during last rites, when Christ "presses one's mouth against the wound in his side."[133]

Gourdan's fellow Jesuit, Louis Bourdaloue, developed the schema in even greater detail. Bourdaloue was a professor of rhetoric, philosophy, and moral theology whose collected works were published in editions throughout the late seventeenth and eighteenth centuries. He was renowned for his mastery of homiletics. Having enraptured the Sun King, he was hailed by his contemporaries as the "founder of Christian eloquence."[134] With stylistic brilliance and spiritual profundity, his sermons articulated the view that Christ, as the Word made flesh, must be grasped not only as a symbol of wealth but also as its consummation.

Bourdaloue took as his point of departure Christ's pronouncement in the Gospel of John, "My flesh is meat indeed."[135] In keeping with Tridentine doctrine and its application by the confraternities, his exegesis clarified that Jesus meant to refer not to "common" sustenance but to its "sacramental," even economic analogue. Bourdaloue admitted that the formula seemed inappropriate at first glance, given the baseness of corporeal forms, but he reassured listeners of its perfect aptitude. The visceral connotations of the metaphor mattered less than how it related to qualities and quantities in the abstract. The miracle of the Incarnation followed from God's will to be reconciled with humanity and anticipated Christ's mortifications in achieving this end. Yet the Eucharist performed a still more remarkable feat in eclipsing the sublimity of Jesus's own body after resurrection. The former, unlike the latter, was "elevated to a distinctly divine order." Transubstantiated bread "possesses a kind of immensity" no longer limited by "space." It exceeded the laws of nature in assuming a visibly physical form even as it "vivifies the spirit." Bourdaloue insisted on the materiality and productivity of the sacramental act. The host carried out its function not merely as "the soul" or "the divinity" of Christ but specifically as "his flesh." It was no longer the soul that served to "conserve the body"; rather, it was a body that henceforth sustained the soul through the sacrifice of the Mass. By displaying the host during processions, as did the confraternities, the savior transmitted his redemptive power so that all might benefit from "the effects of his generosity." Lending still further credence to Eucharistic devotion, Bourdaloue defended public displays as a form of spiritual restitution. Adoration of the host could undo the "outrages" committed against it by Protestants and other heretics, thereby giving "satisfaction [*amende honorable*]" for "all our sacrileges."[136]

It was on this Christian materialist basis that Bourdaloue recommended participation in the Feast of Corpus Christi, the moment of the liturgical calendar in which the labor of Eucharistic confraternities was perhaps most visible. Spectators made themselves worthy of communing with Christ by "prostrating often in the presence of this sacred body and offering there to him a thousand actions of grace." The preacher even offered a verbal formula: each parishioner should acknowledge in the Eucharist "the price of my salvation." As had Gourdan, he called on the faithful, and women in particular, to renounce the "superfluities" of "luxury" and "vanity." Believers should turn their attentions to "enriching the vessels containing" the host and "decorating the tabernacles in which it is stored." The futile energies wasted on the adornment of the human frame would be better spent embellishing the "mystic body" of the church and honoring its most precious possession—"a

God himself in his own substance and with all the fullness of his divinity" that members may "not only approach, but also touch, and eat."[137]

The wonders of the Eucharist likewise preoccupied François-Léon Réguis in the compilation of sermons first published in 1766 as *La voix du pasteur*.[138] Over the course of a career throughout the north and east of France, in Auxerre, Lisieux, and Gap, Réguis preached on an array of subjects related to devotion and comportment but returned time and again to the necessity of sacramental life. Critical of Jansenist parsimony in granting absolution and dispensing communion, but not an avowed partisan of the Jesuits, he prized practical advice over doctrinal speculation. Yet he did not demur from situating his advocacy for the sacraments within a wider framework of production and consumption, which he specifically designated as an economy. The sun proved unquestionably fruitful in the "clothing, commodities, and even pleasures" its rays made possible. It was not for the human mind to grasp the source of the benefits that ensued. "Let us enjoy the possession [*jouir*] of these goods," Réguis advised, even if one lacked full knowledge of the laws that governed them.[139]

La voix du pasteur embraced the semiotic power of the church. "The Word made flesh" operated in a manner reminiscent of a "seal on wax," producing an image with all the efficacy of the being it represented. Through the sacraments, fallen souls were granted "new qualities and new rights" as "heirs" to "all the riches" Christ promised. The Eucharist embodied this patrimony, transubstantiating bread into Jesus's own flesh and uniting the faithful with their savior. In echoes of the liturgies of confraternities in Faverney and Menin, an "excess of love" gave rise to the figure of "man redeemed by a God made man."[140] The Eucharist governed the relations between subjects in avowedly economic terms, through affective expenditure, the generation of bodies, and the redemptive potential of sacrifice.

Réguis held the view that the Last Supper had been anticipated by the multiplication of loaves and fishes at the feeding of the multitude, a miracle enacted in his day at the blessing of the fields, during which the parish priest "commands the fruits of the earth to be reborn without ceasing, and the animals to grow and reproduce in order to satisfy all our needs." The Eucharist pointed up the "infinite providence" that sustained bodies and souls within a discernible order.[141] This universal system defied rational comprehension. Yet once illuminated by the "divine torch of faith," the "*economy* of providence" became apparent.[142] Invoking God's "light," Réguis proceeded with a sense of indebtedness, if not perfect understanding, before "all the economy of your designs," which revealed itself "in the redemption of men, the punishment of the wicked, and the predestination of the just."[143] Likewise, the faithful soul should "exert the greatest order in his affairs," observing "the rules of an honest and prudent economy" with "his salvation" constantly in mind.[144]

These references to economy belonged to a lexical tradition depicting the harmonious, purposeful organization of systems, from the single household [*oikos*] to nature in its entirety. For instance, the *Encyclopédie* referred to the "animal economy," the "ensemble of functions and of movements that sustain the life" of organisms.[145] The work also featured competing articles on "political economy," alternatively transposed into a monarchical register by Nicolas-Antoine Boulanger or a republican one by Jean-Jacques Rousseau.[146] The entry "Œconomie" by Louis de Jaucourt presented the term as referring to the theological distinction between the law of Moses and the soteriological regime inaugurated by Christ's ministry, death, and resurrection.[147] The passage from the old dispensation to the new turned on the management of human sin and the allocation of divine grace.

A spiritual economy, with its attending economic theology, underwrote these concepts. Even the *Encyclopédie* acknowledged this deeper genealogy. According to Réguis, who dutifully outlined its lineaments, religious truth illuminated what natural faculties alone failed to grasp: "an invisible hand" that directed created beings as its "instruments." From the perspective of this ubiquitous agent, the vagaries of chance fell away as illusion. Under its auspices, the "greatest disorders" contributed to "the general order and the universal good." Réguis claimed that even poverty served a purpose, as an occasion for alms-giving. Charity paid dividends to the benefactor as well as the recipient through an "invisible and all-powerful hand, which blesses the commerce and enterprises of this merchant, the lands of this farmer, the labor of this worker, multiplying a hundredfold the profits earned by their toil [*sueurs*]" as ordained by "Providence" itself.[148]

The employment of the metaphor of the invisible hand to describe the workings of the economy is closely associated with Adam Smith.[149] Yet the author of *The Wealth of Nations* did not invent the formula. Nor did Réguis, who followed his clerical forebears in its usage. No later than the 1680s, the Jesuit Claude de la Colombière (1641–82)—noted orator and tutor to the children of Jean-Baptiste Colbert, controller-general under Louis XIV— counseled the faithful in the ways of "the economy" both as it "regards souls" and "regards bodies." Although Colombière did not refer explicitly to the invisible hand, he held that Christians should exhibit greater liberality in giving alms with each child born to a family, since there were then "more persons . . . whose sins must be redeemed." Doing so promoted not only spiritual wealth but also material prosperity.[150] Another preacher of sterling reputation, Esprit Fléchier (1632–1710), the bishop of Nîmes, concurred with such sentiments in a sermon from 1681. Alluding to the Gospel account of the feeding of the multitude, he generalized that "God is the author of all goods, even temporal ones." There was a "secret and spiritual blessing that produces and multiplies them," a "paternal and invisible hand that circulates and distributes them."[151]

The miracle of the loaves and fishes recalled the Eucharist and the treasures of the faith, which Réguis hailed as "the economy of redemption, the marvels of the Gospel, the spiritual riches of the Christian church, [and] the inexhaustible source of graces and blessings that it holds." Although besieged by "unbelieving philosophers," the truth of this order shone like "pure gold, refined a thousand times by fire."[152] Réguis could only stand in awe before such "divine and immortal fecundity," the "womb in which Jesus Christ is perpetually conceived." Its impetus was and would remain the productivity of signs, the "temporal generation" of the "Word." By virtue of an utterance—"This is my body"—the faithful "have enjoyed for eighteen centuries the infinite advantages that the real presence of the God-Man procures for them."[153]

. . .

The Tridentine catechism, the liturgical instructions of the confraternities, and the writings of Gourdan, Bourdaloue, Fléchier, and Réguis sought to enact the economy of the mysteries in theory and practice. Providence governed the distribution of spiritual wealth. Its structural force was an effect of re-presentation, with the sacrament as its currency. The Eucharist embodied this order in a double sense. Not only did the consecrated host come to exist as Christ's real presence in the world; it also projected its value outward, remaking in its own image all those who consumed and communed with it. In this way, endless sacrifice—on every altar, at every hour—gave rise to its apparent opposite: creative destruction around the table of a beggars' banquet. Luxury beyond one's most vivid imagination lay within reach. The faithful were called on to seize it by turning their desire for inferior corruptible riches into wealth without end.

Economic theology proceeded along general rather than restricted lines. This distinction, suggestively posed by Georges Bataille, requires a shift in emphasis from investment to expenditure and the uncoupling of self-interest from the maximization of utility.[154] Yet the Catholic ethic gives the lie to Bataille's account of the religious origins of capitalism, which he located, following Weber, in the rise of Protestantism and the Calvinist desacralization of the world. By invoking the invisible hand, Fléchier and Réguis did not mean to discredit economic activity in this life or divorce it from spiritual dynamics. Practical devotion became a matter of abiding by the divine will that resacralized terrestrial endeavors. As the catechism insisted, theology presumed an economy, a means of administering objects of value from the sacraments and indulgences to metallic treasures cast in gold and silver.

CHAPTER 2

Perpetual Penance and Frequent Communion

IN APRIL OF 1752, at the height of a conflict over the refusal of sacraments, the Parlement of Paris issued an image to accompany the publication of its order that priests administer last rites to dying Jansenists (fig. 2.1). The medallion, etched with the phrase "Custos unitatis schismatis ultrix" (Guardian of unity, Avenger of schism), depicts an allegory of Justice armed with fasces and a sword. She keeps watch over an altar, on which is placed a crown and a monstrance—an allusion to the theological aspect of sovereignty and the court's spiritual pretensions. In keeping with the artistic and devotional conventions I described in the previous chapter, the host radiates light and thus transmits value. A second woman, the symbolic embodiment of the French kingdom, kneels humbly before its splendor in a gesture worthy of the subjects of the *Rex Christianissimus*, or *Roi Très-Chrétien*. A dove, the sign of the Holy Spirit, soars above the scene.[1] Through the employment of myriad devices, the print performed what it depicted—the sacral and Eucharistic display of royal power to be gratefully received by the king's subjects. The parlement asserted itself in the circuit of re-presentation as a third element, along with the church and crown, in a theologico-political and economic-theological trinity. The chronicler Barthélemy-François-Joseph Mouffle d'Angerville grasped the medallion's intended implication, which he lampooned for its resemblance to a devotional object. "There was not a

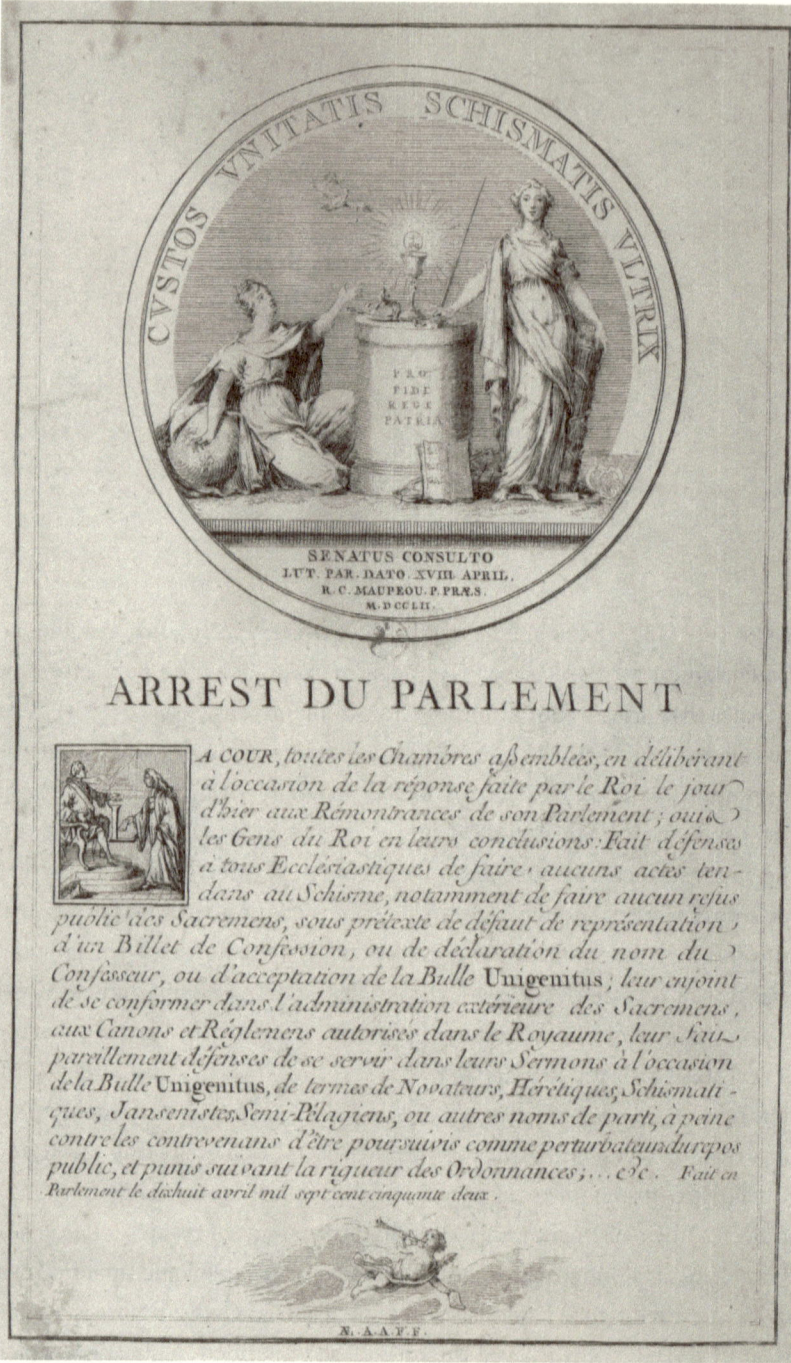

Figure 2.1 *Custos unitatis schismatis ultrix*, 1752. Bibliothèque nationale de France.

Jansenist," he noted, "who did not buy this religious caricature and affix it to the head of his bed with the holy images before which every good Catholic offers the first fruits [*premices*] and the labor of his day."[2]

The engraving further hinted at a field of antagonistic claims between civil and ecclesiastical authority. Despite tributes by Réguis to the invisible hand of providence, the general economy of spiritual wealth did not tend toward equilibrium; theological polemic threatened to undermine sacramental devotion. This chapter will show how the Tridentine directive to commune as often as feasible induced anxieties over the potential for exploitation of the means of salvation. In *De la fréquente communion* (1643), the Jansenist militant Antoine Arnauld subtly challenged Jesuits who recommended continual use of the Eucharist—a position that, in his view, made communion a functional equivalent of penance. The treatise precipitated a long struggle between his allies and the Society of Jesus. More than a century later, the issue remained a *casus belli*. In the 1750s, the Jesuit Jean Pichon came under fire for defending frequent communion, albeit in a vastly different theological landscape. The controversy now arose not from charges of Jansenist parsimony but from Jesuit endorsements of devotional permissiveness. During the same decade, the French crown struggled to adjudicate between the Parlement of Paris and the episcopate in cases involving the refusal of the sacraments to alleged Jansenist heretics. Given that the Council of Trent set the host apart owing to its re-presentational power, it is little wonder the Eucharist featured centrally in debates over the workings of spiritual as well as temporal administration.

The alliance of church and state presumed an economy that it sought to defend in a double sense—as an *oikos* of divine creation and as a framework for conceptualizing and meeting human needs. Kings, judges, and clerics clashed over the most effective means of fulfilling this sacred duty. Jesuits regarded heaven and earth as existing along a continuum, so that a sovereign, whether secular or ecclesiastic, exercised a measure of authority resembling God's. The proliferation of power reflected a surfeit of value so overwhelming that it neutralized the stigma of sin and allowed the faithful to participate in their salvation through consuming the sacraments. These signs of redemption were to be stewarded charitably by the priesthood.

Jansenists countered that Adam and Eve's primordial sin alienated them and their progeny from God, as well as from the divine aspect of their original nature. Earthly passions rushed in to fill the void produced by this irreparable loss. Exiled from paradise, humans struggled for survival in a world beholden to its own corrupt dynamics. According to Pierre Nicole, this perversely stable order was grounded in "enlightened self-love [*amour-propre éclairé*]," an impulse based on deceit and flattery, the need to love and to be loved in turn.[3] Propelled by and abandoned to wayward but countervailing desires, society required little in the way of divine oversight.

Divergent spiritual economies engendered conflict owing not so much to their utter irreconcilability as to the narcissism of small differences. For all their mutual contempt, Jesuits and Jansenists held up the Eucharist as a bottomless reserve of value indispensable for the redemption of sin. To this extent the disputes between Molinist Jesuits and Augustinian Jansenists could never ossify into total schism. François de Sales, who professed the devout humanism associated with the Society of Jesus, cited Augustine in recommending regular, weekly communion as a conduit to the "sovereign source of eternal goods."[4] The progenitor of French Jansenism, Jean Duvergier de Hauranne, the abbé de Saint-Cyran, found in the Eucharist "not only the essence [*abrégé*] of the new world produced by the Incarnation" but even that of "Jesus-Christ himself, in which God has placed all the treasures of his wisdom" and "all the graces of justification and of remission."[5] Sales and Saint-Cyran understood the sacrament as a form of "nourishment" for the soul no less essential than material sustenance for physical health.[6] Both theologians thus endorsed a major tenet of the Tridentine Reform, that the sacraments were necessary instruments in the transmission of grace.

The positing of sacramental plenitude led to compulsive speculations on how or whether its disbursal should be regimented. Questions concerning the frequency of communion and the administration of the sacraments set Jansenists against Jesuits and the Parlement of Paris against the crown. Yet these doctrinal fault lines only cast into further relief their mutual preoccupation with marshaling the wealth of grace. Scarcity was by no means assumed; rather, it was a prospect that occasioned intense soul-searching and fierce contestation. Jansenists counseled restraint when approaching the altar, not because they found the Eucharist wanting but out of deep reverence and humility. In the 1750s, during the refusal of sacraments controversy, the roles were reversed. When denied access to the Eucharist on the orders of the archbishop of Paris, and with the consent of the Society of Jesus, Jansenist partisans alleged that such deprivations were irresponsible if not inhumane. Lawyers pleading their case even considered whether subjects exercised a right to communion akin to that of property. This argument reinforced the implications of the debate for the nature of temporal and spiritual sovereignty. Despite the crown's absolutist ambitions, successive kings demurred from unilaterally imposing their will while also seeking to persuade the parlements against dictating terms to the church. Whether Jansenist or Jesuit, members of the ecclesiastical hierarchy upheld the righteousness of their stance toward the most exalted of gifts, grace itself.

The Passion of Antoine Arnauld

The Jansenists—also known as *appelants* and *anticonstitutionnaires* for opposing papal decrees critical of their spiritual forebears—provoked deep and lasting antipathy. The seeds of dissension were sown in the years immediately preceding Arnauld's forays into Eucharistic theology, with the posthumous publication of *Augustinus* by the Dutch theologian and bishop of Ypres, Cornelius Jansen. As the title implies, the work sought to retrieve Augustine's legacy in the face of Protestant usurpations. Drawing on its cache of arguments, like-minded clerics synthesized Augustinianism with Gallicanism, a doctrinal tendency that asserted the relative independence of national churches from Rome. The Jesuits, who identified closely with the papacy and the French court, found these stances anathematic for ecclesiological as well as doctrinal reasons.[7]

Tensions escalated rapidly from the middle decades of the seventeenth century. The deaths of Cardinal Armand Jean du Plessis, duc de Richelieu, in 1642 and Louis XIII (r. 1610–43) the following year left a power vacuum filled by Louis XIV on his assumption of personal rule in 1661.[8] The pledge to secure religious uniformity in the wake of the French Wars of Religion underpinned Bourbon absolutism in thought and deed. The Sun King undertook this mission with zeal, revoking in 1685 the Edict of Nantes, which had afforded Huguenots a modicum of religious toleration. This audacious move against heresy also contravened Gallican prerogatives won by his royal predecessors and jealously guarded by the parlements. The tradition had long been associated with conciliarist claims that the general church superseded the authority of the popes. In seeming defiance of French custom, Louis XIV embraced direct papal intervention, with the caveat that the monarchy's assent itself stemmed directly from divine right. Hierarchical centralization—political, fiscal, administrative, religious—became the order of the day.[9]

Jansenism was bound to strike a discordant note in these political and religious contexts. Louis XIV suspected its adherents of disloyalty during the Fronde given their anti-Jesuit stance and collusion with rebellious *parlementaires* who questioned the king's right to impose financial obligations on his subjects. As Dale Van Kley has observed, an alliance between the *anticonstitutionnaire* cause and the *noblesse de robe* against royal power coalesced gradually and by the early eighteenth had become an undeniable force.[10] The king responded with shocking belligerence, demolishing the abbey of Port-Royal-des-Champs after Pope Clement XI (r. 1700–1721) ordered its closure. Another explosive catalyst was the papal bull *Unigenitus*, issued at Louis XIV's insistence in 1713 to censure 101 propositions from Pasquier Quesnel's *Réflexions morales sur le Nouveau Testament*. In an irony commensurate with the monarch's arrogance, the parlement found itself in the position of defending Gallican liberties against the encroachments of the French crown itself. For members of this *parti janséniste*, royal absolutism and its Jesuit apologists posed a dire threat, not only to the holy remnant of the faithful but also to the nation's legitimate representatives, the magistrates of the court.[11]

Historians have approached the struggles between Jansenists and Jesuits from multiple perspectives and in varied contexts—as a debate concerning the independence of the French church from papal oversight, a vector for absolutism and its critics, a referendum on entrenched social privilege, clashing styles of biblical and historical exegesis, and a doctrinal dispute over predestination in matters of salvation.[12] The various antagonisms operated simultaneously in so many registers because they all broached a fundamental relationship, that between the human and the divine.[13] Jesuits such as Luis de Molina listed toward anthropological optimism, emphasizing that believers could contribute to their own salvation through the exercise of reason and will. This *humanisme dévot* found favor among members of the Society of

Jesus; the Order of the Visitation, founded by François de Sales and Jeanne de Chantal; and the Society of Saint-Sulpice, launched by Pierre Olier.[14] In contrast, Jansenists followed a strict reading of Augustinianism, which held that the Fall of Adam had decisively corrupted human nature and that no individual could avoid eternal chastisement without express election by God. According to Jansen and his acolytes, only the rare bestowal of "efficacious" grace held out the possibility of everlasting life.

By publishing *De la fréquente communion*, Arnauld wished less to open up a Pandora's box of controversy than to clarify questions of doctrine and devotion that the Council of Trent had raised without answering fully. During the seventeenth century, dereliction of Easter duties became virtually nonexistent.[15] The practice of regularly communing, inspired by Sales, instituted by the confraternities, and incentivized by papal dispensations, attracted rising numbers of adherents who strove to partake at least bimonthly, if not weekly. The abbé de Saint-Cyran commissioned his acolyte Arnauld to condemn the Jesuits for excessive liberality while affirming Sales's rectitude. Arnauld did not intend to reverse prevailing trends in the reception of the sacraments, even if he was later interpreted as taking this stance. Rather, he directed his work at bolstering penance in preparation for the Lord's Supper.[16] Indeed, Arnauld expended far more energy detailing the demands of contrition than he did relating the pleasures of the altar. The drive for absolution aspired to the still loftier, eternal recompense anticipated by the Eucharist.

Arnauld opened his treatise with a synopsis of Augustinian premises defended under the banner of Trent. "In the absence of grace and the movement of the Holy Spirit," he stated categorically, "there is nothing in man that is not evil." Given human depravity, how could one be "well disposed to eat this perfectly heavenly and divine flesh?" The question was purely rhetorical. Arnauld even took care not to deny the possibility of frequent communion outright. Following Sales and Saint-Cyran, he acknowledged that the "bread of heaven" was essential for the "nourishment of souls." Even so, he counseled that deferring participation in "this irresistible [*adorable*] sacrament" might prove edifying if it instilled in the penitent the proper reverence toward "so sublime an action" as that affected by the Eucharist.[17]

De la fréquente communion cast the question in explicitly materialist language, coupling biblical allusions with medical and financial analogies. As was common in the theological literature, Arnauld juxtaposed two accounts from the Gospels. One featured the tax collector Zacchaeus, noted for climbing a sycamore tree to catch a glimpse of Jesus on his way to Jericho. The other praised the faith of a centurion who declined Christ's offer to visit his house in order to heal an ailing servant on the grounds that a mere blessing from the Son of God would suffice.[18] On Arnauld's reading, Zacchaeus characterized "a saintly avidity" for God, the centurion a "respectful fear"; both stances were regarded as potentially appropriate depending on the circumstances. In either case, the "wound of sin" required the "remedy" of penance in the form of "prayers, fasts, alms," and other labors. To be worthy of the Eucharist on a regular basis, the communicant must be without mortal sin and free of all "affection" for venial offenses. The former stipulation was universally accepted, the latter a caveat insisted on by Saint-Cyran and his followers.[19]

Arnauld lingered over the conditions for partaking of the Eucharist, going so far as to approve lifetime penance in rare cases. His treatise painstakingly traced a gradual movement in the administration of the sacrament, which he defined as not only the "pain with which [God] must chastise our own sins" but also "the regret and interior pain of the heart" that followed. Over the course of centuries, demands for physical, often public sanctions had given way to the interiorization of conscience as a self-disciplining agent. Even so, Arnauld cautioned that the Catholic position differed starkly from the Lutheran. While Protestants demanded only a "change of life," the church held up the imperative of "a salutary satisfaction" for one's sins—"redeeming them with alms" and "covering them with good works."[20]

In response to Jesuit calls for liberality, Antoine asserted the daunting price of the sacrament. The dispute turned on rival interpretations of the Council of Trent. The Thirteenth Session had endorsed regular communion so that the faithful "may be able to receive frequently that supersubstantial bread and that it may truly be to them the life of the soul and the perpetual health of their mind." Beyond this general directive, the prelates distinguished between three categories of communicants: (1) those who took communion passively or merely "sacramentally," (2) those who did so "spiritually," or with cognizance of its "fruit and usefulness," and (3) those who received the host in both senses.[21]

According to Arnauld, souls should strive to attain "the greatest reward" and "most loving guarantee" that Christ offered. "Simple confession" proved necessary but not sufficient for reconciliation with God. It was no less vital "to purify oneself by the worthy marks of penance"; otherwise, the sacrament threatened to become a "dangerous poison." Arnauld depicted atonement from sins as a process of "working to expiate them through our mortifications and our good deeds." These efforts ensured "a salutary satisfaction," a way of "redeeming" our trespasses through toil. Such exertions themselves carried advantages by forestalling sin while prompting identification with Jesus's suffering.[22]

Arnauld interpreted the Tridentine decrees as emphasizing transformation via human industry rather than immediate consumption. The Jansenist doctrine of efficacious grace valorized work even if our labors did not contribute to salvation without divine mercy. He rejected the proposition that "Jesus Christ has no greater happiness than bestowing on us the largesse of his favors." His parsimonious attitude extended to the sacraments. "Communion in no way changes the state of those who receive it," Arnauld argued. As a multiplier of grace, the host imparted "only the growth of what one brings to it, whether of good or evil." It did not generate spiritual wealth ex nihilo. Its power derived not from intrinsic value but from "an effective will to please God"—up to denying oneself access to the altar.

Penance mediated between human depravity and divine grace in marking the gulf that separated them. Undue leniency in devotional matters betokened licentiousness. It not only impeded atonement but also accommodated the "love of the world," which "works for nothing but the possibility of allying Jesus Christ with Belial" (a synonym for the devil from the Hebrew adjective indicating worthlessness).[23] The apt lexical choice reflected the Augustinian call to shun the alluring but false goods of the City of Man for the incorruptible riches of the Heavenly City. The latter brought far greater rewards but entailed far more taxing efforts than suggested by the Jesuits. Arnauld concluded on a note of steely determination: "Although the Eucharist should be our most fervent wish, our weakness nonetheless is so great and so staggering as long as we are in this world that we must test our strength with utmost care, lest excessively frequent communion stifle us."[24] In this rendering of the spiritual economy, even the idea of enjoyment threatened to send the soul into a spiral of dissolution. Believers were implored to pursue the moment of redemption tirelessly, as if it might never come.

Arnauld's treatise soon became a theological cause célèbre. Although the author had secured approbations from scores of prelates and doctors of the Sorbonne in advance of publishing *De la fréquente communion*, such measures did not ward off intense scrutiny.[25] The crown did little to dampen the uproar. Louis XIV was a mere child, his government overseen by Anne of Austria, the queen mother. Upon the death of Richelieu in 1642, the position of first minister had fallen to another cardinal, Jules Raymond Mazarin, who lacked his predecessor's theological erudition or grasp of ecclesiastical politics. The Fronde (1648–53), a rebellion against incipient absolutism and the fiscal obligations it imposed, soon heightened political as well as spiritual sensitivities.[26] Jansenists participated in the revolt, earning the young king's lasting scorn. French intervention on the Protestant side against Catholic Austria and Spain in the Thirty Years' War (1618–48) further muddied the religious waters.[27] The stage was set for confrontation. Clashes over frequent communion occurred against the backdrop of ongoing confessional violence and the ambiguous doctrinal legacy of Trent, which upheld the church's role in stewarding the sacramental economy without resolving crucial questions of its administration. To what extent could souls redeem the debt of sin by merit? Was the Eucharist a means or an end of penance? Could one be rightfully denied access to communion? Unsettling debates over such matters periodically shook the church for the next century and beyond.

Refutations of Arnauld's treatise appeared almost immediately, with episcopal censures following for years thereafter. The archbishop of Paris, Jean-François de Gondi, refused to adjudicate the matter. A papal commission appointed to hear the case in Rome fixated on whether Arnauld had contravened common pastoral practice by arguing that priests should grant absolution, and thus approval of receiving communion, only after the completion of penance.[28] The position raised the specter of Jansenism, which had attracted the criticism of Urban VIII (r. 1568–1644) as recently as 1643. The pope decided against ratifying the French approbations given to *De la fréquente communion* but did not condemn the work outright. Arnauld himself made no effort at reconciliation. His father had prepared a brief on behalf of the Paris Parlement against the Jesuits in 1594, and now the son followed suit by firing off a series of works targeting the order. The Sorbonne expelled him when he refused to accede to the bull *Cum occasione* issued in 1653 by Innocent X (r. 1644–55). The constitution, which reiterated the rebukes of the Paris Faculty of Theology against five propositions on predestination in Jansen's *Augustinus*, crystallized the polemical divisions between the Jesuits and the emerging Jansenist movement.[29]

According to the *Remarques judicieuses* (1644), likely prepared by Jacques de La Haye, a member of the Society of Jesus, Arnauld's solicitation of endorsements itself raised doubts concerning his motives.[30] The Jesuit suggested that the entire affair could be explained away as scaremongering, if not a vanity project on Arnauld's part. La Haye's response appealed to mundane facts as well as rarefied theological exposition. Frequent communion was not so frequent after all. He cited the statistic that, in parishes with fifteen thousand to twenty thousand members, perhaps two hundred hosts might be employed on any given Sunday. Besides, rarer communion did not necessarily imply greater rigor. On the contrary, suppressing participation would only embolden "derelicts and idlers" while driving away those who had every reason for "hope in a future conversion." It would appear that Arnauld protested too much. For all his claims to cherish the sacrament, he imposed such exacting standards that most believers would flee in despair. La Haye also raised a practical matter related to the inviolability of the confessional, since directors who advised penitents to avoid communion effectively identified them as guilty of mortal sins.[31]

Following Molina, La Haye asserted the perennial orthodoxy of frequent communion in the joint pursuit of "God's glory" and "our spiritual profit." Whereas Arnauld viewed the alienation of humanity from the divine as nearly impossible to overcome, the *Remarques judicieuses* trumpeted the prospects for reconciliation. The faithful should take advantage of the sacrament whenever possible. Even mortal sin was no hindrance, provided one received absolution in advance. La Haye refuted Arnauld's case and advanced his own via an economic metaphor. Not unlike beggars who seek alms from the rich, the indigent soul should proceed with a sense of hope, perhaps even entitlement. "The more I find myself stripped of grace," he reasoned, "the more boldly I should approach him who has no greater happiness than to dispense the wealth [*faire largesse*] of his favors."[32]

This presumption of liberality flew in the face of Arnauld's understanding of a parsimonious God who held wretched creatures in justifiable contempt. The Jansenist demanded hard-won proof of remorse. The Jesuit offered counsel in a spirit of generosity, accepting the mere desire to reject mortal sin as evidence of contrition. The agony of a long penance led to needless suffering. La Haye advised that in the vast majority of cases, believers should aim to commune weekly. Doing so deepened reverence rather than demeaning it.[33] If the advantages gleaned from the sacrament knew no bounds, neither could one's fervent desire for it be exhausted.

La Haye's premise of absolute abundance served as the point of departure for the reply published by Jean-Pierre Camus. A disciple of François de Sales, Camus held a series of prominent ecclesiastical posts—bishop of Belley, clerical delegate to the Estates-General of 1614, auxiliary to the archbishop of Rouen. He was no stranger to theological polemic on either side of the Jansenist-Jesuit dispute. Before confronting Arnauld, he had quarreled with Jacques Sirmond, a member of the Society of Jesus, over the limits of the pure love of God.[34] Sirmond asserted that concern for salvation necessarily implicated care of self. There was a form of "self-love [*amour-propre*]," he alleged, that made it possible to revere God without losing sight of "one's own particular good."[35] Camus insisted on a still more finely grained distinction between two forms of self-love. As he explained, "we can fully relate our interests to God when they are just. But they cease to be just, however honest they appear, when we reduce them to ourselves through an indomitable sense of ownership [*propriété*]." In contrast, the "supernatural love of self" required that "we love ourselves in charity and according to the order of charity, which is to say, in God, for God, and in reference to God."[36] Sirmond's caveats struck Camus as the machinations of a "servile or mercenary mind" beholden to the fallacy that the soul could exploit the divine to its advantage.[37]

Camus adopted a conciliatory tone with Arnauld, whose work he called "excellent" if "novel" on first reading but still "drawn from the flames of antiquity." His response, *L'usage de la pénitence et communion* (1644), claimed to transcend partisan rivalry. The polemic appeared to him as more a matter of "words and terminology rather than the thing itself." Careful attention to nomenclature might resolve the dispute. As in his exchange with Sirmond, Camus proceeded via differentiation. He likened penance to "a Janus with two faces" or the double-headed eagle associated with the Holy Roman Empire. Not only was it a "virtue" and a "sacrament," but it also had two degrees. The first, contrition, required an abiding regret, inspired by a charitable devotion to God. Its more defective variant, attrition, was motivated by "servile fear, or by a mercenary hope, or by another of our interests." Squaring the circle between the Jesuit and Jansenist positions, Camus stressed the imperative of labor along with the "pure liberality of God." It might be "more severe, but also the surest" standard to demand "perfect contrition" as the ideal penitential state. Ultimately, it remained a question of calculating the relative risk of high penitential expectations and the possibility of success. "Do not act as those merchants," Camus advised, "whose hope for a minor gain leads them down the road to ruin."[38]

Camus devoted a subsequent discussion to the "economy [œconomie] of grace in the conversion of the sinner," which he approached in terms of spiritual self-interest. The "double fear" of exclusion from heaven and eternity in hell marked the "beginning of Christian wisdom" but eventually extended to "the love of God for himself." This moral progression corresponded to devotional practice. Novices might approach the altar four times per year; those more advanced could do so weekly. In another diplomatic gesture, he left it to individual confessors to determine how often their charges should take the Eucharist. Flexibility trumped "two vicious extremes": overindulgence led to "irreverence" toward the sacrament, but hypervigilance instilled "contempt." In matters of communion, one should instead act like a "debtor" who has "recourse to a rich friend" in his time of need.[39]

Camus schematized a form of motivation in which the perception of self-interest remained curiously detached from actions that ultimately redounded to one's personal benefit. By way of example, he took up the case for indulgences. Protestants wrongly accused Catholics of "redeeming their sins in doing certain things that it is commanded to do for gain." Such criticisms failed to apprehend that pardons originated in "the merits and satisfactions of the Savior," which served as the "foundation" and "base" of these donations. Catholics bore a certain culpability for making a vice out of the "abundance and facility" rendered accessible through "the treasure of the Church." This perversion stemmed from a false notion of scarcity—that is, "imagining that one can deplete an infinite treasure." Mixing his metaphors,

Camus approached divine liberality as "a breast overfull with milk" that "is relieved in being suckled." Unlike worldly delights, "one is not afraid of diminishing this treasure in borrowing from its plenitude every day." A "mercenary or servile spirit" had no place among such opulence. If anything, believers "who abandon their interest" for those of God are remunerated a hundredfold, beginning in this life, in addition to the supremely excellent felicity of the next."[40]

In his self-appointed role as mediator, Camus cast a clarifying light on the economic stakes of the debate over frequent communion. He maintained that the pursuit of the glory—not for oneself but for and of God—brought a more valuable reward than wholly self-interested exploits. One should approach heavenly splendor in a spirit of charity, certain in the knowledge of its boundlessness. Camus thus found it revealing to present his case in terms of worldly exchange. He likened God to an affluent benefactor who takes pity on impoverished supplicants. The rewards of piety accrued to the faithful, not only in heaven but also in this life.

Although the prestige of frequent communion never fully recovered from the polemics surrounding Arnauld's work, the concept of plenitude retained its allure. For example, Bossuet and Fénelon clashed in monumental fashion during the Quietist Affair (1694–99), yet another controversy centered on the legitimacy of self-interest in the desire for spiritual goods.[41] Nonetheless, the prelates shared a wonder for sacramental magnificence. Bossuet regarded the Eucharist as a pleasure to delight in without restraint. As he advised his correspondents in remarkably unguarded language, "Devour, quaff, gorge yourself, inebriate yourself on his divine bread." God himself commanded such extravagance. "He wants us to enjoy the possession of him," Bossuet claimed, and had consecrated "his holy flesh" as the "means of this union" so that one might reap "this spiritual profit" to the point of "corpulence."[42] Fénelon, despite his commitment to severing one's possessive attachment to divine gifts, and even to salvation itself, advocated frequent communion, albeit with rather less gusto than Bossuet. The sacrament functioned as our "daily bread," designated by Christ as the medium of the real presence owing to its familiarity as nourishment. To those who pleaded for greater circumspection among communicants, Fénelon answered that "one gives sacred wine even to nursing infants."[43]

The Jesuits and Sacramental Scandal

Frequent communion remained a controversial aspect of the sacramental economy long after the initial debate over Arnauld's treatise had subsided. In a work republished multiple times, the Jesuit Jacques Nouet contrasted God's untold resources with Jansenist penury. The Incarnation resignified poverty as "patrimony" and therefore as the paradoxical means by which believers might "acquire great riches." According to this vision, Father, Son, and Holy Spirit shared "a common good, the enemy of all property." Christ had a distinctive "means of hiding his wealth and his treasures," which rendered them "no less liberal and magnificent." The "faithful man" should appreciate the "utility" of the Eucharist for worshipping God. Nouet reasoned that "the most direct means of possessing all things is to seek and desire him alone." The mind acquired such an understanding in stages. The first resembled mundane "greed" but was soon supplanted by the "foretaste of paradise." Spiritual goods transposed the relationship between desire and fulfillment; fulfillment sustained rather than neutralized the desire, engendering "tranquility" and "inexplicable pleasure" at the same time. If digestion turned "common meats" into nourishment, the Eucharist changed bread into the body of Christ and the sinner into a new being. Similarly, Mass transmitted not only "every spiritual good" but also "worldly goods . . . in relation to the spiritual." Souls should prepare to receive such bounties by suppressing "unruly affections" for "diversions," "conveniences," and "vanities."[44]

The Society of Jesus was not alone in promoting communion several times a month, if not daily. It remained the ideal of the Ursulines and the Visitandines, as well as for the nuns of Port-Royal before the destruction of their sanctuary in 1711.[45] Yet the practice still attracted controversy. In 1745 the Jesuit Jean Pichon published *L'esprit de Jésus-Christ et de l'Église sur la fréquente communion*. He dedicated the work to Catherine Opalińska, consort of Stanisław Leszczyński, duc de Lorraine. Leszczyński owed his position to French patronage. Twice made king of Poland and deposed, his daughter Maria wed Louis XV. On his definitive abdication after defeat in the War of Polish Succession (1733–35), he was granted sovereignty over Lorraine with the proviso that it would be returned to France on his death.

The duchy's religious history was as fraught as its political status. As in neighboring Alsace, Protestantism made early inroads. Huguenots sought refuge in the region's capital, Nancy, after the revocation of the Edict of Nantes in 1685. On assuming the dukedom, Stanisław lent his support to the Catholic cause and placed Jesuits in the vanguard of spiritual revival. Pichon served on a mission to Nancy and its environs, where he encountered not only Protestants but also Jansenists who, following Arnauld and his disciples, opted to abstain from the Eucharist. The Jesuit viewed their reluctance as unnecessary and potentially dangerous.[46] He encouraged believers regardless of devotional aptitude or walk of life to approach the altar daily or as often as possible. Befitting his work's pedagogical aspirations, it takes the form of a dialogue between a doctor of theology and his aptly named acolyte Théophile, who had reached the deaconate but was unsure of his priestly vocation. Another character, an abbé, makes occasional appearances as a Jansenist foil for the doctor.

Pichon rejected outright the argument that deferring communion promoted reverence. Indeed, the opposite was the case. Jansenist self-denial eventually led to "indifference" and then to "disdain" and "infidelity." The only obstacle to communion was mortal sin. No other offense, even if habitual, should cause the least hesitation; on the contrary, frequent communion served as a corrective. Taking direct aim at Arnauld, Pichon argued that "great sins" did not necessitate "great penance." Despite the grumblings of "heretics," God had no need to maintain a strict balance of accounts. The apostles had acted with a "gentle spirit." Their successors should follow this example.[47]

Through the character of the doctor, Pichon criticized his opponents' devotional parsimony. The more one sinned, the more one should commune as a means of discharging obligation and affecting transformation. On Pichon's reckoning, "a golden chalice does not cease to be gold owing to a few specks of dust." Through communion, "the gold of charity will forever grow more and more in your soul, and the specks of dust or minor faults will soon disappear." The "poor and rich" alike were called to the "blessed table." Otherwise, the doctor explained, Christ would not have issued at the Last Supper the general command to "Take and eat," words that "regulate *the entire economy, sacrifice, and sacrament of the Eucharist.*"[48] The spiritual and material economies thus converged in transubstantiation, which redeemed the trespasses of believers from every walk of life.

L'esprit de Jésus-Christ amplified pastoral and theological arguments in favor of frequent communion to an exceptional degree. Like La Haye and Nouet, Pichon characterized the Eucharist as a quotidian form of luxury, the "living bread" that "descends each day from heaven to nourish the Christian people." It had the power to "transform us into Jesus Christ" and render mere humans "living images of the Son of God." The doctor instructed a skeptical Théophile that frequency did not incite contempt when the object in question related to "an infinite goodness." Religion amounted to a "great feast," one incomprehensibly superior to its worldly counterparts. Pichon spared no embellishment in his account of the Eucharist as a banquet at which the "faithful, full of grace and favors, taste at length heavenly delights, drink from the fountain of true felicity, and receive with each communion new wages [*gages*] of eternal happiness." Jesus prefigured this fecundity in his miracle of the loaves and fishes, during which he made seemingly meager provisions not only adequate but more than enough to feed a multitude. Since that time, the early church, patristic sources, the popes, doctors of the church, and the Council of Trent had all advocated regular indulgence in the sacrament.[49]

Over the course of the dialogue, first Théophile and then the recalcitrant abbé find themselves persuaded of the doctor's righteousness. In keeping with Pichon's evident wish-fulfillment, the doctrine grew more emphatic with each new adherent. Early in the text, the doctor contends that no other instrument was "as effective for and as commensurate to our salvation and our weakness. We receive more graces via communion than by any other means."[50] More than 350 pages later, the abbé reiterates and broadens what was already an expansive claim. Communion is further depicted as "the easiest and most pleasant means of salvation," particularly in comparison to the more arduous paths paved by "continual prayer" or "fasting." As Pichon observed, "Everyone can readily participate in this charming sacrament without leaving the world or ruining one's health, without abandoning one's family, one's business, one's occupation." The practice contained hidden depths in which one might glimpse "all the treasures and charms" of "divinity." Lost in "heavenly drunkenness, the soul "forgets the entire world" and is "consumed by fervor for his God alone."[51]

Pichon's work shocked readers. Even fellow members of his order roundly condemned it.⁵² Christophe de Beaumont—the newly appointed archbishop of Paris, who was known to harbor sympathy for the Jesuits—banned the book and advised Pichon to retract it, which the author agreed to do "with all [his] heart."⁵³ *L'esprit de Jésus-Christ* was reprinted in 1747, possibly without the author's consent. It quietly omitted the dedicatory epistle to the duchesse de Lorraine in the original edition but added attestations of the author's orthodoxy—an approbation from the royal censor, a privilege from Cardinal Johann Theodor of Bavaria, prince-bishop of Liège, and a permission from the comte de Rougrave, vicar-general of the diocese.⁵⁴

The reprint edition triggered an even more sweeping wave of protests. Dozens of rebukes, libels, and formal remonstrances appeared in 1747 and 1748.⁵⁵ One indignant polemicist declined to be named but made his objections perfectly plain. His refutation began with a quip. *L'esprit de Jésus-Christ* would have been more aptly named "*L'esprit du P. Pichon et des Jésuites sur la fréquente communion.*" Its pernicious doctrines disseminated the teachings of "an order [*corps*] whose moral laxity has shocked the entire world." Pichon advanced nothing less than a rationalization for "abolishing satisfaction for crimes committed after baptism"—an error the critic associated with Lutheran heresy. In the place of vigorous spiritual labor, Pichon recommended frequent communion. His system thus conflated the "work of penance" with the "recompense" for fulfilling one's obligations.⁵⁶

Official denunciations adopted a less sarcastic but equally damning tone. According to Armand Bazin de Bezons, the bishop of Carcassonne, Pichon had fallen under the spell of "his own dreams" in asserting that frequent communion could effectively produce the moral transformation the practice was intended to reflect. The author misrepresented the church's position on frequent communion, thereby devaluing the other sacraments. Bazin de Bezons also noted Pichon's apparent fondness for the rich, which suggested that they "are more compelled, and in consequence more authorized, to commune daily than those who live in the most exact regularity." The bishop concluded the ordinance by directing his *curés* to prepare penitents for communion through "good works, prayer, reverence, and pious reading."⁵⁷

François de Fitz-James, the bishop of Soissons (and descendent of James II of Britain, through his illegitimate son the first Duke of Berwick) shared many of Bazin de Bezons's misgivings. He denounced Pichon's heretical "new language." The "blessed banquet" of the Eucharist demanded exertion on the part of communicants, who were to "consider seriously . . . whether one is in a state of grace." Pichon erred in minimizing the labor required to commune profitably, especially among those engaged in "worldly occupations." God himself destined all the "children of Adam, without exception," to subsist by the sweat of their brows, a commandment that applied to the religious as well as secular realms.[58]

Given such withering scorn, few clerics came to Pichon's defense. One impetuous theologian, writing under the cover of anonymity, praised the book as "solid and edifying," a bulwark against Jansenist efforts to instill a paralyzing "terror" in the hearts of the clergy and laity alike. Mindful of the deeply partisan nature of the controversy, he further contested the charge that Pichon's doctrines were uniquely Jesuit on the grounds that irreproachable figures such as François de Sales and Vincent de Paul had offered similar counsel. Moreover, Pichon had been unjustly chastised for passing over the "rigors of penance," since the question did not directly pertain to his subject. The Council of Trent lent support to the view that the Eucharist could function as a "work of satisfaction." Read in the proper spirit, the work advised "preparation" and "devotion" by those seeking out the sacrament and thus deserved approbation. For example, the bishop of Sens had hailed the book as "full of piety," and the *Journal de Trévoux* assured readers that it was based on "deep principles, expertly employed arguments, and numerous authorities."[59]

In correspondence with Pichon, Josef Wilhelm Rinck von Baldenstein, the bishop of Basel, expressed horror at Pichon's "violent persecution." Since Baldenstein had penned an approbation for the first edition, he believed himself justified in praising it as a "pious and edifying book." His convictions did not waver even in the face of sustained criticism. "All the holy fathers," he wrote to Pichon, "are united in confirming to me what you say." The Jansenists were fanning the uproar in the hope of winning converts to their "dangerous impressions" of penance and communion. Their standards were set so high as to be impossible to realize. If put into practice, the vast majority of laypersons would be denied access to the Eucharist even at Easter and on their deathbeds. Dejected mortals would abandon the sacrament in frustration. Baldenstein expressed admiration that Pichon sought to combat this "false severity."[60]

The Jansenists' formidable press organ, *Nouvelles ecclésiastiques*, reported on the controversy throughout 1748. The near-universal disdain for Pichon's writings was offered as proof positive of the heterodoxy professed by the Society of Jesus and as justification for the suspicion in which their members were held.[61] The repudiations from *appelants* were so persistent as to invite parody. For example, one cutting text was written in the style of an affidavit. The proceedings were staged as a formal complaint on behalf of Arnauld's nephew against the "defamation" suffered by the venerable author of *De la fréquente communion*. The text identified the petitioner as the "abbé de Saint-Médard" in mocking homage to the *convulsionnaires*, a sect that alleged miraculous healing from the intercession of a revered Jansenist deacon. His address was listed as the rue Neuve Saint-Augustin, a nod to the movement's doctrinal ideal.[62]

On February 15, 1748, the *conseil d'état* handed down its ruling. In light of Beaumont's letter and Pichon's disavowal, the king revoked the privilege originally granted to *L'esprit de Jésus-Christ* and prohibited its further printing or sale.[63] As for the author, he drew up his retraction from Strasbourg and then made his way to the Auvergne before fleeing France entirely. The bishop of Sion, in the Swiss canton of Valais, offered asylum and a post to Pichon, who died in 1751.[64] His fate augured that of his order, which was suppressed in 1764 under intense pressure from an expertly organized Jansenist vanguard with agents in the Parlement of Paris, who argued that the existence of the Society of Jesus on French soil constituted an intolerable affront to Gallican sensibilities.[65]

Eucharistic Expropriation; or, The Refusal of Sacraments

Beaumont's repudiation of Pichon coincided with other turns in the labyrinthine career of *Unigenitus*. Accepted as French law in 1730, the bull met with staunch resistance from the *appelants*. In the middle decades of the century, the parties agreed to a tenuous stalemate that allowed the decree to stand while avoiding undue attention to it. The Jansenists had been chastened by the fallout surrounding the *convulsionnaires*, so named for their tendency to convulse when experiencing supernatural healings or prophetic visions.[66] Throughout the late 1720s and early 1730s, the infirm, the devout, and the curious flocked by the thousands to the tomb of François de Pâris in the cemetery of the Church of Saint-Médard. After attracting considerable publicity, the movement lost its support among those Jansenist elites who found themselves repulsed by the sight of "hideous contortions, . . . indecencies, flashes of every sort of madness, falsehoods, and calumnies."[67] The Jesuits looked to the moderate stance of Pope Benedict XIV, who upheld *Unigenitus* but also made overtures toward rehabilitating the Augustinian stance on essential grace.[68] The government, led until 1743 by Cardinal Andre-Hercule de Fleury as first minister, sought to mitigate the dispute by reining in efforts to impose the bull by force.[69]

Pichon's intransigence nonetheless sounded the first salvos in a theological and political battle that claimed casualties throughout the 1750s. The decade had begun auspiciously enough. An informal truce was approved at Plombières in 1748 by four bishops, including Fitz-James and Bazin de Bezons. An accommodation amendable to both sides appeared feasible, even sustainable. It was not to be. Fleury's death paved the way for Beaumont's elevation in 1746 over candidates more receptive to the Jansenist cause. Although he had sought to keep the peace in his first years as archbishop, he soon adopted a less conciliatory position, especially in the administration of the sacraments.[70]

The quarrel preoccupied the Sorbonne, the Parlement of Paris, and the crown for several years. Attempting to outflank the Jansenists, Beaumont established in 1749 a new system of *billets de confession*. The practice had long been employed as a means of ecclesiastical oversight; the archbishop announced that uncredentialed priests in Paris made such expedients necessary once again. Wayward Jansenists stood forefront in his mind. Before receiving extreme unction, the sick and dying were required to produce an attestation of fidelity to *Unigenitus*, duly signed by their parish priest. A declaration to this effect was issued in 1751.[71] The same year, the clerical establishment was rocked by an incident involving the abbé Jean-Martin de Prades, who was accused of denying the existence of miracles in a thesis to the Faculty of Theology. This new threat—which implicated the burgeoning *philosophe* movement and conflated it with the Jesuit proponents of

Lockean sensationalism and Malebranchian occasionalism—only heightened the general sense of disquiet.[72] The Parlement of Paris lashed out violently, registering the royal act regarding the sacraments only under duress.[73] Beaumont's fellow prelates denied the charge that he was responsible for "openly declaring himself in favor of schism."[74] A protracted debate with grave religious and political ramifications ensued. For individual subjects, their very afterlives hung in the balance.

The anti-Jansenist campaign unfolded along legal as well as theological lines from the outset.[75] French law enshrined the axiomatic distinction between spiritual and temporal authority without clearly defining the relations between these expanding and expansionist hierarchies. As a contemporary jurist observed, "there is nothing more important than not confounding that which belongs to each of these two powers. It is a matter of conscience and of probity, a decision on which the entire management [*bon ordre*] of religion depends." The anonymous author of this brief, apparently drawn up at the request of the episcopate, endorsed the principles of Charles Loyseau and French canon law more generally. "Each of the two powers is sovereign in its domain of jurisdiction," he noted, "and independent of the other in the rights that it has received from God himself." The parlements had no right to interfere in the sacraments since they were "purely spiritual goods," or "visible signs of grace that are invisibly conferred on us." The affirmation of church teachings on the re-presentational prowess of the sacramental sign underpinned legal precedent, which the jurist also duly cited. For instance, Louis XIII's edict of 1610 prohibited secular magistrates from ruling on "the sacraments and other spiritual matters," an order upheld in 1629, 1695, 1724, and 1727. The parlement's claims to act out of a "fear of schism" or "separation from the Church" depended on a *question mal posée*. Tradition demanded that the king "declare himself incompetent" to address the issue at the heart of the current crisis.[76]

This motion approached the conundrum in both theologico-political and economic-theological terms. Royal authority had divine origins yet manifested itself in temporal institutions. From one perspective the arrangement would appear to grant primacy to the clergy, or First Estate, given its role as mediator between the heavenly and terrestrial realms. Yet, from another, kings, as God's "lieutenants" (to cite Bossuet's expression in *Politique tirée des propres paroles de l'Écriture sainte*), replicated the functions of the supreme being on earth.[77] As Loyseau himself had stated, the prince stood as "God's ordained distributor of the enduring honor of this world," a prerogative that could be argued to extend through the crown to the church itself.[78] The goods in question, penance and the Eucharist, were indisputably sacred. Whether the crown should mobilize its power to intervene in how ecclesiastical authorities regulated these possessions remained a point of dispute.

Priests and parlements waged a long, tortuous war of attrition aimed at forcing a settlement. Its first victims were local clergy caught between their own convictions, whether in favor or against the *billets de confession*, and Jansenists desperate to secure last rites in their dying hour. The *curé* of the Parisian parish Saint-Étienne-du-Mont, a man named Bouettin, had denied the sacraments to suspected opponents of *Unigenitus*, among them Charles Coffin, a retired rector of the University of Paris. On March 23, 1752, the parlement ordered him to desist on pain of the confiscation of his property.[79] The king responded tentatively, expressing appreciation for the court's vigilance but calling for restraint in the name of "the just order and peace."[80] After he vacated the magistrates' ruling, they answered on April 18 with a stern judgment renewing the threat to prosecute fomenters of religious division. The decree, which circulated widely, carried the engraving featured in this chapter's introduction that pompously hailed the court as the "avenger of schism." The same month Louis XV reaffirmed the "edicts, declarations, and rulings of the kingdom," especially legislation in 1695 banning the parlements from interfering in "doctrine, the administration of the sacraments, and other purely spiritual matters."[81]

The order fell on deaf ears. In Paris, one Dubois, a former deacon from the parish of Saint-Eustache, was arrested with an Irish priest for withholding the sacrament from the chevalier de Valibouze. The parlement showed relative mercy on the foreigner, who was merely banished from the kingdom for life. Dubois, condemned as a "disturber of the public peace" and for having "aroused a popular emotion," was to be branded with a hot iron and condemned to the galleys.[82] The vicar of Notre-Dame de Louviers in Évreux was arrested on the orders of the parlement for avowing the "unity and infallibility of the Church," which was interpreted as a statement in support of the *billets de confession*.[83]

The contest did not merely pit the worldly against the holy, the parlements against the episcopacy. At issue was the adjudication between competing claims over the sacred. As the magistrates put it to Louis XV in a case heard in 1752, "Never has so important a matter brought your parlement to the feet of your throne. Religion, the state, and the rights of your crown are equally menaced" along with the "fundamental laws of the monarchy." Clergy who "arbitrarily judged their brothers" threatened despotism within the church by deeming the Jansenists "unworthy as such to participate in its goods," of which they have been "deprived with ignominy."[84] From this perspective the sovereign had failed in his duty by breaking with the parlements and even with his own will, which was characteristically divided between the crown's multiple functions. The court took on itself the task of defending the divinely sanctioned rights of the Gallican church and the nation as a whole from threats foreign and domestic—the papacy, the Society of Jesus, even the monarchy itself.

Unigenitus was an apostolic constitution but also French law. The king could not withdraw support from the bishops without negating his previous maneuvers on behalf of the bull. At the same time, the memory of Fleury's gestures of accommodation loomed large. Louis attempted to force a compromise. When the Paris Parlement persisted in its objections, he had its members exiled in May of 1753 to Pontoise and other towns, where they would remain until the following year. On September 2, 1754, he recalled the magistrates and issued a declaration pleading once more for "tranquility" and respect for "the silence imposed for so many years on matters that could not be raised without harming equally the good of religion and the state."[85]

Despite these measures, or perhaps because of them, discord resounded throughout the realm. Case after case followed a predictable pattern of dogged indeterminacy. The hostilities between spiritual and temporal authorities proved especially fierce in Troyes, a diocese where, in the 1760s, Jansenist *curés* militated for the right to represent themselves in fiscal matters.[86] The seeds of contention had already been sown at least a decade earlier. The bishop, Mathias Poncet de la Rivière, from a family with deep ties to the Society of Jesus, expressed incredulity over the parlement's arrogation of power. He demanded to know how "so enlightened a tribunal" could allow itself to forget that the clergy had been granted its power "from Jesus Christ alone," to whom priests and parishioners alike remained "accountable."[87] The plea followed the condemnation of a pastoral instruction he issued in March of 1755 charging the Jansenists of his diocese with fomenting schism. Given that this was the very accusation that the opponents of *Unigenitus* had leveled against Beaumont for imposing the *billets de confession*, the parlement was bound to respond with annoyance. The magistrates banned Poncet de la Rivière's protest, an action he in turn denounced as a "most criminal usurpation." If the precedent were allowed to stand, he warned, the church itself would falter: "seduced peoples will no longer listen to their pastors" and will "seek the rules of their faith in the decrees of the secular tribunals." The parlement asserted that its actions conformed to the royal edict of September 1754. Poncet de la Rivière replied in a subsequent episcopal directive that the measure was never intended to apply to "bishops themselves," who he insisted were the "defenders of the king even at the price of our blood."[88]

Citing the Gospel imperative to "render unto God that which belongs to God, and to Caesar that which belongs to Caesar," the prelate rebuffed parlement's censure of his work.[89] Notably, he amplified this assertion of spiritual will with an appeal to the Eucharist, ordering Forty Hours of prayer "for the pressing needs of the Church, for the conversion of its enemies, and for the consecration of its august monarch." Over three successive days, beginning on Wednesday, July 28, the observances began with the "Benediction of the Most Blessed Sacrament."[90] By July 30 the Paris judges had paid the obstinate cleric in kind, consigning his pastoral mandate to flames. In their view, the call for prayers was a ruse carried out "under a veil borrowed from religion." The magistrates further accused the bishop of Troyes of conjuring up "an imaginary persecution in the very bosom of the Church" while Jansenists who were kept from the sacraments suffered excruciating infractions against their rights as good subjects and faithful Catholics.[91]

The provincial parlements followed the example set in the capital. Judges in Toulouse condemned Me Granet, *curé* of the Montpellier parish of Notre-Dame-des-Tables, as a "disturber of order" for "an unjust and public refusal of the sacraments." He was to be exiled from the kingdom for life.[92] His colleague in the neighboring parish of Sainte-Anne fared even worse. After withholding the sacraments from an ailing woman, he was not only banished but also stripped of all his benefices and other property.[93] In yet another case from Montpellier, an official in the présidial, one Me Lagarde, had fallen gravely ill. He sought extreme unction from four different priests, none of whom were available. His physicians deemed him to be in "imminent danger," which prompted the court to order the bishop to resolve the matter. The prelate supported the alibis of the local clerics. According to canon law, one's parish priest should give last rites if possible. The parlement overruled this requirement and dispatched another ecclesiastic for the sake of Lagarde's imperiled soul.[94] With this action the magistrates commandeered the sacrament in defiance of church tradition and statute. Yet their arrogation of power was no less in keeping with the idealized vision of themselves as guardians of Gallican liberties—even against the encroachments of French bishops.

Numerous canon lawyers, jurists, and theologians issued opinions over the course of the controversy. According to the anti-Jansenist *Consultation de plusieurs canonistes et avocats de Paris, sur le compétence des juges séculiers* (1753), it was essential to delineate jurisdictional boundaries. Did the Eucharist, and with it the spiritual economy, transcend the divided sovereignty of church and state? The learned authors explained that the ecclesiastical judge held competence in purely civil cases involving clerics. The parlements had standing only in criminal matters. The question, then, was whether the refusal of sacraments belonged to the civil or criminal domains. Here another distinction was necessary. If the case turned on the "refusal in itself," the *juge d'Église* presided, given the church's monopoly in administering the sacraments. If, however, there were "extraordinary circumstances," the secular magistrates had the right to intervene—not in the refusal itself but in the conditions under which it was imposed. The authors of the consultation asserted that "bishops receive their power from heaven alone, which flows from no other source but the infinite plenitude of God." As such, civil tribunals were barred from infringing on episcopal authority. It followed that the parlements had no oversight in the "dispensation of sacraments." The axiom had been upheld in multiple judicial decrees and confirmed in the works of "the most erudite authors in the canon law of the kingdom."[95]

The magistrates and their supporters did not allow such claims to go unchallenged. The parlement denounced the consultation not only as "seditious" but also as "falsely and libelously attributed to certain lawyers of the court." They duly ordered the work to be shredded and burned by the royal executioner.⁹⁶ A more fulsome rejoinder attacked its arguments on legal principle. The anonymous *Réponse à la Consultation de plusieurs canonistes et avocats de Paris* affirmed the distinction of civil from criminal cases and the act of denying sacraments from the circumstances in which such decisions were made. The author diverged, however, in how he figured the relationship between the ecclesiastical and temporal domains. The church could only impose "spiritual penalties." If a priest were found guilty of also violating the laws of the state, then additional sanctions should be levied.⁹⁷

This condition applied in the withholding of sacraments for myriad reasons. There were clear precedents of kings and parlements having intervened in such matters; the author cited decrees from 1531, 1651, and 1742. Positioned at the confluence of natural and divine law, the state maintained an interest in the administration of the sacraments precisely because they constituted a form of property. Here the author directly opposed the argument of the original consultation. "Public refusals," he claimed, led to a "disturbance of a citizen in the tranquil possession of participating in the holy Eucharist." Since all impediments of this nature "must be reprimanded by the magistrates," the actions of clerics could not be left to church judges alone. Property in every sphere deserved the vigilance of worldly powers on the grounds that *"the possession of the most spiritual thing in the world is purely temporal."* The monarch had a sacred duty to "maintain his subjects in all their possessions." He was also bound to offer protection to Christians in their time of need. "To deprive a man in agony who is about to die" was "an inhumane act revolting to nature as much as to religion." The king could not ignore these appeals for aid. Moreover, such outrages sparked "trouble in a parish, and in a town," which provided a social rationale for intervention. Thus, "an offense of this nature" was a "privileged case" that involved "the most precious goods." It indubitably required oversight by the civil as well as spiritual authorities.⁹⁸

Several fundamental issues were at stake in the struggles between priesthood and parlement during the refusal of sacraments controversy. It was necessary to determine the status of the Eucharist as a good. Could it be possessed? If so, did the right to property apply? The Jansenist position, as defended by the parlements, answered these questions in the affirmative.

Since the Eucharist counted as the property of individual souls to be used in their moment of need, the church could not legitimately withhold it. Should *curés* act otherwise, both ecclesiastical and secular judges had a responsibility to come to their defense. The pro-*Unigenitus* clergy grounded their arguments in a different vision of the social order. Its agents did not dispute the pricelessness of the Eucharist as a spiritual possession. But they rejected the notion that it belonged to individuals alone. Rather, the church dispensed its wealth according to its own protocols, by its own authority, and without interference from temporal rulers.

Another consultation, prepared by doctors of canon law from the Faculty of Paris, considered the refusal of sacraments from a moral standpoint. A "public sinner," they maintained, should rightfully be denied the Eucharist and extreme unction. Since all "Appellants" or "Quenellistes" committed offenses in the eyes of the church, their exclusion was valid. As evidence the theologians pointed to Christ's prohibition in the Gospels against "giving holy things to dogs." The church observed this rule in regard to the host on the authority of patristic sources, as well as the Synod of Nîmes (1284), the Council of Lavaur (1368), and the Council of Trent. The Jansenists fell under the ban given their penchant for "artifice, fraud, calumny, defamatory libels, outrageous prints, nocturnal assemblies, and obscene convulsions."[99]

A response to this consultation countered that not only had such judgments been deemed "seditious" by the parlement but also that they rested on a series of fallacies. It was impossible in France to recognize public sinners by "a simple publicity of fact"—that is, without the findings of canon and civil law. Sacraments could only be refused in the event of a criminal conviction or if the communicant clearly lacked the necessary "exterior dispositions." For instance, attending Mass in a nightgown or when visibly intoxicated were obvious grounds for exclusion, as was being a "public usurer." Merely speculative failings were insufficient. Failure to accept *Unigenitus* was not in and of itself a crime, according to the *anticonstitutionnaires*, since the bull's propositions were themselves flawed. A "respectful silence" should reign, although the author did not specify the ways in which the parlement's actions would affect such an outcome.[100]

These deliberations hearkened back to previous debates over frequent communion. Another published letter of the time made the connection explicit. The author, supposedly a priest, marveled in his correspondence with a countess under his direction that "it is Arnauld's book on frequent communion that has given rise to your doubts, has nurtured and developed them." The woman, who had Jansenist sympathies, agonized over whether to abide by Beaumont's orders as her bishop and "pastor." At first glance it would seem that there was no "middle ground": either Beaumont was in the wrong, or the parlement was. A possibility for compromise revealed itself if one kept the archbishop's "velvet politics" at a distance. Heretical views might serve a purpose, as Arnauld himself had noted, and the countess reiterated, in "clarifying the truths of the faith." The priest determined that Beaumont's orders were "contrary to the holy canons." Parlement functioned as the "faithful dog" that watched over the church when the "pastors have been sleeping." The metaphor befitted the magistrates' image of themselves as guardians of religious unity. The cleric ultimately concurred with his charge insofar as he regarded the scandal as the work of "providence," a means of "awakening the zeal of defenders of grace."[101]

Despite glaring continuities from the 1650s to the 1750s, not all had remained unchanged in debates over the relative scarcity of the sacraments. For instance, the *reductio ad absurdum* of the Jesuit position espoused by Pichon had met with swift condemnation from not only the disciples of Port-Royal but also the Society of Jesus and the archdiocese of Paris. Arnauld had famously cautioned against allowing frequent communion to become a stumbling block to penance. In a curious reversal of roles, the Jansenists now found themselves arguing for a certain laxity in the possession of the consecrated host—against Beaumont's official policy of strict regulation and accreditation.

The war of words even captivated the attention of Turgot—the future intendant and controller-general. He had begun his intellectual career as a theology student at Saint-Sulpice and the Sorbonne before turning to a legal career. In 1754, while master of requests in the parlement, his works appeared in print for the first time.[102] *Le conciliateur* addressed the struggle between civil and ecclesiastical powers during the clashes over the refusal of sacraments. Turgot grasped the peculiarities of the situation clearly, which he described as a "bizarre project to persecute Calvinists and the clergy at the same time." The parties had failed to differentiate two sorts of tolerance, the civil government's granting of liberty of thought and the church's granting of similar liberties in religion. Although he averred that "there is but one path to salvation," that of the Catholic faith, the state could not compel "intimate persuasion" by force. To the church alone belonged the duty to punish wayward souls. It had every right to excommunicate heretics, but the Jansenists were wrong to appeal to the "corporeal punishment" meted out by the courts since "the kingdom of Jesus Christ is not of this world." Turgot cited Tertullian, Athanasius, and Augustine as authorities for his stance against the arrogation of spiritual authority by the civil magistrates. Religion was in its essence "separated from government." Neither the king nor parlement, then, should intervene in doctrinal affairs. It fell to the episcopate to discipline believers—not in a cruel or petty manner but in the spirit of charity. Turgot justified his views by emphasizing the contrasting characters of the celestial and terrestrial spheres, "the one and other having its distinct laws, as the things of heaven ought to be [distinguished] from the things of the earth."[103]

Learned opinion notwithstanding, the decision ultimately rested with the king. How would he reconcile the demands of *Unigenitus* with the imperatives of religious peace? After considerable stalling and vacillation, he issued a declaration in December of 1756 that in many respects echoed sentiments expressed two years previously by Turgot. His guiding principle would be "absolute silence on questions that could tend only to disturb public tranquility."[104] He lauded Benedict XIV for his encyclical from October, *Ex omnibus*, which reiterated the policy of refusing sacraments to professed *appelants* but did away with *billets de confession*. Louis did so, moreover, even though the papal decree triggered a new wave of indignation.[105] The articles of the royal declaration affirmed that *Unigenitus* carried the force of law. Prelates were to retain the prerogative to instruct the clergy and their parishioners as well as the sole right to decide cases "concerning the administration and the refusal of the sacraments." However, "criminal complaints and proceedings" fell under the purview of the crown. This did not necessarily imply a concession to the parlement as a sovereign law court. On the contrary, the king declared null and void all its previous "decrees and procedures," "sentences or judgements."[106] In light of the legislation, prosecuted clerics like the bishop of Troyes sought restitution for fines imposed by the sovereign courts and local officials.[107]

The Declaration of December effectively overrode the pastoral mandate Beaumont had issued three months previously, in which the archbishop denounced "laws of silence" as "precious to heresy." He complained to his clergy that "after more than seventeen centuries of possession, we are again obliged to prove the independent authority of the church in that which touches on the teaching of the faith." Louis upheld, if only indirectly, Beaumont's threat of excommunication to all Catholics who appealed to "secular judges."[108] Yet there would be no reversion to the *status quo ante*. A monarch who could not assure the religious peace of the kingdom, much less the spiritual well-being of individual subjects, undermined his own *raison d'être*. His sacral credibility suffered further erosion with each passing trial. Despite the challenges posed on all sides—by impending military defeat in the Seven Years' War (1756–63), the ascendency of the *philosophe* movement, cries of despotism from the parlement, and seemingly irresoluble fiscal deficiencies—the regime's gravest wounds were perhaps self-inflicted.[109] Divine-right absolutism asserted a Eucharistic model of power that was vested in an omnipresent, indivisible, immortal body. A king forced to vie for jurisdiction over the sacramental economy cast doubt on his claims not only to religious legitimacy but even to political sovereignty itself.

. . .

Historians continue to view the fate of the eighteenth-century Gallican church and state through the prism of degenerative processes: dechristianization, desacralization, disenchantment.[110] Yet symptoms should not be confused with causes. As this and the preceding chapter have argued, disputes in the economic-theological field involved no small measure of creative destruction. Without Arnauld's provocative treatise on frequent communion, it is uncertain whether Jansenism would have assumed its distinctly French aspects or sheer prominence on the spiritual and social scenes. Likewise, but from the opposite end of the doctrinal spectrum, Pichon's attempt to encourage the practice, which came seemingly as a bolt out of the blue, elevated the already high stakes of the refusal of sacraments controversy. This bitter feud laid bare the constitutive tensions of absolutism under the Old Regime. Struggles between the church, the crown, and the parlements for preeminence would continue down to 1789—in debates over the Eucharist, to be sure, but also over money, usury, and luxury.

Among this book's central theses is that theology and economy were deeply imbricated from the outset. Theology was always already economistic. As the refusal of sacraments controversy made clear, it could not be otherwise in a world where sovereignty and property were inexorably bound up in one another. To cite once more the *Réponse à la Consultation de plusieurs canonistes et avocats de Paris*, the possession of all goods, even the most spiritual, fell potentially under the purview of civil authority. Yet the obverse of the statement held equally true, framing a problematic with conspicuous economic-theological aspects. As the universal equivalent in the production and distribution of grace, the plenitude of the Eucharist gradually extended to consumption in all its forms, belying a unidirectional, teleological transfer from the theological to the economic. Even hardened materialists conceded that economic verities were steeped in theology—not least because of the role played by clerics in their articulation.

Frequent communion and the refusal of sacraments revolved around the vexing possibilities of intervention in a seemingly boundless field. The complete abandonment of oversight remained inconceivable, even for prophets of laissez-faire, such as Turgot, who demanded the ministrations of both the absolutist state and the universal church to actualize reform. Theologians, prelates, and *parlementaires* clashed over how to embed (as Karl Polanyi might have it) the sacramental economy in political, ecclesiastical, scientific, and commercial institutions.[111] Although Jansenism had recognized the existence of a debased but autonomous world, its acolytes readily accepted judicial review in spiritual matters, especially when under assault. The professed enemies of Port-Royal, from Bourdaloue to Pichon to Réguis, infused their thought with an optimism predicated on the bounty of divine largesse, which was granted communally but nevertheless enjoyed exclusively by individual souls. The conceptual and practical tasks of economic theology required determining the most pious means of mobilizing these riches.

CHAPTER 3

The Spirit of Speculation

THE PRINT *ARLEQUYN ACTIONIST* (*Harlequin the Stockjobber*) graces the pages of *Het groote tafereel der dwaasheid* (*The Great Mirror of Folly*), a Dutch work lampooning the mania for economic speculation in the late 1710s (fig. 3.1).[1] Although the wave swept through the United Provinces and Britain, it issued from a French epicenter, where a naturalized subject from Scotland, John Law, presided as controller-general of finances. The business adjacent to the platform is named Quincampoix, after the Parisian street that served as the marketplace for stock in the Company of the Indies (Compagnie des Indes). Above the throng squats Law, who is seen vigorously carrying out the chief ritual of his enterprise (fig. 3.2). Two assistants pour gold coins into a funnel and down his throat. Like the golden fowl of myth, he produces riches, but of a novel kind. Rather than bars of bullion, Law's digestion yields a slip of paper bearing his name. A speculator pulls anxiously at the note, ready to enter it into circulation. The satire seemed to speak for itself: the share certificate, although duly signed, amounted to shit. Yet the print's gesture toward a literally vulgar material base engaged the viewer in no less essential a function—that of accounting for the desire aroused by a tawdry object that had passed itself off as credible.

The Great Mirror of Folly synthesized multiple traditions and genres (*commedia dell'arte*, Greco-Roman mythology, Rococo), with alchemical transmutation

Figure 3.1 *Arlequyn actionist (Harlequin the Stockjobber).* In *Het groote tafereel der dwaasheid*, ca. 1720. Beinecke Rare Book and Manuscript Library, Yale University.

furnishing a prime element in the work's iconography.² *Harlequin the Stockjobber* knowingly drew on a semiotic context in which distinctions between the scientific and the sacramental had not solidified and in which alchemy entailed far more than lead's conversion into gold. Joseph Chambon, a disciple of the Swiss sage Paracelsus, described digestion as a "transmutation that occurs in the stomach," the "first operation" on which all other bodily processes depend.³ René Descartes honed the analogy further, likening the consumption of nourishment to a natural form of transubstantiation—that is, Christ's embodiment under the signs of bread and wine.⁴ Indeed, Law, who publicly converted to Catholicism, is portrayed kneeling to receive the coins as if in the act of communion. His stance even recalls the mystical mill of medieval spirituality, a trope depicting the Eucharist as a mechanized, metabolic process (fig. 3.3).⁵ The sheer ubiquity of alchemical applications facilitated parody, which in turn sent up but also unveiled a faith in Law as the miraculous vessel of wealth. The engraving thus reiterated, albeit obliquely, what its literal meaning opposed: the convergence of the theological and the economic.

Figure 3.2 *Arlequyn actionist* (detail). Beinecke Rare Book and Manuscript Library, Yale University.

Figure 3.3 Workshop of Bartolomeus Zeitblom. Panel representing a mystical mill, n.d., ca. 1455–1522. Museum Ulm and the Archive for Research on Archetypal Symbolism.

This chapter argues that a Eucharistic-alchemical complex of representation and practice lent intelligibility to the effects of what contemporaries referred to as Law's "System." The Scotsman devised paper money and stock shares as a means of revitalizing French finances through credit, which depended not only on abstract economic mechanisms but also on the willful belief of participants. "The public," he remarked of his bank, must have "complete confidence in its bills."[6] It is by no means incidental that references to the host and to the philosopher's stone proliferated in works of the period. The reception of Law's proposals took place within a specifically French, Catholic, sacramental framework. The church defended the dogma that consecration actively gave rise to priceless effects. The Eucharist was understood to elevate simple bread into the real presence of Christ. The philosopher's stone attracted adherents on a similar basis: transmutation, like transubstantiation, breathed new life into inferior substances. By the same token, the dualities of paper—abundant yet valuable, unobtrusive yet palpable—seemingly enabled it to create riches through circulation alone and, in so doing, to perpetuate the motion of the entire economic apparatus. Lead turned into gold, gold into paper, bread and wine into the body and blood of Christ.

What emerged on the streets, on the printed page, and in the minds of traders was a new economic theology of money, with financial instruments accredited by the regent as its sublimely material base. Law's admirers and critics appealed to a vast number of French subjects accustomed to comprehending transmutation and transubstantiation within a single symbolic matrix. The abbé Jean Terrasson, a major spokesman for and investor in the new fiscal regime, drew on his previous Eucharistic writings to bolster confidence in Law's bank and companies. Terrasson's efforts resonated in journals, memoirs, and songs playing on the generative potential of notes and stock, albeit in a more satirical mode. More than five hundred thousand claimants sought relief after the System faltered; their papers were ceremoniously burned in 1723 to preserve the "secret of families."[7] Given the scant archival record, popular accounts offer a compelling glimpse into the epistemological basis for assent among readers, listeners, and viewers. As these sources suggest, Eucharistic and alchemical aspirations underwrote the furor for paper money and shares, which propelled French subjects to invest themselves in the dream of boundless accumulation.

. . .

As a Dutch work, *The Great Mirror of Folly* adopted an implicitly Protestant perspective, associating excessive financial credulity with suspect religious convictions. Pagan deities and devils, but also alchemy and Catholicism, attracted ridicule owing to their misplaced materiality and disregard for reason. The Janus-faced nature of the Mississippi Bubble, at once perspicacious and reckless, has similarly beguiled economic historians who have endeavored to distinguish the presumably sound elements of the System from its excesses. Scholars acknowledge the program's flaws while underscoring its far-sighted logic. Although Law came to be reviled in the eighteenth century, he also proved the superiority of fiat currency and signaled a prescient application of the quantity theory of money.[8]

According to historians of political culture, Law's economic reign provided ammunition for detractors of divine-right politics. In the eyes of its opponents, his System marked an attempt by the crown to seize subjects' gold under the cover of social confusion, setting the stage for later conflicts between the king and the parlements.[9] These struggles raised the specter of public debt that haunted the military-fiscal apparatus: states that compulsively spent beyond their means on conventional and economic warfare might exploit the power to declare bankruptcy, which effectively legalized theft.[10] For a brief moment, Law featured centrally in efforts to renegotiate the European balance of power through financial innovation rather than force of arms, with the aim of shifting the geopolitical advantage in France's favor at the expense of the British.[11]

In keeping with eighteenth-century observers such as Hume, who likened the "obligation of promises" to "*transubstantiation*," historical scholarship has frequently remarked on the relationships between communion, alchemy, and paper money.[12] As Carl Wennerlind demonstrates, Samuel Hartlib and his circle pursued abortive alchemical experiments before endorsing plans to introduce credit money, culminating in the establishment of the Bank of England in 1694.[13] Recent scholarship on Law's scheme has underscored how it effectively performed transmutation in reverse by changing precious metal into paper. For instance, Jonathan Sheehan and Dror Wahrman depict Law as an adept of "a kind of alchemical magic." His downfall precipitated soul-searching on the part of social theorists and political economists such as Hume and Smith, who reckoned that market mechanisms functioned with providential soundness, if not with perfect predictability, since financial bubbles triggered corrections.[14] Arnaud Orain argues that the propaganda devised for the System in the *Nouveau Mercure*, the Regency's semiofficial newspaper, knowingly exploited popular fantasy. Evocations of the untold riches to be had in the "earthly Eden" that was Louisiana affirmed the power of the sovereign, whose persona contemporaries likened to "the image of God."[15]

According to these narratives of supersession, alchemists failed at transmutation but performed the indispensable task of conforming economic thought to the procedures and aims of the scientific and financial revolutions.[16] Of equally crucial significance, such accounts demur from integrating alchemy into the more expansive theological paradigm from which it emerged.[17] The atheist Hume had taken considerable care in choosing the metaphors by which to describe the seemingly miraculous functions of credit. In word and in deed, transubstantiation and transmutation shared a religious context that amplified the resonances between the Eucharist, alchemy, and money. Early modern experiments in generating sacramental and worldly riches should not be reduced to a proto- or pseudoscience, a literary trope, or a means to an end in political propaganda. Behind these speculative feats stood an economic-theological endeavor that was profoundly theorized and comprehensible to a broad public.

The present chapter delves into the French theological past, which encompassed the Eucharist and alchemy as iterations of a comprehensive sacramental regime. Under this symbolic order, the metaphors engendered by metamorphosis captured not only a manner of speaking but also a mode of being structured around the inherent correspondences between things.[18] The reception of Law's program in Catholic France verifies that certain exceptional signs were thought to transform the nature of the thing signified and, in so doing, endow it with fecundity. The Tridentine catechism extolled the rituals by which bread and wine were turned into the body and blood of Christ, a doctrine that confraternities spiritually grasped and viscerally enacted through perpetual adoration. Alchemists who remained in communion with Rome claimed that the philosopher's stone performed a mediating function comparable to the consecrated host. Viewed through the same spiritual lens, Law's paper money assumed an air of the miraculous.

The Eucharistic-Alchemical Complex

Long before the Mississippi Bubble, sacramental and alchemical precedents engendered confidence among French subjects in a world where the spectacular was routine. As we have seen, theologians bestowed moral authority and institutional weight on a form of re-presentation according to which the treasure of grace could be circulated and augmented in value through otherwise common substances. The laity pledged themselves in rising numbers to liturgical practices honoring the host. Alongside these efforts, adepts in the occult arts marshaled orthodox teachings to commend the philosopher's stone as a crucible of perfect abundance that not only produced gold but also purged the world of sinful corruption. Although under scrutiny, the hermetic tradition drew on doctrinal associations with the Eucharist. Investors in Law's companies imbued commercial ventures with a parallel desire. Belief in transubstantiation lent plausibility to transmutation in its various guises. A Eucharistic-alchemical complex conferred prestige on Law's plan while also exposing the credulity that precipitated its collapse.

The priestly consecration of the host and hermetic techniques of converting metals had long informed each other. The Scholastics responsible for the doctrine of transubstantiation incorporated knowledge from Arabic-language sources. Schoolmen found the impetus to innovate Christian thought through the recovery not only of Aristotelianism but also, more generally, of systems of classification that stipulated the conditions under which one substance changed into another. In 1202 the papacy approved the usage of the term *transsubstantiatio* to describe the process by which mere bread and wine were converted into the body and blood of Christ. Although clerics developed the lexicon themselves, they drew on the findings of alchemists to elaborate the mechanics of substantial mutability. The treatises *De Eucharistia* and *De Alchimia*, attributed to the Doctor of the Church and acclaimed adept Albertus Magnus (1200–1280), exemplified the transferability at work between these domains of knowledge.[19]

Throughout the medieval period, alchemy encompassed transmutation as well as a host of techniques related to distillation, extraction, fermentation, generation, and the creation of *homunculi*, or human figures in microscopic form. The mere theoretical possibility of making new beings gave practitioners pause, lest they arrogate to themselves the divine right exercised by priests during Mass.[20] As natural philosophers turned to more specialized experiments in mineralogy, metallurgy, and medicine, prefiguring the modern discipline of chemistry, alchemists drew fire for the potentially heterodox implications of their art. The religious orders had begun to prohibit alchemical experimentation by the 1270s. Thomas Aquinas (1225–74) harbored doubts concerning the fabrication of precious metals. In 1317 Pope John XXII (r. 1316–34) condemned such ventures as aberrant.[21]

Adepts responded by seeking legitimation in scripture and orthodox religious teachings while also emphasizing the practical utility of their work.[22]

Eucharistic dogma offered promising ground for such efforts owing to the intellectual genealogy of transubstantiation. Now, however, the directionality of appropriation was reversed. The celebrated physician and alchemist Arnald of Villanova (1240–1311) claimed that his labors proceeded in stages symbolizing Christ's life, death, and miraculous resurrection.[23] In the late fifteenth century, Arnald of Brussels employed the terms transubstantiation (*transsubstantiatio*) and alchemy (*alchimia*) interchangeably.[24] Theophrastus von Hohenheim (1493–1541), better known as Paracelsus, passed between self-professed vocations as an itinerant preacher of the Gospel and esoteric seeker who oriented alchemy toward pharmaceutical as much as spiritual healing.[25] Even as Paracelsian alchemists expanded their intellectual mission and secured prominent positions in early modern courts, they persisted in affirming resemblances between the consecrated host and the philosopher's stone.[26]

In France, Pierre Jean Fabre (1588–1658) meticulously elaborated this standpoint. A Montpellier-trained *médecin ordinaire du roi* notable for his research on the plague, he was also a fervent Paracelsian and self-professed "philo-chimiste," whose numerous treatises were cited by, among others, Isaac Newton.[27] His career thus epitomized the medicalization of alchemy and its halting transition to iatrochemistry and related disciplinary successors. At the same time, he reiterated the hermetic tradition's theological significance as a means of defending the Catholic view of the Eucharist.[28] His approach in *Alchymista christianus/L'alchimiste chrétien* (1632)—a work he dedicated to Pope Urban VIII as the "alchemist of all Christians"—adopted the principle that the sacred meanings of transmutation ran along a continuum with more worldly pursuits.[29] Alchemical science aimed at returning created beings to the closest approximation of the perfection of their origins.

To this end, Fabre's treatise viewed the world via correspondences—between the divine and human registers of existence but also between metaphysical and physical economies. Knowledge of nature depended on knowledge of the supernatural. The "defective, impotent, and imperfect" elements of the mundane world cast into sharp relief God's "eternal, infinite, and omnipotent" existence. For all its frailties, the mind could identify these attributes in the "immutable order" that reigned among "all the parts of the universe." God remained visible, then, in the "surprising progression [*enchaînement*] of things."[30] Crucially, Fabre approached resemblance not as a passive reflection but, in the late Renaissance spirit of the Tridentine catechism, as a productive means of generation. The "salt of the world" exhibited the "most perfect virtue, power, and energy." Alchemy thus constituted the science of representing life in its "infinite efficacy."[31]

In the beginning there was unity, or the "substantial Trinity that is found in the first and last matter of all things." Every created being was believed to emerge from the "chrysalis [*ébauches*] of this mystery." God saw fit to "imprint externally a striking image" of his being onto mercury or primal matter, which "possesses all generations, corruptions, and alterations." Likewise, Christ as Logos signified the "spirit of life" through creation, "the virtue of all of nature, the faculty of the universe, its energy and power, the seed of the heavens, the stars and the elements." A "natural mirror" reflected the figure of a "tri-unity [*Tri-unité*], which is of such infinitude in divine things, and of such vastness in natural things, that nothing could be added to it."[32]

The principle of divine economy governed relations among beings and precluded scarcity. The "light" of heaven emanated from "its inexhaustible source" down to the "center of the earth," thereby conducting the warmth that stimulated the "propagation of the universe." As the Father begat the Son, so did physical forms derive from mercury. Adam's Fall and Christ's passion foretold that humanity's triumph over sin would lead ultimately to the attainment of paradise. In dialectical fashion, "corruption" was necessary to "excite the generations" that characterized the spiritual as well as natural world. Jesus's crucifixion was no less essential in that it "communicated to us the immortal fruits of the Roman Church, by which we receive eternal life, the remission of our sins, glory, grace, and sanctification."[33]

The passage from death to eternal life was facilitated by the philosopher's stone, which Fabre described as "a deep red powder, more brilliant and radiant than rubies," more lustrous than "gold and silver so pure and beautiful that they carry no metallic stain." It thus simulated the Eucharist in that the "transmutation of lead and iron into gold," like the "transmutation of ourselves," bore witness to the awesome changes wrought through "divine art." Fabre specified that the host served as the key to the other "mysteries" of the faith, which were "useful and profitable in it alone." At the Last Supper Jesus had referred to himself as "flesh," but he was also a "kind of physical stone that transmutes impure metals." Again, Fabre employed hermetic language to describe a state of becoming at once human and divine, alchemical and mystical. "This is my body," Christ declared in the Gospels. "There," Fabre answered, occurred "this miraculous and surprising transmutation, . . . by which God makes himself man, and by which the God-man gives himself as true nourishment to all men, to change them into saints and into god-like beings."[34]

Following the catechism, Fabre codified alchemical science in reference to "instruments" or efficacious symbols that projected the power they represented into and onto the world. Each of the seven sacraments found an analogue in the hermetic arts, but Fabre reserved pride of place for the philosopher's stone, given its Eucharistic character. Communion was "divine and heavenly nourishment," the base of "eternal and spiritual life." It conferred "the marks of distinction of Christ," thus setting the elect apart from the reprobate. The savior was "infinite, immense, incomprehensible"; he was "grander and more admirable" still when embodied under the "veil of the accidents of bread and wine." The Eucharist replicated the "incarnation of the Word" through "many and varied miracles." Calvinists and other "heretics" denied this "real and substantial transmutation" at their peril.[35]

According to Fabre's self-professed "*Economic method*," which he claimed had been established by God to defend the church from internal and external enemies, communion revealed the transformative power of the sacraments. Hermetic and sacerdotal adepts specialized equally in the manipulation of debased substances. Alchemists "convert corrupted, putrid, and foul mixtures" with the heat of "natural fire." "Priests" turn "sinners" into "pious, holy, virtuous men" by applying the "true Christian elixir." This analogy of function demonstrated an essential truth. To potential critics who might doubt the legitimacy of the metaphor, Fabre answered that he offered it "with respect and honor." The structural similarities between transubstantiation and transmutation proved the "depth and supernatural height of these mysteries," the "divine as well as natural secrets" that are "contained under the surface [*écorce*] of things." The polyvalent character of words enacted the fecundity of the universe and foreshadowed the "eternal gifts" awaiting "those who obtain supreme beatitude."[36]

Jean-Albert Belin, the Benedictine monk and bishop of Belley, likewise understood the philosopher's stone as a means of elevating spirit and matter.

In his *Apologie du grand œuvre* (1659), he noted of transmutation that "its effects are so miraculous" as to render "the health that it procures and conserves among the living, the perfection it bestows on all the compositions of Nature, and the great riches that it produces in most divine fashion" secondary among "its most exalted marvels." It "cleanses all things of their original stains," as did redemption through Christ.[37] According to Belin, creation arose incrementally, beginning with "a universal and general mixture," the "seed of gold" from which all else was born. The "composite" occurred naturally before being corrupted by "original sin." The philosopher's stone, which Belin upheld as the "treasure that contains all the others," sought to remove this blemish.[38]

Belin extended his research to other instruments that conveyed representational power, publishing a *Traité des talismans* in 1658. By definition, a talisman was a "seal, figure, character, or image of a celestial sign" that had been "imprinted, engraved, or chiseled on a sympathetic stone or metal." The object owed its value not to its material composition but to a capacity to summon spiritual wealth. This efficacy stemmed from the principle that "superior bodies continually transmit their power in order to conserve, aid, and assist inferior bodies." Harnessing their force required that the image be reproduced with as much verisimilitude as possible. For instance, the god Mercury shared an affinity with the metal of the same name. Similarly, talismans made to conjure terror or love should feature a depiction of Mars or of Venus, respectively. Under the right conditions, the amulets took on a life of their own, granting the "intelligence that moves them" to their bearers.[39]

Belin's treatise noted in passing that Christians possessed their own "divine talismans."[40] He had explored this insight in a previous work entitled *Les emblèmes eucharistiques* (1647). Divine "power" worked through "delicate images" and "remarkable symbols" that "gently lead our thoughts to greater things." Like a celestial painter, God gave us a "figure" of Christ, the "richest work of his omnipotence," the "most beautiful star of his heavens." Fittingly, the Eucharist enchanted the faithful with "emblems that warrant as much respect as they do adoration." Like the savior's body, which manifested itself in the form of humble bread and wine, these signs allowed one to perceive "immense wealth in extreme poverty." As a heavenly father, God distributed two forms of treasure among his creatures. The first, which Belin compared to "furnishings," "money," and other movable possessions, bestowed "his wisdom, his knowledge, his justice, his providence" on human heirs. The second, not unlike the capital held in land, comprised "temporal and spiritual goods that he assigns and imparts to men." The Eucharist, or "most wonderful of transmutations," contained both sources of splendor.[41] No material luxury could rival the sacrament, which, like the philosopher's stone, encompassed the germ of all that counted as precious.

The Eucharistic-alchemical complex articulated by Fabre and Belin cast re-presentation as a profitable endeavor, thereby explicating otherwise impenetrable mysteries. Catholic responses to Protestantism only strengthened the reverence of French subjects for the host. The doctrine of transubstantiation likely originated alongside transmutation. Adepts duly elaborated these correspondences in terms of the sacramental life of the church, which posited the body of Christ as a general equivalent—or, to repeat Belin's expression, the treasure that contains all the others. As we will see, Law's System demanded that economic actors accept the common matter in banknotes and stock shares as a universal means of exchange and store of value. His supporters followed suit by glorifying objects believed to give rise to wealth in the very act of signifying it. Paper was hailed as the reincarnation of the philosopher's stone, with the capacity to spawn precious metal if not render its possession obsolete.

Figuring the Infinite: Cartesian Variations on the Eucharist

The new natural philosophies of the seventeenth century—Cartesianism in particular—developed ingenious ways to account for transubstantiation and transmutation. Descartes himself had been steeped in the occult as a youthful seeker of the *philosophia perennis* before developing his model of the world as mechanism. Much to his disdain, contemporary hermeticists later appropriated Cartesian physics, as they did the Eucharist, for their thought experiments in the manipulation of metals.[42] Although wary of such attempts, Descartes classified transmutation among the enigmas "subject to the research of human reasoning."[43] Likewise, it was incumbent on him as a Catholic to reconcile his theory of matter with tenets of the faith, the Eucharist chief among them. Eager to defend him from charges of irreligion, French acolytes elaborated his theological musings in their own creative applications of Cartesianism. The abbé Terrasson, who later made a star turn in extoling the virtues of Law's System, featured prominently in these efforts.

The mature Descartes adhered to the principle of intellectual modesty, never formulating a consistent Eucharistic doctrine.[44] In letters to the Jesuit Denis Mesland, he claimed that the substance of Christ's body replaced the substance of the species of communion. He departed from Aristotelian models, however, in denying that attributes commonly used to identify bodies actually existed. Matter was defined by the abstract properties of extension (size, shape, motion, and rest). Seemingly concrete traits such as color, odor, taste, and temperature stemmed from the sense impressions occasioned by the space between a body and the air surrounding it.[45] In the case of the Eucharist, the observer's eyes continued to perceive the surface or *superficies* associated with what had been the substance of bread but that now lingered "between the bread (or in actuality the body of Christ after consecration) and the air that surrounds it." If joined to this material trace, Christ's soul could appear in the shape of bread, thereby fulfilling the principal criterion of transubstantiation. Despite rejecting the Scholastic distinction between the essentially divine substance of the host and the nonessential properties or accidents of bread and wine, Descartes insisted that his view conformed to the Council of Trent.[46]

In describing how the body and blood of Christ could assume the characteristics of bread and wine, Descartes also drew on his understanding of natural processes. Human beings changed throughout the course of their lives but retained their identities through the body's enduring relationship with the same soul. For instance, when one consumed bread, it became part of oneself through digestion. A similar outcome transpired during communion but through supernatural means.[47] In an exchange with his editor and translator, Claude Clerselier, Descartes stipulated that transubstantiation did not entail merely changing out the matter contained in the host with divinity as if it were "a piece of gold in place of a slice of bread." The alteration he had in mind was far nobler, since it required union with a new soul.[48]

Descartes ran afoul of clerical opponents who charged that denying substantial forms and real accidents undermined church teaching, which held that the sensible qualities of bread and wine could exist independently of their substance. Yet he found kindred spirits among Jesuits such as Mesland and the Jansenist Arnauld, who engaged Descartes in a sustained dialogue.[49] On reading the *Meditationes de prima philosophia* (1641), Arnauld raised a glaring objection: how could one reconcile the Cartesian system with the doctrine of real presence? Descartes answered in his Fourth Replies to the *Meditationes* by elaborating his theory of the *superficie*. He understood the species of communion as more properly referring to the "surface which is in between the individual particles of the bread and the bodies surrounding them." Far from challenging Catholic dogma, Descartes had the audacity to claim that "orthodox theologians ... will thank me greatly for putting forward in my physics opinions that are in far greater agreement with theology than the traditional ones."[50] Arnauld accepted Descartes's explanation despite its apparent boastfulness and the unstated implication that consecrated bread remained in some sense bread. Nonetheless, his works were placed on the Index in 1663, almost certainly owing to his foray into Eucharistic theology.[51]

Hoping to vindicate Descartes, the Dominican Robert Desgabets (1610–78) published his treatise *Considérations sur l'état présent de la controverse touchant le Très-Saint Sacrement de l'autel* in 1671.[52] The work began with an account of how Christ's body came to replace bread and wine, an issue that had divided theologians both before and after Trent. Thomas Aquinas stressed the total conversion of the Eucharistic species. In contrast, Duns Scotus held that the substance of bread must first be completely annihilated before it was then supplanted.[53] Desgabets directly refuted the Scotist position and proposed Cartesianism as a more plausible philosophical framework for transubstantiation than the Thomistic alternative. There remained the crucial issue of how to preserve Descartes's supposition that "quantity alone" explains "all the other Eucharistic accidents." In response, Desgabets advanced the theory of indefectibility. What appears to the human mind as "destruction" actually entailed "the change or dissolution of certain parts of matter, which forever persists in nature." If accidents could endure in the absence of substance, then the human mind would soon descend into an abyss of doubt, uncertain of the reality of any physical object. What theologians erroneously called "Eucharistic accidents" were nothing other than "true modes and appearances of substances." Although such language implied that bread remained after consecration as Christ's body, Desgabets stipulated that the host was radically altered in being united with "the soul and the divinity of the Savior." In effect, the matter of the bread took on a new aspect without necessarily assuming a different physical form. Desgabets thus allowed that the full nature of transubstantiation remained "a mystery" but one that need not "shock reason."[54]

The Paris Faculty of Theology was scandalized by such claims, which prompted its members to uphold a royal ban on teaching Cartesianism. Desgabets nonetheless continued to give lectures and prepare manuscripts that circulated among his students.[55] An exposé of "Eucharistic philosophy" specified the route by which the consecrated bread became Christ.[56] He was adamant that the transformation in question was not "metaphorical and figurative." To understand "substantial change" in the proper sense meant recognizing what conferred identity on a being in the first place. Following Descartes, he claimed that "the essential form of man" is "the rational soul" joined to a particular body. This relationship occurred miraculously during the Eucharist. Priestly consecration fused the species of bread and wine to Christ's soul, affecting these once purely material substances through a "*transmutative* action." Thereafter, "bread ceases being bread" and "becomes the body of Jesus Christ" without a "pure and simple annihilation" or "production of substance."[57]

Desgabets offered a more fulsome statement of his position in the *Traité de l'indéfectibilité des créatures* (ca. 1653–74). Persons and things willed into existence by an omnipotent deity could not simply perish without a trace. "There is a contradiction," then, in "saying that they are annihilated, or that they could lose the being that God has given to them." Properly understood, "all these productions and destructions are in effect merely new movement or new moments of rest in the parts of matter." God could even create new worlds as desired. The universe constituted a "true expanse" that knew no "limit" except for "our imagination."[58] In Desgabets's view, then, the universe was both fully abundant and expandable to infinity. From a merely human perspective, which was limited to present realities understood at a given time, the world might appear closed. However, the constant recombination of elements into different arrangements revealed God's perfect liberty to engender new spiritual and corporeal forms.[59]

Desgabets took care to defend and enhance the Cartesian position that infinity was both possible and imaginable, while stipulating that the identification of matter with extension did not obviate the necessity of a supreme being. As he observed in *Le guide de la raison naturelle*, one should maintain a distinction between the divine and "created" iterations of infinity. The latter, which Descartes termed the "indefinite," served as an approximation of the former. Whereas the infinity of God possessed an "absolute simplicity," its counterpart in the phenomenal world required "addition" and "accumulation." The most dearly held religious beliefs proved that the human mind could conceive of infinity in both senses. The "learned" and the "ignorant" alike grasped the "eternity of the glory of the blessed." Likewise, "common sense" understood the Trinity in generative terms, as (1) the Father, or divine self-knowledge, (2) the Son, or "the word or idea that is produced by this act of knowledge," and (3) the Holy Spirit, or the "love" that joined "the Father who gives perfections and the Son who receives them."[60] Desgabets thus accentuated the boundless fecundity of the theological economy as representative of God's infinite scope and power.

Desgabets's fellow Cartesian Terrasson pursued even further the associations between boundlessness and the sacrament as representative of the infinite power of divinity. The son of a counselor in the sénéchaussée-présidial court in Lyon, Terrasson first trained for a life in the church, studying at the Oratory and receiving ordination as a subdeacon. His participation in the Quarrel of the Ancients and the Moderns vaulted him to literary fame. By 1707 he had secured membership in the Académie des sciences and in the following decades assumed the chair of Greek and Latin philosophy at the Collège de France. In 1732 he joined the ranks of the Académie française.[61] Jean Le Rond d'Alembert praised Terrasson as the "head of practical philosophers of his age," citing his imperturbable devotion to Cartesian natural philosophy as well as to Law's System, for which he served as publicist.[62]

At the Oratory, Terrasson prepared studies on theology and metaphysics, which were revised from the 1710s to the 1740s and published in 1769 as the *Traité de l'infini créé*.[63] As its title suggests, the abbé aimed at elaborating Descartes's arguments in favor of the relentless extension of matter and spirit, which in his view followed from the bearing of its all-powerful creator. Descartes himself preferred the term *indefinite* to describe the dimensions of creation, reserving absolute infinity to God alone. His denial of the void also led him to demur from insisting on the endless plurality of distinct worlds, since there were no chasms in which such bodies could form.[64] Terrasson held that the tenets of infinity and terrestrial plurality not only conformed to "the new philosophy" but were also essential for its advancement: "All that there is in nature, matter, spirit, number, and duration, is actually and positively infinite." To profess otherwise entailed doubting God's omnipotent fecundity on every scale of being.[65] As had Desgabets, then, Terrasson grounded his natural philosophy in the power of the divine, which he conceived in terms of an all-consuming abundance.

To reinforce the claim that humans were mentally equipped to imagine infinity, Terrasson specifically cited Catholic doctrine against the Scholastic critics of Cartesianism. "The theology of which we have need" proved the necessity of the infinite while exposing the "false and limited" misconceptions of the "Thomists." The capaciousness of the category recalled the stature of the Eucharist, an analogy that Terrasson had clearly in mind. He expressed hope that, with the victory of Cartesianism, the theory of real accidents "will one day pass for inconceivable opinions among those who know God, who are Christian and Catholic." The endless divisibility of matter established the seemingly paradoxical notion that infinity was "an abyss of grandeur that encompasses other grandeurs." He then promised "an explanation of the holy sacrament of the Eucharist" as proof for the certitude of limitless extension.[66]

The text made the case for the infinity and durability of material and spiritual forms, which prompted Terrasson to embrace Fontenelle's defense of the plurality of worlds. Not only did these worlds exist, but their inhabitants were beings in need of redemption. "The eternal Logos [*Verbe*]" could "be united hypostatically to several men" at once. If the body of Christ appeared simultaneously on altars around the world, multiple "God-men" could secure the salvation of an untold number of planets. Terrasson likewise endorsed Desgabets's notion of indefectibility, arguing that "all there is of matter in the world must always endure" even though "each configuration" proved finite. God did not find himself constrained by his own creation; he could produce "an infinite work all the sudden" and then choose "to augment it infinitely."[67]

The *Traité de l'infini créé* referred to a forthcoming account of the Eucharist that did not appear in the text itself.[68] The published edition of 1769 duly appended related writings on the sacraments that, although attributed at the time to Malebranche, were in all likelihood written by another Cartesian fellow traveler. Whether or not Terrasson was the actual author of these works, their arguments and approach closely resembled his own.[69] The first, entitled *Explication de la possibilité de la transsubstantiation*, adapted the theory of infinity via indefectibility to the Eucharist. The tract proceeded as a thought experiment, with an omnipotent divinity electing to destroy and recreate a being at will. Since "there is no contradiction that God, by an eternal and unchanging will, had wanted the same thing" from one interrupted moment to the next, "a being that has been reproduced is the same as the one produced, and not a likeness." This claim applied immediately to transubstantiation, when God effectively fathered his son at multiple times and in multiple places. The soul inhabited a "certain part of the brain"—that is, according to Descartes's speculations, the pineal gland. Physical laws did not obviate the possibility of this organic seat "being reproduced under the appearances of bread." Despite the unassuming physical attributes of the host, "Jesus Christ will in truth be there completely, which is to say, his divinity, his soul, and his body, all that is essential to him, and the same as is in heaven, and that was born of the Virgin." According to the logic of infinite divisibility, Christ's body could even be "reduced to an imperceptible point," as in a mere crust of bread, without compromising its presence.[70]

The *Explication* was followed by a separate *Traité de la communion*, which emphasized the semiotic nature of the Eucharist within the spiritual economy. The author extoled frequent communion so long as one followed the "ways of God" and the "rules of his Church." Those who hoped that "this divine nourishment may profit them" should eschew "brutal sensuality" and espouse a fervent wish "to be changed into Jesus Christ in order to grow in him as his members by imitating his virtues."[71] The Eucharist functioned as an "animated monument" commemorating Christ's existence throughout time and space. It was a "representative sign" of historical communion with Jesus and an "efficacious sign" of the present communion of the faithful

Finally, it served as the "prophetic sign" of their future beatitude, or a "wage" of the "plenitude" in the life to come.[72]

Catholic practitioners of the new philosophy understood the miracle of the host in terms consistent with the definitions of matter as extension and personal identity as the contingent union of body and soul. Desgabets and Terrasson argued that the capacity for transformation could assume heavenly forms, as in the Eucharist, but nonetheless remain intrinsic to the workings of the physical universe. Christ's glorious body offered mysterious yet undeniable evidence of the wondrous mutability of reproduction *in toto* without the loss of qualities. When Terrasson took up Law's cause in 1720, he specifically likened the public's reception of the System to the unsettled fate of Descartes's teaching. Eucharistic theology, Cartesian metaphysics, and even alchemical transmutation provided Terrasson with an intellectual framework in which to justify the virtues of paper, a medium that at once stood for and projected wealth in abundance. French subjects, for their part, found themselves receptive to the idea that credit might breathe new life into moribund riches.

Law's Sacraments of Finance

Law's System seemed to herald the end of chronic scarcity. Its agent of regeneration was money, enigmatically defined by Georg Simmel as "the adequate expression of the relationship of man to the world, which can only be grasped in single and concrete instances."[73] Traditional investments in land, rents, and venal offices were prized for safeguarding wealth under precarious conditions.[74] Paper money promised far more—to augment riches in a rapidly expanding economic field. Law's banknotes and company shares thus realized a long-held desire for a universal equivalent of value that, like the philosopher's stone and the consecrated host, produced wealth in the act of representing it.

The fiscal regime was inextricably bound up with the political and religious fortunes of the kingdom. In *Six livres de la république* (1576), Jean Bodin asserted that "the right of the mint is of the same nature as the law."[75] In actuality, lack of coin necessitated recourse to alternative mechanisms. The crown, despite its reliance on complex credit instruments (the amount of interest-bearing financial paper in circulation by the turn of the eighteenth century ran to nearly 372 million livres), obsessed over accumulating precious metals at the expense of foreign rivals.[76] It repeatedly devalued and revalued metal écus, louis, and other denominations in relation to the livre tournois, the official money of account. Between 1602 and 1709 the amount of gold corresponding to a livre tournois fell from 995 to 374 milligrams.[77] Since the livre did not correspond to a physical coin, these manipulations could be performed by royal edict. Neither sovereigns nor subjects, then, found nonmetallic currencies or shocks to the monetary system beyond the depths of the imagination.

Among government officials, the Cartesian call to render humans "masters and possessors of nature" drove a search for the rational principles behind the political-economic order.[78] For instance, Pierre Le Pesant de Boisguilbert published a series of memoranda on how to alleviate the crushing poverty he observed as a magistrate in the *bailliage* of Rouen.[79] A committed Jansenist and follower of Descartes, he viewed the world as a machine that should operate with minimal intervention but within the bounds of charity.[80] Bolstering consumption would realize the ideal of equilibrium across economic life, with wealth as the horizon and subsistence as a right.[81] Boisguilbert thus rejected the mercantilist orthodoxy associated with the former finance minister Jean-Baptiste Colbert, which championed bullionism, dominance in international trade, luxury manufacturing, and imperious coordination by the state.[82]

In the *Dissertation sur les richesses* (1707), Boisguilbert denounced the fetishistic attachment to gold, a false "idol" with no essential utility of its own. He argued that since money served merely as "a guarantee of the future delivery of a commodity," a variety of media could fulfill its function. Paper held out particular promise. He even ranked banknotes as superior to gold and silver, given their greater availability and velocity of circulation. Breaking the spell of precious metals would lead to the realization of a felicitous "equilibrium" between buyer and seller and thus to the circulation of wealth between both parties.[83]

The *Dissertation sur les richesses* starkly portrayed the various dilemmas confronting France—budgetary, commercial, moral, and religious. The economic situation turned critical after the death of the Sun King in 1715

Philippe, the duc d'Orléans, stewarded the government for a child-king. The debt, a legacy of Louis XIV's ruinous military spending, stood at nearly 2 billion livres, with another 600 million issued in government paper. Revenues through 1721 had already been allocated.[84] The regent entertained a flurry of proposals on how to meet the challenge but ultimately implemented a "Visa," or partial bankruptcy, through the unilateral devaluing of obligations by nearly two-thirds. As if heeding Boisguilbert's proposals for paper currency, the balance of the floating debt was converted into *billets d'état*, which, despite bearing 4 percent interest, soon were trading well below their nominal value. A *chambre de justice* pursued unscrupulous financiers who had profited at the crown's expense.[85]

This was the stage onto which Law made his entrance. Born in 1671 to a Scottish goldsmith, he embarked on a life of gambling after fleeing an English prison on the charge of murder. Amassing a fortune playing basset and faro, he studied the banking institutions of the cities he visited, including Amsterdam and Venice. Around 1700 he returned to his native Edinburgh, where he lobbied for the establishment of a land bank.[86] He formalized his observations in *Money and Trade Considered* (1705), which asserted that "an addition to the money, whether the imployer [sic] gains or not, adds to the national wealth" by stimulating the production and consumption of goods. As a result of importation from the Americas, the value of gold and silver had fallen sharply, while nations without sufficient mines remained chronically short of money. To overcome these defects, Law called for a bank that would issue currency backed by land, which he believed "in all appearance will keep its value best." Paper money held a key advantage as the medium of exchange. Since it had no "intrinsick value" and its "extrinsick value" stemmed from an unexportable resource, the bank could maintain sufficient quantities to support agriculture, manufacturing, and commerce.[87]

Law's proposals met with resistance in Scotland. After a period of further travel, he relocated to Paris and entered into negotiations with the regent. His memoranda discussed the functions of money in an economy under an absolutist government with enormous obligations and vast resources. As he observed, "the richest states lack sufficient species to employ their people and push commerce to the point it could otherwise reach." His bank would remedy this inconvenience through the use of "credit."[88] Law elaborated the point in a subsequent petition: "Money is for the state what blood is for the human body.... Circulation is necessary to the one and to the other."[89] In Law's hands, the well-worn metaphor marked a theoretical and tactical shift from upholding conservation to promoting velocity.[90] A land-backed currency did not figure in the proposal; instead, Law emphasized the bank's role in expanding the availability of money as a means of spurring the realm's demographic and productive might.[91]

To skeptics who objected that a divine-right monarchy would be tempted to abuse its credit, Law responded with a paean to royal power, claiming that a king "who knows how to govern can extend his credit further ... than one limited in his authority." Since the operation provided the regent with much-needed funds, he would feel obliged to protect it. Subjects would place their confidence in paper money if it could be used readily in transactions and exchanged for coin. Those capable of "reasoning according to principles" would soon come to understand that "it is the experience of the virtue [bonté] of paper that attracts confidence and public credit to it."[92] In a variation on Pascal's wager, Law promised that acting out belief, even involuntarily, fostered belief in the long run.

The prediction at first seemed borne out by events. Letters patent from May of 1716 duly authorized Law to found a General Bank (Banque générale). Although the new bank was barred from loaning funds or engaging in commercial activity, the crown authorized it to issue notes that bearers could exchange on demand for specie. The regent lent his support as its official protector and forbade on pain of death the counterfeiting of notes.[93] Additional letters patent from May 20 set the bank's capital at 6 million livres and stipulated the issue of twelve hundred shares at 1,000 écus each (the equivalent of 5,000 livres). Investors could pay three-quarters of this sum in *billets d'état*.[94]

Despite initial skepticism, private and public confidence gradually gained momentum. By September of 1717 the government ordered all tax revenues to be deposited in banknotes.[95] On December 4, 1718, the General Bank was rechristened the Royal Bank (Banque royale) and permitted to issue notes as required.[96] The crown had previously opted to convert the bank's original capital into shares of Law's Company of the West (Compagnie d'Occident), established in 1717 to oversee settlement and commerce in French Louisiana. In July of 1719 the Company of the West merged with the Company of the East Indies (Compagnie des Indes orientales) and the Company of China (Compagnie de la Chine), thereby forming a single enterprise, under the name of the Company of the Indies (Compagnie des Indes), which took charge of the mint and the general farms (*fermes générales*). The nascent behemoth lent the crown 1.5 billion livres to retire the debt. It funded acquisitions through the sale of stock on partial credit. After an initial offering in August of 1717 for 300 livres a share, the price in December 1719 approached 10,000 livres. New issues of paper money tended to accompany that of stock, so that by early 1720, more than 2 billion livres in banknotes had entered circulation. On January 8, three days after Law was appointed controller-general of finances, stock traded at 10,100 livres.[97]

Speculators fantasized about the profits to be gleaned from the colonies' mythic abundance.[98] Maps from the 1710s depicted French Louisiana as within striking distance of New Spain, a territory synonymous in the popular imagination with metallic wealth. Jesuit missionaries had already noted the presence of lead mines.[99] Law traded on such hopes—Parisian shop windows displayed gold bars purportedly from Louisiana—while also seeking to deflect acquisitive desire away from silver and gold and toward paper banknotes and shares.[100] Even if French colonies failed to produce the bullion of Mexico or Peru, the sheer volume of goods circulated through paper instruments would multiply their value. As Law observed in his *Mémoire sur le discrédit* to the Regent, "it is in the interest of the king and his peoples to assure the money of the bank," which represented the collective wealth of the metropole and colonies, and "to abolish gold money," which was essentially a "foreign product." The economic power of Spain, Portugal, and China depended on the value of metal, a substance that "produces nothing." In contrast, Law's scheme for France held that the "value of stock must increase" along with the "commerce of the company." Since paper money and shares were financially linked, "the bill is money"—a form of currency that, unlike the exhaustible wealth of mines, had no physical limit.[101]

The truth was far less dazzling. Despite the capital raised from the sale of stock, Louisiana languished. Colonial economic power derived from codes that favored European traders, constant imperial warfare, and ever-rising numbers of African slaves. The Mississippi River region remained underutilized, underpopulated, and unevenly governed. Law attempted to reverse such trends. Granted a twenty-five year charter to manage the territory, his Company of the West founded the city of New Orleans in 1718. It pledged to populate the colony with six thousand new immigrants and three thousand enslaved persons.[102] Nonetheless, the settlers struggled against the deprivations of hunger and disease. Men complained in particular about a lack of women, suggesting a link between the financial and libidinal economies.[103]

These structural difficulties did not warn off investors. Law made multiple but contradictory adjustments to cool the stock market. On January 9, 1720, he established a premium of 1,000 livres to buy one share at 10,000 livres within six months. The maneuver backfired: speculators pounced in the belief that stock values would continue to rise. Law also redoubled his efforts to curtail the possession of specie. An edict from February 27 prohibited subjects from retaining more than 500 livres in gold and silver. Decrees issued in March announced the reduction in the value of bullion and its demonetization on May 1, while fixing the price of stock at the inflated figure of 9,000 livres.[104] Such measures imagined Louisiana not as a new El Dorado but as an empire of paper.

In concert with these efforts the *Nouveau Mercure* published a series of letters by Terrasson, a heavy investor in the company who clung to his beliefs until he lost his entire fortune.[105] The correspondence typifies the strategies employed to promote the System, which intimated the seemingly miraculous powers of banknotes to generate the wealth they represented. Terrasson advanced claims resembling those developed in his treatises on metaphysics and theology, the first published reference to which appeared in 1715.[106] For the abbé, economic and religious faith followed one from the other, sharing the same unshakable conviction.

The first letter, from February, echoed Law's sentiment that credit served as a "source of circulation and plenty," in contrast to the ossifying effect of annuities.[107] The second letter, published the following month, predicted that the company would forge the kingdom into "a body of traders" and compared its stock favorably to landed assets. Terrasson also observed that the System had met with approval from the regent and esteemed experts. Now it faced challenges posed by "prejudice," which the abbé denounced as the "habit of pure instinct." History assured him that "reason" would prevail by winning converts among "superior minds" before gradually becoming "public sentiment." The same, he noted, had been the case with Descartes's philosophy.[108] Law's views were likewise bound to triumph in good time.

The third letter, which appeared in the pivotal month of May, adopted a less conciliatory tone. Terrasson posed a sharp distinction between "reason" and "common sense," between the "just mind" and the "false." The former calmly deliberated, and, "having admitted a principle, never deviates" from the "constant truth" before one's eyes. In contrast, the "prejudiced man" darted about from denial and rage to intellectual paralysis. Again, Terrasson expressed confidence in vanquishing dissent. The rational course, one that might appear counterintuitive in hindsight, validated stalwart support for the System and its principles. But if the people failed to recognize their own interests, the crown stood ready to impose enlightenment from above. As Terrasson observed, "the credit of this bill is doubtful, and its circulation limited, only when its acceptance remains free." From this perspective, "only the sovereign could have real credit, and particular traders never have but the shadow of it."[109] According to absolutist theory, the king did not merely symbolize power; like the Eucharist, he projected it. In Cartesian terms, royal credit, like extended matter, had no limit but that imposed by its originator.

Terrasson reaffirmed that paper resurrected the economic body in a manner recalling his analogue between the Eucharist and infinite creation.[110] As Law himself had noted, economic life depended on money passing from hand to hand. Confronting the objection that "forced credit" amounted to a pyramid scheme, the abbé answered resolutely in the name of timeless circulation—the "last holder will never be found." The regent would preserve the System by force of will. Paper represented landed, commercial, and colonial riches but owed its status as legal tender to the government. The crown was entitled to manipulate the value of coin for the common good and even "to change the species of gold and silver into other signs more advantageous to the public." Directly confronting skeptics, Terrasson ended on a prophetic note. "One will soon see," he claimed, "the fruits that only this imaginary good can produce."[111]

The language of species carried sacramental as well as monetary connotations. When inflected through the grammar of Cartesianism, it further suggested the possibility of infinite creation. In his memoranda on the establishment of a bank, Law had remarked critically of precious metal that "the same coin cannot come to be in the same place at the same time."[112] Paper money overcame this physical impossibility. Not unlike the supersubstantial bread of the Eucharist, which could be conjured at will, the banknote's reproducibility guaranteed its omnipresence. Both currencies enabled a simultaneous and seemingly miraculous generation.

If money's virtues are replaced with those of a prolific deity, the sacramental dimensions of Terrasson's claims become evident. The abbé argued in his metaphysical treatises that God "creates in every moment an infinity of spirits" since his "power is inexhaustible." He openly admitted that "the rest of my system demands" such an attribute.[113] One of the texts that circulated in manuscript with the *Traité de l'infini créé* marveled at the divine aptitude for bringing forth boundless qualities as well as quantities. Terrasson claimed that material bodies were capable of extension without preconceived limits, thus rendering intelligible the "reproduction of Jesus Christ on all the altars where one celebrates his sacrifice." With the consecration of bread and wine, his soul "merely acquires new relations that the Creator poses between it and certain portions of matter" to the point that "the same person will be really and effectively in a thousand different places."[114]

Like the host, then, which the *Traité de la communion* considered an "efficacious sign," the bills amplified, as "signs of the transmission of real wealth," wealth's very existence.[115] They served not merely as a passive, abstract referent—to gold, land, or other commodities—but as evidence of their purification and expansion. The priest blessed. The alchemist fermented and distilled. Law induced circulation. These processes called for a substance that remained visible yet also transparent in order not to obstruct the activity being represented.[116]

Terrasson's task was to convince buyers and sellers to embrace a medium that did not impose its own form on commercial exchanges. He argued that paper fulfilled this criterion far better than minted money, owing to the latter's inherent scarcity, thereby justifying Law's proposal to confine the use of metal coin to minor transactions. As the third *Nouveau Mercure* letter stated, if "the banknote never produces specie [*argent*], which it is not, no bearer of this note can ever suffer a loss, since he has the same claim to the corresponding goods as the first who had received it." This "sovereign remedy" liberated princes and paupers alike. Since paper could be sourced domestically, it allowed the crown to "increase and decrease the quantity according to the needs of the state."[117]

In the *Traité de l'infini créé*, Terrasson observed with wonder that "the eternal Logos" functioned on innumerable planets at once.[118] Like his readers, he understood that clerics summoned the body of Christ at will. If the generative power of the Eucharist could be harnessed in such a manner, it was not beyond the realm of possibility that Law could reconfigure the religious and economic domains that reigned on Earth. However, his success depended on trusting hearts and open minds. Accordingly, Terrasson proclaimed a new gospel. The kingdom's credit would grow under the auspices of a devotional paradigm that authorized French subjects to regard the currency of the Royal Bank as a readily discernible and infinitely sustainable sacrament of finance.

The Mysteries of Economic Conversion

Like abbés, alchemists were a regular presence at court and in royal academies who drew on priestly expertise to justify their ventures.[119] For instance, during the final years of his reign, Louis XIV made numerous attempts to enlist the services of a man known as Delisle, an illiterate locksmith from Provence thought to have mastered the art of transmutation. The prior of Châteauneuf tested Delisle's competence by means of a secret powder. The bishop of Senez found himself swayed by the evidence, as did the president of the mint in Lyon. In 1710 an official certificate was prepared for Nicolas Desmartes, the controller-general at the time. After Delisle repeatedly evaded the king's summons to Versailles, he was arrested and thrown into the Bastille, where he admitted his fraud.[120] Louis de Rouvroy, duc de Saint-Simon, noted Philippe d'Orléans's delight in forging stones from charcoal.[121] Pierre Narbonne, the police commissioner for Versailles, reported that his experiments involved attempts to discover the philosopher's stone. He is also believed to have consulted with alchemists early in his regency, before accepting Law's proposal for the General Bank.[122]

Skeptics disparaged the allure that alchemy held for the king, the regent, and their subjects. The physician François Pousse grumbled that "of all nations," the French were "the most ardent and persistent" in their enthusiasm. He took direct aim at efforts to purify and regenerate created things, which, to his mind, imputed defects to divine workmanship. It was impossible, even sacrilegious, to believe that one could "give a new perfection" to nature by affecting "the passage of one species into another."[123] Étienne-François Geoffroy, master apothecary and member of the Académie des sciences, prepared an exposé detailing the tricks of the alchemist's trade, including the use of hollow-bottomed melting pots and the mixing of mercury, copper, and other nonprecious metals to simulate gold. Motivating their victims' belief, Geoffroy surmised, was "the idea of immense riches," which "vividly strikes men's imagination."[124] Taken together, these remarks rehearse a critique of the prevailing economic theology: hope for miraculous accumulation incited desire and then heedless action.

During the Law affair, popular songs captured the experience of being adrift in a sea of banknotes, with alchemy—and its Eucharistic associations—serving as a symbolic buoy. Transmutation and transubstantiation offered a range of antecedents describing the spontaneous generation of wealth. An anonymous composer wondered how "an architect without reason," not unlike a priest or adept, had "changed form and matter" by constructing a palace with an "attic" made of "silver" and a "foundation" composed of "paper." How could the inscription of "three or four words"—"variable, uncertain, obscure"—come to replace the solidity of minted metal (or, one might add, how did liturgical utterances convert bread into the body of Christ)? Another lyric answered that in the "admirable mine" where "all paper becomes excellent," wealth stems from "trafficking in it." Verses penned in homage to "the Mississippi" told of a man who "had discovered the secret for the philosopher's stone" in the land's enchanted soil. If alchemists distilled their tincture from gold, their successor's banknotes contained the "quintessence of paper," which possessed still greater luster. Another epigram hailed Law as a "mind that a divine power enlightens" and a "creator who makes all from nothing." His powers were believed to sway the thoughts of others. "Your genius is our treasure," the verse concluded with a sarcastic air, "and you know how to reveal to us gold where there is only a chimera." Not unlike King Midas—who fulfilled his desire for precious metal, but at a terrible cost—"everything in our hands is changing into gold."[125] These observations betray a sense of bewilderment that writers sought to overcome with reference to Eucharist-alchemical principles, which furnished the means of understanding paper as a universal medium, a new talisman to rival the philosopher's stone or the consecrated host.

While allusions to alchemy dominated musical and iconographic portrayals, church ritual also made an occasional appearance, often in reference to Law's conversion to Catholicism in December of 1719 by the abbé Pierre Guérin de Tencin, vicar of the archbishop of Sens, future cardinal, and uncle of d'Alembert. One ditty alleged that Law had given Tencin 200,000 livres in company shares before observing that, since "Law has become Catholic," France "has become Capuchin" (an order of friars notable for poverty).[126] Another song further derided the episode, adding that Law's appointment as honorary churchwarden of Saint-Roch proved that he "wants to be canonized" and that "heaven will be reimbursed" for the privilege. The same lyricist parodied money's reputation as the royal equivalent of the real presence. Louis XV's image was slated to appear "in miniature" on Law's devalued coinage and then grow in size with the king's physical body. Clerics were said to have recommended such abominations to their parishioners without "scruple," in defiance of traditional doctrine. "Where does scripture prohibit gaining all that one can," the casuist argued, "when one gains with ease? This good comes to us from God, let us not doubt it in the slightest."[127]

Jean Buvat, who, as a copyist at the Royal Library (Bibliothèque du roi), observed events within a stone's throw of the Bank's headquarters, memorialized Law's apogee by invoking the church's signature rite. He related the observations of the British ambassador, John Dalrymple, the Earl of Stair, mocking the controller-general's monetary policies and embrace of the Roman faith: "At present, one can no longer doubt Law's Catholicism, after he has thoroughly proven transubstantiation and even availed himself of the Inquisition to establish both perfectly in France."[128] Lord Stair's droll comment leveled ridicule first at the financial logic of the System, which he likened to a spurious point of religious doctrine, and then at its mechanism of enforcing compliance. Lest the reader fail to grasp the joke, Buvat offered to dissect it, explaining that "Law had changed the species [*espèces*] of minted gold and silver into banknotes."[129] In so doing, he expressly confirmed an analogy between bread and wine, the species of communion, and the species of money, gold and silver. Buvat's pun on the word *species*, which carried both liturgical and economic meanings, served to translate Dalrymple's original remark into a French, Catholic context. Moreover, the choice of words reiterated Terrasson's claim—that banknotes represented and reproduced wealth in transubstantiated form.

Law's conversion to Catholicism and elevation to the post of controller-general coincided with tales of enormous sums made and lost from one day to the next. The omnipresence of luxury violated the hierarchical principle that material signs projected social status in and onto the world rather than passively reflecting it.[130] Private individuals and corporate bodies followed the state in leveraging stock to raise capital and reorganize debt.[131] The surge in social mobility occasioned a neologism for an unprecedented class of subject—the *millionaire*.[132] Memorialists and journalists trucked in hyperbole to depict the immense, albeit in certain cases temporary, transfer of assets. The fantastic elements in their accounts did little to dampen the enthusiasm of contemporary witnesses. The *Nouveau Mercure* reported how the popular mood shifted from "disbelief" to "faith" as "persons of status" and commoners "passed rapidly from indigence to opulence."[133]

The chevalier de Piossens likewise told of how speculators "believed that paper would change itself into ingot," so that "the millions that this paper produced in theory [*en idée*] delighted more than the least sum in specie." Investors "made their fortune almost while sleeping." He repeated the tale of a lackey who earned enough in profits to buy a carriage from his former master, only to continue taking the seat behind the coach.[134] Barthélemy Marmont Du Hautchamp, who traded in company shares, declared that Law had established an alternative universe. "Never was a better system invented," he quipped, "to put a nation in perpetual motion." In the final months of 1719, the rue Quincampoix became a captivating "theater," where "the grandest lords did not have the slightest difficulty selling the most beautiful lands in the world to trade them for paper." Even the chill of the season brought "more splendor and brilliance than the most beautiful springtime." The streets glittered with "velvet costumes in every color, lined with cloth of gold and silver." Such displays of fortune drove speculation to dizzying heights by "attracting public confidence." As stock prices peaked in December of 1719 and January of 1720, paper eclipsed gold as the measure of wealth, with the formerly destitute said to earn "twenty, thirty, forty, and up to sixty million" livres in banknotes.[135]

As winter turned to spring and summer, cracks began to appear in the facade of Law's impressive edifice. According to Buvat, the new year brought the first signs of inflation that later terrorized consumers.[136] Fire was sighted in the sky above Rouen. Reports of the Company's forcibly sending colonists to Louisiana provoked public outrage. The comte de Horn, a distant relative of the regent, was accused of murder, with theft as his motive.[137] The Parlement of Paris tenaciously questioned the legality of the System, eventually leading the crown to exile the magistrates to Pontoise.[138] In May a ship from the Levant brought plague to the vital port city of Marseille. The epidemic would eventually claim some ninety-three thousand victims in Provence alone. Facing pestilence of biblical proportions, clergymen ministered to the sick and dying.[139] In a feverish bout of soul-searching, they also drew up various *cas de conscience* involving the use of banknotes to discharge obligations contracted in species. For instance, should it be regarded as a "good work" to free a debtor from prison by this means?[140]

Theologians differed in their response to questions concerning the moral implications of the System, anticipating many of the charges leveled against colonial commerce later in the century, especially in the *Histoire des deux Indes* compiled by the Jesuit abbé Guillaume-Thomas Raynal.[141] The Jansenist Joseph Lambert, doctor of theology and prior of the Church of Saint Martin in Palaiseau, lamented an "affair" that "throws so many consciences into scruple and embarrassment." He upbraided his fellow clerics for their failure of moral courage. The Company of the Indies wantonly promoted usury, financial uncertainty, the dehumanizing effects of the slave trade, the corruption of ecclesiastics, and—most grievous of all—social disorder. "The last have become first," and the "providence" of the "diversity of estates" have been scorned out of deference to the "idol of fortune." Whereas the Gospel served "to moderate and dampen the passions," the ardor for stock had the effect of "awakening and sustaining every one," especially the drive to "make money." Such corruption stemmed not only from the malfeasance of "dishonest traders" but from the very nature of stocks, a cause "so pressing and immediate that it inevitably produces its effect."[142]

The abbé Terrasson rebutted Lambert's charges. As in his letters to the *Nouveau Mercure*, he noted that Law's bank and company exercised "public authority" on the crown's behalf. The law permitted parties engaged in commercial transactions to charge "modest interest" on capital lent in the pursuit of profit. Likewise, the king could in all justice expect his subjects to make "a contribution to the expenditures of the state." Although admitting that "it is rare that one can innocently grow rich in a short time," he emphasized the exceptional nature of events. Money operated according to its own forces, with no consideration of hierarchy or "the rules of order [*police*]." "That shocks you," he wrote to Lambert, "but God permits it." Law's plan might confound "feeble reason" but nonetheless carried divine sanction.[143] As d'Alembert reported, Terrasson likened the founding of a new economic order to a revelation of religious truth. In both instances, "faith is truly necessary."[144]

Alternatively admiring and irreverent in tone, these pronouncements conveyed how French subjects grappled with extraordinary financial change. Eucharistic-alchemical verities took the form of what Robert Darnton identifies in his work on libelers and scandalmongers as a "metanarrative," a cultural code "powerful enough to stamp itself on the collective imagination."[145] In light of alchemy's continued appeal in the highest echelons, and its resemblance to the church's most fundamental sacrament, contemporaries could endow paper with the powers of transmutation and even the effects of transubstantiation. Unlike gold, but rather more like the host, it represented treasure under a banal sign. The material's sheer convertibility seemed to precipitate metamorphosis for and among its bearers, including Law himself.

A realm abounding with banknotes and company shares thus augured nothing less than the dawn of a new age—albeit one that swiftly receded into darkness. On May 21, 1720, Law announced a massive devaluation of paper money and stock—by 50 percent and 44 percent, respectively. The reaction was cataclysmic. "The same spirit of vertigo that had given such great favor to the papers," noted *La vie de Philippe d'Orléans*, "made their decline [*dépérissement*] seem the greatest of misfortunes."[146] The parlement prevailed on the regent to countermand Law's order on May 27. Two days later, the controller-general was dismissed from his post and placed under house arrest. He was recalled on June 2 to oversee the demolition of his

System. After several runs on the Royal Bank, the currency was revoked as legal tender in October. By year's end, his spell now broken, Law fled Paris, never to return.[147]

The Enlightenment and the Catholic Ethic of Capitalism

Historians have tended to salvage the kernel of rationality in Law's theoretical apparatus while identifying the practical complications that besieged it.[148] The Scotsman's immediate contemporaries, however, fixated on the enthusiasm that both justified and subverted his ambitions. Saint-Simon cited the "extreme folly" and "enormous cupidity" sparked by "transmutations of paper" in the "incredible markets" of the rue Quincampoix. He condemned Law as "a peddler of systems [*un homme de système*]" whose plans fell prey to a despotic sovereign and his covetous subjects.[149] Voltaire granted that Law had induced a zeal for acquisitiveness across the social spectrum but regarded this development as potentially beneficial to commerce. Law's bold agenda, though destructive in the short term, "enlightened minds like civil wars excite courage."[150] Saint-Simon's and Voltaire's acknowledgment of the role played by avarice thus presumed an economic-theological faith in the capacity of paper to augment wealth at all times, in all places, ad infinitum.

Montesquieu's *Lettres persanes* (1721), a founding text of the French Enlightenment, made no allowances for the "finesse" and "mystery" of so-called geniuses who inflicted their "miraculous designs" and "novel systems" on public finances. The character Rica expressed his astonishment at a topsy-turvy world in which the rich found themselves poor and the poor rich, before remarking, in contrast to Terrasson, that "God does not create men from nothing with such speed." Montesquieu caricatured these reversals in a tale about a charlatan from the Orkney Islands, off the northern coast of Scotland. His father, Aeolus, the god of wind, taught him the art of balloon-making—that is, of blowing hot air. The young man traveled to Betica (a land symbolizing France), imploring all who would listen to surrender their "vile metals" and take refuge in the "empire of the imagination." As if to highlight the phantasmagorical aspects of Law's reforms, Montesquieu's account preceded a letter on the hermetic arts of chemical distillation and talismans.¹⁵¹ By arranging the text in such a fashion, he effectively replicated, as did *Harlequin the Stockjobber*, the very mode of analogical thinking that he sought to condemn. Parody created a distance from the object of scorn while also reaffirming its fascination for readers, investors in the Company of the Indies among them.

Law's reforms continued to enthrall writers on economic questions in the decades that followed.¹⁵² In his *Essai politique sur le commerce* (1734), Jean-François Melon famously endorsed Law's conviction that a nation's wealth depended more on the circulation of commodities than the accumulation of gold and silver. As a "common measure of exchange," paper instruments proved no less useful than metal coin, a possibility that the System had abundantly demonstrated.¹⁵³ Melon's charitable postmortem aroused the ire of Nicolas Dutot, whose *Réflexions politiques sur les finances et le commerce* (1738) interpreted the System's demise as a morality tale warning of the inflation facilitated by overprinting paper money. The practice favored debtors and paved the way for rampant usury because creditors harbored reasonable fears of timely payment. A sound monetary policy maintained a balance between "real" sources of wealth and "wealth of confidence or opinion."¹⁵⁴ Montesquieu developed this position further in *De l'esprit des lois* (1748), which denounced the excessive issuing of shares in Law's company and the bills of his bank as proof that such ephemeral tokens "would destroy themselves in the same manner in which they were created." The degradation of financial instruments epitomized the hollowing out of the social substance of the legal regime that made despotism possible.¹⁵⁵

In 1749, Turgot, then on scholarship at the Sorbonne, penned a scathing review of Law's System that specifically targeted Terrasson's monetary theory.¹⁵⁶ The young seminarian had avidly read *De l'esprit des lois* despite its condemnation by the Paris Faculty of Theology, and he embraced Dutot's and Montesquieu's claim that money's utility as a medium of exchange depended on keeping its quantity within equitable bounds. In a letter to his fellow student, the abbé Jérôme Marie Champion de Cicé, Turgot ridiculed what he regarded as the magical thinking behind Terrasson's claim that paper bills authorized by the government were not only self-sustaining but also conducive to economic expansion. "If all these reasonings were correct," Turgot suggestively noted, "it would be as great a good as the philosopher's stone." Law and his supporters neglected the crucial task of maintaining the money supply relative to the "proportion of commodities, industry, land, and real wealth of each private individual, or rather of revenues on his wealth compared with his expenditures."[157] In place of exigent calculation, they had followed the siren's song of economic theology, with its promises of infinite riches demanding only a belief in their imminent creation.

. . .

Turgot's criticism hit its mark. Adherents and opponents of Law's System ascribed to financial instruments the potential of measuring value and conjuring riches from base elements. In the minds of French subjects, the consecrated host and the philosopher's stone shared the power of rendering common elements uncommonly valuable. This Eucharistic-alchemical complex prefigured a regime of paper in which the portrayal of wealth led inexorably to its production. Investors seized on the power of currency not merely for what it could purchase but also out of a wish to experience *jouissance* without restriction.[158] The pleasures of the banknote defied mundane hierarchies and the laws of nature. In Catholic devotion, consuming the host anticipated eternal beatitude, a state of self-perpetuating, radically transcendent fulfillment. The alchemist's art emulated the drive for regenerative wealth by underscoring the associations of transmutation with transubstantiation. Terrasson himself recalled the Eucharistic elements of money in his letters to the *Nouveau Mercure*, which Turgot translated into alchemical terms for parodic effect.

The deification of money signaled less a transfer of sacrality than its doubling.[159] Economic theologians evinced an intimate knowledge of this dynamic. In their view, the graven images of Mammon had long mimicked the miracles of the one true god. Perhaps it was only fitting that self-consciously enlightened minds such as Montesquieu and Voltaire sought to stand the idol on its feet. Nonetheless, their efforts failed to exorcise the longing for repositories of celestial and temporal wealth that knew no bounds. At the same time, the coexistence of multiple claimants to the status of universal equivalent—the host, the philosopher's stone, bullion, paper bills—gave rise to protracted conflicts over the means and ends of the economy.

The rise and fall of Law's System thus qualifies as a historical event in the sense understood by William Sewell. It was "a ramified sequence of occurrences" that produced "a durable transformation in structures." It gave rise to "acts of collective creativity" marked by "their ritual character."[160] That is not to say that the articulation of sacramental and financial value was predestined or depended purely on elective affinities. The operative elements of this outcome—the Eucharist, alchemy, paper money—were originally regarded as incongruent. The System seemed to defy the natural order of creation. As Lambert made clear, God would not have wanted such a scheme to turn a profit. Terrasson found himself in a prime position to defend the workings of Law's banknotes and company shares along the lines of no less fraught a venture—his earlier attempts to reconcile transubstantiation with the Cartesian concept of infinity. Once the synthesis took hold, it coalesced into ideas and practices that seemed fated in hindsight and that produced new perspectives on the past and future.[161] It became a force to be reckoned with in its own right, compelling enough to alter the course of Enlightenment-era speculations on the generative faculties of money, the righteousness of usury, and the irresistible attraction of manufactured commodities.

CHAPTER 4

Usury Redeemed

IN 1717, as Law consolidated his System, an almanac published an engraving to celebrate the kingdom's triumph over usury (fig. 4.1). The scene was set in the chamber of justice (*chambre de justice*), an extraordinary body convoked by the regent to try cases involving "illicit profits and usurious transactions."[1] The assembled magistrates, who included the chancellor, masters of request (*maîtres de requêtes*), and representatives from the parlement and the courts of account (*chambres des comptes*), presided sternly over the session. Before the tribunal grovels a convicted usurer surrounded by his wretched brethren. A moneylender bearing a torch begs forgiveness in keeping with the redemptive ethos of public punishment. As the judges look on in haughty approval, a royal secretary writes out the sentence of the court.

Festooned with fleurs-de-lis and other trappings of monarchical power, the print's symbolism conveyed not only the king's authority over the world of finance but also the principles that guided his pursuit of justice.[2] The righthand side of the composition features a virtual tour of economictheological iconography. Under a banner trumpeting "Vive le Roy" hangs a painting of the crucified Christ, whose sacrifice was memorialized by the Eucharist. The viewer's eye follows a line indicated by the base of the cross down to an allegorical representation of religion's triumph over usury. A cherub hoists the scales of justice in one hand, a sword in the other, toppling

Figure 4.1 *Les ordres du roy exécutez par sa chambre de justice pour punir le vice, abolir l'usure et faire regner l'abondance et la paix dans ses états*, 1717. Bibliothèque nationale de France.

a dishonest trader who clutches his ill-gotten gains. A decree condemning rogues and counterfeiters reproduced in the lower right corner codifies these actions in law.

A series of juxtapositions structure the image's meaning. The ornamental framing device that dominates the bottom third of the print announces an act of sovereign restitution both human and divine. Figures portraying justice rest atop a massive vise decorated with a ribbon proclaiming, "Render unto Caesar that which belongs to Caesar."[3] The broken body of Christ looms over the mangled figures caught in the snare of reparation—an image that recalls Eucharistic depictions of Jesus in a wine press.[4] The mechanism crushes the perpetrators of financial abuse, out of whose mouths pour gold coins that fall into the royal coffers. Both manners of torment presage untold abundance. Christ's sacrifice saved the world but left humankind with a debt that could never be repaid. The fate of usurers yielded more immediate riches: cornucopias overflowing with precious metals, medallions, and jewels. It is a stunning vision of justice duly executed. Through an apparent reversal of the feats depicted in *Harlequin the Stockjobber*—where Law stands, or rather squats, as a channel of transmutation—here France is purged of excess with brutal efficiency. On either side gather grateful subjects, whose appearance confirms the work's stated moral. According to the caption, "It is necessary to return with wailing the blood that your tributes have pressed out of the veins" not only of the "merchant" and the "nobleman" but also of "the clergy."[5]

Elements of realism punctuate the revenge fantasy. Reviled in scripture and prohibited by canon and civil law, usury remained a crime under the Old Regime. Merchants accused of lending at exorbitant rates were liable to be brought up on charges and, if convicted, levied with sanctions ranging from loss of property and exile to corporeal punishment. As in the print, the guilty were frequently made to wear placards, carry torches, and perform public acts of penance.[6] The crown and the parlements periodically renewed the ban. Between 1673 and 1764, the government issued no fewer than eight edicts and decrees to this effect. The need for doing so suggested an inability and even unwillingness to impose the royal will on a kingdom that existed in a permanent state of indebtedness.

Indeed, the law permitted the charging of interest under certain conditions.[7] A king celebrated for vanquishing usurers could not subsist without constant borrowing, often on disadvantageous terms. Nor could he abide by the scriptural dictate to "render unto Caesar." The monarchy was beholden to a system of venal officeholding that brought in capital sums at the expense of future tax revenues, since fiscal privileges accrued to the purchasers of posts. The crown's dual role as the fount of glory in a society of orders and the head of an administrative apparatus only further entrenched chronic insolvency. The sovereign had no choice but to punish excessive usury with one hand while engaging in it with the other. He found an accomplice in the church, which not only lent funds to the state but also borrowed on its behalf. This political, fiscal, and moral conundrum triggered an intense debate in the second half of the eighteenth century, prompting the abbé Prigent, a doctor of theology and canon of Léon, to observe in 1783 that "the legitimacy of interest-paying loans in business has been the burning question for the past ten years. It is discussed in all publications."[8]

Although a pan-European phenomenon, the obsession with usury took a distinctly French cast. The crown's debts remained a vexation of mammoth proportions in a realm that lived and died by the balance sheet.[9] The failure of Law's System ensured that, unlike Britain, France did not have recourse to the credit mobilized by a national bank in its pursuit of military, fiscal, and colonial hegemony. Instead of the Bank of England, there was the Gallican Church. Insofar as France experienced a financial revolution akin to its English counterpart, it occurred within as much as outside existing corporatist frameworks.[10] Political theology had long depended on the imbrication of clerical and royal sacrality. Economic theology followed a similar course, with debt functioning as its currency and prime mover. In the spiritual economy, sin necessitated grace. Among worldly actors, trade deepened mutual obligations, both moral and monetary.

Voluminous scholarly literatures address the role of penance in devotion and usury in economic transactions; however, curiously few historians have sought to comprehend these intricately related subjects in tandem.[11] During the medieval period, the church routinely arbitrated questions of financial and spiritual interest as part of what Jacques Le Goff called the "labor pains of capitalism." The doctrinal formulation of purgatory in the twelfth century made it thinkable for the usurer to ply his trade in this life without incurring damnation: he could repent on his deathbed and hope to gain eventual admittance to heaven through the prayers of loved ones.[12] Until the sixteenth century, ecclesiastical courts played a role in the enforcement of financial agreements by threatening derelict borrowers with excommunication. Far from prohibiting credit, the church sought to police the practice with the aim of buttressing moral and social bonds.[13]

Theological concepts of sin and redemption persisted in dominating the early modern social imaginary. As we have seen, communion, indulgences, and the Jubilee all affirmed the necessity of the sacraments for the production of celestial wealth. The same spiritual and moral economy structured relations that would now be thought of as effects of the market. The Catholic ethic made it permissible, even desirable, for expenditure to surpass investment. In the early eighteenth century, 65 percent of day laborers owed money; most died in debt. Farmers depended on advances to obtain seed. The butcher and the baker sold their wares mainly on credit. Artisans in the luxury trades often operated on paper-thin margins and waited months if not years to be paid for their wares by well-to-do clientele. The dictates of reciprocity and charity competed with and frequently took precedence over the brute calculation of profit. From the richest noble landowner to the most humble peasant, men and women honored obligations to lend to family, friends, and other dependents without demanding interest or even repayment. Debt could become a gift of protection, and a past gift could prompt subsequent acts of liberality.[14] In a word, grace infused the moral and material economies alike.

This chapter illustrates how, in devising economic theology, ecclesiastics drew not only on their moral standing but also on their long experience in absolving sin, granting pardons, and administering communion. The boundless nature of divine largesse informed the management of debt—whether as offenses against God or financial obligations to one's neighbor. Catholic orthodoxy had long characterized usury (in practice, interest over commonly accepted rates) as a violation of natural and divine law on the grounds that money could not reproduce itself and that time was not for sale. Such reservations were not without ambiguities. The Bible contained passages that alternatively condemned and made allowances for lending at interest. Luther and Calvin were denounced as heretics for their relative laxity in commercial affairs. Pope Benedict XIV (r. 1740–58) sowed seeds of confusion with an encyclical from 1745 that seemed to justify usurious contracts. No less than penance and indulgences, the First Estate contended with deficits in the temporal sphere. Usury by no means precluded the reconciliation of the church and commercial bourgeoisie.[15] On the contrary, priests stood at the forefront of theorizing lucrative endeavors by virtue of their moral and intellectual acumen.

The conception of sin as redeemable debt permeated Old Regime society. Borrowing at interest found a spiritual analogue in the carefully calibrated practices of forgiveness. When economic theologians advanced positions for and against usury, they did so in a manner that recalled the mechanisms of penance and the Eucharist. Their theories of credit depended on a familiar model: the employment of media capable of augmenting themselves through exchange. Usury's champions seized on the possibility in disputes with clerical critics who denied that the re-presentational productivity of the sacraments extended to terrestrial wealth. As the French history of usury makes clear, economic modernization required faith in money's wondrous facility to bear fruit.

The Catholic ethic cast the believer in a cycle of perpetual debt and redemption, with grace as an exalted form of credit. Financial actors found themselves in a comparable situation. It was only fitting that their spiritual advisers articulated a theory of interest grounded in the ways of absolution. Economic theologians approached the legality of financial interest in light of the virtues of faith, hope, and charity. The church mobilized the limitless capital endowed by Christ and the saints in canceling out transgressions. The question remained whether the laws of God and nature permitted terrestrial beings and institutions to create wealth along similar lines.

The Arbitration of Interest

The canonist Jean Pontas examined the moral life of merchants in a vast compendium of cases of conscience. His work sought to police the boundaries between licit and usurious practices in moneylending. The litany of sinful actions ran the gamut, from dishonoring the Sabbath or feast days without "a pressing necessity" to overindulgence in drink or games of chance. The lion's share of potential offenses related to a "pernicious maxim": that "a merchant can sell his merchandise for as much as possible" and thus set "traps for those who do not know the value of that for which they ask."

Pontas admonished merchants for charging interest on loans "under the false name of a fraudulent company in which you have not risked your capital" or claims of a "loss from the delay of your payment." There was also the "usurious contract," known as *mohatra*, by which a trader sold goods only to repurchase them at a later date for a lower price. Another unscrupulous tactic involved demanding interest for the cost of diverting one's capital from a profitable enterprise.[16]

Pontas's dilemma—the necessity of money despite its patent dangers—had exercised theologians since the Patristic period.[17] In the *Book of Tobit*, Saint Ambrose affirmed the scriptural ban on interest, a position reinforced by Saints Jerome and John Chrysostom. Their objections cited various errors in logic. First, usury posed a false equivalence between the object loaned and interest paid in addition to the principal. Second, the return on investments rightfully belonged to the borrower as the fruit of his labor. Third, a lender could not expect more than the original sum because the money was consumed in use.[18] Gratian endorsed these principles in the *Decretum* (ca. 1145), his manual of canon law. Later commentators mitigated the ban depending on the intention of creditors and by justifying compensation owing to losses sustained (*damnum emergens*), the forfeiture of potential gains (*lucrum cessans*), or delinquency on the borrower's part.[19] Louis-Joseph Carrel reproduced Thomas Aquinas's influential condemnation of usury as "unjust in itself, because one sells what does not exist, from which arises an inequality that is opposed to justice." According to the *Summa Theologica*, a merchant who sought to force money into becoming fecund engaged in a sin no less deviant than sodomy, which likewise perverted the natural order of reproduction.[20]

Aquinas exemplifies a deeper dynamic: natural law originated in the work of canonists and evolved alongside ecclesiological as well as theological innovations. With the commercial renaissance of the twelfth century, the church abjured its hostility to profit per se so long as one did not take advantage of the poor.[21] The ideal of *aequalitas* in exchange, with due allowances for indemnification, held sway throughout the medieval period and remained the linchpin of economic-theological rigorism in future centuries.[22] Claiming competence over all questions concerning justice, clerics such as Peter Olivi and Marsilius of Padua drew on the Franciscan ideal of voluntary poverty to devise the first fully realized framework for mercantile transactions, which posited a willful soul capable of the ultimate act of ownership—that is, renunciation. By asserting divine voluntarism, the so-called nominalist revolution led by William of Ockham fortified a theory of subjective rights inhering in human persons.[23]

After the Reformation, the church took a hard line against usury out of a desire to pathologize Protestant teaching.[24] Lutheran and Calvinist polities—or, as Louis Bulteau wryly observed, "states where heresy reigns"—had legalized "moderate usury."[25] After denouncing the extortionist practices of Catholic institutions in the German-speaking lands, Luther alighted on a compromise whereby princes were counseled to keep interest within humane bounds (no more than 8 percent). Calvin proved more permissive, arguing that the biblical strictures set out in Deuteronomy no longer applied and that the Scholastic theory of sterile money defied logic. He noted that "if we wholly condemn usury, we impose tighter fetters on the conscience than God himself."[26] Confessional disputes informed not only financial transactions but also the relationship between ecclesiastical and secular power. Luther and Calvin allowed that political rule might diverge from revelation. Civil governments thus had the right to regulate the charging of interest. Such accommodations were more difficult to justify in France, where the monarch was bound to honor Catholic orthodoxy.

Faith remained a constant in matters of finance. Over the course of the sixteenth and seventeenth centuries, the Gallican church and state led an episodic campaign against usurious practices.[27] Their efforts gained momentum from dissension among Catholics themselves. Scholars have long suggested that liberal-minded Jansenists offered theological rationales for charging interest, as if performing the role of Weber's Puritans in a French mode. According to historians Arnaud Orain and Maxime Menuet, anti-Unigenitus polemicists showed themselves "more concerned than any of their contemporary Christian believers with the salvation of their soul." This vigilance extended to an inclination toward productive enterprise as a good in itself.[28] Yet the acolytes of Port-Royal often viewed usurious practices with the same jaundiced eye that colored their perception of the human desperation for money. After all, credit required debtors to sustain itself. For instance, the abbé Barthélémi de La Porte laid waste to his coreligionist Étienne Mignot for justifying usury, which he denounced as a "hydra" whose heads "regenerate ceaselessly" and as a "contagion" that "gives to the shadows of sin the name of light."²⁹ A similar dynamic reigned among members of the Society of Jesus, whose views fell along a doctrinal continuum ranging from retrenchment to permissiveness.³⁰ Not even the Enlightenment could deny the ubiquitous presence of religion. As Francesca Trivellato has shown, no less a thinker than Montesquieu accepted the commonplace that the bill of exchange originated in Jewish practice, perpetuating an anti-Semitic trope while championing the civilizing mission of commerce.³¹

The lack of consistency between religious affiliation and attitudes toward usury underscores the problematic that economic theologians held in common, that of reconciling spiritual desiderata with financial expediency. The church's position was revealingly Janus-faced—that is, absolute in theory, mutable in practice. The *Dictionnaire de droit canonique* (1770) offered a purposely anodyne definition: usury extended to "any gain or profit of any kind that one draws from the loan that one makes of something that is consumed in usage."³² The reference to consumption carried metaphysical weight. Following the distinction introduced by Thomas Aquinas, the act of spending a lent sum transferred ownership from the creditor to borrower.³³ Yet various alternatives remained for extracting returns on investments without incurring theological wrath: the purchase of discrete insurance policies, the creation of *rentes perpétuelles* (perpetual annuities) and *rentes viagères* (lifetime annuities), or the patronage of *monts de piété* (pawnshops).³⁴

Theologians frequently authorized indemnification in cases of *damnum emergens*, *lucrum cessans*, and exposure to risk.³⁵ French subjects marshaled such rationales with renewed zeal during the economic recovery from the collapse of Law's System. The demand for credit mounted from the 1730s to the 1780s, with only a slight decline in the aftermath of the Seven Years' War. By century's end, 83 percent of day laborers owed small debts. Merchants, artisans, and landowners dealt in more substantial sums.³⁶ Although one could not legally demand interest on promissory notes, creditors and debtors might list as part of the sum to be repaid an amount that tacitly included finance charges.³⁷ The king defied canon law with impunity, raising tremendous sums from *rentes perpétuelles*, *rentes viagères*, and short-term loans from national as well as international lenders. Notaries guided the private credit market to ever greater heights throughout the period, propelled by expanding trade and manufacturing.[38]

The church was routinely called on to assume financial obligations to the crown's benefit owing to its penchant for timely reimbursements.[39] The interest rate on these loans tended to range from 4 to 5 percent, or within the historical legal limit.[40] But even this concession to propriety did not always suffice. For instance, letters patent dated August 1706, at the nadir of French fortunes during the War of Spanish Succession (1701–14), authorized the diocese of Bourges to borrow 40,000 livres on the government's behalf at an interest rate 6.25 percent. In a typical arrangement, the clerics transferred the capital raised to establish an annuity with the promise of furnishing the dividends.[41] Five years later, the First Estate consented to taking out a loan of 8 million livres in the form of *rentes constituées* at 8.3 percent interest, even though the king had converted the rate on perpetual annuities to 5 percent in 1710.[42] In 1726, the General Assembly of the Clergy agreed to draw on its "inexhaustible credit" by servicing *rentes* on the Hôtel de Ville as part of a contract for the *don gratuit*, stipulating payments of 5 million livres.[43] During the War of Austrian Succession (1740–48), the sum rose to 15 million livres.[44]

As one Père Grangier unabashedly observed at midcentury, the contracting of loans via annuities found great favor "not only among theologians, but also among canonists," and "not only among moderns, but also among the ancients." Accordingly, the First Estate "does not act as though it suspects the least difficulty with the loans one makes to them." The "constant facts" on full display before "the entire universe" revealed otherwise. In public finance, economic theology took precedence over theology *tout court* since the crown and the episcopate alike "believe themselves authorized by the utility" of their transactions.[45]

Prohibitions and prosecutions of usury varied widely. Official interest rates on *rentes perpétuelles* gravitated toward 5 percent, although the government granted exemptions to the city of Lyon, the fairs of Brie and Champagne, and elsewhere, often with the local bishop's consent. Commercial rates trended higher, at 7 percent before 1750, and between 5 and 6 percent from 1750 to 1776. The charging of interest faced less opposition in provinces under the jurisdiction of Roman law than it did in the capital, which operated according to customary law.[46] In 1736 the Paris Parlement convicted an artisan named Chevaucheur of charging "usurious interest" on credit purchases. He was ordered to wear a sign announcing his crime and, "on bended knee, barefoot, in a nightgown, with a rope around the neck, holding a lit torch," plead forgiveness from God and king. He was also fined fifty livres and banished for nine years.[47] Proceedings in 1777 meted out even harsher punishments to a band of suspected usurers from Orléans. One Jeanne Lepage was initially condemned to be "beaten and flayed on her bare shoulders with a cane" and branded by a hot iron with the letter "V," marking her permanently as a *voleur* (thief). Her sentence was ultimately commuted to public ridicule while bound to a stake. A priest named in the scandal, Jean-Baptiste Fouchet, attempted to escape from prison. He was ordered to pay 200 livres in alms before the judgment was reversed on appeal, thereby exposing the futility of the court's efforts.[48]

In a moral economy of status and honor, credit relied on traditional values that strained to accommodate the monetization of social life. Landed property depreciated even as it remained a primary referent in the financial system. Equating secrecy with despotism, political observers looked on royal finances with suspicion.[49] Rising debt also posed the challenge of reconciling lending at interest with Christian ideals. In an effort to address this quandary, Pontas coupled his critique of usury with reflections on the proper employment of benefices and the adoration of the Eucharist. He implored priests to examine their motives not only while undertaking financial engagements but also when receiving God's "excessive charity" through the sacraments.[50] Given their potentially opposing commitments, theologians felt moved to speak in the face of conflicts between divine dictates and worldly exigencies.

Trinitarian Usury

In *Le parfait négociant* (1675), an oft-cited guide to business ethics, the merchant Jacques Savary claimed that commerce could not survive without the motive for gain. Yet he also upheld the Catholic ideal of securing "the abundance of all things" through "the union and charity between men." This commitment led him to denounce usurious exploitation.[51] During the long eighteenth century, theologians elaborated an intricate framework that far exceeded Savary's injunctions. In their view, all commercial obligations could justifiably stipulate interest. Critics responded by denouncing such claims on both doctrinal and economic grounds. The ensuing debate, which reached a critical mass in the second half of the eighteenth century, frequently featured the so-called *contractum trinius* (triple contract, or *trois contrats*). Despite legal rulings against it, which Savary duly reproduced, practitioners claimed to evade the ban on usury by separating the contribution of capital from the guarantee of its reimbursement.[52] The division of financial labor placed interest payments within the context of a sale. The trinitarian contract privileged *société* over *oikos*, threatening to depersonalize networks of production, consumption, and exchange while challenging legally binding religious doctrines.

Since the sixteenth century, banking families such as the Fuggers sought justifications for the *contractum trinius* from Jesuit advisers.[53] The contract required participants to enter into three agreements for (1) a partnership [*société*] between the lender and borrower; (2) insurance on the principal, to the benefit of the lender; and (3) a future sale, whereby the borrower disbursed to the lender a share of the proceeds based on a percentage of the initial investment. The creditor furnished financing and secured a return on his capital without exposure to loss. Triple contracts emulated the logic of annuities in presuming the transfer of property, thus circumventing canon and civil law. Protocols governing simple loans, which required the identity of sums between the original loan and its repayment, arguably did not pertain.

Although the church denounced the triple contract in 1580, theologians continued to debate the question during the next two centuries.[54] Elaborating arguments formulated by Jesuits such as Leonardus Lessius, the Minim polymath Emmanuel Maignan published in 1673 the treatise destined to become a standard reference in usury polemics, *De usu licito pecuniae*.[55] Despite the austerity of their monastic rule, the Minims proved highly amenable to commercial ventures, the sanctity of which friars defended in concert with Jean-Baptiste Colbert's program of financial and industrial revitalization.[56] Maignan marshaled lexical and philosophical evidence to contend that "it is permitted in itself, and according to natural law, to loan one's money on certain occasions in order to realize some honest profit, without usury." Maignan made clear from the outset that his argument cast beyond instances of *lucrum cessans* and *damnum emergens* to encompass "more universal reasons." Since the lender retained ownership over the object ceded to the borrower, he could rightfully charge for the right of "usage." The etymology of the French term *prêt* (loan) offered further justification. According to Maignan, the Latin equivalent *mutuum* did not entail an absolute transfer of property, even though scriptural allusions frequently referred to donation. The lender had a right to remuneration on rational grounds since he had invested the product of his labor and incurred opportunity costs in its engagement. Morally, the borrower shared the lender's desire for gain and so acted as his "auxiliary and agent."[57]

Although money was regarded as moribund by nature, Maignan suggested that in commercial dealings it performed a function comparable to landed assets invested in annuities.[58] According to traditional arguments, since money lent was not identical to money returned, ownership shifted from the creditor to the borrower. Maignan countered that "the usage of money does not only consist in the employment of this same money in species, but also in the trade in the things which come from it." He supported his assertion by denying the Scholastic distinction between goods that "bear some fruit in themselves, and those that do not." No less than a vineyard, a sum of money required human industry as well as good fortune to become productive. The laborer was entitled to a portion of the proceeds. Maignan concluded that the "contract of commission," or triple contract, held the same validity as the *rente consitutuée*.[59]

Not unlike Terrasson, whose theory of Eucharistic currency he anticipated, Maignan envisioned his economic writings as one facet of a totalizing project in theology and natural philosophy. The *Encyclopédie* noted that he devised an explanation of the Eucharist similar to that of Jacques Rohault, a precursor of the radical variant of Cartesianism advanced by Desgabets and his Enlightenment heirs.[60] According to Maignan's *Philosophia sacra* (1664), the superficial appearances of bread and wine should be imagined not as "real accidents" but as effects of the miraculous manipulation of the mental apparatus, having no existence independent of our senses.[61] *De usu licito pecuniae* pursued an analogous approach to economic goods. Under the correct conditions, it should be possible to receive money as if it possessed the generative power of land regardless of the former's sensible qualities. The shift in perspective required a willingness to abandon venerable yet defective understandings of what money represented and how it conveyed value.

Whereas Maignan engaged in metaphysical speculation, André de Colonia, a Minim friar renowned for his prowess at the pulpit, drew up a brief with merchants in mind. His *Éclaircissement sur le légitime commerce des intérêts* (1675) appealed directly to the royal and municipal officials who oversaw the trade fairs of Lyon, a major market for the trade in textiles between Europe, the Levant, and the Atlantic world.[62] "Money is the nerve of trade," he declared, and finance an honorable occupation recommended by *juge-consuls* and archbishops alike. Triple contracts deserved praise for appealing to a sense of "moral security" among participants rather than resorting to coercion. Such mechanisms did not qualify as usury since the loan signaled a deposit entrusted to the borrower rather than a transfer of ownership. Colonia recognized the controversial nature of his position. As he observed, the "true good is very often unknown in this life." Doubt lingered even in our paramount concern for salvation, "which does not have a price." In the absence of certitude, we "buy probability" as a guide to conduct "through diligence and work."[63]

Jean Le Correur, a doctor of theology with Jansenist and Cartesian sympathies, enlarged Maignan's and Colonia's defense of usury on moral as well as economic grounds.[64] His *Traité de la pratique des billets entre les négociens* (1682) identified a matter of "great consequence": whether merchants "will be damned" for their vocation.[65] As the title specified, Le Correur concentrated on bills of exchange, the use of which obviated the need to transport currency while granting access to funds on a speculative basis.[66] At a minimum, bills of exchange involved a payee who deposited a sum of money with a drawer, typically a banker, and received a letter or bill redeemable at another time and place by his designated signatory or signatories. According to Le Correur, bills allowed for interest without facilitating usury. Following Maignan's argument, their deployment did not imply a "complete alienation" of property and thus did not require the charity expected in a simple loan. By ensuring "legitimate compensation" for *damnum emergens*, or the risk of loss, the practice was worthy of "formal approbation" from ecclesiastical and civil authorities.[67]

Le Correur's classificatory maneuvers accentuated the generative capacity of bills. He agreed that the objects of a loan were "consumed directly or indirectly by usage," with the crucial caveat that the goods effectively change their nature and "become fertile" through the act of exchange. "Commerce," then, "presumes the abundance of he who receives." He cited as evidence for this claim the Sermon on the Mount. Jesus's commandment to lend freely applied only to those in desperate need. The parable of the talents, named for the Greco-Roman unit of measure and currency, featured a master who judged his servants on their financial stewardship. The tale seemed to confirm that "the production of money through money in trade" was not only possible but desirable.[68] Christian lenders could sell the use of their capital at a just price, or at "legitimate interest." The decisions reached in scripture and canon law, and by church fathers and magistrates of the parlement, all presented the circulation of bills of exchange as a good "in itself" so long as the poor were not exploited.[69]

The *Traité de la pratique des billets* elicited an ambiguous rebuke from Le Correur's fellow ecclesiastic Louis-Joseph Carrel, who held that even if usury were not inherently evil, it remained opposed to "the entirely supernatural lights of the faith." Bills of exchange did not possess a fixed moral character and could be "just or unjust" depending on circumstances. If the lender failed to share risk with the borrower, he committed "criminal usury." In place of Le Correur's abstract continuum of sterile and productive objects, which he had "forged for no useful reason," Carrel appealed to situational realism. A house or sum of money might be "sterile" in one case, as when lent to the poor, but "fertile" in another, as when engaged in commerce. Likewise, since the church approved of earnings from a *rente perpétuelle*, the only reason for not doing so in other contracts was that it had been "forbidden by divine precept."[70]

Armed with this elastic, empirically grounded theory of sterility, Carrel took his distance from Scholastic bromides that "usury is by nature evil" to advocate a position "more in keeping with businesspeople" and "daily experience." A transcendent, inscrutable deity handed down commandments "as he pleased, and for reasons that are known to him alone." Following Saint Bernard, Carrel distinguished three forms of law: natural law, positive divine law, and human law. Since natural law inhered in the essence of things, it could not be changed. "God himself does not change natures," Carrel noted. Rather, "he destroys them." But the immutable precepts of natural law differed in character from the "inviolable" status of the "positive precepts of divine law," which depended on the "authority of God" alone. If divine will shifted, so, too, would religious commandments.[71]

To exemplify the historical nuances of God's positive precepts, Carrel drew parallels between the status of usury and polygamy in the Hebrew Bible. The Israelites had engaged in both practices "by the word of God." They lent at interest to foreigners but refrained from doing so with their fellows. They married multiple partners without fear of punishment. It was possible to "preserve a true and perfect conjugal love with a double engagement" so long as one followed "divine wisdom" by resisting "the satisfaction of a reprehensible brutality" through adulterous liaisons. Ancient Jewish customs did not correspond to a transcendent, transhistorical reality. God prohibited polygamy among certain peoples but not among others by altering the content of human law. Although Carrel himself avoided Christian stereotypes of the economic behavior of Jews, his criteria could be reasonably extended to myths of their inclination toward profit-seeking through finance.[72]

The treatment of sexual morality had a double signification for the meaning of usury. Accepting patent contradictions between revelation and reason, Carrel deferred to God's mysterious designs. Polygamy served as a reminder that economic theology concerned not only the rational administration of resources but also the comportment of desiring subjects. God's wishes should become our own in both sexual and financial expenditures. Abraham's intention "to immolate his son on God's order" conformed not to "natural precept" but to divine will. Similarly, "if God had truly ordered Hosea [the Hebrew prophet who married the prostitute Gomer] to commit fornication, this would be a sign that, simply put, it is not against natural law, but only against positive law, with which God doubtlessly has the power to dispense."[73] The principle also held in the case of charging interest, which could be either licit or illicit, productive or unproductive, depending on the commandments imposed from one age to the next.

Carrel did not necessarily associate antiquity with veracity. For instance, "scholastic theologians" had obfuscated the mechanics of transubstantiation.

The "new philosophers" rightly challenged the existence of real accidents. Carrel held that "what these philosophers say has a great deal of clarity and solidity," especially when juxtaposed to the "contradictions and confusion" of outmoded authorities. The teachings of Descartes, Maignan, and Rohault "serve religion so favorably" as to lift them above reproach.[74]

Torn between tradition and the innovative arguments of Maignan and Carrel, eighteenth-century theologians such as Père Grangier sought a path between "relaxation" and "rigorism" with the "double torchlight of reason and religion" as their guide.[75] This conceptual terra incognita came to encompass an ever-widening terrain. Debates over the triple contract anticipated heated polemics surrounding pawnshops, lotteries, and annuities—establishments of concern not only to professional merchants but also to artisans and the working poor. Spiritual directors set themselves the task of accommodating religious doctrine to financial practice. In so doing, they effectively theologized finance and confirmed the status of theology as an economic science.

The Universalization of Usury

Perhaps no single work captures the mutual implication of theological and economic affairs more comprehensively than the *Conférences ecclésiastiques sur l'usure* (1717), the published findings of a commission established by Cardinal Louis Antoine de Noailles, the archbishop of Paris, in 1697. The task of summarizing the members' conclusions fell to Jean-Laurent Le Semelier, a priest in the Confraternity of Christian Doctrine.[76] Published in six editions during the eighteenth century, the four volumes instructed priests and parishioners on every matter under the monetary sun: banks, bankruptcy, benefices, bills of exchange, commercial societies, contracts, credit, hunting, inheritance, insurance, investment, leases, loans, pensions, precious metals, property, restitution, sales, shipwrecks, speculation, taxation, theft, the tithe, and wages. The field of usury, like usurers themselves, had "multiplied to infinity" under the guise of "the credit of the prince and the power of the kingdom." Yet the universal scorn of kings, jurists, and clerics offered "infallible proof" that a rising empire of interest threatened the survival of the realm.[77]

The *Conférences ecclésiastiques* began with first principles regarding loans, usury, and money. Whereas the Roman legal term *commodatum* or "loan in use" signified a contract by which one granted the use of a thing that endured, such as a house or a horse, the *mutuum* or "simple loan" involved money or another object consumed in usage. The fine gradations intimated by Maignan and elaborated by Le Correur on the productive nature of money in business struck Le Semelier as specious. The borrower assumed ownership over an object expended during the period of the loan. The lender retained "the right to demand and receive a thing of equal value" but surrendered claims to dividends from capital that no longer belonged to him. The substance of the loan was "sterile" in regard to the lender. Le Semelier thus expressly followed Aristotle in affirming that "loaned money produces nothing naturally."[78]

Le Semelier argued that "the entire injustice of usury consists in taking something appreciable above the sum loaned." The crime assumed several forms: "real" and "express" in self-evident cases, "mental" and "allied" when concealment was involved, and either "active" or "passive," depending on whether one was the lender or borrower in a usurious contract. Risk in and of itself did not legitimize interest, since it was inherent in all monetary exchange. Nor could one claim interest on money handed over to a merchant "to make it grow in value." This sum remained a free loan unless specific conditions applied. Le Semelier cited the case of a man who lent 10,000 livres to a friend with the "simple promise" that it be used to purchase land on which the creditor would receive mortgage payments. Since a "commercial loan" nevertheless remained a loan on "unalienated" property, any interest would be usurious. The same condemnation applied to interest on a loan of 1,000 livres that the creditor claimed would have otherwise been invested, provided he had not sought a formal order from the parlement demanding repayment.[79]

As a practical manual, the *Conférences ecclésiastiques* enumerated the scenarios in which it was permissible to borrow at interest and to profit from economic exchange. For instance, unlike money, which was consumed in usage, one could charge rent on the lease of real estate and movable property on account of depreciation. Following Thomas Aquinas, Le Semelier observed that a person in distress could undertake a monetary loan on usurious terms. Yet the same prerogative was not extended to potential creditors, since usury was an evil in and of itself. The usurer's argument from necessity, as Augustine noted, was tantamount to that of a "magician who earns his living through performing diabolical spells." Thus, even though the crown authorized merchants in Lyon to lend at excessive rates, they remained culpable before God. As tradition dictated, only *damnum emergens* or *lucrum cessans* justified interest. Le Semelier clarified that these situations did not imply "selling the usage of one's money" but rather indemnification for real damages or lost opportunities on the basis of a sincere accounting.[80]

Le Semelier's arguments courted contradiction between theory and practice at nearly every turn. He was compelled to account for the prevalence of *monts de piété* (pawnshops), where borrowers received loans in exchange for personal effects. Pawnshops originated in reforms instituted by Pope Leo X (r. 1513–21), who wished to offer the poor an alternative to unscrupulous moneylenders. Taking root first in Italy, the establishments made their way to France during the reign of Louis XIV. Enterprising members of the regular clergy, primarily Récollet and Franciscan, sought out forms of credit that had economically edifying effects without recourse to alms. Overcoming considerable resistance from local merchants, French *monts de piété* grew in popularity during the second half of the seventeenth century, with Marseille taking an early lead in 1696. Paris came late; its first pawnshop was only established in 1777. The following year, nearly 130,000 objects were pawned; by 1783 the number had risen to 400,000. The clientele, which included rich and poor alike, pawned possessions for sums of money that varied depending on the value of the item but also for grain or advances on seed for the annual crop. Artisans used the *mont de piété* as a means of earning money on unused stock. Customers driven by thrift or desperation pledged items such as winter wear, dress clothing, and jewelry until they were needed. Beyond the collateral, borrowers paid fees depending on the amount of their loans, generally between 3.75 and 5 percent.[81]

Le Semelier argued that *monts de piété* managed to avoid usurious exploitation by limiting themselves to modest loans and treating the collateral as a security in the case of nonpayment. Although conceding that the institutions collected sums over and above the principal, he observed that the charges qualified not as interest per se but as administrative expenses. He also cited the rulings of Leon X and Louis XIV as evidence of the licit nature of such transactions, without considering whether the pope and king had erred in their judgments.[82] The reality of the situation was more complicated. Chronically short of liquid funds, and torn between their roles as banking and charitable institutions, directors of *monts de piété* resorted to borrowing from intermediaries, typically in the form of *rentes constituées*. The costs were passed on to customers, who in turn employed pawn notes as a type of currency that could itself be put up as collateral for a loan from a third party. Unscrupulous financiers also accepted the tickets, thereby compromising the original purpose of the *monts de piété* to banish usury from charitable finance.[83]

Lotteries posed similar difficulties for Le Semelier in that their operation seemed to challenge the Christian dictates of justice. Organized games of chance had long funded monasteries, hospitals, orphanages, church sanctuaries, and other public works. In the middle decades of the eighteenth century permanent lotteries received the approbation of both the miter and the crown, raising millions of livres. The Loterie de l'École militaire, established in 1757, enticed the urban poor with the seemingly miraculous prospect of financial windfalls at deep discount.[84] Two decades later, the government chartered the Loterie royale to support the French Navy. A prize drawing even raised money to construct the facade of the Church of Saint-Sulpice, which counted among the preeminent architectural achievements of neoclassicism.[85] Le Semelier had no choice but to tread lightly in addressing the matter, advising that participants observe the "rules of charity" and refrain from consulting evil spirits to improve their odds. Ideally, lotteries would have as their object a "public good," with a portion of the proceeds set aside for "pious works."[86]

Le Semelier also sought to rationalize the costs associated with the use of bills of exchange, which theological skeptics tended to regard with deep suspicion. After dutifully reciting the common myth attributing the invention of financial paper to banished Jews, he presented unimpeachably Catholic arguments in their favor. Although money itself was sterile, the issuer was entitled to compensation for services rendered in transporting and converting funds, as well as for risks incurred in doing so. A merchant could sell on credit for a higher price or at interest if deferring payment entailed a serious loss, if the buyer was late in settling accounts, or after a year had passed since the original contract. In such cases, he reasoned, money changed hands under the auspices not of a loan but of a sale involving merchandise or the transport of currency.[87]

Annuities presented Le Semelier with a potentially insurmountable stumbling block. If *rentes* did not contravene church doctrine, why could one not enjoy similar benefits from short-term loans? Was property not alienated in both scenarios? According to Le Semelier, the difference turned on the temporal scope of the transaction. Since capital invested in annuities was ceded in perpetuity, interest was permissible. With a loan that must be repaid, in contrast, the usurious creditor aimed to sell time itself, which belonged to God alone. This explanation overlooked other features of annuities—that they could be reimbursed, and that the sum total of payments on *rentes perpétuelles* might eventually exceed the principal. Le Semelier answered such objections only partially. First, he noted that the rate of compensation was established by the prince. Second, the money invested became, not unlike land, a "useful fund that returns revenues." Third, since the lender of the capital sum could only compel reimbursement in cases of default, the debtor dictated how long he would continue making payments.[88]

In keeping with the state's role in the regulation of contracts, legal history became a deeply furrowed, highly contested terrain for debates over interest. As Le Semelier observed, defenders of usury held that only clerics fell under the ban until the tenth century. He refuted this claim with references to ecclesiastical synods and councils from Elvira (305–6) to Trent, the last of which reproached usury in all its forms as a violation of the seventh commandment against theft. French kings observed ecclesiastical precedent in their rulings. During the reign of Louis IX (r. 1226–70), the cardinal Hugues de Saint-Cher referred to usurers as "sorcerers" who seemingly conjured money from nothing through the charging of interest. The royal saint's successors renewed the ban on usury while establishing exceptions in cases such as *damnum emergens*, *lucrum cessans*, and the privileges for the merchants of Lyon. Henri IV (r. 1589–1610) and his Bourbon heirs followed suit. For instance, Louis XIV outlawed terms of repayment for a loan greater than the amount originally borrowed. The parlements approved the charging of interest only in the creation of annuities or as part of a formal sentence against a delinquent debtor.[89]

Le Semelier further chided opponents for asserting that the papacy did not condemn interest until a relatively late date.[90] But events would soon overtake his correction of the historical record. Between the publication of the first edition of the *Conférences ecclésiastiques* in 1717 and the reprinted edition of 1758, a dispute erupted over the vindication of interest by the theologian Scipion Maffei, whose *Dell'Impiego del danaro* (1744) maintained that the crime of usury applied only to extortionist loans taken out by the poor. Maffei dedicated his work to the pope. Now implicated in the scandal, Benedict XIV launched an inquiry into the doctrinal validity of commercial contracts.[91]

The ensuing judgment, *Vix Pervenit* (1745), left many questions undecided. Although the denunciation of usury in the case of the *mutuum* sounded a rigorist note, the text vaguely alluded to "certain circumstances or titles that do not essentially concern loans." These transactions could lawfully yield "annual revenues" and "just profit" in the course of "negotiations and exchanges." The ambiguous finding likely stemmed from the need for strategic tact given the inflammatory nature of the subject, but it also reflected factional divisions among members of the papal commission. In lieu of a definitive verdict, Benedict appealed to "moral theology" in the hope of identifying a golden mean between the "extremes" of absolute prohibition and wanton permissiveness.[92] His overture only deepened the antimonies of the church's tortured position—between traditionalism and innovation, singular authority and moral latitude, biblical proscription and financial realities, the imperatives of the spirit and the requirements of the flesh. Clerics in favor of reforming the traditional ban cited the encyclical in defense of their orthodoxy, a move that provoked outrage among conservatives.[93]

Of the hundreds of works on usury to appear in the wake of Benedict's ruling, the Index only censored a handful. Most titles were listed under the cloak of anonymity.[94] Among them was the *Traité des prêts de commerce*, a work issued by the Jansenist Société des Trente-Trois. Philippe Boidot, a member of the circle, composed the first edition in 1738. Expanded versions appeared in 1759 and 1767 under the direction of Étienne Mignot, a doctor of the Sorbonne and member of the Académie des Inscriptions et Belles-Lettres.[95] Mignot and his collaborators championed usury in the midst of a vertiginous expansion of international trade, which quadrupled during the eighteenth century. Their aim was to liberate economic exchange from traditional strictures while remaining within an orthodox framework. To this end, they drew on arguments from Dutch theologians in Utrecht, who held that annuities should be reimbursable by both creditors and debtors as a form of financing.[96]

The misconceptions and obscurantism of the Scholastics served as a red thread throughout the four volumes of the *Traité des prêts*. Citing Emperor Theodosius and even Thomas Aquinas, Mignot went so far as to rehabilitate the term *usury* itself, which he claimed was "neither odious nor shameful" but merely a means of "signifying all increase or interest of money." Whether usury was licit or illicit depended on the condition of the borrower. The rich creditor had an obligation to lend freely to the indigent even if the transaction left him vulnerable to loss. In such cases God made good on the magnanimous gesture with recompense in heaven. Lenders obtained "infinite riches" in the future merely by sacrificing "a small sum of money" in their fellows' present moment of need. The spirit of Christian fraternity spurred the founding of *monts de piété*, which had long garnered papal support. Mignot lauded such efforts in general while criticizing pawnshops that charged interest to their impecunious clientele. To his mind, Scholastic theologians who defended such practices all but admitted their fundamental hypocrisy, whereas he remained an advocate of charity in giving and consistency in reasoning.[97]

Among the most dogged critics of the *Traité des prêts de commerce* was the Jansenist cleric Barthélémi de La Porte, who in 1769 published his *Principes théologiques sur l'usure* as a refutation of the 1767 edition of Mignot's work. According to La Porte's pessimistic vision, "artifice and trickery" lorded over the disenchanted economy as "the fundamental means of making a more certain and considerable profit in an enterprise." He targeted justifications of the generative power of money as "the firmest and cruelest support of this passion that the Holy Spirit calls the root of all evil." Addressing himself to the "pastors of souls," he bemoaned the temerity of clerics who "speak of divine and ecclesiastical precepts" to rationalize unbridled greed.[98] Seeking refuge in Scholastic doctrine, he condemned the triple contract on the grounds that it defied the principle "that money is by its nature incapable of producing anything." At the same time, he defended the fees assessed by *monts de piété* as necessary for supporting the charitable mission of these institutions. Shifting from religious to practical considerations, he alleged that usury undermined agriculture by diverting investment away from land, which ultimately drove up the price of commodities.[99]

In sharp contrast, Paul-Timoléon Laforest, a parish priest from Lyon, hailed Maffei and Benedict as evangelists of a new social gospel that would vanquish Scholastic prejudices for the good of all believers. The preface to his *Traité de l'usure et des intérêts* (1769) noted that the work had already given peace of mind to merchants concerned with the state of their souls. Laforest acknowledged on the very first page that "the sole objective of every Christian must be to attain his salvation, and that of pastors to obtain it." However, excessive severity in the policing of loans imperiled the faithful parishioner's pursuit of celestial bliss by fomenting a sense of despair. *Vix Pervenit* broke through the impasse by distinguishing usury from permitted business. On Laforest's reading, the pope had admitted, first, that "there are titles that can be united to a loan and grant the right to legitimate interests," and second, that "there are contracts other than loans that can also authorize the drawing of interest," including the triple contract. Laforest rejected Mignot's earlier argument that a transaction could be assessed as licit or illicit depending on the wealth of the parties, turning instead to the uses of money—one of "consumption and destruction," the other of "employment and growth." If one posited the transfer of property for the duration of a financial arrangement, the ensuing alienation demanded a "just price" as compensation for the gains made on the investor's wealth. Priests could minister in good conscience to merchants, who served their own interest and the commonweal without forfeiting eternal beatitude.[100]

The justification of the triple contract with reference to money that perpetuates itself through use met with a hostile reception. Père Carpuac classed Laforest among those who "have for a century prostituted their pens in defense of this impious opinion that usury is not prohibited." He rejected the argument that "the lucrative employment" of money justified interest, citing Benedict XIV as an authority.[101] Similarly, the abbé Prigent attacked Laforest for advancing "novel, dangerous, and false" ideas about the use of financial instruments. The distinction between "consumption" and "growth" in business matters struck him as tantamount to claiming that "money in commerce is a fructiferous thing," a sentiment that ran counter to the doctrines of Thomas Aquinas.[102]

Vix Pervenit opened a Pandora's box of casuistry under the veil of catholicity.[103] The pope's call for economic-theological speculation resounded in an echo chamber framed by the writings of Maignan and Laforest's allies on one side and those of La Porte and Prigent on the other. Le Semelier's lumbering text memorialized positions that, while ancient in provenance, acquired a radically new charge in the aftermath of Law's failed reforms and Benedict XIV's halting apologia for commercial practice. Given its massive wealth and role in state finance, the church had no alternative but to grapple with its fraught relationship to riches, both worldly and celestial. In so doing, theologians found themselves returning to the question of the fecundity of money. It was an issue of overwhelming metaphysical as well as fiscal significance that had long moored anti-usury convictions. If the sterility of money lost its status as dogma, then the most powerful condemnation of interest risked falling into anachronism.

The Fecundity of Money

The Catholic claim that money could not produce money had its origins in the church fathers and was significantly buttressed by Aristotle, whose statements on the subject were taken up and extended by Thomas Aquinas and his Scholastic heirs.[104] The doctrine of sterile money—which coalesced in the thirteenth century, at the same time as transubstantiation—equipped opponents of usury with a formidable weapon. Economic theologians such as Maignan and Le Correur approached the question obliquely but with ever greater boldness. Initially, they conceived of the triple contract and similar arrangements in terms that did not necessitate a complete rejection of Aristotelian-Thomistic verities. Yet their disdain for Scholasticism, strengthened by Cartesian assaults on the tradition, opened the path to a more direct engagement with the issue. Mignot intimated a shift in terrain with his argument that commercial contracts altered the nature of things. It fell to later commentators to complete the logical circuit by attesting to the fructification made possible by financial instruments. They did so in light of Benedict XIV's 1745 encyclical and the resurgence in debates over frequent communion, polemics that concentrated attention on the productivity of the sacraments. The conjuncture of economic realities and theological speculation gave rise to a situation in which casuists invoked heavenly riches to support their position on the charging of interest.

The essence of money had figured in previous clashes over usury. Maignan engaged the question in the 1670s, reversing the Thomistic injunction with his claim that capital, "far from being consumed, will grow and multiply considerably."[105] Le Semelier explicitly censured Maignan in light of the dictates of natural jurisprudence as handed down by the church fathers. For instance, Gregory of Nyssa taught that profits stemmed from human labor rather than the attributes of the good employed. According to John Chrysostom, money differed from land in that it was "not destined by its nature to a definite lucrative use, like a field or a house," but was instead a measure of value. For Le Semelier, the "eternal law of God" did not change merely because Europeans had discovered a new source of gold and silver in the mines of Spanish America.[106] Over the course of the eighteenth century, skeptics alleged that such venerable doctrines had lost their credibility, speculating whether economic signs possessed the power of self-replication.

For instance, the 1738 edition of *Traité des prêts de commerce* attested that money employed in commercial exchange not only "subsists" but "bears fruit."[107] The strident Jansenist Nicolas Le Gros attacked the proposition on the basis of Patristic and Scholastic dogmas before asserting that usury remained deplorable whether or not money was sterile.[108] Mignot and his collaborators subtly made the case for interest-generating financial mechanisms. In the 1759 edition of their work, they claimed that in enjoying the "fruits and revenues of the land," the purchaser of an annuity profited "in a mediated fashion" from the "fruits of money." If a man borrowed 50,000 livres to invest in land, the once dormant proceeds "changed condition" through gainful employment. Turning the authority of Gregory of Nyssa, John Chrysostom, and other fathers against traditionalist accounts, the *Traité* held that money should be regarded as sterile when given to the poor but fertile in dealings with the rich. Not only was this property in keeping with natural law, as Mignot had argued; it even operated as an extension of the golden rule.[109]

Mignot ultimately endorsed the formulation of the *avocat de parlement* Guillaume Raviot: money was "nothing by itself" yet representative of wealth generally. Its value remained "arbitrary and extrinsic," determined by sovereigns who consecrated universal equivalents to measure "the price of all that is venal on the earth." In accordance with the voluntarist credo that "all is fictional in jurisprudence," civil legislation treated mortgages as if they were "real beings" and "minted silver," which "represents all goods," as having the status of "real property." Princes acted in such a manner because scripture itself allowed it. If natural law forbade the charging of interest, then God would not have permitted the ancient Israelites to do so when trading with foreigners. Extrapolating from both legal precedent and principle, Mignot concluded that "usury is a production of money by money, which is not sterile in commerce."[110]

Mignot's *Traité des prêts de commerce* cited his opponents' own arguments as evidence for the belief that wealth creation altered the status quo ante. For example, he countered Carrel's analogy between usury and polygamy with a long disquisition on Hugues de Saint-Cher, who employed the prevalent medieval strategy of likening usury to the "sodomy of nature" because it "makes grain grow where it has not been sowed." Both crimes were at bottom *contra naturam*. Hugues's accusation played on a rich paradox: the unproductive expenditures implied by nonprocreative sex opened the possibility of a mode of enjoyment freed from sheer necessity or utility. In a fascinating move, Mignot next equated the promise of sodomy with that of alchemy. Citing Hugues's comparison of the usurer's art to "the transmutation of metals," he offered a jarring quip: "Nature is surprised that gold gives birth to gold."[111]

These seemingly disparate allusions followed a common economic-theological rationale. Like sodomy, which gave sexual pleasure without responsibility for offspring, alchemy promised riches with minimal labor. The same facility held for lending at interest, which "changes species against the order of nature, in making silver from gold, and oat from wheat." Usury even seemed to transcend mortal existence, given that it "sells the time of which God alone is master."[112] As appropriated by Mignot, Hugues's terminology recalled yet another deviation from natural law that he did not himself name—the Eucharist. Transubstantiation elevated common matter via a miracle that could be replicated ad infinitum, auguring the moment of bliss when time itself would dissolve into eternity.

Rigorist arguments against usury held that the act of lending transferred the property of a thing to the borrower, as in the case of rents and other commercial transactions. Mignot responded by noting that these arrangements nevertheless contravened the natural law of the sterility of money and its prohibition against selling time. The Scholastics could only proceed by making all manner of exceptions to their own rules. Even Aquinas authorized the charging of interest under certain conditions. Usury was said to defy divine and civil law, yet wealth-creating institutions such as *rentes constituées* and *monts de piété* were permitted. Both conditions could not hold true simultaneously: either money was sterile in all cases, or one must admit that it possessed some measure of fecundity.[113]

Mignot sought to impose a legible order on what he regarded as the "caprice" and "particular opinions of theologians," or what Raviot dismissed as their "metaphysical distinctions."[114] The seeming collusion of the cleric and the jurist against their Scholastic predecessors did not signal a disenchanted view of finance but rather of an economic theology of money. Capital changed its nature depending on whether the rich or the poor mobilized it. Coin, annuities, and bills of exchange affected transmutation without end by converting consumption into production, liquid assets into a substance that had the legal standing of land, and the future into the present. Yet this message gave even its most avid defenders pause. As Mignot noted, it was "an injustice that revolts nature itself to profit from the misery of another to enrich oneself."[115] He insisted on shielding the poor from money's effects precisely because he respected its power.

After 1750 theologians felt emboldened to question the sterility of money without resorting to metaphor. In his *Traité de l'usure*, Laforest explained away doctrinal resistance to monetary fertility by emphasizing the Thomistic taxonomy of "money loaned" and "money entrusted . . . for profitable employment." He explained: "it is the circulation and depositing of money that makes wealth, that forms the nerve and support of commerce." Since the discovery of gold and silver in the New World, "minted money has multiplied to infinity," allowing it to be bought and sold like any other good. In a passage reminiscent of Terrasson, Laforest marveled that "commerce, and thus wealth, have expanded without proportion through the perpetual circulation of money." Even so, given that simple loans should be made without the expectation of gain, "money is sometimes sterile, sometimes fertile" depending on "the use one makes of it."[116]

Pro-usury writers made a virtue out of mutability. Money's use value derived from its variable exchange value, which demanded reproducibility and distribution without physical limit. Antoine-François Prost de Royer, a municipal officer [*échevin*] in Lyon, argued in 1763 before the archbishop of Lyon that currencies procured not merely "physical necessities" but also "pleasures, luxury, consideration, distinctions, favor, nobility, dignities, titles." On a still vaster scale, "its balance becomes that of the earth," sustaining "the equilibrium of all of Europe." The occasion for Prost de Royer's appeal to Archbishop Antoine de Montazet was a dispute over usury among Lyonnais clergy. Citing Montesquieu's affirmation in *De l'esprit des lois* of money's sterility alongside the Gospel parable of the talents, Prost de Royer appeared to endorse the principle that "it is not money that produces money, but the labor of the borrower." Yet his encomiums betrayed a deeper faith in what he called the financial "sign," which was for "commerce what blood is to the human body." This function did not depend on the "effigy and arms of the sovereign" but rather on commodified matter itself. The circulating "mass" of money could turn into all things for all people: it "serves to pay for the silks and the raw materials that one must buy in cash, to settle accounts, to purchase at the best price." Its power coursed through "an unbroken network of demands, operations, needs, a rapid and perpetual shock, the effects of which cannot be foreseen and which continually forms voids that money alone can fill."[117]

The apotheosis of money as a potentially productive substance met with resistance from clerics fearful of deviating from both reason and revelation. Did metal coin and paper notes possess a value in and of themselves? As La Porte answered, the theories of Prost de Royer and Mignot implied that money minted for circulation could be traded on the market "like ingot" and thus loaned at interest. It defied logic that "what is the price of all things would have a price other than its own intrinsic value." The wayward ideas disseminated by "corrupting missionaries" had given rise to the delusion that "seeds reproduce, multiply, perpetuate themselves in the very heart of money." Prost de Royer "doubtlessly recognizes in metals an active virtue that animates plants and causes growth." La Porte could only respond with exasperation, "What a bizarre physics!"[118]

Debt and Demystification

The intense speculation over the fecundity of money contradicts narratives predicated on the sequestering of the economic sphere from other domains of life. In the 1760s France groaned under the massive debts and economic displacements occasioned by the Seven Years' War. Secular authorities found themselves all the more beholden to theological scruples. While Prost de Royer extolled the marvels of commerce to the archbishop of Lyon, Turgot made a similar case as intendent of Limoges. A region that would later become synonymous with fine porcelain, at the time it languished as an impoverished hub for paper manufacturing and *eaux de vie*. In nearby Angoulême the lack of coin and credit drove up interest rates, which rose as high as 12 percent (surpassing the nominal rate by 8 points). Businessmen wanting for capital resorted to accommodation bills drawn on each other's credit, which they sold for ready money at a discount. Unwilling to repay the obligations as they came due, the borrowers accused their lenders of criminal usury, prompting Turgot to intervene.[119]

The resulting *Mémoire sur les prêts d'argent* (1770) appealed to the "true principles" of natural law over the doctrines peddled by "rigorist theologians." Following pro-usury clerics from Maignan to Mignot, Turgot held that the right to property and the imperative of utility sanctioned the charging of interest. God would not have "forbidden a thing absolutely necessary for the prosperity of societies." Turgot thus rejected the "false subtleties" of the Scholastics, among them the claim that "money cannot produce money." As he noted, if this metaphysical supposition held true, then the Old and New Testaments would not have recommended productive investment. The ban on interest thus originated in the "cry of nations" rather than divine fiat. Material conditions had since advanced to such a level that borrowers acted not out of desperation but in the pursuit of "great profits."[120] Even the church benefited from the rising tide, which Turgot or a sympathetic commentator wryly demonstrated in an addendum to the manuscript version of the *Mémoire* with a survey of contracts between the clergy and its receivers that called for the payment of interest.[121] His argument persuaded the Conseil d'état to dismiss the usury charges against the defendants in Angoulême. But the government did not lift the official prohibition of usury.[122]

The *Mémoire sur les prêts d'argent* approached interest on a temporal as well as financial plane. Value conveyed not a fixed quantity but "the preference of each of the contracting parties for the thing he receives over the thing he gives." This inclination, Turgot explained, "presumes that each one attributes to the thing he acquires a greater value than to the thing he cedes relative to his personal utility and to the satisfaction of his needs and desires." A relation of nominal equality took the form of a self-interested gain. The debtor consented to an obligation because he valued money in the present more than the same money at a future date. Turgot then posed a rhetorical question: "If a sum possessed presently is worth more, if it is more useful, if it is preferable to the assurance of receiving the same sum in one or several years," then "why should this difference not be offset by assuring an increase in the sum proportionate to the delay?"[123]

Turgot's musings anticipated and amplified the economic doctrine of time preference toward which the theology of pardons had merely gestured.[124] A believer seeking indulgences did so with a similar rationale in mind, exerting himself in this life to shorten the period his soul would otherwise spend in purgatory. Pastors extolled the Jubilee as a chance not only to discharge current debt but also to avoid future obligations through renewing one's moral commitment to God. As Turgot made clear, the difference between a market and a treasury of merit depended on the temperament of the creditor. Unlike a worldly merchant who lived and died by trade, Christ and the saints gave freely of their spiritual capital without expectation of personal gain in the future. Even so, borrowers in both instances shared a conviction that time was of the essence. The penitential regime had long measured indulgences in the exacting terms of days and years. Political economy abstracted time further still by quantifying the price of money at a given moment in the form of interest rates.

Turgot accepted that an economic actor might elect to give "something for nothing" out of "generosity."[125] More concretely, he proposed—in terms reminiscent of Joachim Faiguet de Villeneuve, who contributed the *Encyclopédie* article on usury—the establishment of merchant networks that would allow the poor to aggregate their meager savings into "capital." The collective mobilization of these funds offered more remunerative potential than existing institutions such as the *monts de piété*. Money would not only beget money; it would also serve as an "encouragement to thrift and sobriety," since workers would have a compelling reason not to dissipate their earnings on drink or frivolous pastimes.[126] The movements of the social system thus oriented individual interests toward collective ends. Worldly restraint led not to despair but to freedom from financial bondage.

Turgot imagined the economy as a self-organizing, self-regulating sphere of action.[127] Yet his secular schema coexisted with models of providence drawn from religion. The *Mémoire sur les prêts d'argent* included a chapter on the true meaning of Jesus's commandment to lend without expectation of gain. Although the "duties of Christianity" called for benevolence, theologians had erred by "converting the precept of charity into a precept of rigorous justice." Turgot's reading of the Gospel of Luke harmonized generosity and profit-seeking. Jesus taught that "you have, verily, a means of rendering interest legitimate: lend your capital for an indefinite period." In cases of real need, "allow your purses to be open to one another, and do not sell the assistance that you owe each other."[128]

Faiguet de Villeneuve advanced still more forceful arguments in his *Légitimité de l'usure légale* (1770), which described the price of money as "a sovereign that once reigned throughout the world and has become odious." The time for restoration was nigh. He ridiculed the theory of sterile money as a "childish tale" and sought to unseat metaphysics in favor of calculations of utility. "Nothing is more profitable in the state," he claimed, "than the equitable relation between affluent persons, provided that the loan that makes it possible offers advantages to each party." If civil authorities committed to nonintervention, free trade and "moral equilibrium" would prevail. As Faiguet de Villeneuve assured readers, "the usurious contract in no way attacks divinity. . . . God is not concerned with it except to maintain the precious equity that is necessary for mutual advantage."[129]

Légitimité de l'usure légale foresaw a future in which Christian principles complemented the ideal of equality before the economic law. Faiguet de Villeneuve confidently claimed that "we have an infallible rule to lead us in all matters of interest, a rule of justice and charity that Jesus Christ taught us." In this rendering of the golden rule, one had a financial as well as moral obligation "to treat others as we wish them to treat us." The imperative applied to more than loans by which both parties expected to benefit. Faiguet de Villeneuve viewed magnanimous donation as a means to a greater, eternal end. Business dealings, although "sterile acts" in regard to "salvation," were not in and of themselves "damnable." Rather, Christ counted "the commercial loan" among the "good offices of those one calls *honnêtes gens*." The "free loan" put one in even better stead. It was "an act of perfection, assured of a reward in heaven."[130]

During the same years that Turgot and Faiguet de Villeneuve presented their briefs in favor of usury, François-Léon Réguis reaffirmed the "economy of providence" along general rather than restricted lines. Lenders had a right to indemnification in cases of loss but were expected to consider the borrowers' means to pay. A sense of solidarity attenuated the desire for gain. Professional usurers fell into sin even if they charged no more than the legal rate since the earnings remained exempt from taxes such as the *taille*. Borrowers should make every effort to meet their obligation but could consider whether the lender was capable of sustaining a default on the loan. Those needing money had a responsibility to avoid usurers whenever possible lest they perpetuate evil, for the same reason that one would decline "receiving the sacraments from a priest that one knows most certainly to be unworthy of administering them." Réguis observed that, in relation to God, all humans should consider themselves "debtors" who were dependent on his "infinite mercy."[131]

The history of early modern credit practices cannot be reduced to a narrative of secularization in which the state progressively converted the moral economy into a political economy.[132] Economic theology continued not only to mediate between but also to preside over these realms. Even Turgot's campaign to legalize usury in Angoulême, however portentous for subsequent developments in financial theory and practice, drew on the religious resources of his time. Faiguet de Villeneuve and Réguis offered significant correctives in their refusals to sequester worldly from spiritual aspirations. Alms-giving and profit-seeking did not stand in essential opposition. The pursuit of wealth in this life need not preclude opulence in the next.

. . .

Political economy emerged out of the shock of Law's System, which posited *billets de banque* and shares in the Compagnie des Indes as dazzling agents of wealth creation. Its theorists evinced varying degrees of skepticism toward talismans of value. Endless polemics over usury, occasioned by the intractable tendency of French subjects to engage in the practice, gradually tempered the opposition of church and state to loaning at interest. Responding to the rise in maritime trade but also to revisions of Aristotelian-Thomistic certainties, enlightened clerics militated in both the vanguard and the rearguard of a financial revolution. Their efforts found credence in the ambiguous pronouncements of Benedict XIV, whose encyclical opened a space in which to challenge the ban on usury in practical and conceptual terms.

Economic theologians speculated on the origins of the wealth of nations, struggling with and against the power of signs that yielded what they signified in mysterious fashion. The role of human industry remained a particular source of conflict. Although advocates for usury recognized the necessity of labor, they did not regard all profit as the effect of physical and mental exertion. Money itself—by virtue of its composition, but also by nature of its representative function—mediated value, thereby rendering possible its production. Paper currency, which had fallen into discredit after the departure of Law and Terrasson from the fiscal stage, ultimately triumphed in the form of interest-bearing contracts that bound ecclesiastical and civil powers alike. At the same time, critics of usury denounced the fertility of money for arrogating a generative power that rightfully belonged to natural and supernatural acts of procreation.

The preoccupation with money's attributes followed from a dual religious and financial truth: the omnipresence of debt. A spiritual economy that presumed bottomless sin required infinite forgiveness. During Jubilee years, the church issued indulgences that spared believers a portion of the temporal penalties for sin. According to the Catholic ethic, mortals required assistance from God and from each other. One should lend as one had received—liberally and with grace, faithful to what Bossuet referred to as "celestial usury."[133] The field of economic theology clarified a vast middle ground between the poles of personal obligation and impersonal credit. After all, sinners related to God as both intimate and estranged. The church promised to traverse this chasm through the medium of the sacraments. The excesses of human frailty and the splendors of otherworldly abundance found analogues in the cult of usury redeemed. Its adherents offered money as a universal equivalent for the price of all things—even of time itself. In their eyes the science of economy did not lead ineluctably to the circumscription of traditional doctrine. Rather, economic theologians drew together material as well as spiritual possessions in inventive ways, endowing capital with the productive capacities once reserved for the Eucharist and penance.

CHAPTER 5

The Cult of Consumption

THE FRONTISPIECE of *Le moine secularisé* (1678), a scathing critique of the regular clergy by a disaffected Lyonnais priest named Jean Chastain, satirized the purveyors of spiritual luxury (fig. 5.1).[1] A colporteur hawks celestial wares, including a rosary, a scapular (a small piece of cloth strung across the body), the Belt of Saint Augustine, and the Cord of Saint Francis of Paola. Manuals to connoisseurs also swing from the basket, doubling as advertisements. A guide to the rosary is first among them, an indication of its popularity.[2] The accessories were believed not only to bestow spiritual blessings but also to save their owners from perilous childbirth, shipwreck, gunshot wounds, and other misfortunes.[3] According to a contemporary primer, the church approved such devotions to "make the virtues flourish" and "to revive piety" among the laity "by a gentler path" that was "adapted to their weakness" and paved with various "privileges and indulgences."[4] The papacy duly granted thousands of pardons to members, certifying that the advantages they enjoyed on earth would extend to the afterlife.

The image made light of the material dimensions of the spiritual economy but also cast light on the spiritual dimensions of the material economy. Seizing on common anti-Catholic tropes, Chastain voiced the cynicism of a debauched monk who advised churches to publicize their heavenly merchandise "like a sign, or a *bouchon de cabaret* [indicating that a place of business

Figure 5.1 *Le moine secularisé*, 1678. Bibliothèque nationale de France.

sold wine]." By way of example, he cited a confraternity that profited from eighteen thousand years of indulgences on Sunday and an additional ten thousand years for each day of the week.[5] In this instance truth proved even more lavish than fiction: Innocent VIII (r. 1484–14) had offered sixty thousand years for saying the Rosary.[6] Popes presided over a bull market that incited demand for prayer beads, relics, and sacred images.

Scarcity, long regarded as the inescapable fate of a fallen world, gradually gave way to a new faith in heavenly as well as worldly affluence.[7] This sea change came in waves of material profusion and social confusion. Daniel Roche has brilliantly analyzed the growing range of possessions owned by French subjects as a recalibration of needs, from an "economy of salvation" to one of "worldly happiness."[8] The value of Parisian wardrobes increased in real value 163 percent among the nobility, 272 percent among officeholders and professionals, and 321 percent among domestic servants (growing to 436 percent during Louis XVI's reign).[9] French merchants imported Indian textiles by the hundreds of thousands; the crown supported domestic production of similar goods. South Asian calicos and European knock-offs flooded the market for shirts, cravats, skirts, and blouses, offered in a dizzying array of patterns and colors. Washable cotton became the fabric of choice among day laborers and domestics, while manufacturers of woolen and silken garments adapted by pitching well-cut suits and gowns to an elite clientele.[10]

The eighteenth century bore witness to Marx and Engels's claim in *The German Ideology* that "the action of satisfying and the instrument of satisfaction which has been acquired, leads to needs; and this creation of new needs is the first historical act."[11] Faced with a seemingly infinite number of choices, consumers found themselves at once the quarry of advertisers' machinations and the ultimate arbiters of style, with women setting the trends of the season both as designers and as customers.[12] Demands on the buyer's time and powers of discernment instilled in consumer goods a heightened sense of worth.[13] Fashion called for stylistic emulation even when the quality of materials proved wanting, a predicament that propelled the rise of "populuxe" goods ranging from textiles and furnishings to watches, snuff boxes, and umbrellas.[14]

Pious possessions make rare cameo appearances in the plotline of this history, serving an additive or illustrative rather than explanatory function.[15]

For instance, although the clergy popularized the use of tobacco, scholars overlook that sociability among smokers was expressed in terms of the theological virtue of charity. Likewise, an emphasis on the state and efforts to circumvent its monopolies glosses over criminal assaults on the Catholic Church, an equally formidable economic power with no less global a reach.[16] In 1756 the Parlement of Bordeaux decided the case of a "band of villains" that had launched an expedition from the Pyrenees to plunder churches of "holy things," some of which were sold to Jews. The thieves drew direct inspiration from the notorious transatlantic smuggler Louis Mandrin, whom the verdict expressly named as a "model" for criminal syndicates. After a rampage across hundreds of miles, the men were caught stealing "riches" from the sacristy of the Église des Cordeliers. Besides chalices and other ornaments, they had even taken the ciboria used to hold the Eucharist after discarding the consecrated hosts inside. Although spectacular justice had fallen out of fashion, such wanton blasphemy could not go unanswered. The court ordered forty-seven offenders to be "burned alive in iron cages." In an especially sadistic variation, domestic cats were placed alongside the condemned, presumably so that the animals' clawing, biting, and sheer panic might intensify their suffering, if not approximate the agonies of hell.[17]

While often remarked upon, the conversion of luxury into necessity has likewise elicited scant analysis.[18] Scholars tally prerequisites and repercussions without plumbing the depths—economic and cultural, but also psychic and spiritual—out of which the consumer revolution emerged. Christian missionaries contributed to the popularization in Europe of new products such as chocolate and created demand for rosaries and other artifacts among recent converts from North America to East Asia. Yet leading scholars such as Frank Trentmann give pride of place to "an expansionist state system" that, once coupled with Enlightenment doctrines of progress, facilitated "a climate of ideas and institutions that encouraged men and, especially, womento join the ranks of wage earners and consumers."[19] Trentmann's arguments are well-suited to Britain and the Dutch Republic but less so to France, where administrative centralization coexisted with a hierarchical society of orders and where the Catholic Church remained vital to public finance.

The present chapter returns devotional objects to the front rank of accessories that spurred consumption in the eighteenth century.[20] Their accumulation often preceded that of decidedly secular goods and heralded a more perfect pleasure. The rosary in particular offers a revealing glimpse into the circuits of consumption at multiple sites, from the stocks of artisans to manuals that expounded on the satisfactions to be gained from its use. This artifact, which resembled jewelry, was believed to cure spiritual, physical, and social ills. It also affected the mental state of owners through prayerful meditation. A "psychoactive revolution" led by tobacco and coffee anticipated the consumer revolution.[21] Religion—the "*opium* of the people," in Marx's memorable phrase—had long acted in an analogous manner and on a vaster scale.[22] Mysteries and rituals assuaged fear, structured experience, and altered the mind through a host of new needs, the meeting of which assured not merely survival but also exquisitely blissful, eternal life.

Mindful pastors insisted that one could seek heaven in the midst of earthly pursuits. As Réguis claimed, "a man filled with the spirit of God . . . is a great treasure in society, whatever position he occupies, whatever profession he practices."[23] Confraternities, which originated in trade corporations but came to accept men and women from all walks of life, furthered this ideal through the circulation of indulgences. With the rosary, pardons were deemed interchangeable not only among members of particular brotherhoods but also across Catholic Christendom. Spiritual directors debated among themselves the nature and extent of work required to gain indulgences, from hard penance to the mere donning of an accessory.

As a mode of cultural production, capitalism depends on perpetuating desire, which in turn generates sources of pleasure to the point of mystification.[24] Economic theologians reflected intensely on this state of affairs. Their founding premise, that worldly goods offered nothing more than a simulacrum of eternal riches, interrogated the genesis and fate of satisfaction. The market for devotional objects made manifest this dynamic. Not only did cheaper models recall more sumptuous productions, but the artifact itself, in all its forms, was believed to serve as a conduit to an eternal life of infinite indulgences that surpassed mortal understanding. Objects manufactured and circulated for celestial purposes provide a telling point of departure for how this economic-theological nexus came to be, not least because the clergy produced detailed manuals outlining how the faithful should employ and even desire them. Since devotional guides set out to delimit the use and abuse of instruments of piety among thousands of believers, their authors left behind an empirical source base illustrating how specific acts of consumption were believed to operate in practice.

As a field of knowledge, Catholic economic theology at once projected, established templates for, and even overdetermined the rise of the so-called consumer revolution. That is to say, consumption was endowed with transformative effects within a religious matrix rather than in opposition to it. There was nothing anticipated or teleological in this outcome, just as there is nothing self-evident about the historically inflected and culturally conditioned phenomenon of consumption. The terms of what qualifies as an object worth pursuing have taken radically different styles and forms over time. The church posited an economy deeply embedded in spiritual and material structures. The sacraments upheld a re-presentational ideal in which the outward splendor of things transmitted hidden values. This sacred semiotics marked the decoration of altars and buttressed the conviction that houses of worship should reflect the grandeur of God. Diverse forms of celestial wealth assumed physical form in gold, marble, and semiprecious substances, the circulation of which had worldly and otherworldly consequences.

The renewed economization of Catholic devotional life, which alternately inspired hope and attracted derision, occurred in tandem with a surge in material consumption along a range of fronts. Seventeenth- and eighteenth-century observers recognized the social as well as spiritual dimensions of this conjuncture. It is not a matter of claiming on the basis of mutual exclusion that either religious ideas caused a rise in affluence or that theological writings merely reflected more basic economic realities. Rather, the interpretive task demands attention to the distinct practices that bound together material objects and desires understood in avowedly spiritual terms. The church's evangelizing mission in the wake of the Protestant Reformation gave new impetus to the acquisition of prayer beads, scapulars, books, prints, reliquaries, religious art, Jubilee medallions, and crucifixes. These possessions did not in and of themselves cause the craze for tobacco, chocolate, cotton, or other commodified novelties. Rather, instruments of piety engendered the belief that having them in ever vaster quantities brought contentment and that deprivation amounted to torment. The consumer revolution held out the prospect that the material economy would fatefully converge with its spiritual analogue.

Deus Faber: Graven Images and Gilded Vessels

Catholicism adopted an enigmatic stance toward wealth. It was either a curse to lament or a blessing in which to luxuriate with an eye to serving the poor and securing salvation. Although the clergy took vows of poverty, the church itself owned vast terrains—along with urban holdings, as much as 10 percent of the total arable land in the kingdom, and upwards of 30 percent in the northern provinces of Picardy and Cambrai. Cathedrals, chapters, abbeys, and convents awed visitors with their sheer physical grandeur and ornamental magnificence. Notre-Dame added architectural weight to the center of Paris, balanced in the eighteenth century by the monumental reconstruction of the Church of Sainte-Geneviève, named for the patron saint of the capital. Priests donned sumptuous robes and performed their rites to the accompaniment of soaring choral and instrumental music.[25] The laity participated in the embellishment of sanctuaries as members of *fabriques*. These councils raised and disbursed funds to pay for new edifices and major renovations to existing buildings, from altar pieces and sacristies to statues and stained glass. The sums involved could run to the thousands of livres for a single parish.[26] Ecclesiastical opulence was justified with references to the biblical antecedents of the patriarchs and the priestly king Melchisedech, as well as Christ's largesse in feeding the multitude. As the author of an anonymous tract on the subject explained, since God is "equally the author and master of spiritual and temporal goods," he is empowered to "distribute to the church the riches that could contribute to its preservation and progress." The evangelical imperative to aid the destitute sanctioned boundless accumulation in accordance with the "reign of charity."[27]

Lavish receptacles held the sacraments in anticipation of heavenly splendor: tabernacles of finely carved wood, gold and silver chalices, masterfully crafted monstrances. Jewel-like vessels stored the relics of saints, whose labors underwrote a treasury of merit. The Council of Trent instructed believers in "the veneration of relics and the legitimate use of images, teaching them that the saints who reign together with Christ offer up their prayers to God for men." The church repudiated the iconoclastic claim advanced by Protestants that "our invocation of them to pray for each of us individually is idolatry" and that "these and other memorials are honored by the faithful without profit." Worshippers could kiss or kneel before the artifacts, provided that "all superstition shall be removed, all filthy quest for gain eliminated, and all lasciviousness avoided."[28]

This expressive materiality furnished a leitmotif of *Tableaux sacrez*, a work published in 1601 by the Jesuit Louis Richeome (1544–1625), an educator, administrator, and early exemplar of devout humanism who sought to enliven the Catholic imagination through word and image.[29] In keeping with the teachings of his order, he upheld the Incarnation as the work of a divine iconographer who reflected eternal mysteries in every facet of terrestrial creation.[30] Precisely because every other "work of God" seemed lacking in comparison to the Eucharist, "no human language or even that of angels" adequately described it. Richeome thus proposed the formulation of "tableaux that place before the eyes sacred images and prophetic figures." Pictorial representations should bear a physical resemblance to what they depicted, albeit through "artificial" means. The "speaking painting" communicated by way of textual signs. Allegory, "a thing or action instituted to represent a mystery," served as the third and final medium. Beyond the allegorical "signification of the literal," one discerned two further registers of meaning: the "tropological," or moral, and the "anagogical," or purely mystical realm of interpretation.[31]

These elements converged in likenesses of "the greatest mystery of our religion," the Eucharist. Its artistic renderings followed from the prodigious effects of communion. "Triple painting"—that is, "of the brush, the word, and signification"—replicated the generative capacity of the sacrament.[32] The consecrated host, decorated canvas, and scriptural text all served as conduits to a bounty of artistic and spiritual riches. God had commanded the ancient Israelites to grace their altars with what was known as the bread of the presence. The divine ordinance in the Hebrew Bible prefigured rituals set down by the church. Christ revealed himself as "a soul adorned with charity"—a sublimated successor to "the gold of God's temple" used for the tables on which the Israelites placed their offerings.[33] Only the most sumptuous setting could rightfully receive such a priceless sacrifice.

Richeome justified the use of sacred objects in his polemics with Huguenot iconoclasts such as Jean Bansilion, who turned the Jesuit's methods into confirmation of "papal idolatry." Bansilion's argument took the form of a syllogism: idolaters worship "the representation of a holy deity," and the "Roman Church adores images" such as relics, which its followers mistake for the holy subject being illustrated. It followed, then, that Catholics were idolaters.[34] Richeome countered the charges by opposing the logic of active re-presentation to that of passive representation. Biblical precedent and the "law of grace" held that the physical remains of canonized men and women merited the same honor as their pious actions in life, thus warranting the expenses lavished on their display. God had further seen fit to bestow on their bodies miraculous qualities of incorruptibility that could be transmitted as a power of healing maladies and inculcating virtue. If, according to the Second Council of Nicaea, relics were "profitable [*salutaire*] fountains" through which "God causes his goods to flow," it was only fitting that material luxury anticipate the celestial treasures conveyed by saintly corpses.[35]

Unlike a static image, and in a manner reminiscent of the consecrated host, relics literally embodied the exalted person and exercised agency on the bodies and souls of petitioners seeking intercession. Heeding the call of evangelists such as Richeome, the faithful undertook long and costly pilgrimages, not merely to reflect on the piety of celebrated saints but also to seek delivery from epidemic diseases, ruinous weather, religious unrest, and war. For instance, more than fifty unveilings of the reliquary of Sainte Geneviève took place in Paris between the Fronde and the French Revolution.[36] When Louis XV fell dangerously ill with smallpox while on military campaign in 1744, he likewise prayed to the patron saint of Paris, vowing to construct a church in her name should he recover.[37]

The church joined the crown in policing the boundaries between divine magnificence and indulgent self-display.[38] The king and the parlements frequently issued sumptuary laws to regulate the possession of gold and silver jewelry, lace, fur, carriages, and furnishings. Priests found themselves implicated more frequently as a consequence of Tridentine discipline. From 1599 to 1629, more than a quarter of antiluxury statutes targeted ecclesiastical excess. Sumptuary legislation peaked during the reign of Louis XIV: eighty-six laws were passed between 1600 and 1737, double the figure of the previous century. The legal crusade then fell into gradual abeyance as proposals for duties on luxury expenditures gained favor.[39]

This long line of royal edicts should be taken not as ideological posturing or the futile expression of outmoded scruples but rather as a means of directing economic forces through privileged channels. Colbert's mercantilist ambitions of increasing the stock of precious metals and promoting domestic manufacturing buttressed laws aimed at harnessing luxury consumption in accordance with national interests. By discouraging foreign competition and instilling a sense of French superiority in fashionable wares, the government hoped to create vibrant markets in textiles and other desirable goods.[40] The crown attempted to rein in commerce to spur development through the manipulation of trade privileges, guild regulations, and direct financial subsidies. For instance, Louis XIV's regulation of March 29, 1700, cited the dangers posed by "the consumption of useless things" imported from "the most distant countries" during a time when the kingdom found itself at war "against almost all of Europe."[41] Thus, sumptuary laws operated in tandem with state investment. The Royal Plate Glass Company of Saint-Gobain was established in 1665 to outclass Venetian preeminence in mirror-making, an art it soon put to brilliant use in decorating the palace of Versailles. The Gobelins manufactory in Paris became synonymous with exquisite tapestries and furniture.[42] The profitability of these enterprises varied. The Saint-Gobain glassworks declared bankruptcy in 1702 but was soon reorganized under new ownership. The masterpieces of the Gobelins were intended primarily for the monarchy's consumption. Nevertheless, their reputation galvanized the status of French luxury industries throughout Europe.[43]

The revival of manufacturing coincided with the popularity of devotional objects sought after by men and women during religious pilgrimages. Although the Tridentine clergy hoped to curtail the practice, the faithful continued flocking to Rome, Santiago de Compostela, Mont-Saint-Michel, and other famous European destinations.[44] Artisans fashioned Passion bottles in which miniature figures of Christ and Mary were suspended, medals, pious images, crucifixes, rosaries, jewelry, snuffboxes, and even ephemera such as dolls and paper ornaments. These goods confounded the opposition between sacred and secular, traditional and modern, provincial and global. Their production employed engravers, goldsmiths, and sculptors, as well as workers in a protoindustrial putting-out system. Cities and towns that depended on pilgrimage, such as Saumur in the Loire Valley and Saint-Claude in the Jura, drew visitors across the kingdom and Continent.[45]

The Colbertist policies pursued by Louis XIV and his successors did not signal a disenchanted *raison d'état* presaging the triumph of commercial interests over spiritual authority.[46] The lavish pomp surrounding the Sun King assured his subjects that their sovereign, as God's lieutenant on earth, projected divine splendor through the veneration of the monarchical person, bringing into proximity his mortal and everlasting bodies.[47] The enactment of majesty depended on the tireless mobilization of resources: the patronage of the arts and sciences, massive construction projects, the performance of power in court ritual, medals, statues, and paintings.[48] Richeome's development of Tridentine semiotics again proves illustrative. A century before Bossuet employed similar language, his diatribe *L'idolâtrie huguenote* (1608) likened kings not merely to "public persons" but also to the "living images of God" and "terrestrial divinities." The resemblance was active—that is, tropological and mystical—rather than merely passive.[49]

Over the course of the next two centuries, Catholic apologists struggled to uphold the distinctions between the legitimate and illegitimate veneration of graven images and spiritual riches. Scientific trends lent credence to such efforts. As Jessica Riskin has shown, "sentimental empiricists" anthropomorphized the natural world as an expressive domain that acted with feeling. Their views found analogues in the economic theology of the period, which was in turn built into the decoration of churches. Alongside the emotive images advocated by Richeome, mechanized Christs, Magi, angels, and nativity scenes captivated the imaginations of visitors to houses of worship, as well as admirers of the inventor and entrepreneur Jacques de Vaucanson's automatized novelties.[50] The Enlightenment conception of nature thus reinforced the penchant of the Catholic ethic for endowing seemingly lifeless substances with the power to sway human minds.

Instruments of Piety

In the *Dictionnaire philosophique* (1764), Voltaire lampooned the fashion for devotional objects and relics from a comparative perspective. He labeled as primitive the obsession with trinkets and baubles among Buddhist monks and in Christian disputes over iconoclasm, gesturing with approval toward the standard Protestant line that the worship of relics had pagan roots and financial motives. "The miracles forged on the subject of relics," he wrote, "became a magnet that drew wealth into the church from every quarter." Although "enlightened bishops and philosophers" had long bemoaned the practice, the uneducated masses could not break their attachment to "false gods," which manifested itself in "material" rituals unbecoming of a "pure spirit."[51] Voltaire's quest to eradicate superstition in its institutional guises led him to ridicule popular devotions as suspect, corrupt, and anachronistic. Yet in *Le mondain* (1736) and other writings, the *philosophe* did not hesitate to cast his lot with commodities that he associated with the economic uplift of the luxury trades—to the exclusion, apparently, of instruments of piety.[52]

Such glaring ironies aside, Voltaire's comments suggest an enduring demand for religious goods. Merchants avidly sold textiles, candles, jewelry, and other artifacts to pilgrims, who in turn used them to adorn domestic spaces for worship. According to after-death inventories, in the sixteenth and seventeenth centuries the number of Parisian households across the social spectrum with a rosary, image, or related accessory rose from 38.6 percent to 62 percent. Even the lowliest subjects might own a cross made of ebony and ivory or another valuable piece. The variety of goods also expanded. For instance, whereas rosaries and figurines predominated in the sixteenth century, by the seventeenth, diamonds, pearls, and other jewels, medals cast in gold and silver, paper images of Christ and the saints, and other devotional accessories become increasingly common.[53] Between the years 1711 and 1726, 63.3 percent had purchased such objects, whereas only 21.1 percent owned the implements for serving coffee and tea.[54] The poor were well represented. For instance, the wife of a floor polisher left fourteen reliquaries at her death in 1751. Among inventories listing religious possessions during the seventeenth and eighteenth centuries, more than 50 percent list crucifixes, often of ivory, copper, or wood; 17 percent list reliquaries, which were frequently obtained during pilgrimages; and 12 percent list holy water fonts, whether of silver or a more common metal.[55]

These expenditures facilitated encounters with the sacred, yet scholars often view the confluence of religious and commercial interests from the standpoint of the Protestant ethic, which implies gradual but inexorable disenchantment. An enduring fixation on conflicts between more popular, sensual forms of worship and the disciplinary rigor of the Tridentine church obscures the ways in which spiritual and material imperatives were not merely reconcilable but also mutually constitutive.[56] Along similar lines, historical narratives have long foregrounded Jansenism, the offshoot of Catholic theology that most closely resembles the Weberian ideal type.[57] The tendency has been bolstered further in arguments that pose the gradual interiorization of spirituality against Michel Vovelle's thesis of unrelenting "dechristianization."[58]

Despite evidence to the contrary, scholars continue to labor under the misapprehension, inherited from Weber's thesis, that spiritual belief ultimately diverged from acquisitive desire and that economic expansion signaled the retreat of religion in the face of the Enlightenment. Social historians of religion have made powerful contributions to our understanding of the market for devotional objects throughout the period.[59] Yet they have been hesitant to approach these commodities as part and parcel of the transition from subsistence to superfluity. At the same time, the rising tide of scholarship on consumption has often discounted if not ignored entirely the attraction of rosaries, crosses, medals, and sacred images, which were produced in impressive quantities and diverse qualities well into the eighteenth century.[60]

To a greater degree than many of the goods identified with the so-called consumer revolution, such as fashionable calicoes and watches, religious artifacts like the rosary incited exhaustive commentary on how and why they should be used. As Michael Kwass has argued in the case of wigs, "convenience, nature, and physiognomy" motivated consumption, as did emulation.[61] Instruments of piety point to a still more fundamental impulse beyond use-value. The faithful were taught in no uncertain terms that the acquisition of specific goods would resurrect the dead labor of the saints and bring forth unimaginable riches for eternity.

The mundane conditions under which devotional objects were produced and sold belied their ethereal value. Depending on locale, religious institutions either oversaw their own workshops or negotiated terms with artisans who in turn appealed to the civil government for protection of their privileges. Nuns toiled diligently to construct paper reliquaries, glass receptacles displaying holy scenes, and wax figurines. A host of professional craftsmen likewise turned their talents to making all manner of goods, such as rosaries, statues, prints, and crucifixes.[62] The merchandise was widely available for purchase at artisans' shops, fairs, and, as the illustration for *Le moine secularisé* suggests, from colporteurs who traveled high and low in search of customers. Of the inventories left by goldsmiths in the seventeenth century, 80 percent listed rosaries among the commercial capital of the deceased, as well as figurines, crosses, and bénitiers. Jewelers, mercers, and occasionally moneychangers also participated in the trade.[63] Clerical and secular merchants both did a brisk business on pilgrimage routes, from major destinations like Mont-Saint-Michel to sites of local interest. Although the concerns of the ecclesiastical establishment occasionally diverged from those of merchants, churches and religious orders found lucrative opportunities to evangelize and to raise necessary funds. The manufacture of devotional objects likewise became economic mainstays in Saumur, Liesse, Saint-Claude, Alise, and many other towns down to the Revolution.[64] The clergy also distributed medals and rosaries to believers as a reward for diligence in catechism instruction, during missionary expeditions, and on admission to a confraternity.[65]

In the case of rosary-makers [*patenôtriers*], different trade corporations originally held monopolies on the manufacture and sale of prayer beads, the popularity of which rose exponentially under the auspices of the Catholic Reformation.[66] Each guild specialized in a particular material (enamel, glass, precious metals and stones, etc.). Conflicts inevitably broke out among antagonistic competitors. In 1599 the king ratified a request by master rosary-makers in enamel that the government issue an injunction against master enamelers and fair merchants who encroached on their business.[67] A century later, the police intervened in another dispute between the rosary-makers in enamel and workers in jade, amber, and coral over which guild had the right to use imitation pearl. It was decided that both groups could do so provided they employed different techniques (the former could use heat treatments, while the latter could not).⁶⁸ To minimize further litigation, and in recognition of the "extent of their professions, which are growing," Louis XIV ordered in 1706 that the communities of rosary-makers in enamel and glass-earthenware workers form a single entity, the *patenôtriers-boutonniers d'émail et verre*.⁶⁹ Their merger was confirmed in 1718. Until the end of the Old Regime, this united guild coexisted with two others, rosary-makers in wood and bone, and those who worked in amber, jet, and coral.⁷⁰

Philippe Macquer's *Dictionnaire portatif des arts et métiers* (1766) presented an overview of the trade and its social implications to an audience primed for skepticism by the *Encyclopédie*.⁷¹ The article "Patenôtrier," contributed by Claude-Marc-Antoine Varenne de Beost, a correspondent of the Academy of Sciences and former secretary of the provincial estates of Burgundy, divided the labor into two main tasks, making rosaries and fashioning necklaces for "women of station" to wear.⁷² Varenne de Beost observed that "these two kinds of merchandise" appeared to be "of a use infinitely opposed" yet remained part of the same profession. Indeed, the beads and the necklaces were "ordinarily made of the same substance." Various powders were mixed with perfumes to form the beads, then frequently treated to imitate the appearance of pearl or dyed to resemble precious and semiprecious stones. Rosary-makers sold their namesake devotional object alongside "necklaces, bracelets, and earrings in enamel of every color." Varenne de Beost wistfully commented that "such were the modest joys with which women of quality contented themselves before luxury was introduced into manners [*mœurs*] and in dress." Betraying his own Enlightenment prejudices, and apparently on the basis of works in enamel alone (that is, without considering wood, silver, gold, or other materials, which fell under the purview of different guilds), he claimed that the sale of rosaries had fallen owing to the rise of printing and increased opportunities for education in the countryside.⁷³ In reality, artisans who produced them maintained considerable stocks: at the height of the Terror, 150,000 livres worth of rosaries were gathered up to be burned in the public square of Saumur, a major pilgrimage site.⁷⁴ Moreover, the *Dictionnaire portatif* noted how the invention of "essence of pearl" in the 1680s appealed to buyers "greedy for novelties," anticipating the demand for goods that gave the impression of grandeur at prices accessible to a wide buying public.⁷⁵

Varenne de Beost's article suggested the close associations between pious possessions and other forms of consumption. Yet his narrative of supersession could not account for the persistent allure of rosary beads or the prayers one recited in employing them. As a material artifact, the device ranged from simple wood productions costing only twenty deniers—slightly more than one and a half sous, a fraction of a laborer's daily wages—to more elaborate pieces in gold and silver that sold for dozens if not hundreds of livres (fig. 5.2).[76] Rich and poor alike, and women in particular, made a priority of obtaining an accessory that conferred spiritual and social status. As a liturgical instrument, the rosary was a simple yet remarkably effective way to secure the church's abundant grace. Like the populuxe commodities that attracted Varenne de Beost's commercial attention and cultural scrutiny, the aspirational and the expedient converged in the keeping of devotional objects.

As prayer became a more central element of religious life, laywomen and -men set about furnishing their homes accordingly. The faithful accumulated portraits and prints of Christ, the Virgin, and the saints: around half of the inventories surveyed for the seventeenth and eighteenth centuries mention at least one pious image. Rosaries themselves, however, are conspicuously underrepresented, appearing in only 3 percent of samples from Parisian archives. This faint presence is all the more surprising given that buyers of a painting or engraving for personal devotions could also be expected to have prayer beads, especially in light of their status in the popular religious imagination and in the indulgence regime of the church. Nonetheless, notaries had various reasons to omit them, from their small size and often negligible economic value to the practice of burying them with their owners.[77] Moreover, their sheer ubiquity likely contributed to their being taken for granted in financial record-keeping.

The practice of reiterative prayer was closely associated with the Dominicans; Pius V (r. 1566–72) granted the order an exclusive right to establish confraternities in 1586.[78] Their founder, Saint Dominic, likely gave the cycle its classic form: fifteen decades or ten Ave Marias prefaced by the Pater Noster and followed by the Gloria Patri.[79] The physical instrument supplemented mental and vocal effort with tactile sensation. Each decade had a theme drawn from a mystery of the faith, such as the Annunciation, Christ's birth, crucifixion, and resurrection, or the Assumption of the Virgin

Figure 5.2 Rosary with reliquary, South German folk art, eighteenth century. The pendant is of a double-sided heart, showing the Baptism of Christ and St. George; the attached reliquary is inscribed: "ex carn. S. MAR. CLEOPHAE. SOR. B. UM." Silver, brass, paillettes, glass. 52.2 × 8.4 × 1.3 cm. Photo: Virginie Louis and Anne Maigret. Musée des Civilisations de l'Europe et de la Méditerranée, Marseille, France. © RMN-Grand-Palais/Art Resource, NY.

Mary. The model prayers were sufficiently brief to be mastered by those who had not been taught how to read. So not to lose one's place in the sequence, rosaries were made up of clutches of ten smaller beads (fig. 5.3) for the ten Ave Marias followed by a larger one to mark where to say the Pater Noster at the beginning and the Gloria Patri at the end. The ensemble recalled the shape of a hat or crown of roses, from which the names *chapelet*, *couronne*, and *rosaire* were derived.

In France, the rosary did not become an object of mass devotion until the seventeenth century. Royal officials mandated public observances in gratitude for divine intercession. By the mid-seventeenth century, devotional societies had inaugurated the practice of perpetual recitation. Between the years 1644 and 1647, 12,866 Parisians committed to pray during one of the 8,760 hours of the year, in addition to the 50,665 persons who had joined the rolls during the three preceding decades. After Rome had granted several partial recognitions, Clement XI established in 1716

Figure 5.3 Rosary (consisting of ten beads), France, eighteenth century. Amber, crystal. 1.26 cm. Inv. ECL2859. Photo: Benoît Touchard. Musée nationale de la Renaissance, Ecouen, France. © RMN-Grand-Palais/Art Resource, NY.

a feast day for the Rosary to be celebrated by the universal church.[80] As Marie-Hélène Froeschlé-Chopard has expertly documented, the Rosary, like the Eucharist, inspired the creation of hundreds of confraternities.[81] Members hailed from all social classes, from grand aristocrats and priests to artisans, merchants, and domestics. Even as philosophical assaults on the utility of revealed religion reached a critical mass in the 1760s and 1770s, confraternities acquired new adherents—especially among women, who could perform their devotions at home. The number of associations dedicated to the Rosary grew during the eighteenth century, particularly in northern and eastern France. Likewise, the rolls of the Confraternity of the Holy Sacrament in the diocese of Cambrai nearly doubled from 1720 to 1783, from 243 to 439. Between 1775 and 1779 the sodality in Saint-Nizier expanded from 315 to 522.[82]

The manuals of these confraternities emphasized the scope of their spiritual wealth while affirming the efficacy of material devotion. In *Le triple Rosaire augmenté* (1676), Jean-Vincent Bernard remarked of the Rosary that "after the sacraments" there was "nothing in the Church more august than this holy compound [*composé*], of which it is the ornament and the luster." Whereas communion required exacting preparations, all believers were enjoined to take part—the advanced and mere novices, the great and the lowly, women as well as men. To found a confraternity, it was first necessary to receive approval from the Dominican Order as well as the local bishop. On drawing up a contract of institution, the clerical representative appointed officers and a director to oversee the association's activities. Membership was granted free of charge. Brothers and sisters further consented to hold "their spiritual possessions" and "good works" in common for mutual benefit.[83]

A manual published in the 1750s, the *Abrégé de la dévotion du Saint Rosaire*, echoed these sentiments. Members incurred no expense beyond the acquisition of devotional objects. The reason stemmed from the nature of "spiritual goods, which it is permitted neither to buy nor to sell," although the material means of procuring them could be purchased. Rich and poor alike were welcome to join regardless of their ability to pay. Tellingly, however, grants made to subsidize the decoration of the chapel made one eligible for particular indulgences.[84] While the abolition of spiritual privilege universalized the economy of grace, distinctions endured on the basis of financial contributions. The manual's warning about commodifying celestial profits in terms of monetary exchange pointed at a deeper complex. Even if the heavenly economy could not be reduced to its purely material counterpart, it remained embedded in relations of consumption as well as production—Christ's sacrifice, the merits of the saints, the labor of the members—that manifested themselves in terrestrial form.

Duties centered on the recitation of prescribed prayers. Brothers and sisters said fifteen decades, or the full Rosary, on a weekly basis. They confessed and communed the first Sunday of each month and on the principal feast days of Christ and the Virgin. They were similarly encouraged to visit the confraternity's chapel and to attend processions for deceased members. Another "most useful practice" involved habituating oneself to praying in moments of distress, "to elevate one's heart to God so as to offer to him the prayers that brothers throughout the world say without ceasing." The *Abrégé* made clear that its guidance should not be regarded as a formal directive. Dereliction of duty did not constitute sin, either "mortally" or "venially." A lapsed member remained at liberty to "commit himself without scruple" or fear of punishment, save for a suspension of the "incalculable graces and favors" one would otherwise accrue.[85]

According to the *Abrégé*, the totality of the experience reflected "divine wisdom, which has made everything with weight, number, and measure." In keeping with the Catholic logic of re-presentation, saying the Ave Maria ten times honored the place of the Virgin Mary in the tenth rung of heaven. The separation of the Rosary into three parts reflected the childhood, passion, and glory of Christ. Each set of beads also allowed one to reflect on mysteries corresponding to the joy, pain, and apotheosis of Jesus and his mother.[86] Like the sacraments and Catholic iconography, the Rosary facilitated communion between not only the human and the divine but also between the soul and body of the believer. Its power even extended to the world stage. The authors of the *Abrégé* attributed a role to the saying of the Rosary in Saint Dominic's victory over the Albigensian heresy, the defeat of the Ottomans at the Battle of Lepanto, and the vanquishing of the Huguenots in France. Among observant Christians the practice had the edifying effect of "destroying vice, causing virtue to shine, preserving and increasing the piety and holiness of the Church," as well as "dispelling the shadows of error and unfaithfulness." It further performed miraculous healings and other regenerative feats not only in Europe but in Catholic missions around the world.[87]

The economy of devotions was general rather than restricted in a double sense. First, it encompassed the faithful as a whole, without regard to temporal hierarchies or even individual proprietorship. The principle of mutual labor allowed each soul to benefit from the recompense acquired by all. Second, their common inheritance knew no bounds, whether mortal, temporal, physical, or spiritual. To convey the potential of eternal consumption, Bernard recounted a miracle certified by the archdeacon and vicar general of Toulouse. The events bear a striking resemblance to those five decades earlier in Faverney. In 1659 a nun cast a sacred image of the Rosary into the fire to prevent it from being defiled. Remarkably, the paper did not burn when held to the flame.[88] The soul "embraced by the love of God" would grasp fulfillment in a related manner, "as from a perpetual experience of his goodness and enjoyment of the possession [*jouissance*] of his riches."[89] It was a desire that, unlike bodily urges, persisted in spite of or even owing to its gratification. The more one consumed, the more one longed to consume.

An Infinity of Indulgences

The Holy See encouraged such devotions by authorizing indulgences in ever greater quantities and qualities. In a bull issued on February 6, 1657, Alexander VIII (r. 1689–91) stipulated conditions for the use of devotional objects. Pardons were issued under a number of pretexts, including if one said no less than a third of the Rosary before confessing and communing or prayed before a crucifix, cross, or other blessed image in his home.[90] Medals were required to be cast in a durable metal such as gold, silver, or copper, rather than pewter or lead, and to represent officially canonized saints. A medal lost its efficacy if broken into pieces; however, rosaries with missing beads retained their saving power. Decorations could not be bought, sold, bequeathed, or loaned out to third parties. Moreover, one received the associated indulgences only by keeping the objects on one's person.[91] In 1775 the theologian Pierre Collet explained the logic behind such regulations, which turned on the distinction between "personal" and "real" indulgences. As in the governance of property under civil law, personal pardons applied to individuals. Real indulgences adhered in "certain things, such as crosses, images, and rosaries."[92]

Theologians drew deeply on monetary metaphors to describe the workings of the spiritual economy. An eighteenth-century compendium of real indulgences stressed the supplemental, even superfluous, nature of the exchange. Pardons presumed a surfeit of sin, the temporal penalties for which could not be expiated in a single lifetime. God offered sinners the possibility of forgiving the original offense as well as the punishment it brought upon the soul. The compiler marveled at the "generous goodness of the Church, which procures for us so sure and so abundant a means" of salvation in the "depository of an inexhaustible treasure." He urged readers to seek fortunes so freely given: "Let us never lose an occasion to profit," he wrote, from privileges that "keep us in a spirit of fervor."[93] The analogies formulated between temporal and heavenly wealth transformed both registers of meaning. Economic references designated devotional objects as a means of conveying value without end. The economy in question was founded not on scarcity but abundance, with the rosary mediating between infinite indebtedness and infinite redemption.

As Pierre Forestier, canon on Avalon, observed, "the sovereign pontiffs seem to have wanted to surpass each other in the liberality with which they enriched the Rosary with indulgences."[94] In 1686 Pope Innocent XI directed Antoine de Monroy, Master of the Dominican Order, to publish a compilation of grants issued during his predecessors' reigns. The quantities of indulgences varied widely: Sixtus IV (r. 1471–84) promised five years and five quarantines for saying the Rosary. As noted in the introduction to this chapter, his successor, Innocent VIII, increased the amount to a staggering sixty thousand years, provided one confessed before praying; the reward of five years was also retained, now merely for uttering the name of Jesus after each Ave Maria. Clement IX (r. 1667–69) guaranteed that Catholics in the Spanish Antilles enjoyed the same benefits as subjects residing in the metropole. Gregory XIII gave plenary indulgences to members who confessed and communed before participating in a procession with their rosaries; men and women too infirmed to participate could recite the prayers at home. Still further dispensations accrued for visiting the Chapel of the Holy Rosary in Rome or elsewhere, for giving alms, caring for ailing friends, attending services, and performing other pious actions.⁹⁵

Several popes, including Innocent VIII, Pius V, Clement VIII (r. 1592–1605), and Clement X (r. 1670–76), offered to forgive all outstanding temporal penalties at the moment of death. This was an especially valuable asset, since it opened the possibility of avoiding purgatory altogether. For the most part, one needed only to have received last rites, or, less frequently, to have said the rosary either regularly during one's lifetime or in one's final hours. In drawing up the terms for gaining an indulgence, popes made allowances for the ill and indisposed, who often could recite prayers as a substitute for another good work.⁹⁶ Clement X and Innocent XI also authorized petitions to bestow the advantages enjoyed by the confraternities on the "souls of the faithful departed in union with God."⁹⁷

Such expansive generosity across papal reigns invited theological speculation. For the Jesuit Paul de Barry, rector of colleges in Aix and Nîmes and provincial of Lyon, Marian piety secured a "precious key" to heaven that one could not buy with "millions in gold."⁹⁸ His guide, *Le paradis ouvert à Philagie*, first published in 1636 and reissued eighteen times over the next five decades, instructed readers in "easy devotions for gaining Mary's good graces," such as thinking fervently of the Virgin throughout the day, communing on her feast day, abstaining from meat on Wednesdays, and donating gambling winnings to the poor. Barry dedicated several chapters to wondrous effects transmitted by the Rosary. On saying 150 Ave Marias, the Benedictine nun Gertrude of Helfta had a vision of Christ with "a pile of gold" at his feet, one coin for each of the "graces and favors" that God would provide her against "invisible enemies." When illness prevented her from praying the entire sequence, she was nonetheless rewarded with a "beautiful crown of roses" for uttering a single phrase. In Mary's eyes, each word of the prayer was "worth more, as small as it is, than all the gold in Peru." Likewise, the Seraphic Rosary or Franciscan Crown originated in the wish of a novice to persist in his custom of each day adorning a statue of the Virgin with flowers. Distressed that he could no longer do so on entering the order, she gave him a formula for prayers that would be "no less pleasing to her" nor "profitable" to him.⁹⁹

In a telling rhetorical, as well as theological, gesture, *Le paradis ouvert* fell back on the analogues between heavenly and terrestrial wealth even in denying their equivalence. The least quantity of devotion conveyed greater value than the sum total of precious metals, yet Barry could only express this belief via references to priceless works of art and nature. Elaborating on the materiality of the practice, he specified that the mere possession of a rosary functioned like an emblem projecting re-presentative power. "A soldier never goes without his sword," nor an "officer of the king" without "the mark of his office." Those who wore prayer beads put on the "livery" of "our princess," which is "her crown, her rosary." In imitation of François de Sales, who recited the prayers more than thirty-two thousand times during the final years of his life, the faithful were advised to carry a rosary on their person at all times as a "token of love." One could also emulate the venerable Dominican monk Louis Bertrand by sleeping with the necklace at night.[100]

In *Lettres provinciales*, Blaise Pascal denounced *Le paradis ouvert* for the "extreme facility" of devotions fulfilled with cheaply hewn, mass-produced baubles. Mocking the Jesuit position, he observed that only a "truly wretched" soul could neglect "putting a rosary around one's arm, or in one's pocket, thereby assuring salvation with so much certitude that those who tried it have never been wrong regardless of how they had lived."[101] Although Barry did not intend to make the rosary an immediate substitute for virtue, his counsel left him vulnerable to charges of introducing a false economy in the accumulation of grace. "We often lose a great deal," he exhorted readers, "for lack of a moment's devotion and reflection on the profit one can make at little expense." Citing the order of Leon X (r. 1513–21) to grant a thousand days' worth of indulgences each time one said an Ave Maria as the bell struck the hour, he likened the favorable terms to being offered a hundred pistoles for a similar observance. Even lack of time posed no obstacle, since the first few words of the prayer sufficed to meet the conditions.[102]

The *Abrégé de la dévotion du Saint Rosaire* (1754) adopted the solicitous view taken by Barry. Its authors likened ecclesiastical liberality to the provisions made in "well-governed states [*États bien-policés*]" where "there are stores and reserve funds opened in times of great need." The church, similarly "enlightened by the spirit of God," had its own "precious treasure," which the "sovereign pastor" distributed according to the dictates of "prudence."[103] The political economy of the kingdom of men converged with the economic theology of the kingdom of heaven. The sovereign could draw on financial surpluses or credit to assuage the people's suffering in a moment of crisis. The church, which ministered physically as well as spiritually to the infirm and destitute, exercised the same charity in its care of souls. The model presumed not a zero-sum game among antagonists but rather the sharing of plenitude among brethren.

A competing manual, the similarly named *Abrégé des fruits du Rosaire de la Sainte Vierge* (1696), urged greater circumspection. The Rosary, while facilitating the "special communication of every spiritual good," transformed souls only by indirect means through spurring frequent recourse to the sacraments of penance and the Eucharist. The anonymous author observed that "in these last depraved centuries the church shows itself more liberal in granting indulgences." He lamented but did not condemn outright the shift toward permissiveness. Since "the world tends toward decline," with "sins coming to multiply," the papacy responded dutifully by "compensating for what we lack through the abundance of the satisfactions of Jesus Christ" and by "imparting more generously the treasures of indulgences." The Rosary was amply suited to act as a means of conveyance, given that it "is comprised of all the merits" of the Savior and "his most Holy Mother."[104]

In *De la plus solide, de plus nécessaire, et souvent la plus négligée de toutes dévotions* (1702), the Sorbonne-trained theologian and parish priest Jean-Baptiste Thiers ridiculed the proposition that indulgence-bearing rosaries could transmit spiritual rewards. A learned firebrand who had made a name for himself by railing against the brisk trade in devotional objects around the cathedral in Chartres, he now set his sights on practices regarded as theologically unsound and scandalous to Christian reason.[105] The "vogue in the Church ... for earning indulgences," he speculated, stemmed from the misapprehension that sinners need only perform the works specified in bulls and briefs. But as Thomas Aquinas had taught, it was imperative that recipients also experience "real suffering" while "conscientiously working to purify themselves of their crimes." Otherwise, one acted "like those who declare false bankruptcies." Pardons were intended "to assist debtors in paying" for redemption, not as a substitute for their own efforts. Thiers qualified Trent's defense of indulgences by setting down the conditions that could nullify their validity: (1) the lack or loss of papal authorization, (2) benefits that "exceed the power of those who grant them," as when popes granted pardons measured in centuries, and (3) dispensations that circumvented the sacrament of penance.[106]

Likewise, Thiers specified that the terms of an indulgence must be in "proportion" with the penalties being forgiven. One could not expect a spiritual windfall from "saying a *Pater* or an *Ave*, for example," much less from "kissing or carrying on one's person a medal, an image, a rosary, a cross," or a "blessed bead." These desultory exertions failed to realize the true purpose of indulgences, which was "to excite the piety of the faithful to work for their salvation" rather than "raking in money" by a "shameful commerce." The "superstition" peddled by Jesuits and the deluded directors of confraternities lured credulous souls into investing their faith in mere "instruments of piety" as the "certain path" to beatitude.[107]

Thiers's warnings failed to dampen papal exuberance. On the eve of issuing his anti-Jansenist bull *Unigenitus*, Clement XI (r. 1700–1721) announced plenary indulgences to celebrate the canonization of several new saints, including the former pope Pius V, Felix of Cantalice, and Catherine of Bologna. The faithful could meet a range of conditions, from saying the Rosary or the Penitential Psalms to assisting the poor or engaging in another good work. To obtain the pardons through the employment of devotional objects, "it suffice[d] to have on one's person a rosary or medal, etc., blessed by His Holiness" in accordance with Alexander VIII's decree of 1657.[108] The following year, Clement XI granted plenary indulgences to those who recited at least five decades each day for a year with *brigitains*, prayer beads named for the Order of the Most Holy Savior founded by Saint Bridget of Sweden. Later in the century, Benedict XIV, the pontiff who more than any other infused Enlightenment sensibilities into the Tridentine spirit, reduced the obligation to say five decades once a week, rather than daily, but added the requirements to confess and commune on the Feast of Saint Bridget, visit an approved church, and pray for peace and the end of heresy.[109]

The brothers and sisters in Rosary sodalities specialized in a task for which they received invaluable remuneration. Pastors, directors, and authors of pious manuals duly catalogued the advantages to be gleaned from their efforts. The Dominican François Mespolié began his *Exercices spirituels* (1703) by stipulating the general terms of exchange: "The grace and gifts of the Holy Spirit are these solid and permanent treasures that we must amass on earth to possess the riches of divinity in heaven." Spiritual accumulation in this life determined one's fate. Men and women lavished attention on "ephemeral and perishable goods" that were "incapable of satisfying us" rather than striving for "infinite and immense goods, goods that encompass all goods, which are bound to made us eternally happy." According to the hierarchy of pleasure, more exalted assets established the model for lesser ones. This reasoning rejected a binary opposition between temporal and celestial advantage. The Rosary served as a means to ease the terror of dying and the torments of purgatory. It also deepened devotion, expanded knowledge of "sacred science" among the learned and ignorant alike, and hastened the victory of Christian princes against their enemies. The practice changed the course of history by delivering queens from infertility, miracles that Mespolié credited with the births of Louis IX and Louis XIV. Far beyond the shores of Europe, in Asia, Africa, and the Americas, "innumerable" believers had embraced the Rosary as a form of Marian devotion. Fittingly, Mespolié's praise for the custom was without limit. It communicated, among other virtues, "the antidote that fortifies weakness and heals sickness," the "holy library of theology," the "treasures of divine wealth that God uses to distribute his gifts to the poor," and even a "worldly paradise filled with roses and heavenly fruits."[110]

As if reenacting the fecundity of the Rosary, Mespolié's account of its boundless worth occupied several chapters of the *Exercices spirituels*. He devoted a separate section to all the "great possessions, both spiritual and bodily," that the practice yielded, which he prefaced with a remark by the Minim François Giry that the task of "relating the marvels" in their entirety would require many "heavy volumes." The Rosary heartened the sinner, converted heretics, and restored the morals of cities and kingdoms. Its recitation had attended all manner of miraculous healings—curing blindness, deafness, paralysis, even raising the dead. It brought rain in the time of drought, peace to war-ravaged lands. It gave debtors relief from their creditors and freed slaves from bondage. It liberated souls from purgatory and provided "prodigious and wholly supernatural aid." Quoting Solomon's description of wisdom, Mespolié claimed that "every sort of good has come to me with it."[111]

The Dominican Louis Berny's *Instruction pour les confrères du Rosaire*—a generic guide first published in 1701 and reissued in 1740—specified the manner in which believers should approach this cornucopia.[112] Berny reminded readers that membership in the confraternity ranked among "the greatest possessions that the faithful can procure." As evidence he likened the "infinity of graces and indulgences" granted by the church to the happiness that money could buy. If gold and silver provided for the "necessities of life" through the purchase of "commodities," so much more so did indulgences save souls from the "necessity of suffering in purgatory." The abundance of pardons transmitted via the Rosary offered a luxurious supplement to the exigencies of divine justice. The *Instruction* further recommended the "devotion of fifteen Saturdays," a ritual named in honor of the decades of beads strung on the necklace and the mysteries each represented. Brothers and sisters communed weekly during the prescribed period, either on Saturday, a day associated with Mary, or on Sunday if they were "too occupied during the week." Devotees committed themselves to "something great and of importance to the glory of God." Berny did not exclude worldly concerns, such as a favorable outcome in a lawsuit or a "good choice of station," provided that one hoped for "temporal benefits" piously, "with a profound submission" to "divine will." Even if one's prayers went unanswered, members of the confraternity could rest assured that "God gives us something better in exchange."[113] Like Mespolié, Berny maintained that spiritual self-interest and obligations in the here and now fell among a continuum of sin, redemption, and final reward.

The rosary, like the economy in which it figured, was at once spiritual and material. The attending economic theology had as its base the bottomless wealth capitalized by the sacrifices of Christ and the saints. As did nearly every other manual of the period, the *Abrégé de la dévotion du Saint Rosaire* emphasized the incalculable quantity and quality of indulgences that the church placed at the disposal of believers. Serving as stewards for sinners "charged by divine justice with a great number of debts" that were impossible to repay by purely natural means, God's "administrators" drew on "infinite treasures" to "compensate for this failing." The rosary served as a key to these riches, not only as an aid to prayers but as a source of value in its own right. Tellingly, the first privilege claimed by members of confraternities on admission was the blessing of their beads. Following the traditional salutation, the director invoked the "most sacred womb" of the "Blessed Virgin our Lady" as the embodiment of fecundity.[114] Through the miracle of the Incarnation, the divine *oikos* of Father, Son, and Holy Spirit, joined by Mary as mother, endowed the economy of devotion with a limitless excess crystallized in the form of rosaries and indulgences.[115]

The Superfluity of Religion

Jean-Frédéric Bernard and Bernard Picart opened their massive compendium on world religions by outlining the conception of divinity against which these traditions would be judged. According to the *Cérémonies et coutumes religieuses de tous les peuples du monde*, God exists as "a most simple Being, sovereignly perfect through his Essence, his virtues, and his immense capacity." Bernard and Picart thus sought to discredit religious mediation that struck them as unnecessary. In their view, true worship did not require byzantine administrative hierarchies, nor should it take concrete form in "sacrifices," "feasts," "confraternities," "cloisters," or mortifications carried to "dangerous excess." On the contrary, a "love of virtue and purity of life" sufficed to fulfill human obligations to God.[116]

As noted in the introduction to this book, Bernard and Picart went to great lengths to sensationalize what they viewed as the vulgar economization of spirituality in the Catholic Church. Believers in the eleventh century paid tributes to patron saints as if they were feudal lords and donned necklaces or chains bearing their holy likeness. Monks claimed to have discovered, however improbably, the wedding band, garments, cooking utensils, and domestic furnishings of the Virgin Mary, which the faithful flocked to see despite their evident lack of authenticity. As the main author of the text, Bernard tread carefully in his remarks on indulgences, long a target of Protestant ire. After pointedly noting the "half-Jewish" and "half-pagan" origins of the Jubilee, he referred to pardons in general as the "touchstone" of a spiritual economy that "assured the conquest of paradise." The temptation to mock ultimately proved overwhelming. His stated "intention" not to "ruin the advantages of indulgences" led to the cutting observation that the Crusaders went into battle hoping for "the expiation of their sins" by means of the "the crosses and swords" with which they "armed themselves against the Infidel." According to Saint Bridget, there was "no shorter way of satisfying one's sins." Citing Thiers, Bernard dismissed various pretexts for issuing indulgences, such as "carrying on one's person a medal, an image, a rosary, a cross, a blessed bead." The "Apostolic Chancellery," he quipped, had "taxed sins at reasonable enough prices" when "it only cost ninety livres tournois and a few ducats for certain sins." In the face of rising scrutiny after Luther's denunciation of indulgences, the church now resorted to sources of revenue less immediately lucrative than cash payment.[117]

The discussion next turned to the rosary and other "instruments of piety." Bernard and Picart laconically but damningly claimed that Christians had adopted the use of prayer beads from Muslims, who in turn might have learned the practice from faiths originating in India. As in the frontispiece of *Le moine secularisé*, the Scapular of the Carmelites, the Cord of Saint Francis, and the Belt of Saint Augustine prompted comment as objects revered among members of a plethora of new orders appealing to the "devout man and the man of the world." Although prayer alone sufficed to satisfy one's duties toward God, members of confraternities indulged in drawn-out displays of apparent self-mortification while showing "no scruple in abandoning themselves to vice."[118]

According to Bernard and Picart, Catholic excess served as the basis for a comparative critique of religious observances in Europe and across the world.[119] Various engravings portray in rich detail the coronation of popes, Masses, the proclamation of the Jubilee, the benediction of devotional objects, pilgrimages, but also victims of the Inquisition.[120] The pictorial case for denigrating the Roman creed threatened to overwhelm their project, occupying one and a half volumes out of seven in total. No other faith received an equally exhaustive treatment, perhaps because the recriminations leveled against relics and rosaries set parameters for discussions of the primitivism of American, Asian, and African traditions. For instance, stereotypical images of mendicant Chinese monks (fig. 5.4) present them "in the fashion of Catholics." Bernard lingered over reports of "dishonest persons" who extort "public alms" through outrageous acts such as striking their heads against rocks or appearing to set themselves alight with substances that do not burn.[121]

Figure 5.4 Bernard Picart. *Religieux en noir avec un chapelet à la façon des catholiques*, 1728. In Jean-Frédéric Bernard and Bernard Picart, *Cérémonies et coutumes religieuses des peuples idolâtres*. Bibliothèque nationale de France.

Picart and Bernard took a stand against confessional violence that was likely informed by their persecution in the wake of the Edict of Fontainebleau. They adopted the role of neutral observers engaged in devising a taxonomy of religious needs. But the impression of toleration should not be confused with a laissez-faire permissiveness in spiritual matters.[122] Their sweeping account condemned Catholic traditions with an uncompromising gaze that viewed them as crude and morally retrograde. During a period of extensive scholarly inquiry, rival monotheisms—Islam, in particular—garnered erudite praise for theological sublimity, the repudiation of iconography, and liberal-mindedness toward other faiths. These attributes cast Catholic dogmatism in an even paler light when compared to the sober devotions prescribed by Luther and Calvin.[123]

Although less virulent than early seventeenth-century polemicists such as Jean Bansilion, Bernard and Picart were not above trucking in elements of Protestant iconoclasm or European cultural chauvinism. Their volume on Amerindian beliefs argued that "idolatry" has historically assumed two forms. The first, the worship of the stars, displaced God with astronomical bodies. The second "had men for its object." Vain passion served as the foundation for "a superb edifice" in which the mind "has enclosed an infinity of things that it believed to be pleasing to the gods, without forgetting the least trinket [*colifichet*]." Bernard and Picart likened this ensemble of beliefs to a "store [*magasin*] open to all the peoples of the universe."[124]

The men drew from personal experience in framing their theories. Bernard had made his first fortune by speculating on the stock in Law's companies, his second in the publishing enterprise of *Cérémonies et coutumes religieuses*.[125] Picart was responsible for *Le véritable portrait du très fameux seigneur Messire Quinquenpoix*, one of the more notorious caricatures of the controller-general. In a doubly ironic twist of fate, their critique of economic theology yielded financial as well as intellectual profits by capitalizing on readers' fascination with the bizarre yet recognizable customs of another world.[126] The volumes on Catholic devotion piqued the customer's interest by presenting rosaries, scapulars, and the Agnus Dei as goods for sale. Later installments on New World fetishism portrayed both divine and human agents as spellbound consumers. Anticipating Voltaire, Bernard and Picart not only converted the mystery of faith into a category of social and cultural analysis.¹²⁷ They also affirmed the economic dimension of theology by projecting it onto the newly minted rubric of religion *tout court*.

· · ·

In *Capital*, Marx wrote that even a "common, every-day thing, wood," after becoming "something transcendent" through commodification, "evolves out of its wooden brain grotesque ideas, far more wonderful than 'table-turning' ever was."¹²⁸ His derision reproduced with parodic emphasis the logic of Catholic economic theology. The most modest rosary, carved from wood and purchased at negligible expense, could wield the power to move heaven and earth. As such, it beckoned its owners to recite prayers, examine papal briefs, buy related accessories (manuals, prints, paintings, crucifixes, bénitiers), and stake expansive hopes out of all proportion to the thing in question. That is to say, the rosary acted like a commodity. A countess might believe that her gilded and jewel-encrusted necklace would bring greater favor from God, while the widow of a glassmaker could rest assured in the knowledge that the church did not differentiate between real and imitation pearl in granting indulgences.

A commodity produced for markets—whether terrestrial or celestial or both—gave rise to a belief in its capacity to multiply money, time, and even one's very being. After all, the Eucharist imparted the body of Christ under the physical accidents of bread. In the wake of the consumer revolution, the host revealed the quintessence of the populuxe good: mundane substances treated or arranged in such a manner as to signify value far beyond their purely material means. Women and men who wished to employ their sacred belongings to the fullest were called on to exercise discernment by scrutinizing their consciences, receiving pastoral instruction, meditating deeply on the subjects of prayer, and keeping themselves apprised of the pardons for which they were eligible. Their efforts magnified the "added fashion value" of the object in which they invested their faith.¹²⁹

Unsatisfied with the brute sentiment insisted on by Protestant iconoclasts such as Bernard and Picart, Marx's critique did not begin and end with the recognition that "*Man makes religion*, religion does not make man." He also acknowledged that "*religious* distress is at the same time the *expression* of real distress and also a *protest* against real distress," the "sigh of the oppressed creature, the heart of a heartless world."[130] From this perspective, the full flowering of devotion to the Rosary and to prayer beads did more than prefigure a rise in spending on personal adornment. The granting of pardons allowed petitioners to participate in their own redemption individually and collectively through membership in confraternities. The regime of indulgences socialized the labor of the saints but ultimately disbursed to particular souls a currency measured in quantities of time subtracted from a sentence in purgatory.

Marx's statements on religion would seem out of character for the founder of historical materialism. The Enlightenment, rather than the Catholic Church, tends to receive credit for valorizing pleasure as a spur to progress. In this instance, however, the *philosophe* movement figured as one element in a complex constellation. Priests and pastors instilled a longing for celestial riches that simultaneously bestowed honor on wealth employed in the praise of God. Moreover, this theological work coincided with two intellectual developments that, although closely associated with the Enlightenment, also had religious exponents: (1) ruminations on the possibilities of active mechanism in natural philosophy, which could be extended to the agency that pious objects exerted on believers, and (2) explorations of a sensible middle ground between pure asceticism and rampant hedonism that recalled the counsel of pastors such as Réguis.[131]

Economic theology functions as an alternative prism for interpreting the principles and practices that brought about the consumer revolution and were transformed by it in turn. The Catholic ethic identified the sacred with expenditure, provoking and sustaining an epoch-making market for goods. Its logic informed how subjects oriented themselves toward the panoply of possessions at their disposal. One witnesses in the conjuncture of economized theology and the proliferation of material goods what Rousseau described in the *Discours sur l'inégalité* as the "coming together of several unconnected causes that might never have come into being."[132] This chance encounter transformed both religion and capitalism, giving rise to a new force—the commodity fetish—that worked in mysterious ways. Even men and women largely indifferent to matters of faith were, by virtue of their upbringing, steeped in sacramental culture. Devotional objects held out prospects of fulfillment far in excess of the article being consumed or the labor invested in its production. The anticipation of riches, whether eternal or mortal in cast, perpetuated desire by drawing out to infinity the moment of possession. If needs have a past, their futures were imagined as lasting forever.

CHAPTER 6

Luxury and the Origins of the Fetish

COMMISSIONED FOR 3,000 LIVRES, the painter's highest fee, Hyacinthe Rigaud's portrait of Charles d'Orléans de Saint-Albin (1723–24) radiates ecclesiastical luxury at the dawn of the Enlightenment.[1] The newly appointed archbishop of Cambrai (fig. 6.1), seated on a gilded chair, balances a weighty tome on his knee. He is enveloped in solemn luster. Rich velvet drapes, barely contained by cords and tassels, lap the room's cool marble columns. The finest trappings are reserved for the cleric's person, resplendent in his silken cassock, embroidered rochet, and azure cappa magna of moiré. The pectoral cross, a symbol of episcopal authority, hangs from a broad ribbon suspended around Saint-Albin's neck. Beneath it rests his hand, pressed firmly into the plush fur of his ermine hood. His gaze extends away from the volume he is reading and toward the adornments that surround him.

Rigaud posed his subject in a manner that accentuated worldly as well as spiritual endowments. Saint-Albin's visage—almond eyes, aquiline nose, and generous chin—all bear the marks of his Bourbon paternity. According to Saint-Simon, he was the illegitimate son of the duc d'Orléans and Florence Perrin, a dancer at the opera.[2] Destined for a career in the church, Saint-Albin defended his thesis at the Sorbonne in February of 1718. As reported in the *Nouveau Mercure*, the assembled doctors fawned over the "superior brilliance" of the royal bastard and the "precise and detailed knowledge of each subject

Figure 6.1 Hyacinthe Rigaud. *Charles de Saint-Albin, Archbishop of Cambrai*, 1723. Oil on canvas, 146.1 × 113 cm (57 ½ × 44 ½ in.), 88.PA.136. J. Paul Getty Museum, Los Angeles.

that he addressed."³ His elevation at the tender age of twenty-three—first as bishop of Rouen (1721), then of Laon (1722), and finally of Cambrai (1723)—shocked his contemporaries. A sexual affair with Margaret Josepha, wife of the Old Pretender James III's devoted servant Daniel O'Brien, Earl of Lismore, cemented his reputation for audacious profligacy.⁴

Nevertheless, Rigaud's portrait immortalized the projection of power under a symbolic regime in which material wealth conjured its celestial equivalent. Saint-Albin's thesis offered commentary on Psalm 65, an encomium to the terrestrial abundance established by God's fecundity: "You visit the earth and water it; you greatly enrich it," the scripture proclaims. "You crown the year with your bounty."⁵ These references to divine largesse carried implications for the relationship between wealth and status. The cleric's tonsure, the sword identified with nobility, and the fulsome robes of the *parlementaires* manifested the gradations of hierarchy. This sartorial regime met with greater skepticism over the course of the eighteenth century. In a period marked by rising consumption along with clashes over sacramental and financial currencies, the correspondence between material signifiers and social realities no longer garnered immediate assent.⁶

Eighteenth-century luxury migrated from a fixation on the social status and moral constitution of persons to a more general reckoning of what counted as superfluous.⁷ The pursuit of pleasure spurred commercial exchanges and the fashioning of personal identity among aristocrats and commoners, men and women alike.⁸ Consumers with sufficient means or credit could purchase clothing, wigs, jewelry, crockery, writing desks, or accessories for coffee, tea, and tobacco—goods that made life not only bearable but even satisfying. They brought their tastes to market in feats of stylish, rank-defying self-presentation that rendered nature an agent of artifice.

French thinkers, even those who considered themselves in the vanguard of progress, kept a wary distance from the leviathan of luxury.⁹ As in the case of usury, few writers embraced the concept without numerous caveats. They weighed their words carefully to evade—or at least to accept with a resigned air—classical and Christian fears of enervation. The guarded approach betrayed a certain obsessiveness: no fewer than a hundred works appeared on the subject during the reigns of Louis XV and Louis XVI.¹⁰ Denis Diderot cited the "infinity of objects of every kind" classifiable as luxurious in justifying the *Encyclopédie*, a work intended to "establish the meaning of the terms of a language."[11] Gabriel Sénac de Meilhan observed in 1777 that a century of fervent debate had failed to define "so vague and so abstract a word." To his mind, luxury could only be known "in the physical order it destroys, in the morals it corrupts."[12]

This chapter contends that the problem of terrestrial luxury necessitated a spiritual intercession. Sénac de Meilhan quoted from Fénelon's *Télémaque*, a primer on Christian agrarianism, even while allowing that luxury inevitably followed economic progress.[13] *Télémaque*'s appeal precludes a linear passage from traditional religious strictures to modern liberalism. Theological conceptions of wealth and abundance furnish the missing link between the hierarchical complementarity of the society of orders and an economy set in motion by abstract financial instruments. Even Mandeville did not so much reverse Jansenist moral philosophy as find new applications for it.[14] As we have seen, Nicole followed a similar course. Given that original sin had corrupted the world to a seemingly irretrievable degree, reason itself counseled that "enlightened self-interest" offered the best hope for peace in this life. Led by Jacques-Joseph Duguet, second-generation Jansenists marshaled Nicole's Augustinian anthropology in defense of commerce, agricultural reform, and lending at interest.[15]

Historians of economic thought, insofar as they consider religion at all, tend to emphasize the workings of a radically transcendent *deus absconditus* who effectively abandoned the earth to its own corrupt yet self-sustaining devices. But this model does not account for the economy in all its conceptual and material fullness. According to Enlightenment-era political economists, God ordained the laws that governed the natural world and testified to the enduring character of divine presence. Claims of the potential for infinite growth required elaborate justifications, the symbolic resources for which followed sacred precedent—the Incarnation, the Eucharist, penance, and indulgences.

Even as the Catholic ethic rendered impossible a definitive judgment on luxury, it framed a critique of the economy that assumed a prophetic air. Commodity fetishism had long been an open secret among economic theologians, who required no intellectual *deus ex machina* to recognize that manufactured idols exerted a disquieting agency on their human worshippers.

The magnitude of Marx's discovery notwithstanding, the clergy shared such reservations with the *philosophes*. The relationship between worldly and otherworldly possessions, a perennial question in a Christian polity, provoked intense spiritual and cultural speculation. What distinguished true reverence from idolatry, or faithful stewardship from pernicious luxury? Time and again, economic theologians entered the fray, whether to denounce human avarice or to recommend lavish expenditure in the church's name.

Tellingly, priests and pastors issued rebukes featuring the sins of women, who were regarded as particularly prone to sumptuous exhibition. According to the Book of Genesis, history began with an act of deviant consumption—Eve's theft of the fruit from the tree of knowledge. God punished the first humans by casting them into a world of scarcity. The narrative of the Fall gendered economic matters from their inception. Throughout the eighteenth century and beyond, the imputed desires of women continued to figure centrally in efforts to distinguish enlightened luxury from decadence. Progressively if paradoxically universalized, the specter of feminine profligacy became a model for and motor of the discourse of political economy, from Fénelon and Rousseau to Quesnay and Turgot.

Clerics stood on all sides of the polemics surrounding luxury but shared a common preoccupation with the vagaries of desire—masculine and feminine, human and divine. To the minds of critics such as Jean Pipet, Pierre de Gourdan, and François-André-Adrien Pluquet, luxury deluded its victims to such an extent that they sought in worldly trifles the fulfillment that celestial riches rightfully procured. Saint-Albin's predecessor as archbishop of Cambrai, Fénelon, formulated a singularly influential indictment of exorbitant consumption as a crime against God's law and a false promise of liberation from want. According to his disciple Rousseau, commodities enslaved their owners more oppressively than the cruelest tyrant. Although Rousseau is often regarded as a theorist of sovereignty, his contributions to political economy proved no less fateful for the intellectual history of the Enlightenment.

Denunciations of luxury as idolatry acquired new force and meaning in the middle decades of the eighteenth century. Mindful of Fénelonian and Rousseauian critiques, Diderot and his fellow *Encyclopédistes* struggled to distinguish dangerous from salutary forms of expenditure. The Physiocrats, who had their own theological commitments, asserted the primacy of agriculture while identifying *jouissance* as the prime mover of history. Their contemporary Georges-Marie Butel-Dumont established a religion of superfluity on sensationalist principles, according to which every new want revealed a potential need. Against such claims, ecclesiastics elaborated their critique of luxury in historical-materialist terms, equating illegitimate commerce with slavery in the colonies and despotism in the metropole. These various perspectives imagined the terrestrial sphere to be a bottomless crucible of generative desire. Theologians had long feared that idolatry would triumph over pure devotion. Their predictions came to pass not in the secularization of religious doctrine but in the deification of the economy itself.

Before Fetishism: Luxury as Idolatry

Historians frequently trace the beginnings of the eighteenth-century luxury debates to Mandeville, who shocked contemporaries by avowing that the worst of individual intentions produced felicitous outcomes in the aggregate. As he observed, the so-called virtues bore no relation to eternal truths but were rather "the political offspring which flattery begot upon pride."[16] Even before the translation of *The Fable of the Bees* in 1740, French readers found themselves scandalized and intrigued by a work almost universally regarded as a threat to established morals.[17] In Mandevillian fashion, they might have even been flattered. The anthropological premise of *The Fable of the Bees* resembled that of Jansenists such as Nicole and Pascal, who held that the human desire for recognition converted pride to utilitarian ends.[18] This moral philosophy trucked in the conviction that humans were ruled by their passions, prideful self-interest above all, and that spiritually damnable urges could be harnessed to socially edifying effect.

Nicole, Pascal, and Mandeville are often featured in genealogies of political and economic modernity, albeit at the cost of obscuring equally formative currents of thought. The Augustinian paradigm played a role in the emergence of society as an autonomous domain of human action.[19] Yet narratives of Jansenism's influence have their limits. Nicole might have been expected to embrace luxury as a necessary evil. Yet he resisted the siren's song, holding that emulation should restrain rather than foster immoderate displays of wealth. "There is nothing more capable of inspiring modesty in persons of middling station," he wrote, "than seeing persons of great quality... whom they do not wish to displease in a state of scrupulous modesty."[20] In contrast, Jesuit thinkers often vindicated moderate pleasure on the grounds that "nature invites us to it."[21] Their calls for bounded enjoyment presaged the "Epicurean Stoicism" that became a defining feature of Enlightenment ethics and aesthetics.[22] In its Catholic guises, the hierarchy of spiritual and material goods was reinforced by economic theologians, who also advanced a critique of idolatry that would resonate throughout the eighteenth century and beyond.

Although austerity is often associated with Jansenism, members of the Society of Jesus did not hesitate to denounce conspicuous consumption that exceeded the circumscribed bounds of respectability. In the popular manual *La cour sainte* (1624), the Jesuit priest and royal confessor Nicolas Caussin depicted unbridled luxury as the confusion of persons and things. Like contemporary sumptuary laws, 40 percent of which concerned game animals and banqueting, he trained his eye on sins committed at the table. Gluttony, in particular, was an "effeminate god" lacking the "heart to undertake the good." Caussin's remarks show a familiarity with reification: the act of bodily consumption transformed men and women into objects of devotion for a deity devoid of feeling. Overindulgence was simultaneously inhumane and unmanly, thus effeminate; likewise, the "luxury of clothing" proved especially malignant in the case of women. Anticipating Rousseau's critique in the *Discours sur l'inégalité* (*Second Discourse*), and adopting the same language, Caussin directed his ire and his irony toward "victims of vanity who have no other knowledge [*étude*] except of adorning themselves above their station" and no other "desire but seeming to be what they are not." Caussin counseled modesty in all things, attention to social propriety, and the avoidance of "useless expenses." All Christians should preserve "some mark of mortification"—be it ill-fitting garments, unpalatable food, or poorly appointed lodgings.[23]

La cour sainte was published in numerous editions and inspired various imitators. For instance, the abbé Jean Pipet cited Caussin in his *Instructions chrétiennes* (1678), a work that took a stance against luxury at once uncompromising and ambiguous.[24] Luxury had its origins in the Garden of Eden, where the serpent tempted Eve with the forbidden fruit of knowledge. Pipet wondered whether "God seems to have displayed excessive severity" in imposing banishment from Eden. He nonetheless followed contemporaries in deriving luxury from idolatry. Worldly possessions were "in truth goods" but nonetheless "uncertain, deceptive, and perishable." Covetousness led to "thefts," "frauds," and "irreligion and irreverence toward the most holy mysteries." Since women were especially susceptible to the temptations of fashion, Pipet counseled them to style their hair and dress themselves with reserve as a sign of preference for God over the self.[25]

Pipet's fixation on women prompted a series of powerful displacements. By reducing the apparent scope of idolatrous self-regard to particular manifestations, clerics preserved a separate heavenly sphere in which splendor reigned.[26] For instance, Jacques Boileau took offense at the fashion for *décolletage* in gowns not only at balls and in the streets but also "at the feet of altars." Exhibitionism had the effect of "profaning the sanctity of churches" and "wounding the eyes of the most innocent." Boileau vilified the perpetrators as "idolaters of vanity" whose luxury "makes all the saints groan." Oblivious to the source of true wealth, "they consume the goods of fortune" yet "lose the goods of grace." The first humans had sought to clothe themselves out of shame for sin. Now the "nudity of the bosom" kept reprobate women from partaking in the spiritual wealth of penance and communion.[27]

Feminine vanity touched followers of religious vocations as well as the devotees of high society. According to Nicolas Héron, chaplain of the queen and treasurer of the royal chapel of Vincennes, candidates for the nun's habit counted among the worst offenders. Dressed as if attending a ball, their appearance "scandalizes an infinity of persons" in a manner unbecoming of a "bride of Jesus Christ." Héron advised that "it is better for you to appear only in simple dress and achieve your salvation than to risk it through vain magnificence." He rejected every possible justification for indulgence, from a misguided sense of familial honor to the false belief that marriage to God demanded the trappings of a conjugal union. None of these rationales overcame the shameful truth that "the majority of nuns love the sumptuousness of taking the habit."[28]

Claude Joly's sermons as parish priest of Saint-Nicolas-des-Champs in Paris adopted a somewhat more lenient tone toward his audience, which, according to the noted Jesuit orator and poet Charles de la Rue, featured "the most dazzling" personages of the capital and at court.[29] Although Joly assured his listeners that "affluence is not incompatible with holiness," he also counseled that no fleeting earthly pleasure was worth jeopardizing the reward of heaven, which God promised to the elect in "abundant and magnificent" largesse. The wealthy should recognize the role of providence in their good fortune as a debt that could not be repaid. Those who looked to themselves for credit "forget the true God and make false deities of themselves everywhere." The pious soul acknowledged that "you give me . . . not only bread to eat, but also the greatest delicacies of the seas and the forests," merely for serving as the "steward of the poor, the surrogates of the providence of God."[30]

The Jesuit Gourdan, whom we encountered in Chapter 1, placed manufactured goods along a continuum with sacramental wealth. Affirming the Eucharist as a universal equivalent, he observed in *Le chrestien heureux* that it "simultaneously enriches us with the pleasures of this world and the delights of heaven." Given the liturgical significance and material trappings of the Mass, its celebration served as a point of convergence between these sources of value. It constituted "a paradise rather better and more enchanting [*délicieux*] than that which our first parents possessed." This second "earthly paradise" promised "an infinite happiness to be augmented by desire, action, and sacrifice with one's Redeemer."[31]

Despite the voluptuousness of Gourdan's praise, he avowed a pressing need for "chasing luxury from the Mass and from the Church." Pastors could elect to withhold the sacraments from parishioners who flouted the standards of "propriety, modesty, and chastity." Like his contemporaries, Gourdan expressed particular concern for women, whom he expected to display "decency, modesty, and chastity" during worship. Luxury constituted a mortal sin that led perpetrators to "make illicit gains and contracts" at the expense of almsgiving. Furthermore, it concealed "all the demons in their last redoubt, and every wrongdoer in the first principle of his reprobation." Material licentiousness corrupted the representation of heavenly glories, posing a dire threat not only to the church and "all the happiness for which it hopes," but also to Christians and "all the bliss they demand."[32]

If the Eucharist functioned as the currency of sacramental life, luxury served as the coin of the sinful realm, a manifestation of "the idolatry that *amour-propre* wants to establish in our heart." Like the false gods worshipped by the Israelites, "luxury is as insatiable in its crimes as the devil, because it always breathes and burns for the pleasures of the eyes, for the indulgence of the flesh and for the splendor of life." As we have seen, Gourdan diagnosed the practice of wearing "magnificent dress" as indicative of "a double idolatry, active and passive." It was active insofar as sufferers "idolize themselves from every perspective" and passive since they comport themselves only "to be idolized."[33]

Gourdan's theological elaboration of luxury privileged a distinctly Christian form of materialism writ large in the Eucharistic devotions of the period. Along with his fellow Jesuit Caussin, he suggested that the perversions of luxury endowed mere objects with agency and reduced persons to the status of things. Fear of loss gripped victims in the "panicked terrors of necessity," "crueler than the furies of Hell." It seemed to "besiege them on all sides" like a "magical enchantment." Gourdan reappropriated the metaphor of demonic possession for pious purposes, asking, "Is it not a visible enchantment to make a profession of believing that Jesus Christ is the sovereign good that encompasses and surpasses all goods?" Devout souls chose to "break the spell that has blinded them" and overcome "the fears of their false prudence." It did not suffice to have faith, which was "nothing more than a great esteem for heavenly goods." One must further cultivate "confidence," or the "experience anticipated by a constant possession."[34] Celestial treasures cast their own spell of fulfillment, the effects of which should alter the believer's outward appearance and hidden depths.

The tradition represented by moralists from Caussin to Gourdan established vital terms for the eighteenth-century luxury debate, which opposed feminized, degenerate luxury with its more edifying, presumably masculine counterpart. In *The Fable of the Bees*, Mandeville observed that "what the Prosperity of *London* and Trade in general, and consequentially the Honor, Strength, Safety, and all the worldly Interest of the Nation consist in, depends entirely on the Deceit and vile Stratagems of Women."[35] Montesquieu's *Lettres persanes* reiterated these sentiments. The character Usbek noted that "a woman gets it into her head that she must wear a particular outfit on some occasion, and at once it becomes impossible for fifty craftsmen to get any sleep or have leisure to eat and drink."[36] As the exchanges between the Persian and European characters made clear, a state given over to luxury depended on a dialectic of commercial enlightenment, with women at its center.

The preoccupation with feminine consumption endured not only as a discrete theme, itself a reflection of the role women played in setting fashion, but also as a structuring ideological principle. Theologians and *philosophes* alike grappled with the challenge of distinguishing between positive and negative forms of superfluity. One means of doing so posited a difference between exclusively egoistic pursuits and the legitimate longing for riches promised by God. This conceptual operation proved remarkably adaptable. The task of separating worldly from otherworldly goods informed efforts by Fénelon and Rousseau to define a sovereign arbiter of decisions related to the production and distribution of material goods. Their writings, which defined the luxury debate throughout the eighteenth century, projected sacrality onto the emerging field of political economy.

From Fénelon to the *Philosophes*

At the turn of the eighteenth century, theologians and pastors issued increasingly urgent warnings against the political, economic, and moral consequences of luxury. Their disquiet arose from Louis XIV's massive financial outlays on wars of conquest and personal aggrandizement—ambitions that compounded each other with devastating effect.[37] In *Traité contre le luxe des hommes et des femmes* (1705), Jean du Pradel rehearsed arguments favoring costly and ever-shifting fashions: that the taste for novelty suited French customs [*mœurs*] and was even a "necessary abuse" that contributed to "public utility."[38] He discredited these claims as theologically flawed and historically inaccurate. The ancients, who were "strong, gallant, cultivated, with fine taste in all manner of things," exhibited a glory that did not depend on constant infusions of money. They understood that "nothing signals the general corruption of *mœurs*" more than "the luxury of clothing and the table." The citizens of Rome rushed to give their wealth, and even their very lives, when the city faced peril. An early sumptuary law, which limited women's spending on their dress and means of conveyance, led to "a return of modesty inspired by love of country." Peace, however, brought a restoration of feminine decadence. Over time, luxurious wants crystallized into needs that fostered dependence on a single ruler, gradually but irreversibly undermining the military and financial strength of the empire.[39]

Du Pradel dedicated his *Traité* to Paul de Beauvillier, duc de Saint-Aignan, the director of the Royal Council of Finances and a member of the High Council (Conseil d'en Haut).[40] Along with Charles Honoré d'Albert, duc de Chevreuse, he joined Fénelon in a cabinet of advisers for Louis XIV's grandson and heir, the duc de Bourgogne. Their platform outlined a model of Christian agrarianism that promised to save France from financial disaster through comprehensive political and economic reform.[41] According to Fénelon and Chevreuse, a major stumbling block to the kingdom's redemption was luxury, an evil that compromised the "customs [*mœurs*] of the entire nation." Salvation lay in the establishment of strict sumptuary laws for all subjects. The state should rein in expenses through a massive reduction in the size of the army. The makers of frivolous novelties had long received needless subsidies; henceforth, policy would favor agricultural produce and manufactured goods for which the French held a natural advantage. Once the demon of conquest had been cast out of the body politic, the crown could repeal consumption taxes such as the *gabelle* along with the *capitation*, a nominally universal income tax that ran counter to Fénelon's ideal of hierarchical complementarity. Nobles would recover their prominence in government, leading provincial estates and tempering the monarchy's ambitions.[42]

In his popular spiritual writings, Fénelon treated the problem of pride with bracing clarity. One should look on goods "without passion," "making a sober use of them, not wanting to enjoy the possession [*jouir*] of them and put them in one's heart."[43] Virtuous souls were to maintain constant vigilance lest they exploit the sacraments as a means of aggrandizement that put the desires of self before God. Fénelon's identification of spiritual self-ownership with idolatry led to his break with Catholic orthodoxy. His theological contemporaries' critiques of luxury aimed to instill a preference for the treasures of the church over worldly riches. For this reason they alluded to the satisfaction of acquiring grace. Fénelon's refusal of this axiom ultimately brought him into conflict with Bossuet, leading to his condemnation by Pope Innocent XII and exile to his archdiocese in Cambrai.

Fénelon's star continued to rise in the intellectual firmament despite his official censure.[44] As a former tutor to the duc de Bourgogne, he had the ear, if not the soul, of an heir to the throne. Even after Bourgogne's untimely death in 1713, the archbishop's legacy was assured by the unauthorized publication of *Télémaque* (1699), a work originally written for the young prince's edification. This mythic and mystical adaptation of Homer's *Odyssey* became the greatest best seller of the eighteenth century. Some 450 editions appeared, eclipsing titles by Voltaire, Montesquieu, and Rousseau.[45] In an irony that would not have been lost on Fénelon, the tale's unprecedented success reflected its diagnosis of social ills. It was a populuxe version of Quietist moral theology, written for a child and thus accessible to a wide audience.[46]

Télémaque established the template for approaching luxury during the Enlightenment.[47] The character Mentor teaches the eponymous protagonist that "the ambition and avarice of men are the sole sources of their misfortune: men want to have everything, and their desire for excess makes them unhappy. If only they would want to live simply, and to content themselves with satisfying their true needs, there would be plenty, joy, peace, and union everywhere."[48] Fénelon thus confronted his readers with a deceptively stark choice. The Bourbon dynasty could pursue the ruinous course set by Louis XIV and Colbert or opt for a fundamental reorientation of both the self-owning subject and the goods regarded as the essence of existence. Tilling the soil should take precedence over the luxury trades. The preening despotism of the Sun King should give way to the virtues of natural right under a regime that was monarchical in form but republican in spirit. Otherwise, the French would collapse under the weight of their own avarice.[49] Yet Fénelon's calls for moderation nonetheless assumed that well-cultivated land could produce more than was necessary for mere subsistence. Abundance, not scarcity, made possible the social harmony central to his vision of reform.

Partisans of the luxury debate learned the axioms of *Télémaque* by heart along with its heady combination of utopian myth and classical values.[50] Excepting Voltaire, who in *Le mondain* (1736) brazenly proclaimed that "the superfluous is the most necessary thing," few if any *philosophes* dared advance an unqualified defense of luxury.[51] In *De l'esprit des lois*, Montesquieu advocated a mutually beneficial division of labor between republics specializing in the "commerce of trade" and monarchies devoted to the "commerce of luxury."

The "principal object" of the latter was "to procure for the nation engaged in it all that can serve its pride, its delights, its fantasies."[52] Jean-François Saint-Lambert's article in the *Encyclopédie* was indicative of prevailing sentiments on how France might follow its natural economic inclinations without falling into ruin. Adopting the terms of sensationalist psychology, he defined luxury as "the use one makes of wealth and industry to procure a pleasant existence." Since superfluous consumption buttressed the "strength of nations" and the "happiness of citizens," government should not merely "encourage it" but seek "to enlighten" and "direct it" by privileging the domestic production of luxury over foreign imports.[53] This approach, which Diderot followed as well, reconciled sumptuousness with equity and self-interest with virtue. The *Observations sur le Nakaz* (1774), his commentary on the guidelines for new Russian legal code written by his patron, Catherine II, distinguished between a harmful type of luxury, which drives one to labor ceaselessly for little gain, and another that, through "excellent administration," promoted "the splendor of the sciences and the liberal and mechanical arts."[54]

The advent of the Enlightenment did not signal a decisive shift in the polemics surrounding luxury. Fénelon's soul lived on through Rousseau, who shot to literary fame with his *Discours sur les sciences et les arts* (*First Discourse*), a work arguing that superfluity produced moral exhaustion and economic tumult.[55] Rousseau's denunciations of unfettered commercialism followed in the long tradition of theologians who wrote about economic matters while also casting an inescapable shadow over his contemporaries. As Melchior Grimm wrote of the *First Discourse*, "Monsieur Rousseau has converted almost all the *philosophes* here. They all agree, with some qualifications, that he is right."[56] The admission suggests that, alongside the movement toward a purportedly secular political economy, there were no less inventive attempts to resacralize its dynamics by collapsing the distinction between the heavenly city and terrestrial sphere and by seeking redemption in this life rather than in the world to come.

Rousseau and the Resacralization of Political Economy

Rousseau expanded the scope of economic theology inherited from his predecessors. Like Caussin, Gourdan, and Du Pradel before him, he held that the fate of the soul and society depended on toppling false deities fashioned by human hands. Rousseau's most distinctive innovation came in generalizing the plasticity of human nature and theorizing its susceptibility to modes of existence-altering possession. These conceptual advances led to his conjecture that commodified humans might again remake themselves but only once their collective reification had broken the psychic bonds between love of self and the bonds of property.

As had Du Pradel's *Traité* and Fénelon's *Télémaque*, Rousseau's *Discours sur les sciences et les arts* (1750) marshaled evidence from ancient history, contrasting the decline of Athens and Rome with Sparta's militant temperance. He then trained his critical gaze on the eighteenth century. The glories of Louis XIV and Louis XV on the throne, and of Voltaire on the page, concealed the progress of a polite form of despotism. He observed that "a vile and deceitful uniformity reigns in our customs [*mœurs*], and every spirit seems to have been cast in the same mold." Like Caussin, Rousseau bemoaned the tyranny of appearance over reality in a world where "no one will ever truly know those with whom he is dealing." Coupling the rectitude of the ancients with a Christian sensibility, he considered "luxury, dissolution, and slavery" as the just "punishment for the arrogant efforts that we have made to leave the happy ignorance in which eternal wisdom had placed us." Renouncing the ostentatious cult of learning, he called on "almighty God" to "deliver us from enlightenment and the lethal arts of our fathers." Tellingly, Rousseau's rhetoric followed the Lord's Prayer. Jesus had taught his disciples to forgive their debtors and to petition God for freedom from the bondage of sin. Likewise, Rousseau implored his readers to seek out "ignorance, innocence, and poverty, the only goods that can secure our happiness and are precious in your sight."[57]

Rousseau drew out the implications of his antiphilosophy in a rejoinder to Stanisław Leszczyński, the deposed king of Poland and current duc de Lorraine. Leszczyński took issue with what he viewed as Rousseau's devaluation of science, of which he considered himself an enlightened patron. Rousseau assured Leszczyński that he rejected not learning per se but rather the selfish ends it had been made to serve. Despite their shared moral premises, the *First Discourse* dismissed Leszczyński's claim that one's "first discoveries increase the avidity" to learn ever more. Rousseau cast doubt on progress not only in the natural and mathematical sciences but also in theology. "The puerile subtleties of Scholasticism," he observed, had bestowed unwarranted legitimacy on "scientific pride" over the "Christian humility" that Jesus taught to the "twelve poor fishermen and artisans" whom he had entrusted with "converting the world." As this recounting of ecclesiastical history made clear, apparent innovations in the sciences converged with those in material production. "Luxury corrupts everything," Rousseau affirmed: soul and body, church and state, "the wealthy who enjoy its possession, and the poor who covet it."[58]

Rousseau delved further into the devastating invention of new material needs in the *Discours sur l'inégalité* (1755). This conceptual history traced the emergence of primitive humans out of a purportedly self-sufficient state of nature into the successive tragedies of civil society: the reification of being into having, the emergence of moral and sexual differences, the division of labor, and the entrenchment of despotism. The individual who defined others according to physical attributes, intellectual powers, and material possessions was himself "subjected by a multitude of new wants . . . to his fellows, to whom he has in a sense become a slave, even in becoming their master." Overcome by the "burning desire to raise one's relative fortune," the creature of society harbored "a secret jealousy" hiding under a "mask of benevolence." He was left in a state of estrangement, conditioned to remain "always outside himself" and to derive "the sentiment of his own existence" from external authorities.[59]

In a review of the *Second Discourse*, Smith seized upon Rousseau's paradoxical engagement with Mandeville, observing that, despite their seeming opposition, both thinkers appreciated the transformative effects of social exchange.[60] On this view, Rousseau's work had performed a feat of "philosophical chemistry," whereby the "principles and ideas of the profligate Mandeville seem in him to have all the purity and sublimity of the morals of Plato, and to be only the true spirit of a republican carried a little too far."[61] Remarkably, Smith alluded to the alchemical tradition in describing Rousseau's rhetorical and logical feats. In light of the powerful resonances between transmutation and transubstantiation throughout the early modern period, one could extend the metaphor further. The *Second Discourse* concluded with an account of how, through bonds of mutual dependence, "the souls and the human passions are imperceptibly altered, and change, as it were, their nature."[62] Rousseau had not only turned the natural law tradition on its head but also recast the Augustinianism of *The Fable of the Bees* into a brief for natural virtue. Society, as he understood it, triggered a process of degradation by which material enrichment led to psychic impoverishment. His later writings imagined the possibilities of avoiding this fate. Worldly salvation depended not on Mandeville's disenchanted realism but on the potential for metamorphosis.

The *Encyclopédie* article that Rousseau wrote on political economy—also known as the *Third Discourse*—synthesized elements of the Fénelonian critique of luxury and his own analysis of the increasingly impersonal nature of social relations. This heady combination spoke to the fears of provincial elites wary of the power accumulated by financial and commercial interests.[63] Rousseau began by noting the derivation of the term *économie* from *oikos* and *nomos*, thus signifying its etymological origins in the administration of the household. Yet he cautioned against merely expanding the techniques of a single family to the "*general* or *political economy*," which must operate according to its own transcendent principles. A "political body is thus a moral being that has a will," a "general will" corresponding to a mysterious abstraction from the wills of each associate in his or her capacity as a citizen, even if the particular will of an individual deviated from that of the whole. Rousseau paused to contemplate the seeming paradox of his position. Men and women formed political societies to protect "the goods, life, and liberty of each member through the protection of all." On what grounds, then, would they consent to the "altering of private property" that necessarily ensued? Rousseau emphasized the difficulty of resolving the problem before claiming to find it in "the first inspiration which taught man to imitate here below the immutable decrees of the divinity." One should marvel at the transformation of equality from a primordial condition into a "civil right," and of alienation from a psychic tragedy into a social virtue. Underscoring the religious premises of "the work of law," he hailed "the celestial voice that dictates to each citizen the precepts of public reason."[64]

According to the *Third Discourse*, property stood as "the most sacred of all the citizens' rights." Nonetheless, members of the body politic had a duty to "contribute their goods toward its maintenance." The sovereign established a common fund or "public domain" for governmental expenditures and appointed administrators to ensure its solvency. Financial stewardship required curtailing "useless desires," above all the "taste for conquests." The populace would accept taxes levied at "proportional rates that leave nothing arbitrary." Rather than duties on land or foodstuffs, revenues should come from tariffs on the "products of useless and inordinately lucrative arts." Not unlike the daily miracle performed in reconciling particular wills into the general will, the economy worked in mysterious ways. Rousseau maintained that "industry would have nothing to suffer from an economic order that... brought all fortunes imperceptibly closer to the middling quality [*médiocrité*] that constitutes the true strength of the state."[65] Progressive and socially strategic taxation furnished the material needs of the commonwealth while neutralizing the threats posed by luxury and inequality.

Rousseau's economic theology enshrined the experience of "peaceful enjoyment [*paisible jouissance*]" as its overarching principle.[66] This stance, announced in the *Second Discourse* and reiterated in the *Third Discourse*, introduced a variation on the Catholic ethic drawn from the "enlightened Orthodoxy" of his youth in Geneva, which broke with Calvinist precedent in stressing the soul's responsibility for salvation through moral action.[67] Rousseau elaborated on the ideal in his best-selling novel *Julie, ou La nouvelle Héloïse* (1761), a work that followed Fénelon by diminishing the significance of individualist property in favor of the generalized enjoyment of possession. Contentment depended not on ostentatious trappings such as "gilt paneling, luxury, and magnificence" but rather on a state in which "you see order reign without gloom, peace without slavery, plenty without profusion." The bliss of self-sufficiency endowed the good steward with the air of divinity or, in Rousseau's evocative description, "happy like god himself, without desiring anything more than what he already had."[68]

At Clarens, the model estate that furnished the setting for *La nouvelle Héloïse*, perfectible pleasure demanded the exercise of restraint and even a moderate affinity for dispossession.[69] The protagonist Julie's willingness to forsake her beloved Saint-Preux in marrying Wolmar assured domestic tranquility. Whereas her medieval namesake lived out her days in unrequited, embittered obsession, the new Heloise charts a via media between decadence and abstinence. Pleasure reigns in a subdued manner. Julie embraces virtue in the full knowledge of lesser enjoyments. "Now that she experiences that supreme delight in peace," Saint-Preux observes, "she denies herself none of those that can accompany it." According to this "art of enjoyment," which is also "that of privations," she takes all things in moderation, not out of misplaced scruple but in the name of pleasure itself. "This simple soul thus preserves her primary drive" so that "her taste does not go flat" and "she never needs to revive it through excess." Far from the labors of worldly asceticism featured in Weber's *Protestant Ethic*, the characters in *La nouvelle Héloïse* embraced an "epicureanism of reason."[70]

Within the materialist framework established by the *Discours sur l'inégalité*, *Du contrat social* joined the concept of general will introduced in the *Discours sur l'économie politique* to the practices of psychic and cultural conditioning lauded in *La nouvelle Héloïse* and *Émile* (1762).[71] Rather than a more circumspect *art de jouissance*, citizens of a popular government engaged in "the total alienation of each associate, with all his rights, to the entire community." Rousseau qualified the severity of the pronouncement by likening it to an advantageous exchange. Since one submitted without reservation, "the condition is equal for all." On weighing the "balance" of the moral, political, and economic transaction, it became clear that what one loses in natural prerogatives returns in a higher form: "faculties are honed and developed," "ideas are expanded," "sentiments are ennobled," the "entire soul is elevated." Natural autonomy is converted into "civil liberty and the property rights to all one possesses." Even then, the exercise of ownership is kept "forever subordinate to the right of the community over all," thereby preserving the equality stipulated by the social contract."[72]

As justification for the "absolute power" wielded by the "body politic," Rousseau appealed to the heavens in his theory of the legislator. After all, "gods would be necessary to give laws to men." The founder of a republic "must feel that he is in a position to change, so to speak, human nature." His vocation deprives the individual of "his own forces in order to give him forces that are alien to him and that he cannot make use of without the help of others." In this transformative exchange of thoughts and desires, the more one's "natural forces" become "dead and annihilated," "the greater and more lasting are those acquired." Neither brute force nor gentle persuasion accounted for the mechanisms by which such changes were wrought. Sheer ritual failed to reproduce "the true miracle" effected by the "soul of the legislator."[73]

This otherworldly figure surpassed the bounds of the political realm as humans had originally entered it to give them a new mode of being. As

Rousseau explained in *Émile*, "civil man is nothing but a fractional unity dependent on the denominator whose value is determined by his relation to the whole." The reference to value was by no means incidental. It signaled the primacy of a general over a restricted system. That is to say, Rousseau tempered the autonomous market of free individuals with a sublime form of economy in which the self, the most intimate possession of all, is mortgaged to the "common unity."[74] The divine legislator returns to the citizen in a more exalted form all that he has stripped away.

It is tempting to trace from Fénelon to Rousseau the secularization of the luxury debate and even of politics tout court. Rousseau appropriated Malebranche's doctrine that God operates according to simple, uniform volitions and employed it to describe the workings of a temporal sovereign.[75] In relocating the Fall to the origins of society, Rousseau also contradicted scripture. Yet he did not cast faith into the outer darkness.[76] The theological precedent of equating luxury and femininized decadence deeply informed his writings. Moreover, the theory of the general will preserved a divine kernel of rights within the rational shell of civil society.[77] Rousseau invoked God at critical junctures of his thought, effectively resacralizing the political and economic domains.[78] Subsequent attempts by the Physiocrats and Turgot to distinguish the veritable economy from misconceived modes of production and consumption testified to his influence. Although rejecting his amalgam of Christian spirituality, classical republicanism, and the natural law tradition, these interlocutors continued to work the same conceptual terrain.

The Physiocratic Gospel of *Jouissance*

French economic thought in the eighteenth century took its distinctive cast by prioritizing agriculture over manufacturing and resisting a wholesale rehabilitation of luxury. The introduction of new cultivation practices, the rising prospect of a commercial nobility, and calls for a more equitable tax system had existential consequences for a regime grounded in the logic of privilege. Modernization marched under the sign of a patriotic zeal that sought to reconcile ancient virtue with pecuniary interests.[79] The polity assumed a preeminent place in the economic imaginary not by severing its ties to the celestial realm but by affirming the relationship between natural law and divine will. In a word, the "economy" was the continuation of both politics and theology by other means. Quesnay and Turgot inaugurated a science of commerce that presumed the resacralization of the material domain intimated by Fénelon and Rousseau. Rather than demarcating a separate and secular economic field, debates over luxury continued to draw on persistent tensions within the Catholic ethic of *jouissance*. Writers brooded over whether the motive of material gain might be harnessed for a greater end through the revivification of agriculture, industry, and the entire fiscal apparatus.

Pierre-Samuel Dupont de Nemours devised the term *Physiocracy*—literally, "the rule of nature"—to encapsulate Quesnay's teachings. A royal surgeon and favorite of the marquise de Pompadour, Louis XV's powerful mistress, Quesnay advocated entrepreneurial, large-scale farming, domestic free trade, the loosening of traditional bonds of aristocratic privilege, and the legal despotism of an enlightened monarch.[80] His career took a fateful turn when he met Victor Riquetti, the marquis de Mirabeau, whose *L'Ami des hommes* (1756) developed a program of reform inspired by the prescriptions of the duc de Bourgogne's circle.[81] Mirabeau fell under Quesnay's spell, while Mirabeau's celebrity gave Quesnay a platform from which to popularize his views. Their encounter marked the founding of Physiocracy as an identifiable school of thought. The Physiocrats borrowed liberally from Fénelonian agrarianism and the natural rights tradition while seeking to forge a new synthesis out of these elements.[82] Whereas Fénelon espoused Christian universalism, Quesnay and Mirabeau joined Malebranche and Rousseau in arguing for the binding nature of the general will.[83] This commitment meant that the desires of particular subjects remained at the mercy of divine ordinance, in contrast to the liberal tradition as conceived across the English Channel.

Rousseau's contributions to political economy have attracted only halting scholarly attention. He foreshadowed the Physiocrats in at least three respects, despite his subsequent critique of their arguments for enlightened despotism.[84] First, Quesnay's circle of *économistes*, as they were commonly known, embraced the principle that laws—whether human or divine, positive or natural—operated at a general rather than particular level. Second, they emulated both Fénelon and Rousseau in privileging agriculture. Third, they further advanced a shift in the aim of economic knowledge from subsistence to *jouissance*.⁸⁵ The Physiocrats defined the pleasures to be gleaned from possession in keeping with God's sovereign dictates. As with Rousseau, an economic theology underwrote their political economy. Agricultural produce did not merely provide for bare needs; rather, bread and wine sold on the market generated a self-perpetuating surplus.

Historians have alternately hailed the Physiocrats for their embrace of laissez-faire and dismissed them as retrograde for their defense of landed wealth and absolutist politics. Recent trends in the scholarship challenge such assessments, which rely on teleological narratives of the transition from statist mercantilism to liberal modernity.⁸⁶ The eighteenth-century vogue for agronomic experimentation, while encouraged by Quesnay's circle, drew together ideologically disparate support from the royal administration, reform-minded members of provincial academies, local improvement societies, and even the Gallican church.⁸⁷ Likewise, Physiocracy itself, for all its doctrinal rigor, remained an assemblage of ideas with heterogeneous origins. As Dan Edelstein has recently shown, scholars wall off its political philosophy from its economic doctrines at their peril. The same lesson holds true for its theological sources. In a daring move, Quesnay and Mirabeau collapsed the distinction between the state of nature and civil society on which natural rights theory was founded, allowing for a nearly imperceptible passage from primitive social organization to fully formed government. Political institutions safeguarded property in the way that God intended, by enforcing the laws that a divine sovereign bestowed on the natural order at the moment of creation.⁸⁸

Quesnay rejected a positivist account of wealth despite the seemingly mechanical mode of exposition favored in his *Tableau économique* (1758), with its somewhat mystifying diagram of zigzags employed to illustrate the benefits of agricultural surplus. The schema depended on intuition as much as calculation, art as much as science, faith as much as reason. The master imposed his ethos of laissez-faire from above on a cohort of followers who embraced its principles despite lapses in demonstrable evidence.⁸⁹ As Quesnay himself declared in the *Encyclopédie* article "Évidence," "faith cannot contradict the certainty of evidence, and evidence, limited by natural knowledge, cannot contradict faith." The human mind arrived at an understanding of its own freedom by reflecting on the "divine intelligence" that established the "natural order" according to which all "moral determinations" were made.⁹⁰

The *Tableau économique* divided society into three categories: the "productive class," which engaged in cultivation; "proprietors" of the land, including the crown; and the "sterile class," which made its living by manufacturing and commerce. As the terminology suggested, the power of the productive class stemmed from the transformation of expenditure into revenue. Their tastes, preoccupations, and disposable income drove the market for commodities. The sale of agricultural produce on the free market supported landowners, artisans, and merchants while "being reborn annually" with each harvest. Acts of "simple consumption," which "destroy themselves without a return," qualified as "luxury spending if they are superfluous and prejudicial to agriculture."[91]

Theologians in favor of usury had long adopted the strategy of likening the gains made from money to that of rents. Quesnay developed their logic into specific policy prescriptions, arguing that the government should permit the charging of interest but fix the rate to returns on *rentes perpétuelles*. This approach complied with "natural law," or "the real state of revenues produced by nature."[92] Wealth gained everlasting life not by dint of isolated effort or state intervention but through the conversion of mere nature into truly fertile capital. Given his exaltation of land, Quesnay demurred from asserting money's generative capacities. Even so, the intersecting lines of the *Tableau économique* represented the value of landed assets exclusively in terms of money itself.[93]

Quesnay's disciples interpreted the metaphysical aspects of the *Tableau* through the prism of occasionalism, the theological doctrine holding that God is the unique cause of whatever exists.[94] Among the most influential seventeenth-century exponents of this position was the Cartesian Malebranche, whose work the Physiocrats cited fulsomely. According to their vision of the economy, wealth had one true source: agriculture. God, likewise, was the one true cause of all things, with creatures providing the opportunities or occasions for divine activity to exert itself on events.[95] His decrees, which were regarded as fundamentally general in nature, established and maintained the framework in which particular beings acted.

La philosophie rurale (1763), a sprawling collaboration between Mirabeau, Quesnay, and the agronomic statistician Charles Richard de Butré, duly began with a long chain of quotations from Malebranche.[96] The preface credited him with charting a course to the "haven of moral truth through the development of physical truths" and with illuminating "the full and demonstrated excellence of the laws of eternity." The "regular, multiplying, recurring, fruitful movement" of the physical world confirmed the existence of "the intellect that gives matter such properties" and with it the validity of Malebranche's theory.[97] As these passages suggest, occasionalism reinforced the Physiocrats' conviction that natural law belonged to an all-encompassing order that God himself had willed and in which humans could participate.

The coauthors of *La philosophie rurale* refused to interpret divine commandments as the blind workings of mechanism. Their preface specified that the order of things had analogues in the "laws of worship" and the "precepts of obligation." The *économistes* claimed that they had uncovered the "principle and base of the moral order here below." They also recognized, however, that "perfect government is not a human institution" and that "men can neither add nor subtract from this theocracy." The *Tableau économique* was submitted as evidence of the "eternal decree" that humans must work "by the sweat of [their] brow."[98]

Applying this truth to practical matters, Mirabeau and his colleagues addressed the question of usury. "Interest on money," they asserted, "destroys society by putting revenues into the hands of people who are neither proprietors nor producers." The usurer "throws his morals [*mœurs*] into the ruinous luxury of decoration" and sabotages "industry in subjecting it to his fantasies." Efforts by the church and state to prohibit such abuses arose not only from objective conditions but also from moral concerns and scriptural pronouncements. God himself required the ancient Israelites to celebrate every fifty years a Jubilee in which all debts were forgiven. In the eighteenth century, enlightened souls had devised the "economic means" to revive a tradition "so worthy of a fraternal society, so suitable for turning the greed of the wary into free and charitable aid."[99]

The *économistes* justified the free circulation of goods while rejecting the unfettered exercise of human agency, either mental or physical. Ideally, the reader who encountered their teachings on the natural order would see that, "embraced in the circle of this great law, he cannot refuse playing his part in the universal chorus."[100] Because many minds required guidance from above in grasping the truth, politics was made to emulate the determinism of the metaphysical and epistemological realms. For instance, Quesnay's *Maximes générales du gouvernement économique d'un royaume agricole* (1758) characterized "sovereign authority" as "superior to all the individuals of society and to all the unfair undertakings of particular interests."[101]

Notable critics, the abbé Ferdinando Galiani and Alexis de Tocqueville among them, drew attention to a blind spot in Physiocratic theory: it appeared to make absolutist government the conduit of laissez-faire.[102] This charge presumed the separation of political and economic existence that, while axiomatic of classical liberalism, was by no means self-evident in the eighteenth century. By what rationale, then, did Quesnay join political means and economic ends? One answer presents itself in the Physiocrats' understanding of providence. Yet the movement's religious sentiments far exceeded the serendipitous operation by which sin occasioned the workings of grace. A second component of the Physiocratic creed posited a divine economy that structured its terrestrial counterpart through the medium of the Incarnation.[103] In Malebranche's words (duly cited in *La philosophie rurale*), "the state to which sin has reduced us renders the grace of delight necessary to counterbalance the continual strain of our concupiscence." The text further acknowledged that "the Word," or Christ's presence in the world, "made itself perceptible and visible only in order to render truth intelligible." All divinely created beings were endowed with the "love of order." The Gospel gave fallen souls a lodestar by which to rediscover the truth within themselves.[104]

The Physiocrats translated the miracle of God's appearance as human into the language of political economy. In so doing, they heralded a new conception of commerce predicated on the limitless growth made possible by the enlightened cultivation of the soil. *Jouissance*, the enjoyment of surplus, derived not only from one's own labor but also from the rational circulation of expenditures. The social body drew its sustenance from agriculture, the productive sphere most closely associated with the Eucharistic media of bread and wine.[105] The sacraments affected the transubstantiation of common materials in a ritual that could be performed ad infinitum. Quesnay and his followers likewise applied the dogma of reproducible profit to landed capital, converting the means of subsistence into a crucible of wealth through the faithful execution of the laws of nature.

Turgot as Economic Theologian

Quesnay's sect mounted an intense campaign to see the *Tableau économique* adopted as royal policy. Facing bankruptcy in the financial fallout of the Seven Years' War, the crown proved receptive to their message of reform. In 1763 Henri Léonard Jean-Baptiste Bertin was appointed controller-general of finances. A champion of Enlightenment agronomy, he sponsored improvement societies and liberalized the grain trade everywhere in the kingdom except Paris. A declaration in May of 1764 lifted restrictions on buying and selling cereals; an edict permitting export abroad followed two months later. During the next six years the government stood firm despite popular protests and opposition from the parlements. By the end of 1770, anemic harvests, public outcries of despotism, and the runaway success of Galiani's parody of the Physiocrats in *Dialogues sur le commerce des blés* (1770) at last prevailed on Louis XV to halt the experiment.[106]

The ascension of Louis XVI in 1774 resurrected the Physiocratic cause. The young king appointed Turgot as controller-general, who in turn named Quesnay's acolyte Dupont de Nemours to the position of inspector-general of commerce. Although Turgot's relationship with the Physiocrats was notoriously vexed and should not be overstated, he shared their conviction that God prescribed the physical and human laws of development.[107] After years spent reflecting on the grain trade, taxation, and usury as intendent of Limoges, the new minister sought to implement his sweeping vision on a national scale. Between 1774 and 1776 he issued decrees dismantling market protections for cereals and the monopolistic privileges of the guilds, including those associated with the provisioning of bread and beef for the capital. Convinced of the injustices and inefficiencies of compulsory labor, he also abolished the deeply unpopular *corvée*, the regime of unremunerated work on public service projects, replacing it with a tax.[108]

For all his worldly experience, Turgot was an economic theologian in the most literal sense. Trained at Saint-Sulpice and the Sorbonne, he exemplified the Enlightenment-era theology of intellectual progress and social utility that shone brightest at midcentury, before the so-called Prades affair galvanized the Catholic establishment against the *philosophes*.[109] Remarking on his work to the king, the archbishop of Tours claimed to have "never seen a thesis defended with such distinction." By the time he left the clergy in 1751, Montesquieu's *De l'esprit des lois* had inspired his first writings on money and trade.[110] Yet he never surrendered belief in the reality of a divine cause that set all things in motion. His ideal subject took pleasure seriously while remaining mindful of God's commandments.

At the Sorbonne Turgot delivered his *Discours sur les avantages que l'établissement du christianisme a procurés au genre humain* (1750), a work that argued for the utility of religion in terms of the enjoyment of riches. Scripture revealed that providence sowed "the seed of salvation and the promised happiness of nations," making apparent "the treasures of its goodness." Christ's sacrifice marked "the accomplishment and the justification of the Jewish *economy*" in a material as well as spiritual sense. Turgot chastised sceptics who falsely charged Christianity with constructing an opposition between "the hope for eternal possessions" and the "enjoyment of those that the earth offers." Nothing could be further from the truth, since the "most celestial religion" also offered the "purest source of our felicity in this life." Through preaching the Gospel, pastors had "in some sense rendered it fecund" in the form of moral, intellectual, and technological progress. This faith inspired the "necessary subordination between all the orders of the state" under the "wisdom and equity of the laws."[111]

Turgot's theological musings lingered long after he abandoned his clerical vocation.[112] As we have seen, biblical exegesis and church tradition informed his writings on money and on lending at interest. Furthermore, he left among his papers notes for *Encyclopédie* articles on the nature and love of God. Likely composed between 1753 and 1755, the piece on God's existence identified two ways of approaching the question. Turgot dismissed the first, which involved "examining precisely what God is according to the exact enumeration of qualities attributed to him." The second, more empirical, method gleaned from the "phenomena that surround us" a "single intelligent cause" known by "the name of God." Applying the philosophical *esprit systématique* to the study of religion, Turgot's sensationalist and historicist method took as its point of departure not a speculative abstraction but humans "struck by phenomena" produced by the interaction of physical bodies. Yet the mind perceived a difference between "mechanical and intelligent causes," with the latter providing the "force" that "matter obeyed."[113]

The draft article on the love of God conveyed how one should approach this feeling. Love in general referred to "the desire for enjoyment [*jouissance*]" of a thing perceptible to the senses. How, then, could one love God? Turgot answered that one seeks the divine as an "abstract principle formed according to the particular desires of each good." Since "a certain but imperceptible good" is superior to an uncertain one, it is reasonable that "we prefer eternal goods of which we have neither the idea nor sentiment to the pleasures of the earth." By the same token, one owes to God "a love of gratitude for the goods that we have received." Only "revelation" could impart an understanding of what the soul gains by privileging timeless possessions over transitory objects.[114]

Theologians and their preoccupations even figure in Turgot's *Réflexions sur la formation et la distribution des richesses* (1766), the most complete exposition of his economic theory. He wrote the text during his intendancy in the Limousin region as a manual for two Chinese Jesuits on the eve of their return to Canton.[115] As in his analysis of the love of God, discerning the relative pleasures obtained from goods was of paramount concern. Turgot began by elaborating the division of labor. The farmer's vocation held preeminence as "the unique source of the wealth, which . . . animates all the work of society." Turgot stipulated that cultivators need not own the land they tilled. If the proprietor hired the labors of others, he could "enjoy in tranquility the possession [*jouir*]" of his surplus.[116] Capital triumphed over human exertion. Work held merit not in itself but only insofar as it contributed to the generation of riches—first for landowners themselves and then, through their expenditures, for tenant farmers, domestic servants, and artisans.

The *Réflexions* first appeared in the pages of the Physiocratic journal *Ephémérides du citoyen* over the winter of 1769–70. Dupont de Nemours edited the text in conformity with Quesnay's doctrine, provoking Turgot's ire.[117] Although willing to make common cause with the Physiocrats in support of agronomic reform, he articulated a monetary theory that deviated from the *Tableau économique* in subtle but crucial respects. Turgot reserved his highest praise not for the *grand fermier* but for the aloof *rentier* who leased his land in exchange for a fixed sum. With the tenant taking charge of every aspect of cultivation and assuming all the risks for the harvest, the distant proprietor gained "a more peaceful enjoyment [*jouissance*] of his revenue."

This scenario imagined that it was not only possible but even preferable to "live on what one calls the revenue of one's money, or the interest one draws on money lent."[118] Indeed, there was a calculated advantage to surrendering a share of potential profits for greater leisure.

The indispensability of exchange for human flourishing necessitated the introduction of money, the means by which "a certain quantity" of one commodity became "equivalent to a certain quantity" of another. In theory, any object could serve this function, making each commodity "a kind of universal wage." Turgot conceded that "all merchandise is, in certain regards, money." Nonetheless, he advocated the employment of precious metals owing to their scarcity, divisibility, and stable degree of purity. One should look neither to convention nor legal fiat to justify money but rather to the "nature of things." From this perspective, "any sum of value" found its essential measure in "landed property producing a revenue equal to a definite portion of this sum."[119]

The *Réflexions* anticipated the position Turgot would subsequently take during the usury debate in Angoulême. If land continually generated new wealth, it required a medium that could also reproduce itself. The "useful and fruitful circulation" of financial instruments "animates all the labor of society" and "maintains the movement and life of the body politic." Interest denotes the sale of the use of money, the rate for which should be established according to "the balance of the offer with the demand." Mindful of Scholastic prohibitions, Turgot admitted that "money considered as a physical substance . . . does not produce anything." Yet he immediately qualified the statement, claiming that "money employed in advances for enterprises of agriculture, manufacturing, or commerce procures a certain profit."[120]

Beyond a theory of interest, the *Réflexions* presented a model of the economy according to which exuberance and self-discipline operated in tandem. At the macroeconomic level, frugality precipitated a fall in interest rates by augmenting the money supply. The taste for "foolish expenditures" had the opposite effect for borrowers compelled to pay more for loans. Like Montesquieu before him, who emphasized the complementarity of *commerce d'économie* and *commerce de luxe*, Turgot realized that the "spirit of thrift" and the "habit of luxury" alternated in influence. Money lent for commercial purposes ultimately derived from the "production of lands." Yet the owners of the means of production were not given to economizing. They "have more surplus" but also "more desires" and "more passions." Given their psychic and material dispositions, "they save less" and "think more about pleasantly enjoying" their fortune than "increasing it." Accordingly, "luxury is their lot." In contrast, "entrepreneurs of other classes," who are "removed by their labor from amusements and expensive passions," showed a greater tendency to preserve their revenue.[121]

By reconciling agriculture with finance, and investment with luxury, the *Réflexions* accommodated capitalist values with the Catholic ethic of the landed elite. Turgot defended the fecundity of money, which he compared to the conversion of land into perpetually reproducible capital. Proprietors should resist heedless dissipation; however, they might opt for heightened pleasures over accumulation through delayed gratification. This impulse presumed a longing for luxury that need not hinder economic growth. On the contrary, it could complement the industry of manufacturers, artisans, and merchants. Beyond the division of labor, then, there existed divisions between those compelled to work and those destined for relatively effortless abundance.

Nonetheless, Turgot had no intention of justifying greed. Like Quesnay and Mirabeau, he held that the rich should possess capital and conscience in equal measure. Turgot lived by this principle as intendent. In 1770, to meet the challenges of the economic crisis in Limoges that had precipitated fears of usury, Turgot called for the establishment of *bureaux de charité*. As he observed, "the misery caused by the scarcity of essential goods [*subsistances*] among the people of this province is only too well known." The administration would respond swiftly to ensure that "all true needs are met." According to the directive, "the relief of men who suffer is the obligation and concern of everyone," especially of "notable inhabitants distinguished by their station and all those who enjoy a measure of ease." Each district would organize its own office, presided over by the "first officer of justice" or, in episcopal seats, by the local prelate. Members drew up lists of donors and their respective contributions. When Turgot pledged to donate 500 livres a month from his own purse, the bishop of Limoges followed suit.[122]

Quesnay and Turgot have long been credited with establishing political economy as a radically distinct, fully secular domain. In this view, the doctrine of laissez-faire divorced the economic sphere from traditional authority.¹²³ Such claims fail to consider the dynamics of economic theology at work in the eighteenth century. The sacramental regime was predicated on miraculous transformation, not only of bread and wine into the body and blood of Christ but also of sinners into beings redeemed of their spiritual debts. In an analogous manner, Rousseau, the Physiocrats, and Turgot affirmed the existence of various figures—the legislator, the landowner, the benevolent lender, the enlightened despot—capable of altering the natures of men and matter.

Religion and political economy informed each other throughout the eighteenth century. Rejecting unqualified asceticism, economic theologians offered new variations on the Catholic ethic of tranquil enjoyment. Arable land became the hallowed, resacralized ground of earthly salvation. Labor was necessary but not sufficient for the creation of value. Expenditure remained a commandment from on high. Pleasure counted alongside profit in economic analysis. Quesnay and Turgot differed on the question of lending at interest, yet they concurred on the precept of charity. Their pronouncements recalled not only Rousseau but also enlightened pastors such as Réguis, who held that "the poor sanctify themselves through patience and through the work that furnishes the needs of the rich," and that the rich do so through "sharing with the poor a portion of the goods that Providence has given them on this condition."¹²⁴

The Religion of Superfluity

In 1771, three years before Turgot's rise to the post of controller-general, Georges-Marie Butel-Dumont published his *Théorie du luxe* with an eye to swaying government officials and public opinion in favor of luxury's virtues. A lawyer by training and member of the so-called Gournay circle, Butel-Dumont expanded the jurisdiction of *jouissance* to every good under the sun. "The legislator" must guarantee to each subject "in the most sacred manner the full enjoyment of the possession [*jouissance*] of the fruit of his ideas and of his labor." The widest latitude should be granted not only to the "industry of the laborer" but also to the "fantasy of the consumer." Desire worked like the ghost in an economic machine of "varied enjoyments [*jouissances*] that do not last forever." Over time, even transitory pleasures "become a sort of need that one satisfies with eagerness" and, through the medium of luxury goods, serve as a "mainspring without which a great empire cannot enjoy a full and lasting prosperity."[125]

The *Théorie du luxe* ventured headlong into the motives for consumption. Arguing, as had Saint-Lambert, from the first principles of sensationalist psychology, Butel-Dumont concluded that "the taste for luxury" constituted nothing less than "the essence of man." God himself had endowed his creatures with the instincts of self-preservation and self-improvement, which men and women satisfied through the pursuit of "pleasures, sensations, [and] enjoyments," whether physical or intellectual.[126] Luxury was a perfectly natural and morally neutral category that evolved with human wants. Any innovation or augmentation beyond the minimum necessary to sustain life—including perfunctory shelter and food cultivation—fell within its domain. "One need," then, "engenders other needs" in an endless series of material and psychic investments.[127]

While not targeting the Physiocrats by name, Butel-Dumont wrote with their doctrines in mind. The *Théorie du luxe* embraced the principle of *jouissance* along with its corollary that "a nation is happy in the proportion to which the individuals that compose it have fewer strains, have less harsh labors, more conveniences, more satisfactions, and more pleasures."[128] Yet Butel-Dumont rejected the distinction that "modern economists" posed between the active wealth of agriculture and the sterile returns of industry. "Luxury alone," he contended, "furnishes the satisfactions that can spur the owners of production and their agents in creating diverse enjoyments [*jouissances*]." Motivated more by the promise of pleasurable acquisitions than a wish to increase the net product, farmers redoubled their efforts to generate revenues that could be spent on consumer goods.[129]

The abbé Baudeau issued the Physiocratic reply in the *Ephémérides du citoyen*. His review damned Butel-Dumont with faint praise for adopting a speciously capacious definition of superfluity to encourage agriculture, manufacturing, and "the institutions of the social art." As Baudeau noted, "once one takes the word *luxury* to express even the brownest bread, the coarsest clothing, the most savage hut, it is not difficult to prove that *luxury* is useful." Butel-Dumont had lapsed into contradiction by claiming that everything should be regarded as both extraneous and necessary. Faithful to

Quesnay's teaching, Baudeau retorted that luxury detracted from "productive advances" and was therefore "essentially bad."[130]

Butel-Dumont's position more closely approximated that of Turgot, who, as we have seen, also sought to expand the category of productive expenditure to include capital investment in industry and even finance. In *Valeurs et monnaies* (1769) Turgot foreshadowed Butel-Dumont's premise, which he attributed to Galiani: "the common measure of all value is man."[131] The *Théorie du luxe* elaborated a similar insight to dazzling effect. Value was at bottom a subjective category that emerged from the process of exchange. It followed that the economy itself, rather than land or another particular class of good, generated wealth in its totality. Seizing on this possibility, Butel-Dumont developed the gospel of *jouissance* far beyond what the Physiocrats countenanced. Fantasy counted as a legitimate economic factor that crossed the circuit of production and consumption. What one believed to possess value came to possess it in reality. A new economic theology, the religion of superfluity, summoned the faithful to worship desire as the genesis of historical development.

This creed transposed the formula of the Incarnation into the most literal terms imaginable: The Word must be made flesh. Butel-Dumont's methods reflected the preoccupation with semantics writ large in the *Encyclopédie* and in Enlightenment thought more generally.[132] Luxury had been promiscuous since its etymological conception. As Anoush Terjanian notes, Butel-Dumont traced the term's unacknowledged paternity from the Latin *luxus* (luxury) and its derivative *luxuria* (things that cause offense).[133] The distinction was maintained in French: *luxe* meant luxury, and *luxure* referred to lasciviousness. For Butel-Dumont, this slippage between economic and sexual "intemperance [*incontinence*]" provided the key to understanding the sentiments expressed by both words. "The sin of lust [*luxure*]," he remarked, "has its source in the superabundance of juices that one cannot contain." The "marked penchant for the pleasures of love" presumed excess, as did the desire to accumulate the pleasures of consumption.[134] The economy was libidinal through and through.

Butel-Dumont's foray into historical semantics was no diversion, a pleasure for pleasure's sake. Given the time and place in which the exercise was undertaken, it marked nothing less than the reductio ad absurdum of the Catholic ethic. Whereas churchmen tended to emphasize the threat posed by feminine profligacy, Butel-Dumont recalled that men at once suffered from and enjoyed their own surfeit of vital essences. In drawing such parallels, he directed economic theology's past toward new ends. Medieval spirituality often featured acts of bodily profusion: Mary lactated openly; Christ's blood pooled beneath the cross. The Council of Trent marked a shift to the more abstract formula of redeeming the debt of sin through the expenditure of Eucharistic currency. Corporeal metaphors gradually came to focus on consumption and circulation, processes that were invisible to the naked eye. The *Théorie du luxe* reversed this trend by equating *jouissance* with the satisfaction of conspicuously physical wants and needs. Likewise, the economic organism lived in a state of constant superfluity, necessitating the discharge of excess value.

Theologians Take Their Revenge

Butel-Dumont's boundless optimism notwithstanding, the hopes for Louis XVI's reign were soon dashed. Turgot found himself embattled almost from the outset. The liberalization of the grain trade set off what became known as the Flour War [*guerre des farines*]. Although the French economy performed admirably over the course of the eighteenth century, and agronomic improvement was a fixture on the royal agenda, women and men remained preoccupied with securing their daily bread. Turgot's reforms coincided with poor harvests. Outraged by high prices, disgruntled consumers ransacked bakeries and the granaries of wealthy farmers and merchants. Turgot stood his ground in the face of hundreds of riots during the spring of 1775. The king authorized the duc de Biron to quell the uprising.[135]

The force of arms could not silence opposition to Turgot in the parlements, the public sphere, or the halls of Versailles. He was also drawn into court intrigues with the queen and her favorites. Jean-Frédéric Phélypeaux, the comte de Maurepas, had paved the way for Turgot's rise in his role as chief adviser. He now did nothing to silence the rumors of treachery and dereliction that ultimately undermined the king's confidence. On May 12, 1776, wary of Turgot's imperious means of enacting reform and sympathetic to cries of injustice, Louis XVI removed him from his post. He would be replaced later in the year by the Genevan banker Jacques Necker, who steered the financial ship of state through crisis after crisis for the next four years.[136]

Turgot's departure signaled a pyrrhic victory for the clerical establishment, which loathed his philosophical spirit but could not have welcomed his Protestant successor. Nonetheless, the initial outcome likely heartened members of the Paris Faculty of Theology seeking revenge for Turgot's stance on usury, since the case in Angoulême was settled the same year that his ministry fell.[137] Indeed, the *Mémoire sur les prêts d'argent* attracted controversy long before its publication, with the abbé Prigent blaming Turgot's commodity theory of money for inspiring a new wave of works defending the legitimacy of interest. As he reminded readers in 1783, "theologians have a better memory and better knowledge than Monsieur Turgot would care to suppose." They understood that money could be employed in the purchase of "productive capital" but insisted that it nonetheless "had no germ of fecundity, either physical or moral." Real human labor, rather than some invisible force, generated profits from commercial enterprise. As for Turgot, "his metaphysics [was] not exact." In particular, the argument that interest represented the value of selling money for a specific duration—that is, the theory of time preference—struck Prigent as an exercise in "rarifying [*alambiquer*] ideas" for polemical effect.[138]

The theological backlash against Enlightenment political economy extended to the luxury debate, which showed no signs of abating despite the highly publicized interventions by Turgot and Butel-Dumont.[139] The best-selling *Histoire des deux Indes* reflected and refracted the eighteenth-century tropes related to commerce. Although the anticlerical tendencies of the former Jesuit Raynal ran through the text, his sentiments nonetheless resembled those of economic theologians such as Fénelon. Raynal and his collaborators denounced the church's stance on usury, which he deemed materially regressive, intellectually hypocritical, and socially prejudicial toward Jewish merchants. Yet they also praised Montesquieu for doing "honor to the Christian religion" by advocating the abolition of slavery, which, like Law's theological critic Lambert, struck them as a moral and spiritual aberration that blighted the colonial enterprise.[140]

Their position on luxury shifted over the course of the work's survey of European economic history in imperial context.[141] The early volumes depict material advancement as finding paradise on earth. Britain furnished a shining example of "a free, wealthy, magnanimous, and happy people." The possibility lurked, however, that "the enjoyment of the pleasures [*jouissances*] of luxury" might come to "entirely pervert national customs [*mœurs*]," that "the love of pleasure" would weaken the military, and that "the euphoria of momentary success" and "delusions of grandeur would make the nation susceptible to ventures greater than its forces."[142] Such dangers became ever present with the discovery of the New World, which unleashed the demons of avarice on a global scale. To procure labor for their conquests, Europeans had recourse to slavery, the horrors of which the *Histoire* recounted in gruesome detail: "immense countries invaded and devasted, their innocent and peaceful inhabitants either massacred or laden with chains." The "commerce in men bought and sold by men" had no justification. Raynal implored readers to "renounce a trade that has only injustice as its foundation and luxury as its object."[143] He also criticized what he viewed as antisocial priestly practices, especially the vows of celibacy and poverty, yet he alluded to Fénelon's *Télémaque* as the antidote to poisoned luxury. The "tender pastor of Cambrai" wrote "not for solitary men" such as Rousseau, "who flee from the evils and vices of the world," but for "happy families who intone [*chanter*] the magnificence of God on earth like the stars announce it in the heavens."[144]

Whereas Raynal and Diderot stressed the effects of colonization, French clerics tended to emphasize the extent to which luxury enslaved Europeans themselves. It was as if the fear of creolization, whereby the colonists fell prey to the temptations of African and Native American flesh, had followed Europeans back to the metropole.[145] For instance, the abbé Louis Genty, a doctor of theology and perpetual vice-secretary of the Royal Society of Agriculture in Orléans, submitted an essay for the eloquence competition sponsored by the Academy of Besançon in 1783 on the subject of luxury. The Academy posed a perennial but admittedly leading question on whether "luxury destroys customs and empires." Genty's piece might not have struck the requisite literary tone, but it made up in moral fervor for what it lacked in style. According to the abbé, luxury lends "new energy to the causes that give rise to it" until it completely degrades "the physical and moral constitution of the state."[146]

Like his clerical predecessors, Genty delved into the psychic and social aspects of consumption. He understood luxury as a sign that did not merely reflect decline but also occasioned it, "thereby establishing a continual chain of causes and effects." The quest for superfluity led workers to abandon their fields for "perfectly sterile" expenditures and pernicious debt. Meanwhile, "capitalists ... devise a million artifices to foment this disordered agitation," using money "like a treacherous lover to attract all wealth." Eventually, even the king himself would fall under their spell. These dangers impressed on Genty a truth that Turgot and Butel-Dumont acknowledged and that Marx and Engels later enshrined in *The German Ideology*: "the depraved imagination invents without ceasing new means to enjoy every caprice that transforms itself into needs," leaving only "self-love" and "the vilest self-interest." Ultimately, "there will be nothing respectable or sacred," and "religion will become the object of most bitter irony."[147]

These sentiments permeate the two volumes of the abbé François-André-Adrien Pluquet's *Traité philosophique et politique sur le luxe* (1786). Evincing a vast knowledge of his subject, he charted the theme of luxury in the works of Mandeville, Melon, Montesquieu, Hume, and Helvétius. These philosophers redefined the term as everything beyond subsistence without distinguishing between edifying and destructive ends. Pluquet grumbled that "nothing is more uncertain or more difficult to determine than that which is absolutely necessary to exist." What humans regard as indispensable has changed over time and depends in the present on one's station. The signification of luxury advanced in the *Encyclopédie*, "the usage that one makes of his wealth to obtain a pleasing existence," proved no more illuminating, since it applied equally to all manner of diversions.[148]

Pluquet sought to launch a new line of inquiry founded on the "nature" of things, which required approaching man "in the greatest simplicity" and in a state ruled by "primitive needs." Only then could one trace the evolution "in the use he makes of his faculties and in the progress of his resources to meet his needs." At the end of a long process of historical development, humans had reached a relative "state of abundance" in which luxury became possible.[149] In other words, Pluquet effectively repeated the thought experiment undertaken by Rousseau in the *Second Discourse* without citing the Genevan *philosophe* by name. According to the *Traité*, early humans lived neither in an Edenic paradise nor under conditions of simple self-sufficiency but rather with relentless suffering. Torment forged a being with a mind for technological ingenuity and a heart for sociability. Despite countless hardships, "the love of life, the desire for happiness, [and] knowledge of the strength and industry that he discovered in himself sustained and animated him." The faculty of reason directed these impulses not only in agriculture and animal husbandry but also in strengthening familial bonds. Like Locke and Rousseau before him, Pluquet idealized this stage, defined by "conjugal love," as the happiest epoch of the species.[150]

Yet even when "man enjoyed all that was necessary for life," his anguish persisted, driving him to "seek means against difficulties that seemed to arise from abundance and security themselves." Stultified by "boredom" and "apathy," unsettled more than satisfied by "the exercise of social virtues," humans turned to "a host of arts and sciences all related to the pleasures of the senses." Luxury thrived in a state of insatiability. Humans hope not only "to be happy, but to be always happy." The satisfaction of one need led to the desire for yet another to be satisfied. At this point Pluquet's analysis converges with Rousseau's and anticipates that of Marx. The possession of agreeable things became a means of ensnaring the government and governed alike in a web of dependence. Approximating Turgot's theory of subjective value, Pluquet recognized that luxury was less an objective state than "a moral principle that only exists in the heart of man." The principle operated by the imposition of "*excess*," or "rendering necessary to happiness what nature had not made necessary." But since the pleasures garnered from physical objects lasted only an instant, the "man of luxury" manipulated these sensations again and again, gradually undermining the capacity to experience satisfaction and the "religious respect for virtuous men."[151]

Luxury disturbed the "animal economy" of the first humans along with the spiritual economy established by faith. It also deprived governments of the means of combating such ills. Subjects motivated by superfluity neglected "the needs of the indigent" and ruthlessly exploited them out of greed. Pluquet stressed that luxury stood in moral opposition to religion and its values of "frugality, sobriety, temperance, [and] charity." Traders exported reserves that might otherwise support poor relief. Nonetheless, the church held firm as the last bastion of benevolence, even if certain "religious houses or societies" had fallen prey to the immorality of the age.[152]

Pluquet rejected Butel-Dumont's vision that superfluity led to prosperity. To this extent, the *Traité* retraced the narrative of the *Second Discourse*. Luxury subverted both the material and moral means of providing for the vast majority of subjects. Policy could not compensate for such a loss. The purpose of the body politic was to assure that "members enjoy the possession of things necessary for their subsistence" and that "they procure them reciprocally through the combination of their enlightenment [*lumières*], their cares, and their industry." These efforts depended on "political customs" and the "constant practice of social virtues."[153] Civil penalties alone could not sustain the Christian spirit of the laws. Since Aristotle, philosophers had preached the "utility" of religion for the maintenance of the political order. In contrast, luxury destroyed the bases for faith. Pluquet held that, at a minimum, religion taught respect for a "Supreme Being who created and governs the world" and "prepares rewards for virtuous men." He lauded Catholicism in particular for its commitment to reason, generosity, and mutual obligation. The church taught that believers would be "rewarded after their death with an eternal happiness" and fortified them "through the prayers and sacrifices that it offers." It offered a bulwark against rapacious sovereigns who, desperate for funds, raided the possessions of their subjects through forced loans. In Europe, as in the Americas, "the progress of luxury was inclined toward slavery."[154]

According to the laws of Catholic economic theology, the afterlife promised *jouissance* without end. Unlike brutal need, the desire for celestial recompense could be extended infinitely. This ideal served a regulative function even in Pluquet's schema, which, while avowedly religious, did not make frequent allusions to the sacraments or the mysteries of revealed religion. According to the *Traité*, luxury perverted the motivation for self-improvement at every turn. Humans might ceaselessly invent new physical needs and ways of fulfilling them, but they could not reproduce the everlasting splendors of heaven. Acknowledging the disparity between the City of God and the City of Man, Pluquet mapped a utilitarian theory of government in which the political, the economic, and the moral were part of a complex whole that changed dramatically over time. Luxury was at once a sin and a social evil. The wanton pursuit of wealth by the few kept prosperity out of reach for the vast majority. Expanding upon the themes of Genty's essay, Pluquet's rejoinder to apologists of luxury asserted a fully realized vision of Christian political economy that could dispense with dogma and scripture to defend religion on historical-materialist grounds.

. . .

Successive movements in the political economy of the Enlightenment emerged from the shadows cast by the idol of luxury. *Philosophes* and *économistes* contorted themselves to demarcate the threshold separating productive, patriotic wealth from wasteful, self-destructive profligacy. In so doing, they maintained the oppositions that structured Catholic economic theology—between masculine and feminine desires and, perhaps more crucially, between otherworldly and worldly goods. In his idiosyncratic way Rousseau revealed the contradictions of this system by generalizing its effects. Society debilitated the rich while oppressing the poor. Manufactured possessions turned on their owners, reducing them to a state of tyrannical homogeneity. *Du contrat social* sought redemption in the transformative powers of a quasi-divine legislator. God himself would reveal a new economic theology. The Physiocrats and Turgot shared Rousseau's belief in the primacy of agriculture and the virtues of *jouissance*, while subordinating political will to the order of nature. When Butel-Dumont declared the novelties of the present to be the necessities of the future, he realized the deepest fears of ecclesiastical critics who denounced the religion of superfluity as an affront to God.

Taken together, the works of theologians such as Caussin, Genty, and Pluquet tell the secret history of what Marx called the fetishism of commodities. Its first theorists situated luxury within a sacred structure of beings and things. The *philosophes* repeatedly modified this hierarchy in a desperate attempt to isolate the variable that evinced true wealth. Ultimately, the material economy itself became the object of a fetish, a seemingly infinite field that, no less than the spiritual economy, represented invisible processes of value creation. Money begat money. Growth induced further growth. New commodities imprinted not only new needs but also new rationalizations on the mind. As Terrasson asserted at the height of Law's System, and as Quesnay and Turgot confirmed during the struggle to liberalize the grain trade, the acceptance of economic knowledge required more than empirical verification and mathematical demonstration. It also demanded belief.

EPILOGUE

Encounters with Economic Theology

THE CLASSICIST, ethnographer, linguist, and scholar of comparative religion Charles de Brosses developed a global theory of fetishism to account for the worship of "animals" and "inanimate beings that one deifies." As he specified in *Du culte des dieux fétiches* (1760), these objects do not qualify as gods per se; rather, what matters is that they are "things endowed with a divine virtue." De Brosses noted that the term *fetish* originated in the lexicon of European merchants in West Africa, who employed the Portuguese *fetisso* to signify a "*mythical* [fée], enchanted, divine thing*, or one that *delivers oracles*." Europeans were not necessarily immune to such charms. De Brosses related the story of the indigenous Taíno people of Cuba who, on realizing that gold was the "Spaniards' Fetish," set about appeasing this divinity.[1] Having surveyed cases among Africans, Native Americans, and other "savage peoples," he distinguished "idolatry vulgarly speaking," which more accurately characterized "works of art representing other objects to which the adoration was really addressed," from fetishistic practices that exalted "living animals or vegetables themselves" in an unmediated manner.[2]

According to de Brosses, all subsequent developments in the history of religion involved wrapping the mantle of allegory and regularized ritual around an originally spontaneous impulse. What he referred to as "figurism"—shrouding unseemly origins in formal doctrines and founding myths—was still "a vast field, fertile in explanations." Even enlightened souls could not deny the "long-standing credit it has enjoyed for so many centuries." De Brosses ascribed the veneration of the Kaaba to the fetishization of stones despite the professed commitment of Muslims to monotheism. Ultimately, "one is not obliged to give a reason for a thing where there is none" except the "fear and madness to which the human mind is susceptible."[3] By this standard, Bernard and Picart were profoundly mistaken in positing a pure religion of the spirit that had been corrupted by superstition. The fetish was the sine qua non of faith.

Although de Brosses did not subject Christianity to the same unflinching treatment applied to Islam, the teachings of Jesus of Nazareth were guilty by association.[4] Yet his twin insights—that the fetish was deeply rooted in the past and that it persisted as the hidden essence of religion proper—have clear applications for this book, which similarly traces the interpenetration of two fields often kept distinct: the material and the spiritual. One wonders what de Brosses made of the Eucharist, a ritual that depended on a form of re-presentation at once immediately corporeal and impossibly ethereal. Transubstantiation was no allegory; rather, it actually generated the body of Christ ad infinitum under the sensible qualities of bread. The host exhibited a peculiar power in that it was conjured by humans without being bound by the productive limits of physical labor. Protestant critics inveighed against African religions and the Roman faith for trucking in superstition, whereas Catholic theologians zealously guarded the threshold between legitimate devotion and the worship of idols.[5]

The historical analyses pursued here come full circle when de Brosses is read alongside indictments of Catholic fetishism by Chastain, Thiers, Bernard and Picart, and Voltaire. Even the specific vocabulary of fetishism owed its origins to the work of Catholic traders, who hawked not only worldly merchandise but also devotional objects. De Brosses charged latter-day figurists with willfully forgetting the origins of their beliefs.[6] Such repression was not yet possible in France during the long eighteenth century, when the church dominated public finance through its ideological policing of usury and luxury. As we have seen, the convergences of the economic and the theological have a much richer and more incredible history than even de Brosses recognized.

In the wake of the Reformations, the Catholic Church renewed its efforts to legitimize the sacraments, a mode of production aimed at overcoming the debt of sin with a profusion of grace. The host, banal in its physical composition but miraculous in its effects, promised redemption and fulfillment to believers who partook of it. Heeding the call of popes and local bishops, thousands of men and women joined confraternities during the seventeenth and eighteenth centuries for the perpetual adoration of the Eucharist and the saying of the Rosary. Devotional manuals offered concrete instructions on how to found and fund sodalities, on how to petition God for temporal wealth without compromising one's heavenly reward, and on the means of deploying this wealth in luxury spending and the granting of alms. Earthly delights became a foretaste of pleasures to come. That is not to say that the Catholic ethic rejected sacrifice; on the contrary, its spiritual capital drew on the suffering of Christ and the saints. Yet it approached transitory loss not as a good in itself but rather as one of a litany of exchanges that surpassed all limits, including mortality itself.

The sacramental economy elaborated by the Council of Trent and its ecclesiastical vanguard in France was vehemently contested. The embrace of *jouissance* in spiritual matters posed the problem of identifying the most efficacious means of designating and distributing sources of value. Economic theology emerged as a codified but disputed body of knowledge for fulfilling this task along a range of fronts. The ensuing ideological divisions cannot be reduced to competition between Jansenists and Jesuits. Even Arnauld's qualms about excessively frequent communion stemmed from the need to prepare for the sheer abundance embodied in the Eucharist. Thiers denounced the excesses of indulgences, but he was no Jansenist, much less a Protestant. Neither Terrasson nor Turgot, for all their theological training, aligned themselves with a single doctrinal school. Disciples of Port-Royal stood on both sides of the usury debate. Jesuits like Gourdan caught themselves succumbing to spiritual sensuality before recalling that the soul should ruminate on its divine source, even if colleagues like Pichon showed less circumspection. It was a matter of calibrating the relationship between spiritual and physical goods but always with an eye to the essential superfluity of both.

This book has studied the economic elements of theology and the theological vestiges in economics to recover the contingent combinations that have punctuated their joint history during disputes over the nature of wealth. Terrasson attempted to habituate the French public to Law's System by grounding it in a Eucharistic-alchemical complex. Opponents of the regent's fiscal experiments struck back through parodies that nonetheless confirmed the very relationship they aimed to deride: the intersections of theological and economic life. The same could be said for Bernard and Picart and, perhaps, for the Protestant critique more generally. At the end of the eighteenth century, thinkers like Genty and Pluquet refined traditional condemnations of excessive self-display, especially by women, as a means of challenging Enlightenment political economy on the basis of its own utilitarian ideals.

The decades-long debates over usury and luxury offer a critical mass of evidence for the role played by economic theologians throughout the Old Regime and beyond. Ecclesiastical reflections on the fecundity of money and the idolatry of luxury established the parameters of how the material economy was understood. Given the church's immense wealth, it could not refrain from intervening in public and private finance. Terrasson was an abbé. Quesnay, although no orthodox Catholic, organized Physiocracy along sectarian lines. He defended alms-giving and, more significantly, made *jouissance* the watchword of material development. Following his mentor Fénelon, Rousseau showed how political economy was indebted to religious verities, even if he himself preferred a distant, deist god to its Christian counterpart.

It is no coincidence that the century's single most powerful economic thinker, Turgot, also intervened in many of the subjects addressed in this book, from frequent communion to Law's banknotes. He was even a devoted reader of de Brosses.[7] Although Turgot denounced Terrasson for dabbling in alchemical wish-fulfillment, he outlined a theory of capital accumulation that defied Scholastic prohibitions while maintaining a claim to orthodoxy. He and his contemporaries resacralized the economy by endowing it with a generative capacity that was physically certain and divinely sanctioned. Even if enlightened policy had liberated the mode of production from the strictures of the traditional social order, consumption was still embedded in the gendered logic of the fetish.

The history of economic theology in no way ended with the fall of Turgot's ministry and the rejoinders of clerics such as Genty and Pluquet. The "Catholic question" resonated in wider conflicts over the sacrality of property and the nature of sovereign authority. The French Revolution of 1789 left a divided legacy for liberals and socialists, both of whom drew on religious antecedents in devising their respective platforms. Remnants of the Catholic ethic have also lived on as a spectral form of knowledge that haunts the modern social sciences. The writings of Marx and Benjamin are most suggestive in this regard. My concluding observations thus seek to historicize their critiques of capitalism by situating them in a current of spiritual polemic that runs from the early modern period to the present. Despite frequent pronouncements of God's impending demise, images of celestial splendor still turn profits on the global luxury market. Likewise, the fashion industry perpetuates the fantasy that signposts of wealth can exceed the limits of the mundane.

Revolutionary Economic Theology: Marx and Benjamin

Marx's indebtedness to religious thought has long preoccupied his followers, critics, and commentators.[8] As for Marx himself, in the manuscript *Contribution to the Critique of Hegel's Philosophy of Law* (1843), he defined "the criticism of religion" as "the premise of all criticism," or more poetically, as "*in embryo the criticism of the vale of tears*, the *halo* of which is religion."[9] These pronouncements of the young Marx carry through to the first volume of *Capital* (1867), a work at once thoroughly disenchanted and teeming with supernatural imagery. My brief foray into his writings will emphasize his use of Catholic metaphors in accounting for the dual fetish of commodities and money. This nexus foregrounds the persistence of theological polemic in grasping the mysterious nature of the modern economy. I will then briefly touch on Walter Benjamin's engagements with economic theology, which drew out the ways in which historical materialism belonged to a longer religious history that could be mobilized for both critical and potentially redemptive ends.

If, as Marx asserted, capitalism "converts every product into a social hieroglyphic," critique tore back the veil of ideological obfuscation that shrouded classical political economy. He insinuated that the necessary theological resources could not be gleaned from Protestantism; its "*cultus* of abstract man" rendered the tradition useless for such a task.[10] He thus gestured toward what this book has called Catholic economic theology, practitioners of which speculated on the very possibility that their Protestant opponents rejected time and again: the power of things to transmit value. It is well known that de Brosses's work figured among the sources for Marx's theory of the commodity fetish.[11] What is less understood is the extent to which Marx intervened in enduring disputes between Catholics and Protestants on active versus passive modes of representation and on the role of human labor in the spiritual economy. Viewed through the lens of the Catholic ethic, the religious genealogy of Marx's pronouncements becomes abundantly apparent.

Take as a preliminary example the signal distinction between use value and exchange value featured in the first volume of *Capital*. Whereas the utility of an object stemmed from the exertions of actual men and women, the "unsubstantial reality" of commodities was held together by a "congelation of homogeneous human labor power" measured in terms of "weeks, days, and hours."[12] What was a printed pardon, if not a mass-produced guarantee of mercy acquired through the sacrifice of saints, a bottomless well of spiritual fortune that the church distributed at will? As we have seen, indulgences could inhere both in persons and things. Their exchangeability was a matter of common devotional practice. Commodities would thus seem to share a "two-fold character" with objects of piety: they are banal goods that serve as "depositories of value."[13]

As if exorcizing the commodity form like a demon, Marx adopted theological formulas in describing the allure of goods made for profit. Unsatisfied with the assertion of the equivalence between goods traded in the marketplace, *Capital* took linen as representative of the secret workings of value, which makes a thing "materially different" from itself but also gives it "something common" with every other commodity. To express this alienating yet productive doubling, Marx highlighted the change undertaken by the linen used to fashion a garment. Its value comes from "equality with the coat, just as the sheep's nature of a Christian is shown in his resemblance to the Lamb of God." The statement's bracing irony recalls Picart's staid depiction of the Agnus Dei, which contrasted the manufactured quality of the wax with its power to defend against physical threats in this world and secure salvation in the next. Yet Marx eschewed Protestant iconoclasm for a symptomatically Catholic reading that aimed to apprehend (and criticize) the "sublime reality" of the commodity. As he remarked in an aside, quoting Henri IV, "Paris vaut bien une messe." Inert matter had the potential to become "the visible incarnation, the social chrysalis state of every kind of human labor."[14] This property, which Marx defined as exchange value, is the point of departure for *Capital*, which uses religious language to articulate the commodity's enigmatic nature.

Fetishism bestows on commonplace things the potential to transfix producers and consumers alike. The history of economic theology is also a history of such metamorphoses. At certain moments Marx explained away the fetishized commodity in terms of alienation, "because in it the social character of men's labor appears to them as an objective character stamped upon the product of that labor." Yet he specified that the correct "analogy" for commodification led one to "the mist-enveloped regions of the religious world," where "the productions of the human brain appear as independent beings endowed with life."[15] Marx divorced Catholic economic theology from its divine authorization, yet its logic shines through clearly in his critique of capitalism. Like the Eucharist, the sacrament that served as the general equivalent of the others, the commodity represents value in both a rarefied and physically immediate sense. "This is my body," Marx would have it proclaim to those seeking redemption through its charms.

Marx knew from reading Hegel that theologians had long acknowledged the Eucharistic character of money.[16] His breakthrough was to realize that commodified financial currencies had at last inscribed such associations into the heart of economic reality. As we saw in Chapter 3, Hume likened credit to transubstantiation. Marx extended this metaphor in comments on James Mill from 1844, where he spelled out the theological, even Christological, resonances of money. On the one hand, it works as an "*alien mediator*" of relations within and among men. On the other, it also functions like "a *real God*, for the mediator is the *real power* over what it mediates to me. Its cult becomes an end in itself." Just as Christ is "*alienated* God and alienated *man*," and just as "man has value only insofar as he represents Christ," economic actors are in a position of absolute dependence on their mediator or redeemer. Here re-presentation operated not merely as a passive reflection but rather as the active, material projection of value. Marx ridiculed "modern economists" for harboring a misguided faith in their own formulas, which merely "substituted refined superstition for crude superstition" without seeing that such an enterprise could never be complete. The "sensuous form" persisted despite all efforts to rationalize it away.[17]

In a move evocative of de Brosses's critique of religion as a figurist abstraction from fetishism, Marx took this sensuous form as the key to commodity-money. The first volume of *Capital* grounds the discussion of the universal equivalent in allusions to its seemingly supernatural properties. Gold rose to preeminence because in this medium commodities found "their own value already completely represented. . . . Hence the magic of money." Nonetheless, the presumably natural identification of gold with money required a profound metamorphosis. To become exchange value, the commodity "must quit its bodily shape, must transform itself from mere imaginary into real gold, although to the commodity such transubstantiation may be more difficult" than Saint Jerome's struggles when "putting off of the old Adam." The passage inundates the reader with a flood of analogies ranging from transmutation and transubstantiation to the conversion of the soul (that is, Marx's reference to Jerome's "Letter to Eustochius," in which God has the saint reject both physical and spiritual temptation).[18] Such wrenching changes require feats of supernatural prowess and yet present themselves under capitalism as quotidian miracles. In the act of monetization, "commodities strip off every trace of their natural use value . . . to transform themselves into the uniform, socially recognized incarnation of homogeneous human labor." Currency needs a state-sanctioned, socially acceptable, and tangible substance, which perhaps explains why Marx distanced himself from Law's dream of species-free banknotes. Indeed, "only in so far as paper money represents gold" could it be considered "a symbol of value."[19]

Precious metals perform the mystery of commodification owing to the fundamental illegibility of the commodity itself, which allows the mind to fantasize about the untold marvels occurring beneath their surfaces. "Modern society," Marx declared, "greets gold as its Holy Grail, as the glittering incarnation of the very principle of its own life." The sale of commodities with the aim of gaining surplus value aspires not merely to reproduction but to "automatic expansion," an "occult quality of being able to add value to itself. It brings forth living offspring, or, at the least, lays golden eggs."[20] The objective of infinite growth—which in the eighteenth century took the form of a Eucharistic-alchemical complex and a gendered obsession with fecundity—found its nineteenth-century embodiment in the fetish.

Marx implied that as capitalism became ever more reified, the principles of economic theology did not withdraw into the background. The situation was quite the reverse, in that the ideals of perfectly expanding plenitude and desire became even more pronounced. Capital claimed for itself a power to which the church had only aspired. For all its generative capacity and miraculous agency, the Eucharist required intercession at multiple points: a merciful God, the sacrifice of Christ, consecration by the priest, communion on the part of the believer. The archetypical economic fetishist seized what the Christian expected in heaven and brought it crashing down to earth. Severed from all traditional moorings, everything took on the appearance of a worldly paradise.

Marx clarified the confessional distinctions to which he alluded in the subsequent volumes of *Capital*. "The monetary system," he observed, "is essentially a Catholic institution, the credit system essentially Protestant." Without referring to Hume, he ultimately judged the system as a whole to be indebted to its religious origins: "The credit system does not emancipate itself from the basis of the monetary system any more than Protestantism emancipated itself from the foundations of Catholicism."[21] In *Theories of Surplus Value* (1862–63) Marx made the affinities between Roman dogma and capitalist faith even more overt by referring to revenue as "the *most fetishistic* expression of the relations of capitalist production." More specifically, interest-bearing capital activates the superlative fetish because it is based on "a kind of fiction without fantasy": "money which creates more money." This "*automatic fetish*," or the "self-valorizing value" of "money-making money," occurs without mediation and is "consummated as a relation of things (money, commodities) to themselves."[22]

Fully realized fetishism abandons all pretense to natural productivity. In Marx's view, Quesnay, Turgot, and other theorists of "'enlightened' political economy" tended to "superstitiously confuse use value with exchange value" on the grounds that "land is productive (of use value) and is itself a living productive force." Now, Marx claims, the situation is qualitatively different. No longer occupied with "a relation which is alien to capital" (that is, with land), the "capitalist is impregnated with interest" as in a virgin birth. The alienation of value from its origins in human labor reaches its final stage. One passes from "the simple mystification of commodities" to the "the more complicated mystification of money. The transubstantiation, the fetishism, is complete."[23]

Marx grasped not merely the economic order's dependence on groundless faith but also its specifically Catholic antecedents. If, as I argued in Chapter 5, devotional goods were a privileged agent of the consumer revolution, the reason should now be apparent. Used as intended, objects of piety retained only the faintest suggestion of mundane functionality. Their power stemmed from a series of exchanges related to the redemption of sin and the promise of self-perpetuating *jouissance*. *Theories of Surplus Value* reminds us that such aspirations did not merely dissolve into the ether but went on to infuse capitalist fetishism. To return to a claim made in this book's opening pages: religion's mystification of the economy also reveals a key for demystifying its effects on and through human desire.

In "Capitalism as Religion" (1921), Marx's heterodox disciple Walter Benjamin reflected on the connections I have advanced between the sacramental and material economies of the early modern period. To his mind, capitalism made it impossible to distinguish God and Mammon. Everything becomes subsumed in "an enormous feeling of guilt not itself knowing how to repent." Breaking with Weber, on whose thesis he clearly drew, Benjamin concluded that "capitalism itself developed parasitically on Christianity in the West—not in Calvinism alone, but also, as must be shown, in the remaining orthodox Christian movements."[24] The preceding chapters make a similar case for French Catholicism—that its Eucharistic devotions, market for indulgences, attachment to devotional objects, and formal political-economic musings on usury and luxury sought a way of converting the debt of sin into a source of wealth.

Following in Marx's footsteps, Benjamin explored the allure of the commodity as a means of both damnation and potential salvation.[25] The unfinished *Arcades Project* (1927–40) leads the reader through the glass-covered passages that served as sanctuaries of luxury consumption in nineteenth-century Paris. For Benjamin, they furnished the architectural quintessence of a life organized around the exigencies of commodification. Likewise, the World Exhibitions "are places of pilgrimage to the commodity fetish" where "use value becomes secondary," and even those without the means to buy "are imbued with the exchange value of commodities to the point of identifying with it." Mesmerized by the "phantasmagoria," the "individual abandons himself in the framework of the entertainment industry." Quoting *Capital*, Benjamin notes the "'theological niceties' of the commodity," attributes that he identified with the "*spécialités*" of the "luxury industries." Devotion now takes the form of fashion, which "couples the living body to the inorganic world."[26]

With the advent of fetishism, worship loses its original power insofar as the worshippers themselves are simultaneously called to and estranged from the objects of their desire.[27] Protestant critics such as Bernard and Picart had argued, along similar lines, that vulgar economization would delegitimize Catholic spirituality in the eyes of more enlightened souls. This was not yet the case in the eighteenth century. For thousands of men and women, the holy and the profane still stood in productive opposition, with each realm reinforcing the value of the other. Benjamin likewise preserved some measure of wonder in an otherwise disenchanted world. Following the poet Charles Baudelaire's example, he showed a willingness to reckon with the fate of Catholicism in modern life.

Whereas members of Rosary confraternities emulated the perfect life of the Virgin Mary, a woman born of immaculate conception, the economic fetishist "succumbs to the sex appeal of the inorganic."[28] In "The Paris of the Second Empire in Baudelaire" (1938), the spectacles of capital have their natural devotee in the *flâneur* who liberally consumes narcotics to gauge the effect of the most potent opium of the masses—that is, merchandise for sale. Like an object of piety, the "commodity-soul" is the "most emphatic ever encountered in the realm of souls, for it would be bound to see every individual as a buyer in whose hand and house it wants to nestle." The *flâneur*'s very existence merges with that of the commodity: "Like those roving souls in search of a body, he enters another person whenever he wishes." Commodities seek euphoria in the crowds that swarm to gaze on and be near them, what Baudelaire termed "the religious intoxication of great cities." However, the experience was not one of glorious elevation but sordid decay, reduced to ever further abasement in the "prostitution of the commodity's soul."[29] The state of gratification extolled by eighteenth-century economic theologians followed from Eucharistic materiality, which transcended the known limits of the human body. The commodity-form, in all its ghostly splendor, offered a hollowed-out, staggering ecstasy that needed constant infusions to be sustained.

Far more than Marx, Benjamin was attentive to the gendered aspects of commodification; in this way his work hearkens back to seventeenth- and eighteenth-century theologians who condemned the vanity of women as a form of idolatry. Yet he also turned such criticisms on their head. In place of the saintly mother and the sacred body of her son, Benjamin portrayed in *Central Park* (1938–39) the correspondences between the proletarian and the prostitute.[30] "Prostitution opens up the possibility of a mythical communion with the masses," he observed, but also "the possibility of surviving in a world in which the objects of our most intimate use have increasingly become mass-produced." Even as the commodity "celebrates its incarnation in the whore," hope endures in Baudelaire's use of allegory "to humanize the commodity heroically," despite the thoroughly dehumanizing processes from which it arose.[31] Adapting the Baroque semiotics mastered by Richeome to a fallen age, Baudelaire worshipped at the feet of the commodity. In place of the timeless abundance of heaven, a flood of impressions threatened to make a martyr of the poet while salvaging a kernel of true sensation from jaded superfluity.[32] "Can motifs of redemption be found specifically in fashion?" Benjamin asked. This ray of hope was immediately dimmed by the stipulation that such an outcome would entail unspeakable suffering: "redemption depends on the tiny fissure in the continuous catastrophe."[33]

Via Marx's historical materialism and Baudelaire's poetry, Benjamin confronted commodification as both a fate to lament and an opportunity to seize. In "Capitalism as Religion," he wondered if the sense of guilt pervading the economic and cultural orders might become "to God himself" unbearable enough "to finally interest him in repentance." Only when "religion is no longer the reform of being, [but] rather its obliteration," he answered cryptically, does one see that "healing is expected." Fully implicated in "the fate of man," a formerly transcendent God falls to earth, albeit as the "immature deity" of the capitalist creed.[34]

Benjamin made no secret of his ambivalence toward transcendent ends, noting that *The Arcades Project* could be read from two temporal standpoints. The first leads from the glimmering passages of the French capital in the nineteenth century to an all-consuming sense of despair in the twentieth. The second, however, aims "to have the revolutionary potential of these 'precursors' explode into the present."[35] How might one take the desires on which capitalism feeds and direct them to other ends? Given the radical nature of historical time, perhaps the "eccentric, revolutionary, and surrealist possibilities" of fashion offered the prospect of converting fetishism from within. Or, as Benjamin also put it in his reflections on truth's ragged appearance in the ephemera of everyday life, "the eternal is in any case far more the ruffles on a dress than some idea."[36]

The Arcades Project and the essays on Baudelaire could be seen as experiments in materialist resacralization. Benjamin's atheism did not keep him from drawing on religious methods and sources. His hermeneutic abjured positivism in favor of allegory. His ultimate horizon was apocalyptic reckoning rather than gradual progress.[37] As he himself put the matter, "My thinking is related to theology as blotting pad is related to ink. It is saturated with it. Were one to go by the blotter, however, nothing of what is written would remain."[38] This confession by way of paradox does not ring true in a literal sense. Benjamin could deny being a theologian only by engaging in theology—and, more precisely, economic theology. His work returns to a structuring principle of the early modern luxury debate, the profligacy of women. But it also suggests that, once brought to its most extreme conclusions, the principle could be turned against itself. Enchantment might redeem alienation.

The Catholic Ethic, after a Fashion

Looking back on the eighteenth century from Benjamin's day, one finds arresting descriptions of Paris in a satirical work from 1766 entitled *L'enthousiasme français*. Its author, the lawyer and royal censor Jean-Henri Marchand, was known in his lifetime as an obsessive if reproachful imitator of Voltaire.[39] From his residence in the Marais, he looked with bemusement on the "the activity of a crowd of citizens who daily see themselves without having anything to say of themselves." Jansenists and Jesuits battled in "immense volumes" to the point that "the principal object finds itself nearly obliterated." More practical minds set about creating automata that sold briskly for enormous sums, so that "luxury itself is introduced among these incredible figures." Eventually, however, even this fashion would be replaced by yet another in the spectacle of urban life. Anticipating Baudelaire's *flâneur*, the author wrote of boulevards "filled daily with the curious," who would stop to watch scenes encountered many times before. Self-professed economic thinkers turned heads with their intricate plans. So many systems abounded that "all of France seems to have become a financier." Yet the author defended those who profited from their schemes for disbursing wealth "from hand to hand." Fads came and went interchangeably—Romanian tables, Chinese cabinets, English gardens. There was no end to the cycle, since "when we have exhausted one genre of enthusiasm, we rest in the hope of soon seeing another spring up again."[40]

Tellingly, Marchand saw fit to explain the rage for novelties as an expressly French trait. The choice of title for his work was all the more apt since enthusiasm, like fetishism, carried strong religious connotations.[41] True to form, both church and state in France evinced devotion to a particular vision of commerce. The regimes that succeeded the tumultuous Revolutionary decade—the Restoration (1814–30), the July Monarchy (1830–48), the Second Republic (1848–51), the Second Empire (1851–70), and the Third Republic (1870–1940)—gradually developed an economic policy blending liberalism and paternalism in what David Todd terms "the protection of 'national labour.'" This ideology of industrialization with a human face employed Catholic social thought to shore up the belief that economic vitality need not come at the cost of mass pauperism and self-denial associated with unrestricted free trade.[42]

If France diverged somewhat from Britain in embracing the doctrines of laissez-faire, it showed a truly enterprising spirit in promoting Catholicism through the most fashionable means available. In 1858, the Virgin Mary appeared in a grotto to an unassuming young woman from the Pyrenees, Bernadette Soubirous. The local bishop, Bertrand-Sévère Laurence, commissioned the construction of a basilica and directed a religious order, the Assumptionists, to organize pilgrimages. By 1900, Lourdes emerged as a shrine not only to the Mother of God but also to consumer culture. The town drew hundreds of thousands of visitors, especially women who traveled by rail for miraculous cures and left with souvenirs such as statues, rosaries, postcards, and pastilles containing local water, all manufactured on an industrial scale.[43] As Suzanne Kaufman argues, mass marketing bolstered religious fervor in an age of mechanical reproduction. Put another way, economic theology, with its veneration of devotional objects, bestowed a sacred aura on the memorabilia sold in Lourdes' Grands Magasins des Galeries Catholiques.[44] The exchange of instruments of piety confirmed the spiritual as well as monetary value inherent in the accumulation and circulation of goods. Yet it also had the potential of cheapening such transactions through vulgarization—or, in Marx's terminology, of imperiling an object's "sublime reality as value."[45]

Émile Zola dramatized the secular analogue to religious commerce in *Au bonheur des dames* (1883), a novel that couples a meticulous eye for naturalism with passages portraying the department store as a cathedral dedicated to shopping. Economic statistics bear out Zola's approach: estimates of French income and production growth per head—1.3 and 1.1 percent, respectively—remained competitive with those of Britain for much of the nineteenth century.[46] Preparatory studies led the novelist to the Bon Marché in Paris, a renowned emporium assembling a cornucopia of goods and services under one exquisitely domed roof. The concentrated labor of hundreds of professional purchasers, saleswomen, cash register clerks, and deliverymen made the store a veritable factory of consumption with a seemingly endless parade of wares.[47]

The Bon Marché's fortunes depended on stoking the fantasies of those who passed through its doors, so much so that the edifice itself became a tradable image in the form of postcards and stationery.[48] The power of signs to project their signifiers, a hallmark of the Catholic ethic, was also indispensable to modern consumerism. Zola's shoppers, mainly women, lose themselves in a bourgeois hall of mirrors bathed in light and stocked with products that come alive before their gaze: makeup, perfume, gloves, umbrellas, hats, and gowns of satin, velvet, and lace. The fictional impresario Octave Mouret expresses self-satisfied awe at founding "a new religion" whereby "churches ... were being replaced by his bazaar" and traditional faith "with the divine hereafter of beauty."[49] Yet Zola's secularizing perspective turned a blind eye to the long-standing spiritual capital on which the department store drew. As the sheer marketability of Lourdes indicated, the compulsive shopper did not merely break with religion; rather, connoisseurs of abundance expended what Zola termed their "nervous passion" on mundane yet dazzling artifacts.[50]

France continues to loom in the global popular imagination as a source of refined pleasures, from haute cuisine to haute couture. Joan DeJean has deftly traced the ways in which the magnificence of Louis XIV's court at Versailles established templates for high style that persist to this day in the minds of discerning consumers.[51] With the exception of Dom Pérignon, clergymen make few appearances in her study. Also absent is their critique of the taste for courtly accoutrements, from low-cut necklines to high-heeled shoes, which unsettle the triumphalist tale of how Paris became the fashion capital of Europe and then the world. Economic theologians in the age of the Sun King preached a rather different vision—of corrupt souls slavishly bound to worship themselves in commodified form—that paved the way for Marx to describe the wages of alienation.

DeJean ends her book with what Benjamin called a "wish image": a ritzy gala thrown at the Metropolitan Museum of Art in New York.[52] As if by magic, the institution followed suit in 2018 with a lavish exhibition, *Heavenly Bodies: Fashion and the Catholic Imagination*. A collaboration between the Vatican and The Costume Institute, with sponsors like Versace, it drew a record-breaking 1,659,647 visitors.[53] David Tracy's essay in the catalogue argues for the theological distinctiveness of a "Catholic analogical imagination" that links "faith and reason, human and divine love."[54] According to C. Griffith Mann, the curators aimed to capture "the ongoing dialogue between art and religion, and its importance in transforming and elevating lived experience."[55]

The exhibition's pieces would have intrigued Benjamin. Emblematic is the case of Gabrielle "Coco" Chanel, who after her mother's death was sent to live at a convent, where she learned needlework. Her name is now synonymous with the little black dress (fig. 7.1). In October of 1926 *Vogue* hailed the creation as nothing less than the firm's "Ford," the arrival of a ubiquitous accessory.[56] Despite the au courant reference, the straight-lined, monochromatic design may well have taken inspiration from a youth spent

Figure 7.1 Gabrielle "Coco" Chanel (1883–1971) for the House of Chanel (French, founded 1913). Ensemble, ca. 1927. Front view. Silk, wool, metal. Purchase, New York Historical Society, by exchange, 1984 (1984.28a–c). Metropolitan Museum of Art, New York. Image copyright © Metropolitan Museum of Art. Image source: Art Resource, NY.

Figure 7.2 House of Dior. Wedding ensemble, Fall/Winter 1968–69. Fur, nylon, metal. Gift of E. I. du Pont de Nemours and Company, 1969 (C.I.69.1a–e). Metropolitan Museum of Art, New York. Image copyright © Metropolitan Museum of Art. Image source: Art Resource, NY.

under the tutelage of nuns. She would acknowledge the debt later in life with occasional visits to the sisters and through charitable donations.[57] The garment stands as the sartorial epitome of the populuxe good; simplicity conceals its fine materials and high price as readily as it facilitates cheaper imitations. Religious referents in the House of Dior's wedding ensemble of the 1968–69 season are even more sumptuously explicit. The gown incorporates stylistic elements from a monk's habit in a way that is almost lurid in its purity, especially given the presumed wearer (fig. 7.2). Combining plush fur and a synthetic, mass-produced material, nylon, the piece extends the articulation of the sacred and profane—and of the luxurious and the necessary—that runs through the exhibition as well as this book.

French economic theology emerged from Parisian seminaries in the age of Enlightenment. Now its trappings are on display in the halls of Manhattan museums and in the storefronts of upscale boutiques throughout the world. It seems fitting to conclude this history with images that project spiritual and psychic force along confessional and gendered lines. Although male clerics stood at the forefront of theorizing the Catholic ethic in print, women were ever in the vanguard as consumers, educators, founders of charitable orders, producers of vestments and devotional objects, and members of confraternities. As in the seventeenth and eighteenth centuries, luxury is often coded as feminine. To cite Benjamin once more, fashion establishes, in a manner reminiscent of its Catholic antecedents, "the ritual according to which the commodity fetish demands to be worshipped."[58] The value imparted by this industry remains radically double-edged, like a blade poised to cut through the tissue-thin boundaries separating the celestial from the terrestrial spheres and the supplicant customer from a desired object.

Notes

Introduction

1. On the history and significance of Bernard and Picart's work, see Hunt, Jacob, and Mijnhardt, *Book That Changed Europe*; Hunt, Jacob, and Mijnhardt, *Bernard Picart*; and Wyss-Giacosa, *Religionsbilder der Frühen Aufklärung*.

2. Bernard and Picart, *Cérémonies et coutumes religieuses de tous les peuples du monde*, 1:xxxiv.

3. Bernard and Picart, 1.2:138–39. On the production and distribution of the Agnus Dei, see Troyon, "Les 'Agnus Dei,'" 69–78; and Lepoittevin, "La fabrique romaine des *Agnus Dei*," 89–104.

4. Bernard and Picart, *Cérémonies et coutumes religieuses de tous les peuples du monde*, 1.2:176.

5. Marx, *Economic and Philosophical Manuscripts of 1844*, 290 (emphasis in original).

6. Weber, *The Protestant Ethic*.

7. Connolly, *Capitalism and Christianity*, 13–15, 22–28, 39–67. Recent works that examine the Protestant roots of the market economy include Hilton, *The Age of Atonement*; Waterman, *Revolution, Economics, and Religion*; Valeri, *Heavenly Merchandize*; and Moreton, *To Serve God and Wal-Mart*.

8. Arnoulx, *Du paradis et de ses merveilles*, 75. Unless indicated otherwise, all translations from French are my own. For primary and secondary sources originally published in languages other than French, I have relied on English versions whenever possible.

9. See, e.g., Labrousse and Braudel, *Histoire économique et sociale de la France*, vol. 2, *Des derniers temps de l'âge seigneurial*. For eighteenth-century ruminations on France's economic fate, see Cheney, *Revolutionary Commerce*, 21–51; and Shovlin, *Political Economy of Virtue*, 44–58.

10. For an overview of this historiographical shift, see C. Jones and Spang, "Sans-culottes," 40–47; Grenier, *L'économie d'Ancien Régime*; and Horn, *Economic Development*.

11. Weir, "Les crises économiques," 919–21, 934–39; Sonenscher, *Work and Wages*, 174–209.

12. Cullen, "History, Economic Crises, and Revolution," 639–46; Hoffman, Postel-Vinay, and Rosenthal, *Priceless Markets*.

13. Taylor, "Types of Capitalism," 495; Chaussinaud-Nogaret, *French Nobility*, 104–13; and Crouzet, *Britain Ascendant*, 34–42.

14. Crouzet, *Britain Ascendant*, 18–19; Cheney, *Revolutionary Commerce*, 15–16, 135.

15. On the rise in consumption, see, e.g., Roche, *La culture des apparences*; Roche, *Histoire des choses banales*; and Kwass, *Contraband*.

16. Mercier, *Tableau de Paris*, 1:50, 7:164.

17. This point has received recent confirmation in Piketty, *Capital in the Twenty-First Century*, 4.

18. S. Kaplan, *Bread, Politics and Political Economy*, 1:52–82, 90–299, 2:408–90, 611–96.

19. Grenier, *L'économie d'Ancien Régime*, 417–24.

20. Goldsmith, *Lordship in France*, 11.

21. On ecclesiastical wealth, see Blaufarb, *The Great Demarcation*, 54, 119–22 (quote on 119); McManners, *Church and Society*, 1:95–140; and C. Michaud, *L'église et l'argent*.

22. C. Michaud, *L'église et l'argent*, 12–21, 201–53, 540–45.

23. Kessler, *A Revolution in Commerce*, 74–78; and Kessler, "Enforcing Virtue," 79–89.

24. On this development, see Kselman, "Challenging Dechristianization"; Van Kley, "Christianity as Casualty"; and C. Coleman, "Resacralizing the World." Key works include Van Kley, *Religious Origins*; Sheehan, *The Enlightenment Bible*; Sorkin, *The Religious Enlightenment*; and Burson, *Rise and Fall*.

25. Diderot and d'Alembert, *Encyclopédie*, s.v. "Philosophe," 12:510. The article was written by César Chesneau Dumarsais. On the eighteenth-century invention of society as an independent field of action, see Baker, "Enlightenment," 95–96, 114–20. Baker draws on the conjectural history elaborated in Gauchet, *Disenchantment of the World*.

26. Bell, *Cult of the Nation*, 7. See also Sepinwall, *Abbé Grégoire*.

27. For an overview of this literature, see Larrère, *L'invention de l'économie*; Perrot, *Une histoire intellectuelle*; Kwass, *Privilege*; Clark, *Compass of Society*; Hont, *Jealousy of Trade*; Terjanian, *Commerce and Its Discontents*; and Soll, *The Reckoning*, esp. 87–164.

28. Sonenscher, *Before the Deluge*.

29. Shovlin, *Political Economy of Virtue*.

30. Cheney, *Revolutionary Commerce*.

31. In addition to Roche, *La culture des apparences*; Roche, *Histoire des choses*

banales; and Kwass, *Contraband*, see the following cross section of scholarship on the topic: Brewer and Porter, *Consumption and the World*; C. Jones, "Great Chain of Buying"; Berg, *Luxury and Pleasure*; Vries, *The Industrious Revolution*; Coquery, *Tenir boutique à Paris*; and Trentmann, *Empire of Things*.

32. Boisguilbert, *Factum de la France*, 282.
33. Sewell, *Logics of History*, 150.
34. Sewell, "The Empire of Fashion"; Sewell, "Connecting Capitalism." See also C. Jones, "Great Chain of Buying," 14–15, 19–20, 24–26. On the fashion industry, see also J. Jones, *Sexing La Mode*; Crowston, *Fabricating Women*; and Crowston, *Credit, Fashion, Sex*.
35. Sewell, "The Empire of Fashion," 115–16.
36. Voltaire, *Candide*, 180.
37. Spang, *Stuff and Money*, 1–44, 271–74 (quote on 272). On the material, moral, and social valences of the credit economy, see Crowston, *Credit, Fashion, Sex*, 3–12, 21–55, 166–69, 195–245; Coquery, *Tenir boutique à Paris*, 211–60; and Fontaine, *The Moral Economy*. On the history and semiotics of money, see Vilar, *History of Gold and Money*; Shell, *Money, Language, and Thought*; Goux, *Les monnayeurs du langage*; and, more recently, Desan, *Making Money*; Yuran, *What Money Wants*; and Bandelj, Wherry, and Zelizer, *Money Talks*.
38. Fairchilds, "Production and Marketing"; Fairchilds, "Marketing the Counter-Reformation."
39. On this theme, see also Pietz, "Fetishism and Materialism," 129, 149; and Baudrillard, *The Consumer Society*, 25–33.
40. See, e.g., Konings, *Emotional Logic of Capitalism*; and McGowan, *Capitalism and Desire*.
41. Cheney, *Revolutionary Commerce*, 15–16; Piketty, *Capital in the Twenty-First Century*, 28–30.
42. Marx and Engels, *The German Ideology*, 49. On Marx's understanding of capital accumulation in historical context, see Piketty, *Capital in the Twenty-First Century*, 3–13.
43. Schmitt, *Political Theology*, 36–52. For highly influential critiques of Schmitt, see Peterson, "Monotheism"; and Blumenberg, *Legitimacy of the Modern Age*, 89–101. More recently, Gil Anidjar offers an especially evocative definition of *economic theology* as "the history of religion as political economy" in *Blood*, 141–48 (quote on 142).
44. Blumenberg, *Legitimacy of the Modern Age*, 27–36, 63–75 (quote on 65, emphasis in the original). As he specifies further, "What mainly occurred in the process that is interpreted as secularization . . . should be described not as the *transposition* of authentically theological contents into secularized alienation from their origins but rather as the *reoccupation* of answer positions that had become vacant and whose corresponding questions could not be eliminated" (65).
45. In emphasizing a form of binding contingency over positivist causality, I also draw in part on the "aleatory materialism" of Althusser. See Althusser, *Philosophy of the Encounter*, 167–207.

46. Agamben, *Kingdom and the Glory*. Michel Foucault traces antecedents of governmentality in the Christian pastorate in *Security, Territory, Population*, 115–254. See also Sheehan and Wahrman, *Invisible Hands*, 16–18, 49, 234–35, 245–48, 264–68.

47. Subsequent engagements with Agamben's work have placed greater emphasis on financial matters per se. See Leshem, *The Origins of Neoliberalism*; Singh, *Divine Currency*; and Heron, *Liturgical Power*.

48. Benjamin, "Capitalism as Religion," 259.

49. Bataille, "The Notion of Expenditure" (1933); Bataille, *The Accursed Share*, 19–41. Bataille's contributions to the field of general economy extended arguments formulated by Marcel Mauss in *The Gift* (1925).

50. Weber, *The Protestant Ethic*, xxxi–xxxix, 53–56, 102–25 (quotes on 107, 117, 121).

51. On the reception of Weber's work, see Chalcraft and Harrington, *The Protestant Ethic Debate*; and Swatos and Kaelber, *The Protestant Ethic Turns 100*. For a recent attempt to salvage aspects of the original thesis, see Gorski, "The Little Divergence."

52. See Chalcraft and Harrington, *The Protestant Ethic Debate*, 55–59.

53. Sombart, *Jews and Modern Capitalism*; Slezkine, *The Jewish Century*, 54.

54. Weber, *The Protestant Ethic*, 117, xxxix.

55. Todeschini, *I Mercanti e il Tempio*, esp. 40–45, 89–94, 326–92, 479–86 (quote on 42); Todeschini, *Franciscan Wealth*.

56. Weber, *The Protestant Ethic*, 61, 71, 97, 178n19. For rejections of this view, see Todeschini, *I Mercanti et il Tempio*, 8–9; and McCarraher, *The Enchantments of Mammon*, 6–13.

57. McCarraher, *The Enchantments of Mammon*, 3–175, 361–401 (quotes on 4, 5, 676, 679). For Catholic responses to commodity culture, see V. Miller, *Consuming Religion*, 184–94; Grumett, *Material Eucharist*, 255–58; and Clavero, *La grâce du don*, 163–97.

58. Here I follow Rousseau's speculations on the plausibility of an idealized state of nature devoid of competition over scarce resources, which extended to his assertion that socialized humans cannot recover their prior innocence. See Rousseau, *Discours sur l'origine et les fondemens de l'inégalité*, 122–30, 207–8.

59. On the view that modern economic categories owe their existence to the regular clergy of the medieval period, see Todeschini, *I Mercanti e il Tempio*, 40–45, 349–70.

60. Trivellato, *Promise and Peril*, 49–98, 128–61 (quotes on 68, 95).

61. For an overview of the historical terminology associated with the Catholic Reformation, see Hsia, *World of Catholic Renewal*, 1–7.

62. Here I draw on what Michel de Certeau termed the "formality of practices," whereby "the *content* of practices scarcely changes" even as "their *formality* does"—that is, the manner in which they are deployed. In particular, Certeau claimed that previously autonomous religious referents gave way to "social *utility*" and a "merchant morality" during the eighteenth century. See Certeau, "The Formality of Practices," 148, 173.

Notes to Introduction

63. On resacralization, see C. Coleman, "Resacralizing the World"; and C. Coleman, *The Virtues of Abandon*, 11–12.

64. On historical rates in the granting of pardons, see Tingle, *Indulgences after Luther*, 40. Tingle cites the statistics compiled in Desmette, "Les confréries religieuses," 355–70 (figures on 357–59). See also Froeschlé-Chopard, *Dieu pour tous*.

65. On the publishing statistics, see Duranton, "La ficelle de Law," 112.

66. McManners, *Church and Society*, 2:265.

67. Provost, *Le luxe*, 13–22, 159–63.

68. Cassirer, *Philosophy of the Enlightenment*, 135–36. On historical epistemology, see Sheehan and Wahrman, *Invisible Hands*; Rosenfeld, *Common Sense*; and Matytsin, *Specter of Skepticism*.

69. Edelstein, "Introduction to the Super-Enlightenment," 33.

70. Fleming, *The Dark Side*; Monod, *Solomon's Secret Arts*; Cameron, *Enchanted Europe*; Edelstein, *The Super-Enlightenment*; and Landy and Saler, *Re-enchantment of the World*.

71. See, e.g., Groethuysen, *The Bourgeois*.

72. Palmer, *Catholics and Unbelievers*.

73. R. Nelson, *Economics as Religion*; McCloskey, *The Bourgeois Virtues*. See also Bateman and Banzhaf, *Keeping Faith, Losing Faith*.

74. Groethuysen, *The Bourgeois*, 175.

75. Van Kley, "Pierre Nicole"; Dickey, "Pride, Hypocrisy and Civility"; Hundert, "Bernard Mandeville"; Orain, "The Second Jansenism"; and Orain and Menuet, "Liberal Jansenists." See also Viner, *Religious Thought*, 130–50.

76. Weber, *The Protestant Ethic*, 117, 119, 123.

77. Hirschman, *Passions and the Interests*, 9–43, 58–80, 100–110, 128–31 (quote on 27).

78. Sheehan and Wahrman, *Invisible Hands*, xii, 9.

79. Edelstein, *On the Spirit*, 119–27 (quote on 124).

80. Sheehan and Wahrman, *Invisible Hands*, 252–57.

81. Jameson, "The Vanishing Mediator," 78.

82. On early modern emblematics, see Russell, *Emblem and Device*, esp. 23–111. In the eighteenth century, visual culture (not only portraiture but also engravings, figurines, medals, and the like) also played a crucial role in advancing the figure of the celebrity; see Lilti, *The Invention of Celebrity*, 50–85.

83. Friedland, *Political Actors*, 8.

84. Singh, *Divine Currency*, 104–31.

85. On the affinities between the Eucharist and money, see Shell, *Money, Language, and Thought*, 40–43; and Shell, *Art and Money*.

86. Bossuet, *Politique*, 177–78.

87. Marin, *Le portrait du roi*, 2–21. On the religious character of monarchy, see also Kantorowicz, *The King's Two Bodies*; and Bloch, *The Royal Touch*.

88. Cameron, *The European Reformation*, 249–50; Eire, *War against the Idols*.

89. Réguis, *La voix du pasteur* (1773 ed.), 1:274, 275. A far earlier reference to the "invisible hand" is found in Fléchier, "Sermon de M. Fléchier," 152.

90. *Dictionnaire de l'Académie française*, 4th ed. (1762), s.v. "Jouissance," in *The ARTFL Project: Dictionnaires d'autrefois*, http://artfl-project.uchicago.edu/content/dictionnaires-dautrefois. Here I am drawing on Louis Althusser's definition of *overdetermination* as the "accumulation of effective determinations," at once material, political, even spiritual. See Althusser, *For Marx*, esp. 87–128 and 161–218 (quote on 113).

91. See Matt. 14:13–31 and Luke 9:12–17.
92. Marx, *Capital*, 1:76, 77, 132.
93. Marx, *Theories of Surplus Value*, 494 (emphasis in original).
94. On the theory of the signature, see Agamben, *Signature of All Things*, 33–55.

Chapter 1: The Economy of the Mysteries

1. Luke 22:19.
2. The following survey draws on Stone, *History of the Doctrine*; Bynum, *Holy Feast*; Certeau, *The Mystic Fable*, esp. 79–94; Rubin, *Corpus Christi*; Bynum, *Christian Materiality*; and Grumett, *Material Eucharist*.
3. Berman, *Law and Revolution*; Certeau, *The Mystic Fable*, 79–84 (quote on 84).
4. Grumett, *Material Eucharist*, 156–59.
5. Stone, *History of the Doctrine*, 1:244–50, 393–95.
6. Rubin, *Corpus Christi*, 14–35.
7. On the paradox of "holy matter" in late medieval devotional practice, see Bynum, *Christian Materiality*, 34–35, 215–16, 284–86 (quote on 35).
8. Bynum, *Holy Feast*, 171–82; Rubin, *Corpus Christi*, 45–49.
9. Rubin, *Corpus Christi*, 164–212, 334–46.
10. Grumett, *Material Eucharist*, 144–45, 179–82.
11. Rubin, *Corpus Christi*, 352–55; Bynum, *Christian Materiality*, 269–73.
12. Rubin, *Corpus Christi*, 13–14, 359–61; Grumett, *Material Eucharist*, 159–61.
13. Grumett, *Material Eucharist*, 163–65.
14. On the problem of decay in Eucharistic miracles, see Bynum, *Christian Materiality*, 177–216.
15. Cf. Bataille's notion of general economy in "The Notion of Expenditure" and *The Accursed Share*, 19–41.
16. My discussion of the Council of Trent is informed by Delumeau, *Catholicism between Luther and Voltaire*; Jedin, *A History*; O'Malley, *Trent*; Tallon, *La France et le Concile de Trente*; Stone, *History of the Doctrine*, 86–106; and Hsia, *World of Catholic Renewal*, 10–25.
17. On this point, see Delumeau, *Catholicism between Luther and Voltaire*, 13.
18. Fontigny, *Le catéchisme*, 1:184–85, 187, 188, 190. On the attribution of the translation to Fontigny, see Barbier, *Dictionnaire des ouvrages anonymes*, 1:531.
19. Marin, *Le portrait du roi*, 12–21, 19. See also Kantorowicz, *The King's Two Bodies*; and Santner, *The Royal Remains*, 33–62.
20. Fontigny, *Le catéchisme*, 1:147–54 (quotes on 147, 150).
21. Fontigny, 1:168–80 (quotes on 168–69, 174, 177).

22. Fontigny, 1:194, 197–206 (quotes on 194, 199, 205, 206).
23. Blairye, *Le thrésor des grandes richesses*, 26.
24. Spahn, *From Gold to Euro*, 48.
25. *Canons and Decrees*, 74.
26. Du Bosc, *L'Eucharistie paisible*, 104.
27. Fontigny, *Le catéchisme*, 1:273, 274.
28. Fontigny, 1:199.
29. Fontigny, 1:309, 313.
30. S. Kaplan, *Bakers of Paris*, 24–25.
31. On the manufacturing of hosts for the Mass, see Migne, *Dictionnaire des confréries*, s.v. "Saint-Honoré," 333; and Bouchot, *Histoire anecdotique des métiers*, 64–65.
32. For the Gospel account, see Matt. 26:26–29.
33. Fontigny, *Le catéchisme*, 1:278–79.
34. On controversies surrounding the Eucharist, see Jedin, *A History*, 1:383–91.
35. Fontigny, *Le catéchisme*, 1:280–309 (quotes on 280, 283, 287, 292, 299, 308). Cf. *Canons and Decrees*, 73–75.
36. Fontigny, *Le catéchisme*, 1:310, 312, 313, 314.
37. Fontigny, 1:326; O'Malley, *Trent*, 252.
38. *Canons and Decrees*, 77.
39. Fontigny, *Le catéchisme*, 1:316–25 (quotes on 318, 319, 312).
40. Fontigny, 1:329.
41. On the speech act, see Austin, *How to Do Things*. Tellingly, Austin cites two sacraments, baptism and marriage, to exemplify his theory; see 7–9, 24–38.
42. O'Malley, *Trent*, 164–67, 198–223; Bergin, *Church, Society, and Religious Change*, 2–6; and V. Martin, *Le gallicanisme*, xi, xiv, 345–95.
43. On the financial and political negotiations involved in France's acceptance of the Tridentine reform, see Greengrass, *Governing Passions*, 288–303; and Bergin, *Politics of Religion*, 134–36.
44. Blumenberg, *Legitimacy of the Modern Age*, 65.
45. Arnauld, *La perpétuité*, 2:107–32 (quotes on 115, 130, 132). On the Jansenist interpretation of the Eucharist as it related to the theory of language, see Marin, *La critique du discours*, 59–63, 74–76, 92–100.
46. Vaubert, *La dévotion à Nostre Seigneur*, 1:i, 92, 100, 101, 108.
47. Tallon, *La France et le Concile de Trente*, 766–70, 794–801 (quote on 794).
48. Rom. 5:15.
49. Viller et al., *Dictionnaire de spiritualité*, s.v. "Pénitence," 12:Col. 943.
50. Viller et al., 12:Col. 958–80; Iogna-Prat, "Topographies of Penance," 163–72.
51. *Canons and Decrees*, 88–99 (quotes on 90, 91, 98); Fontigny, *Le catéchisme*, 1:343. On the Tridentine deliberations concerning penance and their consequences for religious practice, see *Dictionnaire de spiritualité*, s.v. "Pénitence," 12:Col. 980–86; Tingle, *Indulgences after Luther*, 23–26; and O'Malley, *Trent*, 132–33.
52. See Tingle, *Indulgences after Luther*.

53. *Canons and Decrees*, 253–54.
54. Tingle, *Indulgences after Luther*, 27–38; McManners, *Church and Society*, 2:121.
55. Bossuet, *Méditations*, 88, 89, 90, 91.
56. *Jubilé universel*, 4. On the significance of physical space in the distribution of indulgences, see Tingle, *Indulgences after Luther*, 138–42.
57. *Jubilé universel*, 5–6.
58. On the financial and liturgical commitments involved in observing the Jubilee, see Tingle, *Indulgences after Luther*, 138–39.
59. *Jubilé universel*, 10–12.
60. Tingle provides an overview of this literature in *Indulgences after Luther*, 33–38.
61. On Joly's life and career, see Hébrard, *Histoire de Messire Claude Joly*; for an account of Joly's work on indulgences and the Jubilee, see 495–97.
62. Joly, *Doctrine des indulgences*, 7–14 (quotes on 11, 12, 13, 14).
63. Joly, 15; cf. Bossuet, *Méditations*, 8–10, 19–20.
64. Joly, *Doctrine des indulgences*, 16, 17, 18.
65. Joly, 32, 33, 34.
66. Joly, 91–94.
67. Gerberon, *Le catéchisme des indulgences*, iii–v, 55–67, 75–95, 104–10, 139–44, 160–65 (quotes on iii, 59).
68. Treuvé, *Instruction sur les dispositions*, iii–iv, 75, 55–59, 66–67, 160–64 (quotes on iii, 59, 164). On Treuvé's career and Jansenist sensibilities, see L-G. Michaud, *Biographie universelle*, s.v. "Treuvé (Simon-Michel)," 42:134.
69. Bourdaloue, *Sermon sur le Jubilé*, 3–13, 20–25, 30–44 (quotes on 3, 5, 8, 10, 25, 30, 42).
70. Rom. 16:18; Bourdaloue, *Sermon sur le Jubilé*, 25.
71. Joly, *Doctrine des indulgences*, 23–32 (quotes on 24, 27).
72. Luther, "Pagan Servitude," 256, 267–76, 295–98, 357–58.
73. Calvin, *Institutes of the Christian Religion*, 495–509.
74. On these devotional tendencies, see Evennett, *Spirit of the Counter-Reformation*, 36–42; and Bergin, *Church, Society, and Religious Change*, 252–76.
75. McManners, *Church and Society*, 1:364–82; Taveneaux, *Le catholicisme*, 1:145–59.
76. Evennett, *Spirit of the Counter-Reformation*, 39–40; cf. Bremond, *Histoire littéraire*, 2:436–41.
77. Viguerie, "La dévotion populaire," 12–13.
78. McManners, *Church and Society*, 2:98; Viguerie, "La dévotion populaire," 13.
79. McManners, *Church and Society*, 2:101–6; Bergin, *Church, Society, and Religious Change*, 258–67; and Viguerie, "La dévotion populaire," 14.
80. Archives nationales, Paris, Minutier central, Étude CV, liasse 796, Saint-Benoît (église) (Confrérie du Saint-Sacrement), Fondation par Claude Sonnius, July 2, 1650.
81. *Mémoire pour les prestres asssociez la confrairie du Très-S. Sacrement de l'autel*, 1.
82. *Fondations faites à la confrairie du Très-Saint Sacrement*.

83. On laicization, see McManners, *Church and Society*, 2:116–18. McManners positions himself against the model of "de-christianization" championed by Michel Vovelle in *Piété baroque et déchristianisation*. For commentary on this literature, see Van Kley, "Christianity as Casualty."

84. Froeschlé-Chopard, *Dieu pour tous*, 149–50.

85. McManners, *Church and Society*, 2:157–58.

86. Viguerie, *Le catholicisme des français*, 162; cited in Bergin, *Church, Society, and Religious Change*, 361.

87. *Occupation intérieure pour les âmes*, 13–14.

88. The overview of confraternities in this paragraph draws on McManners, *Church and Society*, 159–88; Bergin, *Church, Society, and Religious Change*, 339–65; Froeschlé-Chopard, *Dieu pour tous*, 13–23, 149–77; and Gutton, *Les confréries et dévotion*.

89. Froeschlé-Chopard, *Dieu pour tous*, 179–80; Gutton, *Les confréries et dévotion*, 63.

90. Archives nationales, Paris, O¹ * 70, fol. 67–69, Lettres de confirmation de la confrairie du St. Sacrement dans l'Église de St. Eustache.

91. McManners, *Church and Society*, 2:157; Froeschlé-Chopard, *Dieu pour tous*, 179; and Gutton, *Les confréries et dévotion*, 61–68.

92. Froeschlé-Chopard, *Dieu pour tous*, 181–85.

93. Tallon, *La Compagnie du Saint-Sacrement*, 21.

94. On admission to and the functions of French confraternities, see Froeschlé-Chopard, *Dieu pour tous*, 188–200.

95. *Institution de la confrairie*, 3–8, 64–71 (quotes on 7, 67, 69).

96. *Règlements de la confrairie*, 4–14 (quotes on 4–5, 6, 14).

97. *Règlements de la confrairie*, 15–22 (quote on 21).

98. *Règles et statuts*, 7–16 (quotes on 16, 15, 8). On the events at Faverney, see Marchal and Tramaux, *Le miracle de Faverney*.

99. *Règles et statuts*, 18–20 (quote on 19).

100. *Règles et statuts*, 54, 55, 62.

101. *Institution de la confrairie*, 9–15 (quotes on 12).

102. For instance, see also *Statuts et règlements*, 55–70; *Instructions touchant l'adoration perpétuelle*, 111–15; and *Mémoire pour les administrateurs*, 4–9.

103. *Canons and Decrees*, 97–98 (quote on 97, emphasis in the original). The reference to treasuring up wrath is a quotation from Rom. 2:5.

104. *Instructions touchant l'adoration perpétuelle*, 1–16 (quotes on 1, 2, 12).

105. On the baron de Renty and the role of the Compagnie du Saint-Sacrement in establishing the ideal of perpetual adoration, see Tallon, *La compagnie du Saint-Sacrement*, 74–77 (quote on 81).

106. *Instructions touchant l'adoration perpétuelle*, 17–36 (quotes on 36).

107. *Instructions touchant l'adoration perpétuelle*, 68–115 (quotes on 76, 99, 100, 105, 112).

108. *Instructions touchant l'adoration perpétuelle*, 117–47.

109. *Instructions touchant l'adoration perpétuelle*, 147–83, 213–14 (quote on 213).

110. *Instructions touchant l'adoration perpétuelle*, 220, 223, 222.
111. *Instructions touchant l'adoration perpétuelle*, 181–82.
112. *Instructions touchant l'adoration perpétuelle*, 190–93, 198–99.
113. *Statuts et règlements*, 74, 75, 76, 88–89, 96, 97, 113–14 (emphasis in original). For the biblical references, see Ps. 36:8 ("They feast on the abundance of your house, and you give them drink from the river of your delights"); and 27:13 ("I believe that I shall see the goodness of the Lord in the land of the living.").
114. *Statuts, règlements, et prières*, 192, 226.
115. *Statuts, règlements, et prières*, 248, 249, 252.
116. *Statuts, règlements, et prières*, 256–57, 260, 264.
117. *Cy commence ung devot et salutaire traicte intitule La marchandise spirituelle*, Aii.
118. *Cy commence ung devot et salutaire traicte intitule La marchandise spirituelle*, Aiii.
119. Matt. 14–30; cf. La Chétardie, *Homélie VI*.
120. *Cy commence ung devot et salutaire traicte intitule La marchandise spirituelle*, Miv; Matt. 6:21.
121. Arnoulx, *Merveilles de l'autre monde*, 35, 45. I have consulted the 1676 edition.
122. Arnoulx, *Du paradis et de ses merveilles*, 8, 21, 23, 24, 32, 33, 38, 45, 46, 47. I consult here the 1676 edition, which is bound in the same volume as Arnoulx's *Merveilles de l'autre monde* in the collection of the Bibliothèque nationale de France. For the biblical depiction of God's palace, see Ps. 112:3.
123. Arnoulx, *Du paradis et de ses merveilles*, 53–57 (quotes on 53, 54).
124. Arnoulx, 58, 59, 63.
125. Arnoulx, 69, 71, 74, 79, 80.
126. Gourdan, *Le chrestien heureux*, 1:iiii, 339.
127. Gourdan, 1:15, 304.
128. Gourdan, 1:7, 87, 98.
129. Gourdan, 1:197–212, 2:54 (quotes on 1:198, 199, 201).
130. Gourdan, 1:251, 253, 261, 262, 276.
131. See, e.g., Rom. 1:18–31; and Augustine of Hippo, *The City of God*, 548–53. On the origins of the fetish, see Pietz, "Problem of the Fetish II," esp. 26–27 and n. 6.
132. Gourdan, *Le chrestien heureux*, 2:54.
133. Gourdan, 2:450–53 (italics in the original). Cf. Luke 22:15.
134. Bossuet et al., *Les avocats des pauvres*, 1:xi. On Bourdaloue's life and career, see L-G. Michaud, *Biographie universelle*, s.v. "Bourdaloue (Louis)," 5:293–95.
135. Bourdaloue, *Sermons du P. Bourdaloue*, 1:512; John 6:55.
136. Bourdaloue, *Sermons du P. Bourdaloue*, 1:512–27 (quotes on 513, 518, 519, 520, 521, 525, 527).
137. Bourdaloue, 529–40 (quotes on 530, 531, 533, 535).
138. On Réguis's pastoral career, see Julia, "Les sources"; and Dinet, "Une dechristianisation provinciale."
139. Réguis, *La voix du pasteur* (1766 ed.), 2:31, 32. On the economic theology of the Trinity—more specifically, as an administrative paradigm—see Agamben, *Kingdom and the Glory*, 36–46.

140. Réguis, *La voix du pasteur* (1773 ed.), 1:103, 104.

141. Réguis, *La voix du pasteur* (1766 ed.), 2:361. For the miracle recorded in the Gospels, see, e.g., Matt. 14:13–21. On the blessing of the fields, see Delumeau, *Rassurer et protéger*, 52–56. For a recent assessment of clerical interventions in the agricultural economy, see Stockland, "Insects."

142. Réguis, *La voix du pasteur* (1773 ed.), 1:274, 275, 3:343 (emphasis added).

143. Réguis, 3:343.

144. Réguis, 4:320.

145. Diderot and d'Alembert, *Encyclopédie*, s.v. "Œconomie animale," 11:360–66 (quote on 360). On the economy of nature, see Stockland, "Insects," 10–18.

146. Diderot and d'Alembert, *Encyclopédie*, s.v. "Économie ou Œconomie (Morale et Politique)," 5:337–49; and "Œconomie politique," 11:366–83. Diderot solicited the second article by Boulanger in response to Rousseau's critique of his notion of general will in "Économie politique"; see Hulliung, *The Autocritique of Enlightenment*, 26–31.

147. Diderot and d'Alembert, *Encyclopédie*, s.v. "Œconomie," 11:360.

148. Réguis, *La voix du pasteur* (1773 ed.), 1:275, 2:189.

149. Smith, *Theory of Moral Sentiments*, 184–85; Smith, *The Wealth of Nations*, 484–85. On Smith's use of the phrase, and its significance for his thought, see Sheehan and Wahrman, *Invisible Hands*, 264–70. Emma Rothschild argues, in contrast, that Smith's references to the term are meant to be ironic; see Rothschild, *Economic Sentiments*, 116–24.

150. Colombière, "Réflexions chrétiennes sur l'aumône," 266–67 (quote on 266). On his life, see L-G. Michaud, *Biographie universelle*, s.v. "Colombière (Claude de la)," 8:647–48.

151. Fléchier, "Sermon de M. Fléchier," 152. On Fléchier's career, see L-G. Michaud, *Biographie universelle*, s.v. "Fléchier (Esprit)," 14:210–13.

152. Réguis, *La voix du pasteur* (1773 ed.), 1:276, 277.

153. Réguis, 3:155, 156.

154. Bataille, *The Accursed Share*, esp. 19–40, 55–59.

Chapter 2: Perpetual Penance and Frequent Communion

1. Bibliothèque nationale de France, Département des Estampes et de la photographie, Collection Michel Hennin, vol. 101, pièce 8727, Réserve QB-201 (101)-FOL, p. 20, Médaille (*Custos unitatis schismatis ultrix*) [1752]. On artistic representations of the parlement's spiritual claims during this period, see Crow, *Painters and Public Life*, 119–22.

2. Mouffle d'Angerville, *Vie privée de Louis XV*, 2:283.

3. Nicole, *Essais de morale*, 1:240. On this point, see also Van Kley, "Pierre Nicole"; and Grewal, "Political Theology of *Laissez-Faire*."

4. Sales, *Introduction à la vie dévote*, 159–65, 502–13 (quote on 506).

5. Duvergier de Hauranne, *Maximes saintes*, 266–67.

6. Sales, *Introduction à la vie dévote*, 159–60; Duvergier de Hauranne, *Maximes saintes*, 266.

7. On the beginnings of the Jesuit-Jansenist conflict, see Van Kley, *Religious Origins*, 58–61; and Bergin, *Politics of Religion*, 181–86.

8. Bergin, *Politics of Religion*, 186.

9. Van Kley, *Religious Origins*, 33–49; Van Kley, "The Religious Origins," 118–19.

10. Van Kley, *Religious Origins*, 67–71.

11. Van Kley, 77–85.

12. See, e.g., Cognet, *Le jansénisme*; Maire, *De la cause de Dieu*; Van Kley, *Religious Origins*; and Bergin, *Politics of Religion*, 181–205.

13. For an excellent overview of the Jansenist versus the Molinist-Jesuit positions on human nature and grace, see Van Kley, *Religious Origins*, 49–65.

14. The expression is from Bremond, *Histoire littéraire*, 1:187–385.

15. Taveneaux, *Le catholicisme*, 2:342–43.

16. Bremond, *Histoire littéraire*, 9:45–128; for an opposing view, see Hogan, "Jansenism and Frequent Communion."

17. Arnauld, *De la fréquente communion*, preface, n.p.

18. See Luke 19:1–10 and 7:1–10.

19. Arnauld, *De la fréquente communion*, 57–62, 96–104 (quotes on 60, 66, 96).

20. Arnauld, n.p., 87–95, 395–406, 470–506 (quotes on n.p., 396, 401). See also *Dictionnaire de spiritualité*, s.v. "Pénitence," 12:Col. 976–77; and Iogna-Pratt, "Topographies of Penance," 168–71. On confession and truth regimes, see also Foucault, *The History of Sexuality*, 58–63.

21. *Canons and Decrees*, 78.

22. Arnauld, *De la fréquente communion*, 181–91, 370–406 (quotes on 191, 374, 376, 396, 401).

23. Arnauld, 663, 665, 700, 714. On Belial, see *Theological Dictionary of the Old Testament*, s.v. "b^{e}liyya'al," 2:131–36.

24. Arnauld, *De la fréquente communion*, 747.

25. Arnauld, n.p. For instance, approbations came from the archbishops of Sens, Toulouse, Bordeaux, and Tours, among others, but not from their colleague in Paris.

26. Bergin, *Politics of Religion*, 188–90.

27. Van Kley, *Religious Origins*, 66–68.

28. For a history of the reception of Arnauld's work, written from the Jansenist perspective, see Bourgeois, *Relation de M. Bourgeois*.

29. On *Cum occasione* and Arnauld's condemnation, see McManners, *Church and Society*, 346–48; and Nadler, *Arnauld and the Cartesian Philosophy*, 16–18.

30. [La Haye], *Remarques judicieuses*, 5. The work has also been attributed to La Haye's fellow Jesuit Jacques Nouet; see Barbier, *Dictionnaire des ouvrages anonymes*, 4:251.

31. La Haye, *Remarques judicieuses*, 13–15, 20–22, 35–36 (quote on 21).

32. La Haye, 64–65, 85.

33. La Haye, 83, 90–91.
34. On the Camus-Sirmond debate, see also Bremond, *La querelle du pur amour*.
35. Sirmond, *La déffense de la vertu*, 69, 88.
36. Camus, *La déffense du pur amour*, 33, 106–7.
37. Camus, *Théodoxe*, 57.
38. Camus, *L'usage de la pénitence*, pt. 1.3, 6, 11, 15, 20, 34, 36, 115.
39. Camus, pt. 3.8, 9, 10, 41, 58.
40. Camus, pt. 4.87, 89, 168.
41. For overviews of the Quietist Affair, see Cognet, *Crépuscule des mystiques*; and C. Coleman, *The Virtues of Abandon*, 53–75.
42. Bossuet, *Œuvres*, 11:515, 525, 440.
43. Fénelon, *La fréquente communion*, 8, 39.
44. Nouet, *La vie mystique*, 84–98, 142–53, 309–10, 491–94, 502–31 (quotes on 84, 85, 94, 142, 143, 148, 153, 309, 493, 531). According to the catalogue of the Bibliothèque nationale, editions were also published in 1675 and 1766.
45. McManners, *Church and Society*, 2:101–2.
46. Pichon, *L'esprit de Jésus-Christ* (1745), iv–viii. On Pichon's career, see L-G. Michaud, *Biographie universelle*, s.v. "Pichon (Jean)," 33:199. On Protestantism and Jansenism in Lorraine, see Geppert, "The Sillon Lorrain," 80–81; and Maire, "Port-Royal," 345–46.
47. Pichon, *L'esprit de Jésus-Christ* (1745), 3–6, 9–12, 272–73, 304–7, 317–39 (quotes on 12, 338, 339).
48. Pichon, 389–410, 468–71 (quotes on 402–3, 410, 470 [emphasis added]).
49. Pichon, 19–32, 39–46, 142–56 (quotes on 24, 26, 28, 30, 31, 32).
50. Pichon, 10.
51. Pichon, 366–76 (quotes on 369, 372, 373, 376).
52. *Ordonnance et instruction pastorale de Monseigneur l'évêque de Soissons*, 2–4. This text is included in a single-volume compilation of twenty-two texts related to the Pichon affair found in the Bibliothèque nationale de France (Cote E-3652). The catalogue of the BnF gives the title as *Recueil de mandements et autres ouvrages publiés au sujet du livre du P. J. Pichon*.
53. Beaumont, *Lettre de Monseigneur l'archévêque de Paris*, 7. On Beaumont's ultimately self-defeating support for the Society of Jesus, see Worcester, "Friends as Liabilities," 65–79.
54. For the reprint edition, see Pichon, *L'esprit de Jésus-Christ* (1747). Beaumont mentioned the possibility of a corrected version but claimed that it could not proceed owing to "difficulties that the author had not foreseen" (Beaumont, *Lettre de Monseigneur l'archévêque de Paris*, 4).
55. For contemporary accounts of these titles, see *Recueil de mandements*; and *Extraits des assertions dangereuses et pernicieuses*, 199–200.
56. *La fréquente communion du P. Pichon*, 4, 10, 12.
57. *Ordonnance et instruction pastorale de Monseigneur l'évêque de Carcassonne*, 6–10, 12–17, 20–29, 60–61 (quotes on 9, 15, 60).

58. *Ordonnance et instruction pastorale de Monseigneur l'évêque de Soissons*, 4, 5, 23.
59. *Lettre de M ****, 1, 2, 5–7.
60. Von Baldenstein, *Lettre de Son Altesse Monseigneur Joseph-Guillaume de Rinck de Baldenstein*, 1, 2, 3.
61. *Nouvelles ecclésiastiques*, Jan. 9, 1748 (7), Jan. 23, 1748 (13–14), Jan. 30, 1748 (15–22), March 4, 1748 (37–44), March 19, 1748 (48), March 26, 1748 (49–52), June 4, 1748 (89–92), Dec. 4, 1748 (193–96).
62. *Le triomphe de M. Arnaud*, 1.
63. *Arrest du Conseil d'état du roy, qui révoque le privilege*, 1–2.
64. L-G. Michaud, *Biographie universelle*, s.v. "Pichon (Jean)," 33:199.
65. On the suppression of the Society of Jesus, see Van Kley, *The Jansenists*.
66. On the *convulsionnaires*, see Kreiser, *Miracles*; and Vidal, *Miracles et convulsions*.
67. *Consultation sur les convulsions*, 8–13 (quote on 9).
68. McManners, *Church and Society*, 2:482–83.
69. Rogister, *Louis XV*, 77–80.
70. On the midcentury lull in hostilities between the Jansenists and Jesuits, and their resumption with Beaumont's appointment as archbishop, see McManners, *Church and Society*, 2:484–86; and Rogister, *Louis XV*, 77–80.
71. On the *billets de confession*, see Van Kley, *Religious Origins*, 142; and McManners, *Church and Society*, 2:486–88.
72. On the de Prades affair and its significance for the Enlightenment, see Burson, *Rise and Fall*.
73. Van Kley, *Religious Origins*, 143–44; McManners, *Church and Society*, 2:492–93.
74. Archives nationales, Paris, G^8 796 *, *Lettre de MM. les évêques, du 11 juin 1752, en faveur de M. l'archévêque de Paris*.
75. On the political stakes of the debate, see Van Kley, *Religious Origins*, 143–46.
76. Archives nationales, Paris, G^8 796 *, Pièce 1, "Principes du droit sur le refus des sacrements," 1, 2, 3, 12, 13, 15.
77. Bossuet, *Politique*, 65.
78. Loyseau, *Traité des ordres*, 44.
79. Archives nationales, Paris, G^8 796 *, *Arrêt du Parlement de Paris qui deffense de recidiver dans le refus de sacrements*, March 23, 1752, 111. On Bouettin's case, see also McManners, *Church and Society*, 2:493.
80. Archives nationales, Paris, G^8 796 *, *Réponse du roy aux rémonstrances du parlement*, April 18, 1752, 113–14 (quote on 114).
81. Archives nationales, Paris, G^8 796 *, *Arrêt du parlement*, April 18, 1752, 114–15; and *Extrait des registres du Conseil d'état*, 121–22 (quote on 121).
82. *Extrait des registres de parlement*, 1–3 (quote on 3).
83. Archives nationales, Paris, G^8 796 *, "Mémoire sur l'incarcération du vicaire de Notre-Dame de Louviers d'Évreux," July 8, 1753, 155–57 (quote on 155).
84. *L'affaire du refus des sacrements*, 1, 2.
85. *Déclaration du roi. Donnée à Versailles le 2 septembre 1754*, 1, 3.
86. On clerical discontent in Troyes, see Tackett, *Religion, Revolution, and Regional Culture*, 137–38.
87. *Lettre de Monseigneur l'évêque de Troyes*, 1, 2.

88. *Mandement de M. l'évesque de Troyes à Monsieur le procureur général du Parlement de Paris*, 2, 4.

89. *Mandement de M. l'évesque de Troyes*, 4.

90. *Mandement de M. l'évesque de Troyes, pour ordonner des prières de Quarante Heures*, 2, 3.

91. *Arrest de la cour de parlement, qui condamne un imprimé intitulé: Mandement de Monseigneur l'évêque de Troyes*, 2.

92. *Arrest du parlement, du 30 juin 1755, qui condamne Me Granet à un bannissement perpétuel*, 1–3, 6 (quotes on 3, 6).

93. *Arrest du parlement qui condamne Me Aymé*.

94. *Arrest de la cour de parlement concernant le refus de sacrement fait à Me Lagarde*, 1–4 (quote on 2).

95. *Consultation de plusieurs canonistes et avocats de Paris, sur le compétence des juges séculiers, par rapport au refus des sacrements*, 1–3, 6–10 (quotes on 2, 6, 8–9). For a defense of the *Consultation*, see *Lettre à Monsieur ****.

96. *Arrêt du parlement ordonnant lacération et destruction par le feu de l'écrit imprimé intitulé*, 1–4 (quote on 3).

97. *Réponse à la Consultation de plusieurs canonistes et avocats*, 3–5 (quote on 4).

98. *Réponse à la Consultation de plusieurs canonistes et avocats*, 5–10 (quotes on 4, 6 [emphasis added]).

99. *Consultation de quarante docteurs*, 1–6, 12–14 (quotes on 1, 14).

100. *Réponse à la Consultation de quarante docteurs*, 1, 2, 3, 32.

101. *Lettre d'un saint prêtre en réponse à Madame la Comtesse de ****, 1,2 3, 5, 7, 10.

102. On Turgot's early career, see Poirier, *Turgot*, 29–60.

103. Turgot, *Le conciliateur*, 393, 394, 403.

104. *Déclaration du roi. Donnée à Versailles le 10 décembre 1756*, 1.

105. Benedict XIV, *Ex omnibus christiani orbis*. On protests against the pope's order, see *Lettre à M. L. G. P. au sujet du nouveau bref de Benoît XIV*.

106. *Déclaration du roi. Donnée à Versailles le 10 décembre 1756*, 2–4.

107. Archives nationales, Paris, G⁸ 796 *, "Requête de MM. les Agens généraux du clergé pour demander la cassation de la sentence du bailliage du Troyes," 322–24.

108. *Mandement et instruction*, 35, 36, 82.

109. Van Kley, *Religious Origins*, 136; McManners, *Church and Society*, 2:501.

110. See, e.g., McManners, *Church and Society*, 1:3–4 and 2:116–17; Van Kley, *Religious Origins*, 135–248; Merrick, *Desacralization of the French Monarchy*; and Vovelle, *Piété baroque et déchristianisation*.

111. Polanyi, *The Great Transformation*, 141–217.

Chapter 3: The Spirit of Speculation

1. *Arlequyn actionist*, in *Het groote tafereel der dwaasheid*, 1:print no. 12. The print circulated in France and originally served as the frontispiece for Pieter Langendijk's eponymous play, itself based on a Parisian production. See De Bruyn, "*Het groote tafereel der dwaasheid* and Its Readers," 27; and Labio, "Staging Folly," 145–46.

2. De Bruyn, "Reading *Het groote*," 6–13, 25, 33, 35; Spieth, "French Context," 220–24.

3. Chambon, *Traité des métaux et des minéraux*, 209.

4. Descartes to Mesland, Feb. 9, 1645, in *Œuvres de Descartes*, 4:167.

5. On the mystical mill, see Bynum, *Holy Feast*, 67; and Timmerman, "View of the Eucharist," 386–98.

6. Law, *Mémoire sur la Banque générale* (1717), 19.

7. Velde, introduction, xxxv; Chrétien-Deschamps, *Lettres sur le Visa*, lettre 4, 107.

8. Faure, *La banqueroute de Law*; Murphy, *John Law*.

9. Kaiser, "Public Credit"; Kaiser, "Money, Despotism, and Public Opinion."

10. Sonenscher, *Before the Deluge*, 1–21, 108–20; Sonenscher, *Sans-Culottes*, 261–73, 315–24. Sonenscher draws explicitly on Hont, *Jealousy of Trade*, 325–53; and Hont, "The Early Enlightenment Debate."

11. Shovlin, "Jealousy of Credit."

12. Hume, *Treatise of Human Nature*, 524; also cited in Rey, *Le temps du crédit*, 131–32. On credit and religious metaphor, see also Rey, *Le temps du crédit*, 21–25, 123–38.

13. Wennerlind, "Credit-Money"; Wennerlind, *Casualties of Credit*, 44–79, 231–34.

14. Sheehan and Wahrman, *Invisible Hands*, 48–132 (quote on 54).

15. Orain, *La politique du merveilleux*, 177–200 (quotes on 182, 192).

16. As Wennerlind argues, "It was only after the alchemical understanding of nature was infused with the utilitarian ethos of Baconianism that alchemy began playing a prominent role in political economy" (*Casualties of Credit*, 47).

17. See Wennerlind, "Credit-Money," 251–52; Orain, *La politique du merveilleux*, 196–209; Orain and Thézé, "Publicité, contre-publicité, et représentations," 129–40; and Rey, *Le temps du crédit*, 129.

18. The Eucharist and money thus confound the shift from the Renaissance to the classical age plotted by Michel Foucault in *The Order of Things*, 17–25, 51–63, 181–83.

19. Wilson, "An Alchemical Manuscript," 221, 338–40; and Newman, *Promethean Ambitions*, xiv, 99–106.

20. Newman, *Promethean Ambitions*, 6–8, 167–235.

21. Newman, 83–106.

22. On the contested relationship between alchemy and religion, see Principe and Newman, "Some Problems," 396–401; and Nummedal, "Alchemy and Religion," 312–15.

23. Newman, *Promethean Ambitions*, 89–90; Principe, *Secrets of Alchemy*, 66–68.

24. Wilson, "An Alchemical Manuscript," 339.

25. Newman, *Promethean Ambitions*, 9, 107–8.

26. On alchemy and court patronage, see Newman, "From Alchemy to 'Chymistry,'" 506; Nummedal, *Alchemy and Authority*, 73–94; and Smith, *The Business of Alchemy*, 94–140, 173–227.

27. On Fabre's life and work, see Joly, *Rationalité de l'alchimie*, 35–64; and

Greiner, introduction, vii–xxii (quote on xi). Newton's alchemical interests are discussed in Dobbs, "Alchemical Death and Resurrection," 55–87.
28. Greiner, introduction, xxiii.
29. Fabre, *L'alchimiste chrétien*, ii.
30. Fabre, 1–9 (quotes on 3, 4).
31. Fabre, 11, 45.
32. Fabre, 22–36 (quotes on 22, 28, 29, 31, 35, 36, 32).
33. Fabre, 37, 40, 47.
34. Fabre, 58–69 (quotes on 63, 65, 66, 67, 68).
35. Fabre, 170–202 (quotes on 172, 173, 174, 194, 195, 198).
36. Fabre, 215, 218, 226, 231, 236 (emphasis added).
37. Belin, *Apologie du grand œuvre*, 3, 5.
38. Belin, 18–22, 34–55, 115–18 (quotes on 38, 39, 41, 42, 116).
39. Belin, *Traité des talismans*, 20–22, 24–26, 32–70, 87–92 (quotes on 20, 32, 92).
40. Belin, 101–4 (quote on 102).
41. Belin, *Les emblèmes eucharistiques*, 2–10, 221–68 (quotes on 2, 4, 9, 237, 238, 251).
42. On Descartes's early engagement with the occult, see Keefer, "The Dreamer's Path." On his complex relationship to alchemy, see Joly, *Descartes et la chimie*, 45–58; Maillard, "Descartes et l'alchimie"; and Matton, "Cartésianisme et alchimie."
43. Descartes, *Notae in programma quoddam*, 353.
44. On Descartes's understanding of transubstantiation and his status as a theologian, see Adam, *L'eucharistie*, 43–63; Ariew, *Descartes among the Scholastics*, 217–40; Armogathe, *Theologia Cartesiana*; Gouhier, *La pensée religieuse*; and Nadler, "Arnauld, Descartes, and Transubstantiation."
45. Armogathe, *Theologia Cartesiana*, 46–48, 56–58; Nadler, "Arnauld, Descartes, and Transubstantiation," 232–33.
46. Descartes to Mesland, Feb. 9, 1645, in *Œuvres de Descartes*, 4:163–70 (quote on 163). On Descartes's Eucharistic theology, see Armogathe, *Theologia Cartesiana*, 43–80; and Gouhier, *La pensée religieuse*, 221–31.
47. Descartes to Mesland, Feb. 9, 1645.
48. Descartes to Clerselier, Mar. 2, 1646, in *Œuvres de Descartes*, 4: 373.
49. Nadler, "Arnauld, Descartes, and Transubstantiation," 231–35.
50. Descartes, *Meditations on First Philosophy*, 150, 151.
51. Nadler, "Arnauld, Descartes, and Transubstantiation," 239–42.
52. On the ongoing controversy surrounding Descartes's Eucharistic theology, see Jolley, "Reception of Descartes' Philosophy," 397–402; and Watson, "Transubstantiation among the Cartesians."
53. Desgabets, *Considérations*, 3–8. On the tensions between the Thomistic and Scotist positions, see Armogathe, *Theologia Cartesiana*, 7–30.
54. Desgabets, *Considérations*, 8, 9, 12, 14, 15. For an account of his theory of indefectibility, see Armogathe, *Theologia Cartesiana*, 85–113; and Schmaltz, *Radical Cartesianism*, 27–61.

55. On Desgabets's career, see Schmaltz, *Radical Cartesianism*, 3–6.
56. Bibliothèque nationale de France, Département des Manuscrits, Français 463, Desgabets, *La philosophie eucharistique*.
57. Desgabets, 23–29 (quotes on 24, 27, 29 [emphasis added]).
58. Desgabets, *Traité de l'indéfectibilité des créatures*, 15–22, 26–39, 65–68 (quotes on 16, 22, 28).
59. On the metaphysical implications of the new science, understood simultaneously in natural philosophical and theological terms, see Koyré, *From the Closed World*.
60. Desgabets, *Le guide de la raison naturelle*, 137–45 (quotes on 137, 138, 143).
61. For an overview of Terrasson's life and career, see L-G. Michaud, *Biographie universelle*, s.v. "Terrasson (Jean)," 41:169–71; and Paradis de Moncrif, *Lettre première à milady ****, 3–16. On his intellectual pursuits, see also Palmer, *Catholics and Unbelievers*, 104–12; and Orain, *La politique du merveilleux*, 108–11.
62. D'Alembert, *Éloge de Jean Terrasson*, 370–75 (quote on 371). Cf. *Lettre première à milady ****, 5.
63. Del Prete, introduction, 9, 12–18, 127. Although the work was acknowledged as Terrasson's during his lifetime, it has long been misattributed to Malebranche, including in the published edition of 1769. See Malebranche, *Œuvres complètes*, 20:325–26; and Del Prete, introduction, 25–43.
64. On Descartes's theory of the plenum and its implications for conceiving infinity, see Gaukroger, *Descartes*, 238; and Dick, *Plurality of Worlds*, 106–12.
65. Terrasson, *Traité de l'infini créé*, 1–7 (quotes on 1, 3).
66. Terrasson, 11–40 (quotes on 12, 17, 20, 21).
67. Terrasson, 48–60, 100–146 (quotes on 54, 55, 100, 142).
68. Terrasson, 22.
69. On the possible authorship of these texts, see Malebranche, *Œuvres complètes*, 20:323–26.
70. *Explication de la possibilité de la transsubstantiation*, 157–64, 169–71 (quotes on 159–60, 161–62, 170).
71. *Traité de la communion*, 195, 196, 197.
72. *Traité de la communion*, 199–210 (quotes on 199, 200, 203). Cf. Fontigny, *Le catéchisme*, 1:188–90.
73. Simmel, *The Philosophy of Money*, 129.
74. On the multiple stores of value during the period, see Spang, *Stuff and Money*, 11–13, 20–50; and Blanc, "La France de François Ier," 335–44.
75. Bodin, *Six livres de la république*, 150–53, 242, 855–56 (quote on 242); Bodin, *Discours de Jean Bodin sur le rehaussement et diminution tant d'or que d'argent*, 45–51. It would be premature, however, to regard Bodin as an architect of the quantity theory of money; see Blanc, "La France de François Ier," 347–56.
76. Harsin, *Les doctrines monétaires*, 15–18, 69–70, 85–86; Mousnier, "L'évolution des finances publiques," 5–6.
77. Blanc, "La France de François Ier," 336.
78. Descartes, *Discours de la méthode*, 128.

79. On Boisguilbert's career and thought, see Faccarello, *The Foundations of Laissez-Faire*; Meyssonnier, *La balance et l'horloge*; and Roberts, *Boisguilbert*.

80. Boisguilbert's synthesis of Cartesianism and Jansenism has been frequently commented on in the scholarship. See, e.g., Spengler, "Boisguilbert's Economic Views," 73–74; Meyssonnier, *La balance et l'horloge*, 36–41, 46–50; and Faccarello, *The Foundations of Laissez-Faire*, 16–37.

81. Boisguilbert, *Traité de la nature*, 355–61 (quotes on 355, 356). As Harsin points out, even officials and theorists usually considered mercantilists, such as Colbert, advocated free trade, while Boisguilbert, a presumed champion of liberalism, nonetheless recommended assured minimum incomes to protect consumption levels. See Harsin, *Les doctrines monétaires*, 86–87, 106; and Meyssonnier, *La balance et l'horloge*, 26, 39.

82. For an overview of mercantilist principles and policies during the period, see Harsin, *Les doctrines monétaires*, 11–20, 69–87; and Rothkrug, *Opposition to Louis XIV*, 8–19, 30–35, 66–69.

83. Boisguilbert, *Dissertation sur les richesses*, 396, 409.

84. Mousnier, *Institutions of France*, 2:442–43; Norberg, "French Fiscal Crisis," 276.

85. Harsin, *Les doctrines monétaires*, 123–36; and Murphy, *John Law*, 135–37.

86. On Law's early life and career, see Murphy, *John Law*, 14–45, 139–47.

87. Law, *Money and Trade Considered*, 20–34, 110–73, 188–91 (quotes on 23, 158, 190).

88. Archives nationales, Paris, K 884, no. 1/bis, Law, *Mémoire sur l'établissement de la banque*.

89. Law, *Second mémoire sur les banques*, 605.

90. On the tradition of likening the circulation of money to that of blood, see Riskin, *Science in the Age of Sensibility*, 112.

91. Law, *Second mémoire sur les banques*, 578–80. On Law's shift away from his previous land bank proposal, see Murphy, *John Law*, 112–15.

92. Law, *Second mémoire sur les banques*, 582–90 (quotes on 582, 589).

93. *Lettres patentes du roy, portant privilege au Sieur Law et sa Compagnie d'establir une Banque générale*, 1–4; *Lettres patentes du roy, contenant règlement pour la Banque générale*, 1–2. See also Murphy, *John Law*, 148–55.

94. *Lettres patentes du roy, contenant règlement pour la Banque générale, accordée au Sieur Law, et à sa Compagnie*, 1–2. On the stipulation that payment for stock could be made in *billets d'état*, see Harsin, *Les doctrines monétaires*, 150.

95. Murphy, *John Law*, 157–63.

96. *Déclaration du roy, pour convertir la Banque générale en Banque royale*, 1–3; Murphy, *John Law*, 185–86; and Harsin, *Les doctrines monétaires*, 162.

97. On the establishment and rapid expansion of Law's Company, see Murphy, *John Law*, 164–68, 188–230; and Faure, *La banqueroute de Law*, 186–205, 220–28.

98. On the associations of the colonies with abundance, see Orain, *La politique du merveilleux*, 81–91, 174–84; Force, *Wealth and Disaster*, x–xi; and Greenblatt, *Marvelous Possessions*, 78–80.

99. Ekberg, *Colonial Ste. Geneviève*, 143–45.

100. On the use of gold as an enticement to investors, see Parkman, *France and England*, 2:545.

101. Law, *Mémoire sur le discrédit* (June 1720), 163–66 (quote on 165).

102. The survey of French colonization in this paragraph draws on Giraud, *Histoire de la Louisiane française*, 2:129–46, 3:24–27, 222–50; and Parkman, *France and England*, 2:534–51.

103. Parkman, *France and England*, 2:546. On the intersections between erotic, financial, and political desire, see Garraway, *The Libertine Colony*.

104. Murphy, *John Law*, 215–16, 220–30; Faure, *La banqueroute de Law*, 351–60.

105. The authorship of the letters remains somewhat uncertain, although scholarly consensus now attributes them to Terrasson. See Murphy, *John Law*, 232–33; Faure, *La banqueroute de Law*, 364; and Kaiser, "Money, Despotism, and Public Opinion," 17n84.

106. Del Prete, introduction, 13.

107. Terrasson, "I. Lettre," 3–8. I cite from the May 1720 edition of the collected letters rather than the versions from the *Nouveau Mercure*.

108. Terrasson, "II. Lettre," 1–9 (quotes on 5, 8).

109. Terrasson, "III. Lettre," 15–19 (quotes on 15, 17, 18–19).

110. My reading departs from that of Orain and Thézé, who argue that Terrasson's point of reference is alchemy rather than the broader framework of Eucharistic theology; see Orain and Thézé, "Publicité, contre-publicité, et représentations," 134; and Orain, *La politique du merveilleux*, 195.

111. Terrasson, "III. Lettre," 17–20, 23–24, 31–33 (quotes on 18, 19, 24, 32).

112. Archives nationales, Paris, K 884, no. 1/bis, Law, *Mémoire sur l'établissement de la banque*.

113. Terrasson, *Traité de l'infini créé*, 123, 142.

114. [Terrasson], *Explications sur le mystère de l'Eucharistie*, 247–60 (quotes on 251, 252). On the attribution of the text to Terrasson, see Del Prete, introduction, 242–45; and Malebranche, *Œuvres complètes*, 20:321–26.

115. Terrasson, "III. Lettre," 19.

116. Cf. Marin, *La critique du discours*, 51–77.

117. Terrasson, "III. Lettre," 20–23 (quote on 22).

118. Terrasson, *Traité de l'infini créé*, 48–56 (quote on 54).

119. On alchemical experimentation in the Académie des sciences, see Jacob, *Strangers Nowhere*, 50–56; and Principe, "The End of Alchemy?" 100.

120. Dufresnoy, *Histoire de la philosophie hermétique*, 2:68–98. For a similar case involving one Diesback, who found himself the subject of an investigation by the comte de Pontchartrain, the minister of the King's Household (Maison du roi) and the marquis d'Argenson, the lieutenant-general of police, see Pontchartrain to d'Argenson, April 10, 1715, April 17, 1715, and May 2, 1715, in Quétel, *La Bastille dévoilée*, 724–25.

121. Saint-Simon, *Mémoires*, 5:245; cf. Faure, *La banqueroute de Law*, 113.

122. Narbonne, *Journal des règnes*, 78. On the regent's dalliances with alchemy, see also Kerschagl, *Die Jagd nach dem künstlichen Gold*, 64; and Binswanger, *Money and Magic*, 31.

123. Pousse, *Examen des principes*, preface, 12–15, 99–100, 177–96 (quotes from preface [n.p.], 12, 100).

124. Geoffroy, "Des supercheries concernant la pierre philosophale," 61–69 (quote on 61). On Geoffroy's role in discrediting alchemy in the Académie des sciences, see Principe, "The End of Alchemy?" 105–7.

125. *Recueil Clairambault-Maurepas*, 3:144, 151, 133, 139–40.

126. *Recueil Clairambault-Maurepas*, 2:347–48, 359–60; Buvat, *Journal de la Régence*, 1:465–67 and 2:61(quote from 2:61).

127. *Recueil Clairambault-Maurepas*, 3:171, 172, 174, 219, 220.

128. Buvat, *Journal de la Régence*, 2:39. Buvat mistakenly refers to Lord Stair as "Stairs," an error duplicated in Rey, *Le temps du crédit*, 123n51.

129. Buvat, *Journal de la Régence*, 2:39.

130. On traditional representations of wealth as emblematic of the social order, see Shovlin, "Cultural Politics of Luxury."

131. Faure furnishes numerous examples of such transactions in *La banqueroute de Law*, 536–66.

132. The first use I have encountered is from the *Mercure de France*, Oct. 1719, 201.

133. *Mercure de France*, Oct. 1719, 199.

134. Piossens, *Mémoires de la Régence*, 1:preface; 2:321–31 (quotes from 1:preface [n.p.], 2:322, 329).

135. Marmont Du Hautchamp, *Histoire du système des finances*, 2:1–2, 82, 105–6, 217. On Marmont Du Hautchamp's participation in the System, see Murphy, *John Law*, 35–36.

136. Price increases began to outpace rises in wages during the winter of 1719–20 and reached a crisis stage by May. See Hamilton, "Prices and Wages," 49–54, 61–62; and Faure, *La banqueroute de Law*, 297–301, 611.

137. Buvat, *Journal de la Régence*, 1:18, 22, 32–34.

138. For the parlement's resistance, see Saint-Simon, *Mémoires*, 7:667–70, 690–98; Orain, *La politique du merveilleux*, 229–33; and Murphy, *John Law*, 253–54, 279–80.

139. On Law's System and the plague in Marseille, see Takeda, *Between Crown and Commerce*, 106–79; and McCloy, "Government Aid," 298–305.

140. Archives nationales, Paris, K 910, no. 19.

141. Terjanian, *Commerce and Its Discontents*, 18–23, 68–92, 182–83.

142. Lambert, *Décision théologique*, 1–2, 4–15 (quotes on 1, 8, 10, 14, 15).

143. Terrasson, *Mémoire pour servir*, 3–5, 22–50 (quotes on 5, 23, 24, 27, 41–42).

144. D'Alembert, *Éloge de Jean Terrasson*, 377.

145. Darnton, *Devil in the Holy Water*, 295–99.

146. L. M. D. M., *La vie de Philippe d'Orléans*, 2:92.

147. On the collapse of Law's System, see Barbier, *Chronique de la Régence*, 1:77–94, 112; Murphy, *John Law*, 244–311; and Faure, *La banqueroute de Law*, 428–535.

148. See Murphy, *John Law*, 7, 130–35, 164–65, 195–96, 254, 332–33; Faure, *La banqueroute de Law*, 220–42; and Kaiser, "Money, Despotism, and Public Opinion," 4–5, 12–14.

149. Saint-Simon, *Mémoires*, 7:650, 730–31.

150. Voltaire, *Précis du siècle de Louis XIV*, 163–65 (quote on 163). Cf. Voltaire, *Observations*, 359–60.

151. Montesquieu, *Lettres persanes*, 292–94, 305–16 (quotes on 292, 293, 307, 308). On the "Aeolian" trope in Montesquieu's fable, see also Magnot-Ogilvy, "Le Système au miroir," 80–83.

152. For an overview of this literature, see Harsin, *Les doctrines monétaires*, 237–59; Poirier, *Turgot*, 42–46; and Orain, *La politique du merveilleux*, 269–321.

153. Melon, *Essai politique sur le commerce*, 12–13 (quote on 13). For Melon's estimation of Law's System, see 93–98.

154. Dutot, *Réflexions politiques*, 1:17, 210–26 (quotes on 212, 213).

155. Montesquieu, *De l'esprit des lois*, 1:47–48, 3:161–62.

156. On Turgot's brief ecclesiastical career, see Poirier, *Turgot*, 29–50. On his engagement with Terrasson's letters, see Murphy, *The Genesis of Macroeconomics*, 133–54, esp. 139–41.

157. Turgot, "Deuxième lettre à l'abbé de Cicé," 142–52 (quotes on 146, 147).

158. On the discrepancy between money's stated function in classical economic theory and the compulsion it inspires, see Yuran, *What Money Wants*, 2–4, 16–21, 25–31.

159. I adapt the expression "transfer of sacrality" from Mona Ozouf's influential work on the political culture of the French Revolution; see Ozouf, *Festivals and the French Revolution*, 262–82.

160. Sewell, *Logics of History*, 225–70 (quotes on 228, 250, 252).

161. On the tendency of historical events to recast the past, present, and future in their own image, see Sewell, *Logics of History*, 236–44; Edelstein, *The Enlightenment*, 72–74, 100–103; and Chartier, *Cultural Origins*, 4–6, 88–89.

Chapter 4: Usury Redeemed

1. *Déclaration du roy, concernant les justiciables de la chambre de justice*, 5. On the organization and function of the *chambres de justice*, see Mousnier, *Les institutions de la France*, 1041–45.

2. Bibliothèque nationale de France, Département des Estampes et de la photographie, Collection Michel Henin, vol. 171, pièce 7688, Réserve QB-201 (171, 17)-FT 5, *Almanach pour l'année M.DCC XVII*.

3. Matt. 22:21.

4. On the mystical wine press, see Decker, *Technology of Salvation*, 1–5; and Bynum, *Christian Materiality*, 82–84.

5. *Almanach pour l'année M.DCC XVII*.

Notes to Chapter 4

6. See, e.g., *Arrest de la cour de parlement, qui condamne Jacques Boulleau* [. . .].

7. See, e.g., *Édit du roi, portant qu'à l'avenir le denier de l'intérêt de l'argent sera fixé* [. . .].

8. Prigent, *Observations sur le prêt à intérêt*, 1.

9. On the centrality of the problem of debt and credit in eighteenth-century political thought, see Sonenscher, *Before the Deluge*.

10. On the viability and sheer persistence of the prerevolutionary fiscal regime, see Norberg, "French Fiscal Crisis"; and Spang, *Stuff and Money*, 20–56.

11. On religious doctrines concerning usury and credit, see Buckley, *Teachings on Usury*, 85–186; Courdurié, *La dette des collectivités*; B. Nelson, *The Idea of Usury*; Robertson, *Aspects*, 88–167; Taeusch, "The Concept of 'Usury'"; and Taveneaux, *Jansénisme et prêt à intérêt*, 13–51. On the penitential regime in early modern France, see Delumeau, *L'aveu et le pardon*; Firey, *A New History of Penance*; Le Goff, *La naissance du purgatoire*; and Tingle, *Indulgences after Luther*.

12. Le Goff, *Your Money or Your Life*, 9.

13. See Lange, *Excommunication for Debt*.

14. See Fontaine, *The Moral Economy*, 4–99; Crowston, *Credit, Fashion, Sex*, 195–245; and Clavero, *La grâce du don*.

15. This claim runs counter to that of Groethuysen in *The Bourgeois*, 212–25.

16. Pontas, *Examen général de conscience*, 140–46 (quotes on 140, 143, 145, 149, 151).

17. For an overview of these positions, see Taveneaux, *Jansénisme et prêt à intérêt*, 17–23.

18. Le Semelier, *Conférences ecclésiastiques*, 1:101–19.

19. Kaye, *A History of Balance*, 24–41.

20. Carrel, *De la pratique des billets*, 26; cf. Aquinas, *Summa Theologica*, 10:330–31, 13:160–61.

21. Berman, *Law and Revolution*, 1–23, 113–18, 199–261.

22. On the medieval concept of equality in commercial exchanges, see Kaye, *A History of Balance*, 20–75.

23. Tierney, *Idea of Natural Rights*, 43–194.

24. McManners, *Church and Society*, 2:263.

25. Bulteau, *Le faux dépôt*, 96.

26. On Luther's and Calvin's approach to the question of usury, see B. Nelson, *The Idea of Usury*, 29–108 (quote from Calvin on 75); and Buckley, *Teachings on Usury*, 152–59.

27. Bulteau, *Le faux dépôt*, 98–120; Courdurié, *La dette des collectivités*, 56–60; McManners, *Church and Society*, 2:263–64.

28. See, e.g., Taveneaux, *Jansénisme et prêt à intérêt*, 31–94; McManners, *Church and Society*, 2:266–68; and Orain and Menuet, "Liberal Jansenists," 710. Edmond Préclin argues for the variability of Jansenist thought on usury; see "Les conséquences sociales de jansénisme," 386–90.

29. La Porte, *Principes théologiques*, 1:v, xix, xx. See 1:lxii–lxv and 3:22–416 for La Porte's critique of Mignot's *Traité des prêts de commerce* (1759).

30. Préclin, "Les conséquences sociales de jansénisme," 386–87; Taeusch, "The Concept of 'Usury,'" 303–4; Robertson, *Aspects*, 107–10; McManners, *Church and Society*, 2:271–74; Alonso-Lasheras, *Molina's "De Iustita Et Iure."*

31. Trivellato, "Usury and the 'Spirit of Commerce,'" 645–83; and Trivellato, *Promise and Peril*, 128–61.

32. Durand de Maillane, *Dictionnaire de droit canonique*, s.v. "Usure," 4:752.

33. Aquinas, *Summa Theologica*, 10:330–31, 336–37. On Aquinas's theory of the consumption of money, see also Langholm, *Aristotelian Analysis of Usury*, 82–90.

34. McManners, *Church and Society*, 2:263–64.

35. On the theological conditions governing loans, see also Courdurié, *La dette des collectivités*, 35–40; and Le Goff, *Your Money or Your Life*, 73–74.

36. Fontaine, *The Moral Economy*, 95–97.

37. Hoffman, Postel-Vinay, and Rosenthal, *Priceless Markets*, 98; on obligations and provisions for interest, see 15–16.

38. Hoffman, Postel-Vinay, and Rosenthal, 98–100.

39. On the clergy's superior credit in matters of public finance, see McManners, *Church and Society*, 1:142.

40. On interest rates during the eighteenth century, see Rowlands, *Financial Decline*, 76–78; and Velde and Weir, "The Financial Market," 12–15.

41. Archives nationales de France, Paris, O^1 * 50, fol. 84 v°, *Lettres patentes portants permission au clergé du diocese de Bourges d'emprunter 40,000 livres*.

42. *Délibération de l'Assemblée générale du clergé de France, du 11 juillet 1711, portant pouvoir d'emprunter huit millions de livres accordez au roy en l'Assemblée générale*, 3–4. On the 1710 conversion, see Homer and Sylla, *History of Interest Rates*, 168.

43. Archives nationales, Paris, G^8 111, IIIe Armoire, chap. 9, Contrat fait et passé entre le roi et le clergé de France le 8 décembre 1726 pour le paiement du don gratuit accordé à sa Majesté par ladite Assemblée, n.p.

44. Archives nationales, Paris, G^8 112, IIIe Armoire, chap. 9, Contrats passés entre le roi et le clergé pour le paiement du don gratuit de 15 millions de 1745 et pour celui des rentes de l'Hôtel de Ville de Paris, 2 juillet 1745, n.p.

45. Père Grangier, *Examen théologique*, 77–82 (quotes on 77, 80).

46. Courdurié, *La dette des collectivités*, 62–67; Flandreau, Galimard, Jobst, and Nogués-Marco, "The Bell Jar," 161–209, esp. 165 and 196; and Fontaine, *The Moral Economy*, 203–4.

47. *Arrêt de la cour de parlement, confirmatif de la sentence de Monsieur le lieutenant criminel au Châtelet de Paris, qui condamne le nommé François Chevaucheur usurier public*, 2.

48. *Arrest de la cour de parlement, qui condamne Jacques Boulleau* [...], 1–2, 4–5, 13, 26–27 (quotes on 5).

49. Crowston, *Credit, Fashion, Sex*, esp. 1–55, 97–137, 246–82; Fontaine, *The Moral Economy*, 49–62, 138–46; and Spang, *Stuff and Money*, 20–56.

50. Pontas, *Examen général de conscience*, 10–19, 261–73 (quote on 271).

51. Savary, *Le parfait négociant*, 1:1–2, 25–28 (quote on 1).

52. Savary, 2:150–60.
53. On the early practice of the *contractum trinius*, see Noonan, *Scholastic Analysis of Usury*, 203–25; and Buckley, *Teachings on Usury*, 136–42.
54. Decock, "Catholic Spirit of Capitalism?" 25–36; Noonan, *Scholastic Analysis of Usury*, 225–29.
55. On Jesuit rationalizations in favor of the triple contract, see McManners, *Church and Society*, 2:271–72; Noonan, *Scholastic Analysis of Usury*, 212–17; and Buckley, *Teachings on Usury*, 147–52.
56. On the Minims, see McManners, *Church and Society*, 1:580–81; and Whitmore, *The Order of Minims*, 182–84.
57. Maignan, *De l'usage licite de l'argent*, 1–3, 10–12, 15–25, 41–47 (quotes on 1, 3, 11, 47).
58. On the history of this distinction, see Langholm, *Aristotelian Analysis of Usury*, 52–53, 74–80.
59. Maignan, *De l'usage licite de l'argent*, 31, 47–78 (quotes on 31, 50, 70).
60. On Maignan's Eucharist theology and engagement with Cartesianism, see Whitmore, *The Order of Minims*, 165–78; Armogathe, *Theologia Cartesiana*, 109–11; and *Encyclopédie*, s.v. "Transsubstantiation," 16:563.
61. Maignan, *Philosophia sacra*, 867–68, 874–88.
62. Colonia, *Éclaircissement sur le légitime commerce*, dedicatory epistle, n.p. On the fairs of Lyon, see Brésard, *Les foires de Lyon*; and Farr, *The Work of France*, 128–29. On the establishment of merchant tribunals, see Trivellato, *Promise and Peril*, 86–87.
63. Colonia, *Éclaircissement sur le légitime commerce*, dedicatory epistle, 21–43, 271–74 (quotes on n.p., 25, and 273).
64. Taveneaux, *Jansénisme et prêt à intérêt*, 48–49, 210; Orain and Menuet, "Liberal Jansenists," 715–17. On Le Correur and Cartesianism, see Carrel, *De la pratique des billets*, pt. 2.85.
65. [Le Correur], *Traité de la pratique des billets entre les négociens*, Avertissement.
66. On bills of exchange, see de Roover, *L'évolution de la lettre de change*; and Trivellato, *Promise and Peril*, 24–30.
67. [Le Correur], *Traité de la pratique des billets*, 1–7 (quotes on 2, 3, 5, 7).
68. [Le Correur], 8–14, 18–45, 78–88, 143–66 (quotes on 8, 9, 35, 42). For the allusions to lending at interest in the Sermon on the Mount and the parable of the talents, see Matt. 5:42 and 25:14–30.
69. [Le Correur], *Traité de la pratique des billets*, 51–52, 78–88, 94–103, 175–86 (quotes on 52, 103).
70. Carrel, *De la pratique des billets*, pt. 1.i-iii, 1–16, 23–33 (quotes on iii, 2, 3, 7, 23, 24, 30).
71. Carrel, pt. 1.31–34; pt. 2.130–44 (quotes on 1.31, 33, 2.138, 142).
72. Carrel, pt. 2.7–29, 31–32, 146–49 (quotes on 26, 28, 29, 149). On stereotypes of Jewish financial acumen, see Trivellato, *Promise and Peril*, 12–13, 38–40, 107–11.
73. Carrel, *De la pratique des billets*, pt. 2.141–42.
74. Carrel, pt. 1:preface, 104–6 (quotes on 104, 106).

75. Grangier, *Examen théologique*, 4. Grangier's text was first published in 1741.
76. Taveneaux, *Le Jansénisme et prêt à intérêt*, 190.
77. Le Semelier, *Conférences ecclésiastiques*, 1:preface, vi.
78. Le Semelier, 1:1–15 (quotes on 1, 6, 9).
79. Le Semelier, 1:26–32, 173–76, 206–209, 414, 417 (quotes on 30, 31, 32, 206, 414). See 1:144–46 for the regulations of the parlements.
80. Le Semelier, 1:153–54, 190–95, 258–71 (quotes on 193, 262).
81. Le Semelier, 1:297–98. See also Fontaine, *The Moral Economy*, 164–78; and Courdurié, *La dette des collectivités*, 237–41.
82. Le Semelier, *Conférences ecclésiastiques*, 1:299.
83. Courdurié, *La dette des collectivités*, 241–43; Fontaine, *The Moral Economy*, 159–63, 179–82.
84. On the establishment and operations of lotteries, see Kruckeberg, "Wheel of Fortune," esp. 28–31, 59–61, 95–96, 155–57; and McManners, *Church and Society*, 2:268–72. For a discussion of lotteries in light of gambling more generally, see Kavanagh, *Enlightenment and the Shadows*, 29–63.
85. McManners, *Church and Society*, 2:270–71.
86. Le Semelier, *Conférences ecclésiastiques*, 4:92–100 (quotes on 94, 96, 99).
87. Le Semelier, 2:83–86, 111–13, 268–70.
88. Le Semelier, 2:232–37, 318–24 (quote on 323).
89. Le Semelier, 1:87–94, 134–43, 232–37 (quote on 136).
90. Taveneaux, *Jansénisme et prêt à intérêt*, 36–38.
91. Courdurié, *La dette des collectivités*, 47–49.
92. Benedict XIV, *Lettre encyclique*, 276, 277, 287.
93. On the conditions and consequences of Benedict's encyclical, see Courdurié, *La dette des collectivités*, 49–56; and McManners, *Church and Society*, 2:273–74.
94. Courdurié, *La dette des collectivités*, 54.
95. On the composition of the *Traité des prêts de commerce*, see Taveneaux, *Jansénisme et prêt à intérêt*, 69n89, n. 81n50; and Orain and Menuet, "Liberal Jansenists," 721–24.
96. Taveneaux, *Jansénisme et prêt à intérêt*, 81–83.
97. Mignot, *Traité des prêts de commerce* (1759 ed.), 1:1–50, 61–129 (quotes on 21, 62). Note that the *Traité* first appeared in 1738. Revised editions were published in 1759, 1762, 1767, and 1770. I will use Mignot to designate the collective author of the *Traité* in subsequent references, since he published the work under his own name in 1759.
98. La Porte, *Principes théologiques*, 1:vi, x, xiv, xviii.
99. La Porte, 2:303–28, 343–46, 426–34 (quote on 327).
100. Laforest, *Traité de l'usure*, 1–5, 27–44, 95–106, 133–37, 161–71 (quotes on 1, 96, 162, 169).
101. Carpuac, *Examen et réfutation*, i–iv, 2–47 (quotes on ii, 5).
102. Prigent, *Observations sur le prêt à intérêt*, 337–445 (quotes on 339, 349).
103. Courdurié, *La dette des collectivités*, 54–56.

104. Langholm, *Aristotelian Analysis of Usury*, 54–90.

105. Maignan, *De l'usage licite de l'argent*, 150–62 (quote on 159).

106. Le Semelier, *Conférences ecclésiastiques*, 1:5–12, 37–47, 110–19, 209–12 (quotes on 118, 211).

107. Mignot, *Traité des prêts de commerce* (1738 ed.), 92.

108. Le Gros, *Lettres théologiques*, lettre 22, 169. For Le Gros's biography, see Taveneaux, *Jansénisme et prêt à intérêt*, 210–11.

109. Mignot, *Traité des prêts de commerce* (1759 ed.), 1:160–87, 222–33, 2:60–79, 86–34, 148–59, 190–208, 274–76 (quotes on 1:186, 233).

110. Mignot, 3:461–70 (quotes on 463, 464, 465, 467–68). Cf. Perrier and Raviot, *Arrests notables*, 1:414–16.

111. Mignot, *Traité des prêts de commerce* (1759 ed.), 4:30–40 (quotes on 32, 35); cf. Ps. 71.

112. Mignot, *Traité des prêts de commerce*, 4:38.

113. Mignot, 4:112–58.

114. Mignot, 2:337; and Perrier and Raviot, *Arrests notables*, 1:414.

115. Mignot, *Traité des prêts de commerce* (1759 ed.), 4:155.

116. Laforest, *Traité de l'usure*, 107, 205, 207, 208, 235.

117. Prost de Royer, *Lettre à Monseigneur L'archévêque de Lyon*, 16, 58, 34, 37–38. On Prost de Royer's career as magistrate and president of the *tribunal de commerce*, see Taveneaux, *Jansénisme et prêt à intérêt*, 76n15.

118. La Porte, *Principes théologiques*, 1:129–46, 160–74 (quotes on 130, 133, 146, 165).

119. On the scandal in Angoulême and Turgot's response, see Poirier, *Turgot*, 142–45; and Rothschild, "An Alarming Commercial Crisis."

120. Turgot, *Mémoire sur les prêts d'argent*, 167, 168, 172, 183, 187.

121. Archives nationales, Paris, K 910, no. 23, "Avis donné au Conseil le 27 janvier 1770, par M. Turgot, Intendant de la généralité de Limoges, sur une accusation d'usure intentée en la sénéchaussée d'Angoulême, contre le Sr Marat, receveur des tailles, et autres," 85–86.

122. Poirier, *Turgot*, 144.

123. Turgot, *Mémoire sur les prêts d'argent*, 174–80 (quotes on 174, 177).

124. On time preference and the discounting of the future, see Rothbard, "Time Preference," 270–75.

125. Turgot, *Mémoire sur les prêts d'argent*, 180.

126. Turgot, 192–94 (quotes on 193, 194). On proposals for a credit union, see *Encyclopédie*, s.v. "Usure," 17:529–53; and Faiguet de Villeneuve, *L'ami des pauvres, ou l'Économie politique*.

127. On this prominent theme, see also Larrère, *L'invention de l'économie*, 7–8, 214–18; Perrot, *Une histoire intellectuelle*, 9–60, 257–68, 347–52; and Sheehan and Wahrman, *Invisible Hands*, 252–57.

128. Turgot, *Mémoire sur les prêts d'argent*, 181–82 (quote on 181).

129. Faiguet de Villeneuve, *Légitimité de l'usure légale*, 3, 46, 55, 56, 77.

130. Faiguet de Villeneuve, 20, 128.

131. Réguis, *La voix du pasteur* (1773 ed.), 4:334–39, 387–414, 424 (quotes on 339, 409, 424).

132. Even Laurence Fontaine, who argues for the persistence of traditional social relations in economic practice, asserts that "between the sixteenth and seventeenth centuries, the state took charge progressively of the legitimacy of discourse on usury as well as control of credit practices.... In the eighteenth century, the system of theological thinking is markedly detached from any economic dimension" (Fontaine, *The Moral Economy*, 205).

133. Bossuet, "Abrégé d'un sermon de M. Bossuet," 566. For a more recent elaboration of the theme, see Clavero, *La grâce du don*, 49–56, 96–108.

Chapter 5: The Cult of Consumption

1. [Chastain], *Le moine secularisé*. The first edition of the work was published in 1675. On the history of the text and its attribution to Jean Chastain, see Netz, "Grâce à une annotation."

2. On devotional practices related to the Rosary, see, e.g., Berny, *Instruction pour les confrères du Rosaire*.

3. *L'institution et les merveilles du Saint Scapulaire*, 51–101.

4. *Instruction pour ceux de l'archiconfrérie*, 7–10, 24–32 (quotes on 8, 27).

5. Chastain, *Le moine secularisé*, 13–14 (quote on 13).

6. *La bulle de N. S. Père le Pape Innocent XI*, 10.

7. For recent assessments of the so-called consumer revolution, see, e.g., Kwass, *Contraband*; Trentmann, *Empire of Things*; and Sewell, "Connecting Capitalism."

8. Roche, *Histoire des choses banales*, 16–17.

9. Roche, *La culture des apparences*, 110–17. See also the table included in the English edition: Roche, *The Culture of Clothing*, 109.

10. On changing fashions in textiles, see Roche, *La culture des apparences*, 126–38; Kwass, *Contraband*, 31–40; and Sewell, "The Empire of Fashion," 105–14.

11. Marx and Engels, *The German Ideology*, 52. See also C. Jones and Spang, "Sans-culottes," 38–40; and Kwass, *Contraband*, 17–18.

12. J. Jones, *Sexing La Mode*; Crowston, *Fabricating Women*; Crowston, *Credit, Fashion, Sex*, 96–138; and Roche, *La culture des apparences*, 119–48, 247–78, 447–76.

13. Sewell, "The Empire of Fashion," 86–87, 105–6, 116–18. For critical reflections on this claim, see Sonenscher, "The Empire of Fashion," 247–67.

14. Fairchilds, "Production and Marketing."

15. Characteristically, and as discussed further below, Fairchilds posed an early exception to the rule (Fairchilds, "Marketing the Counter-Reformation"). For a more recent overview emphasizing conditions of production and sale over consumption, see Lezowski and Tatarenko, "Façonner l'objet de dévotion chrétien."

16. Kwass, *Contraband*, 26–28; on Mandrin's life and career, see 70–86.

17. *Jugement souverain rendu en la cour du Parlement de Bordeaux*, 1, 2. On trends in corporeal punishment, see Foucault, *Discipline and Punish*; and Friedland, *Seeing Justice Done*.

18. A rare exception is Kwass, "Between Words and Things." Kwass's fascinating discussion of how the eighteenth-century French historical and economic writer Georges-Marie Butel-Dumont recalibrated the meanings of *nécessité*, *commodité*, and *luxe* is focused on what was regarded, strictly speaking, as superfluous.

19. Lezowski and Tatarenko, "Introduction," 17, 22–25; Thanh, "L'économie des objets," 208–10; and Trentmann, *Empire of Things*, 75–81, 95–110 (quote on 76). By focusing on the smuggler Mandrin, Kwass instead emphasizes the oppressive nature of state intervention; see Kwass, *Contraband*, 3–11.

20. On the significance of accessories, see Kwass, "Big Hair," 639–41; and De Vries, *Industrious Revolution*, 135, 140–44.

21. Kwass, *Contraband*, 22–24 (quote on 22). On this point Kwass also cites Courtwright, *Forces of Habit*.

22. Marx, *Contribution to the Critique*, 174 (emphasis in original).

23. Réguis, *La voix du pasteur* (1773 ed.), 2:23. On the compatibility of religious devotion and secular vocations, see P. Martin, "La boutique."

24. On this point, see McGowan, *Capitalism and Desire*, 6–15.

25. McManners, *Church and Society*, 1:97–99, 2:434–35.

26. Bonzon, *L'esprit de clocher*, 255–85, 369–77, 423–30.

27. *Dissertation, si la grandeur temporelle de l'Église n'est point contraire à la loi de Dieu*, 16.

28. *Canons and Decrees*, 218, 220.

29. On Richeome's career and legacy, see Bremond, *Histoire littéraire*, 1:20–66; and Ossa-Richardson, "Image and Idolatry," 41–53.

30. For an introduction to Jesuit visual culture, see Melion, "Introduction"; and Dekoninck, "Jesuit *Ars* and *Scientia Symbolica*."

31. Richeome, *Tableaux sacrez*, 1–6.

32. Richeome, 6, 7.

33. Richeome, 192–93, 233 (quote on 233). Cf. Exod. 25:23–30 and Matt. 12:4.

34. Bansilion, *L'idolâtrie papistique*, 3–6, 283–86 (quote on 3).

35. Richeome, *Défence des pèlerinages*, 41–55, 96–101 (quotes on 42, 100).

36. Sluhovsky, *Patroness of Paris*, 141–42, 217–18. On invocations of the saint, see also Gras, "Les processions"; and H. Williams, "Saint Geneviève's Miracles."

37. Sluhovsky, *Patroness of Paris*, 142; H. Williams, "Saint Geneviève's Miracles," 338–39.

38. On sumptuary legislation, see Lériget, *Des lois et impôts somptuaires*, 69–103; Moyer, "Sumptuary Law"; and Course, "'La façon.'"

39. Moyer, "Sumptuary Law," 68–78, 148–49, 337–69.

40. Moyer, 148–237.

41. *Ordonnance contre le luxe* (March 29, 1700), 20:355.

42. On French investment in manufacturing under Colbert, see D. C. Coleman, "Economic Problems and Policies," 39–41; and Shovlin, *Political Economy of Virtue*, 34–35.

43. On Colbert and the rise of French fashion, see DeJean, *The Essence of Style*, 8–9, 53–54.

44. On the economic impact of pilgrimage during the Catholic Reformation, see Maës, *Le roi*, 313–60, 487–512; Maës, "Légendaires de pèlerinages," 123–43; Maës, "Le pèlerinage de Notre-Dame," 612–44; Burkardt, *L'économie des dévotions*, 139–66; Ammannati, *Religione e istituzioni religiose*, 697–821; Duhamelle, "Le pèlerinage dans le Saint-Empire"; and McManners, *Church and Society*, 2:140–55.

45. Maës, "Artisans et commerçants," 143–51; Subirade, "Commerce et pèlerinage," esp. 122–40; and McManners, *Church and Society*, 2:145.

46. On this view, see Rothkrug, *Opposition to Louis XIV*, 99–110; and Shovlin, *Political Economy of Virtue*, 20–21.

47. Course, "'La façon,'" 116.

48. On these themes, see Burke, *Fabrication of Louis XIV*, esp. 49–69.

49. Richeome, *L'idolâtrie huguenote*, "Épître au roi."

50. Riskin, *Science in the Age of Sensibility*, 69–71 (quote on 70); Riskin, *The Restless Clock*, 12–43.

51. Voltaire, *Dictionnaire philosophique*, s.v. "Religion" and "Reliques," 20.4:357–64 (quotes on 359, 361, 362).

52. Voltaire, *Le mondain*, 83–88.

53. Friant, "Le catholicisme matériel," 459–91. On the use of after-death inventories, and the persistence of devotional objects in these registers, see Pardailhé-Galabrun, *La naissance de l'intime*, 26–33, 437–38; and Cornette, "La révolution des objets," esp. 485.

54. Fairchilds, "Marketing the Counter-Reformation," 31–58 (cited statistics on 36–37). In Pardailhé-Galabrun's sample from 1600 to 1790, 52 percent of the total inventories contain religious images, with the figure declining to 42 percent after 1750. For devotional objects, the figure is 45 percent. See Pardailhé-Galabrun, *La naissance de l'intime*, 429 and 437, as well as Leridon-Segui, "Les objets de piété"; and Colodiet, "L'objet religieux."

55. Pardailhé-Galabrun, *La naissance de l'intime*, 437–49, 468.

56. Burkardt, "Commerce et dévotions."

57. Fairchilds, "Marketing the Counter-Reformation," 52. See also Van Kley, "Pierre Nicole"; Dickey, "Pride, Hypocrisy and Civility"; and, for more recent examples, Orain, "The Second Jansenism"; and Grewal, "Political Theology of Laissez-Faire."

58. On the interiorization thesis, see Ariès, *L'homme devant la mort*; Maës, *Le roi*; and Froeschlé-Chopard, *Dieu pour tous*. For the classic statement of the dechristianization thesis, see Vovelle, *Piété baroque et déchristianisation*, xiv, 325–26; and Cousin, *Le miracle et le quotidien*, esp. 199–208.

59. On this point, see Aerts, "La religione nell'economia," 9–10; Duhamelle, "Pèlerinage et économie dans l'Empire," 714–20; Subirade, "Commerce et pèlerinage," 105–6; and Lezowski and Tatarenko, "Introduction," 13–15.

60. To cite but one example: Daniel Roche does not address devotional objects in either *Histoire des choses banales* or *La culture des apparences*.

61. Kwass, "Big Hair," 657.

Notes to Chapter 5

62. On the manufacture of religious objects, see Friant, "Le catholicisme matériel," 89–108; Subirade, "Commerce et pèlerinage," 111–26; and Lezowski and Tatarenko, "Introduction," 19–22.
63. Friant, "Le catholicisme matériel," 140–60, 163–74.
64. Subirade, "Commerce et pèlerinage," 124–26; Maës, "Artisans et commerçants," 148–51; Friant, "Le catholicisme matériel," 208–39.
65. Friant, "Le catholicisme matériel," 242–52.
66. On the widespread recitation of the Rosary, see Taveneaux, *Le catholicisme*, 2:368n8.
67. *Édit du roy, portant érection et création des articles*, 15–22; *Requeste présentée au roy par la Communauté des maistres patenôtriers-boutonniers d'émail, marchands verriers-fayanciers*, 24–25.
68. *Sentence de police*, 1–2, 3–8.
69. *Arrest du Conseil d'état du roy, du 21 septembre 1706*, 28–32.
70. Varenne de Beost, "Patenôtrier," in *Dictionnaire raisonné universel des arts et métiers*, 3:380–81.
71. Varenne de Beost, "Patenôtrier," in *Dictionnaire portatif des arts et métiers*, 2:326–38. The article was retained in the second, expanded edition of the work, with the addition of a paragraph on the three official communities of rosary-makers. See the preceding note. On Philippe Macquer's work and its relationship to the *Encyclopédie*, see Proust, "Deux Encyclopédistes hors de l'*Encyclopédie*," 330–36.
72. Varenne de Beost, "Patenôtrier," in *Dictionnaire portatif des arts et métiers*, 2:327. Macquer identifies Varenne de Beost as the article's author in "Patenôtrier," 334.
73. Varenne de Beost, 327–28.
74. Maës, "Artisans et commerçants," 150.
75. Varenne de Beost, "Patenôtrier," in *Dictionnaire portatif des arts et métiers*, 2:328–38, 329.
76. On the price of rosaries, see Maës, "Artisans et commerçants," 150; Maës, "Les conditions de voyage," 95; Friant, "Le catholicisme matériel," 170–74; and Mousnier, *La stratification sociale à Paris*, 118, 119, 122.
77. Pardailhé-Galabrun, *La naissance de l'intime*, 32, 438, 443–44.
78. Bernard, *Le triple Rosaire*, 22.
79. On the history of the rosary, see Migne, *Encyclopédie théologique*, s.v. "Rosaire," 27:162–65.
80. Viller et al., *Dictionnaire de spiritualité*, s.v. "Rosaire," 13:951–67; and Froeschlé-Chopard, *Dieu pour tous*, 67, 221–24.
81. Froeschlé-Chopard, "La dévotion du Rosaire," 299–306.
82. Froeschlé-Chopard, *Dieu pour tous*, 63–78, 221–83.
83. Bernard, *Le triple Rosaire*, 2–31 (quotes on 3, 29).
84. *Abrégé de la dévotion du Saint Rosaire*, 75–81 (quotes on 78).
85. *Abrégé de la dévotion du Saint Rosaire*, 10–12 (quotes on 12). Cf. Bernard, *Le triple Rosaire*, 28–31.

86. *Abrégé de la dévotion du Saint Rosaire*, 6–9 (quote on 6).

87. *Abrégé de la dévotion du Saint Rosaire*, 23–32 (quotes on 28–29).

88. "Merveille d'une image du S. Rosaire de simple papier," in Bernard, *Le triple Rosaire*, n.p.

89. Bernard, *Rosier mystique*, in *Le triple Rosaire*, 175.

90. Bibliothèque nationale de France, Département des Manuscrits, Fonds Français, 20344, fol. 345, *Formule des indulgences ordinaires* (Feb. 6, 1657). See also fols. 340 and 344.

91. *Recueil de plusieurs indulgences*, 22–23.

92. Collet, *Traité historique*, 1:14–15 (quote on 14).

93. *Recueil de plusieurs indulgences*, 3, 4, 5–6. Although this edition of the text was published in the nineteenth century, the references to papal decrees would seem to date it to the 1750s or 1760s. Robert Mandrou claims that the work is from the early eighteenth century; see Mandrou, *De la culture populaire*, 100.

94. Forestier, *Histoire des indulgences*, 156; quoted in Tingle, *Indulgences after Luther*, 89–90.

95. *La bulle de N. S. Père le Pape Innocent XI*, 14–15, 18, 21–22, 26–27.

96. *La bulle de N. S. Père le Pape Innocent XI*, 35–37, 39–40.

97. *Abrégé de la dévotion du Saint Rosaire*, 42–43 (quote on 43).

98. Barry, *Le paradis ouvert*, "Au Lecteur."

99. Barry, 5–7, 40–50, 78–82, 104, 207–9, 294–308 (quotes on 104, 296, 297, 298).

100. Barry, 304.

101. Pascal, *Les provinciales*, 1:173–79 (quote on 176).

102. Barry, *Le paradis ouvert*, 50–54, 130–33 (quote on 51).

103. *Abrégé de la dévotion du Saint Rosaire*, 33–34.

104. *Abrégé des fruits du Rosaire de la Sainte Vierge*, 4–8, 16–25 (quotes on 5, 22, 23, 24, 25).

105. See Thiers, *Traité des superstitions*. On Thiers's career, see Feller, *Biographie universelle*, 8:185–86, s.v. "Thiers (Jean-Baptiste)"; Dompnier, *La superstition*, 22–28; and Balzamo, "Une controverse sans débat."

106. Thiers, *De la plus solide, la plus nécessaire, et souvent la plus négligée de toutes dévotions*, 2:686–96 (quotes on 687, 689, 691).

107. Thiers, 2:696–710, 812–14, 839–46 (quotes on 697, 703, 842, 843). Cf. Thiers, *Traité des superstitions*, 4:1–32.

108. *Formulaire des indulgences que N. S. Père le Pape Clément XI*, 2–4 (quote on 4).

109. *Recueil de plusieurs indulgences*, 17–19. On Benedict XIV's role as an agent of the Enlightenment, see Messbarger, Johns, and Gavitt, *Benedict XIV and the Enlightenment*; his commitment to Tridentine reform is described in Kerber, "Vicar of Christ."

110. Mespolié, *Exercices spirituels*, 71–75, 109–50, 183–96 (quotes on 72, 73, 194).

111. Mespolié, 202–8 (quotes on 203, 205).

112. On the work's authorship, see Montagnes, "Les écrits," 140.

Notes to Chapter 5

113. Berny, *Instruction pour les confrères du Rosaire*, 11–12, 31–35 (quotes on 11, 12, 32, 33, 34).

114. *Abrégé de la dévotion du Saint Rosaire*, 8–9, 13–23, 31–43, 48–49, 75–78 (quotes on 35, 36, 77). Cf. Mespolié, *Exercices spirituels*, 334–77; and Berny, *Instruction pour les confrères du Rosaire*, 11–19.

115. On the economic-theological implications of the Incarnation, see Leshem, *The Origins of Neoliberalism*, 92–108; and Singh, *Divine Currency*, 27–38.

116. Bernard and Picart, *Cérémonies et coutumes religieuses de tous les peuples du monde*, "Préface générale."

117. Bernard and Picart, 1.2:153–76 (quotes on 168, 173, 174, 175, 176).

118. Bernard and Picart, 1.2:176–91 (quotes on 177, 181, 187).

119. My interpretation of the significance of anti-Catholic sentiment for Bernard and Picart's critical framework departs somewhat from Hunt, Jacob, and Mijnhardt's argument anticipating the advent of liberal toleration in *The Book That Changed Europe*, 194–213, esp. 198–206.

120. Bernard and Picart, *Cérémonies et coutumes religieuses de tous les peuples du monde*, 1.2:49, 58, 77, 170, 172, 2:96; for the image, see 1.2:115.

121. Bernard and Picart, *Cérémonies et coutumes religieuses des peuples idolâtres*, 2:226.

122. On the limits of toleration insofar as it was advanced as an ideal during the seventeenth and eighteenth centuries, see B. Kaplan, *Divided by Faith*.

123. Bernard and Picart, *Cérémonies et coutumes religieuses de tous les peuples du monde*, 5:106–10, 111–15. On Bernard's treatment of Islam, see Hunt, Jacob, and Mijnhardt, *Book That Changed Europe*, 247–69; and Brafman, "Picart, Bernard, Hermes, and Muhammad," 139–64. On the state of European knowledge of Islam in the eighteenth century, see Bevilacqua, *Republic of Arabic Letters*.

124. Bernard and Picart, *Cérémonies et coutumes religieuses des peuples idolâtres*, 1:12–19 (quote on 12).

125. On Bernard's financial and commercial dealings, see Hunt, Jacob, and Mijnhardt, *Book That Changed Europe*, 107–9.

126. In contrast to Hunt, Jacob, and Mijnhardt, Tomoko Masuzawa stresses that contemporary readers would have been drawn to Bernard and Picart's work for entertainment as much as Enlightenment; see Masuzawa, *Invention of World Religions*, 61–63.

127. On the emergence of religion as a distinct category of analysis, see Feil, *On the Concept of Religion*, 1–35; Stroumsa, *A New Science*; and Masuzawa, *Invention of World Religions*.

128. Marx, *Capital*, 1:76.

129. On eighteenth-century luxury and the "added fashion value" conferred on goods in the process of consumption itself, see Sewell, "Empire of Fashion," 85–87, 104–5 (quote on 87).

130. Marx, *Contribution to the Critique*, 175 (emphasis in original). On Marx's move from simple inversion to a fully dialectical criticism of religion, see Morris, "After de Brosses," 191–95.

131. On these themes, see Riskin, *The Restless Clock*; and Kavanagh, *Enlightened Pleasures*.

132. Rousseau, *Discours sur l'origine et les fondemens de l'inégalité*, 162; for the English translation, see Rousseau, *Discourse on the Origin*, 68. In emphasizing a form of binding contingency over positivist causality, I also draw on the "aleatory materialism" of Althusser. See Althusser, *Philosophy of the Encounter*, 167–207; for his discussion of Rousseau, see 183–88.

Chapter 6: Luxury and the Origins of the Fetish

1. On the commission of Rigaud's portrait, see James-Sarazin, *Hyacinthe Rigaud*, 1:209, 2:477–78.

2. Saint-Albin's life and career are treated briefly in Saint-Simon, *Mémoires*, 5:921, 6:765, and 7:341.

3. *Nouveau Mercure*, Feb. 1718, 211.

4. On the scandals involving Saint-Albin, see McManners, *Church and Society*, 1:50, 211, 238–39.

5. Ps. 65:1–13 (quoted are verses 9 and 11). For Saint-Albin's thesis, which takes Ps. 65:7 as its point of departure, see Saint-Albin, *Quaestio theologica*.

6. On the semiotics of consumption in Old Regime France, see Shovlin, "Cultural Politics of Luxury"; Kwass, "Ordering the World"; Maza, *Myth of the French Bourgeoisie*, 14–68; and Caplan, *In the King's Wake*, esp. 1–9.

7. Berg and Eger, "Rise and Fall."

8. On consumption and identity, see Berg, *Luxury and Pleasure*, esp. 1–16, 25–45; Kwass, "Big Hair"; Goodman, "Furnishing Discourses"; and J. Jones, *Sexing La Mode*, 113–44.

9. For an overview of this diverse and abundant literature, see Roche, *Histoire des choses banales*, 85–91; Kwass, "Big Hair," 633–34; Goodman, "Furnishing Discourses," 73–75; Provost, *Le luxe*; Terjianian, *Commerce and Its Discontents*, esp. 11–16, 26–67; Hont, "The Early Enlightenment Debate"; Berry, *The Idea of Luxury*, 126–76; and Jennings, "The Debate about Luxury."

10. Roche, *Histoire des choses banales*, 88; Provost, *Le luxe*, 7–14, 159–64.

11. Diderot and d'Alembert, *Encyclopédie*, s.v. "Encyclopédie," 5:635. The article was written by Denis Diderot.

12. Sénac de Meilhan, *Considérations sur les richesses et le luxe*, 112.

13. Sénac de Meilhan, 174–75n1.

14. See, e.g., Dickey, "Pride, Hypocrisy and Civility"; Hundert, "Bernard Mandeville"; and Grewal, "Political Theology of *Laissez-Faire*."

15. Van Kley, "Pierre Nicole"; and Orain, "The Second Jansenism."

16. Mandeville, *Fable of the Bees*, 1:51.

17. On the French reception of Mandeville, see Muceni, "Mandeville and France"; and Gottmann, "Du Châtelet, Voltaire."

18. Nicole, *Essais de morale*, 1:240–43. For a survey of thinkers who articulated similar views, see Hirschman, *Passions and the Interest*, 14–31.

19. Baker, "Enlightenment," 96; on Augustinianism, see 119–20.
20. Nicole, *Essais de morale*, 1:158.
21. Quoted in Palmer, *Catholics and Unbelievers*, 51.
22. On the importance of Epicureanism and Stoicism for Enlightenment moral philosophy, see Kavanagh, *Enlightened Pleasures*, 2–4, 218 (quote on 3). I depart from Kavanagh's claim that the *philosophes*' defense of pleasure broke with Christian antecedents. On the compatibility of Catholic and Enlightenment thinking on the question of pleasure, see Palmer, *Catholics and Unbelievers*, 29–52; and Mauzi, *L'idée du bonheur*, 180–97.
23. Caussin, *La cour sainte*, 1:80–83.
24. Pipet, *Instructions chrétiennes*, 562–64.
25. Pipet, preface, 50–58, 116–23, 569–71, 584, 588–90, 631–37 (quotes from preface, 569, 584).
26. Among other works, see Vassetz, *Traité contre le luxe des coiffures*; Philalèthe, *De la modestie des femmes*; and Gerbais, *Lettre d'un docteur de Sorbonne*.
27. Boileau, *De l'abus des nuditez de gorge*, 5–14, 105–6, 108–13 (quotes on 6, 7, 11, 12, 105).
28. Héron, *De la modestie des postulantes*, 1–54, 161–69 (quotes on 2, 6, 9, 50).
29. Quoted in Hébrard, *Histoire de Messire Claude Joly*, 485–86 (quote on 485).
30. Joly, *Prônes*, 1:340–51, 430–36, 2:101–4, 144–46, 165–81 (quotes on 1:340 and 2:101, 144, 172, 178).
31. Gourdan, *Le chrestien heureux*, 1:iv, 288, 339.
32. Gourdan, 1:239–59 (quotes on 239, 240, 246, 250, 251).
33. Gourdan, 1:261, 275–76; cf. Rom. 13:14.
34. Gourdan, 2:201–3.
35. Mandeville, *Fable of the Bees*, 1:228. On Mandeville's rendering of the acquisitiveness of women into a sociological axiom, see Hundert, "Mandeville, Rousseau," 30–32.
36. Montesquieu, *Persian Letters*, 195; cf. Montesquieu, *Lettres persanes*, 221.
37. On the various currents of organized resistance to Louis XIV's policies during this period, see Rothkrug, *Opposition to Louis XIV*, 372–457.
38. Du Pradel, *Traité contre le luxe*, preface.
39. Du Pradel, 1–10, 53–60, 107–15 (quotes on 2, 53, 57).
40. Du Pradel, ii.
41. Rothkrug, *Opposition to Louis XIV*, 234–98.
42. Fénelon, *Plans de gouvernement [Table de Chaulnes]*, 182–94 (quote on 188).
43. Fénelon, *Œuvres spirituelles*, 1:66.
44. Chérel, *Fénelon au XVIIIe siècle*; Kates, "Fénelon's *Telemachus*," (unpublished manuscript).
45. On the publication statistics for *Télémaque*, see Kates, "Fénelon's Telemachus," 31–33.
46. Kates, 5–8.
47. See also Hont, "The Early Enlightenment Debate," 382–87.

48. Fénelon, *Les aventures de Télémaque*, 426.

49. On Fénelon's political thought, see Riley, "Fénelon's 'Republican' Monarchism"; and Edelstein, *Terror of Natural Right*, 57–62.

50. Edelstein, *Terror of Natural Right*, 61–62, 94–101.

51. Voltaire, *Le mondain*, 83–87 (quote on 84). Voltaire appears to have modified his views over time, however; see Gottmann, "The Eighteenth-Century Luxury Debate."

52. Montesquieu, *De l'esprit des lois*, 3:51–52. On the distinction between *commerce d'économie* and *commerce de luxe*, see Cheney, *Revolutionary Commerce*, 67–73.

53. Diderot and d'Alembert, *Encyclopédie*, s.v. "Luxe," 9:763–71 (quotes on 763, 770).

54. Diderot, *Observations sur la Nakaz*, 411–12.

55. On Rousseau's intellectual debt to Fénelon, see Chérel, *Fénelon au XVIIIe siècle*, 393–400; and Riley, "Rousseau, Fénelon, and the Quarrel," 81–89.

56. Grimm to Gottsched, Nov. 25, 1752, in *Correspondance complète de Jean-Jacques Rousseau*, 2:202; also quoted in Cranston, *Jean-Jacques*, 234.

57. Rousseau, *Discours sur les sciences et les arts*, 8, 15, 28.

58. Rousseau, *Observations de J.-J. Rousseau*, 37–52 (quotes on 41, 44, 45, 51).

59. Rousseau, *Discours sur l'origine et les fondemens de l'inégalité*, 174–75, 193.

60. On Smith's comparisons of Mandeville and Rousseau, see, for instance, Force, *Self-Interest before Adam Smith*, 18–35; Hundert, "Bernard Mandeville and the Enlightenment's Maxims of Modernity," 591–92; and Hont, *Politics in Commercial Society*, 18–22. Hont has applied Smith's remarks regarding the similarities between Mandeville and Rousseau to Smith and Rousseau. As he argues, "it seems that Smith the political economist and Rousseau, political economy's arch critic, shared moral foundations"—namely, an acceptance of pity or sympathy as a natural impulse (21).

61. Smith, "Letter to the *Edinburgh Review*," in *The Glasgow Edition of the Works and Correspondence of Adam Smith*, 3:250, 251.

62. Rousseau, *Discours sur l'origine et les fondemens de l'inégalité*, 192.

63. On Rousseau's reception among members of the Second Estate, see Galliani, *Rousseau*; and Shovlin, *Political Economy of Virtue*, 24–26.

64. Rousseau, *Discours sur l'économie politique*, 241–51 (quotes on 241, 245, 248); cf. Rousseau, *Du contrat social*, 360–62.

65. Rousseau, *Discours sur l'économie politique*, 263–78 (quotes on 263, 265, 267, 268, 270, 276, 277).

66. Rousseau, 269; cf. Rousseau, *Discours sur l'origine et les fondemens de l'inégalité*, 185.

67. On Rousseau's religious upbringing, see Rosenblatt, *Rousseau and Geneva*, 11–17. Rousseau's religious views are examined at length in Masson, *La religion de Jean-Jacques Rousseau*.

68. Rousseau, *Julie, or the New Heloise*, 384; cf. Rousseau, *Julie, ou La nouvelle Héloïse*, 467.

69. On this point, see Spector, *Rousseau et la critique*, 117–27.

70. Rousseau, *Julie, or the New Heloise*, 443, 544; cf. Rousseau, *Julie, ou La*

Notes to Chapter 6

nouvelle Héloïse, 541–42, 662. On Julie's *art de jouir*, see Spector, *Rousseau et la critique*, 118–19. On Rousseau's relationship to Stoicism and Epicureanism, see Force, *Self-Interest before Adam Smith*, 48–90; and Hont, *Politics in Commercial Society*, 14–35.

71. On the evolution of Rousseau's views on the general will, see Crocker, *Rousseau's Social Contract*, 49–54; and Riley, "Rousseau's General Will," 124–53.

72. Rousseau, *Du contrat social*, 360, 364, 367.

73. Rousseau, 372, 381, 382, 384.

74. Rousseau, *Émile*, 249.

75. This is the case made for Rousseau's political thought in Riley, *General Will before Rousseau*, 79–98.

76. My argument thus deviates from Ernst Cassirer, *The Question of Jean-Jacques Rousseau*, 70–76. For a recent adaptation of Cassirer's view, see Cooper, *Secular Powers*, 113–16.

77. On Rousseau's synthesis of natural law and legal generality, see Edelstein, *Terror of Natural Right*, 75–86.

78. See also C. Coleman, *The Virtues of Abandon*, 235–40, 246–47.

79. See Shovlin, *Political Economy of Virtue*, esp. 1–12.

80. For overviews of Physiocratic thought, see Fox-Genovese, *The Origins of Physiocracy*; Weulersse, *Le mouvement physiocratique*; Higgs, *The Physiocrats*; Steiner, *La "science nouvelle"*; Hochstrasser, "Physiocracy"; and Vardi, *The Physiocrats*.

81. Fox-Genovese, *The Origins of Physiocracy*, 140.

82. Rothkrug, *Opposition to Louis XIV*, 458–69; Larrère, *L'invention de l'économie*, 8–13, 193–204; and Jaume, *L'individu effacé*, 474–75.

83. Larrère, *L'invention de l'économie*, 196, 202–4; Sonenscher, *Before the Deluge*, 202–22; and Edelstein, *On the Spirit*, 78.

84. On the relationship between Rousseau and the Physiocrats, see Spector, *Rousseau et la critique*, 24–30; and Sonenscher, *Before the Deluge*, 222–33.

85. See also Larrère, *L'invention de l'économie*, 10–14, 196–201; and Rétat, "La jouissance physiocratique." As Larrère notes, Physiocratic theory is opposed to Weber's Protestant ethic (*L'invention de l'économie*, 201).

86. See, e.g., Hochstrasser, "Physiocracy," 419–20; Vardi, *The Physiocrats*, 10–20; and Schachter, "François Quesnay," 313–22. In the vanguard of the revisionist scholarship is Shovlin, *Political Economy of Virtue*, 3, 111–13; Cheney, *Revolutionary Commerce*, 8–10; and Vardi, *The Physiocrats*, 20–22.

87. Shovlin, *Political Economy of Virtue*, 80–117; S. Kaplan, *Bread, Politics and Political Economy*, 1:398–99.

88. Edelstein, *Terror of Natural Right*, 101–5; Edelstein, *On the Spirit*, 74–88.

89. Vardi, *The Physiocrats*, 3–4, 20–21, 124–29.

90. Diderot and d'Alembert, *Encyclopédie*, s.v. "Évidence," 6:146, 157.

91. Quesnay, *Analyse du Tableau économique*, 58–69 (quotes on 68, 64, 67).

92. Quesnay, "Observations sur l'intérêt," 159.

93. Fox-Genovese, *Origins of Physiocracy*, 272.

94. See Nadler, *Occasionalism*.

Notes to Chapter 6

95. On Malebranche's philosophy and the Physiocratic worldview, see Larrère, *L'invention de l'économie*, 196–203.

96. On the composition and publication history of the text, see Sabbagh, "The *Philosophie rurale*"; and Théré and Charles, "Writing Workshop of François Quesnay."

97. Quesnay, Mirabeau, and Butré, *La philosophie rurale*, ii, xvii.

98. Quesnay, Mirabeau, and Butré, xviii, xix.

99. Quesnay, Mirabeau, and Butré, 101, 102.

100. Quesnay, Mirabeau, and Butré, xvii.

101. Quesnay, *Maximes générales*, 81.

102. On the Physiocrats' problematic joining of laissez-faire economics and legal despotism, see Fox-Genovese, *Origins of Physiocracy*, 12–13, 50–52, 235; Hochstrasser, "Physiocracy," 429–38; and Edelstein, *Terror of Natural Right*, 105–6.

103. Sonenscher discusses the moral implications of this doctrine in *Before the Deluge*, 220–21.

104. Quesnay, Mirabeau, and Butré, *La philosophie rurale*, i–xvi (quotes on xiii, xiv).

105. S. Kaplan, *The Bakers of Paris*, 3, 24–25.

106. S. Kaplan, *Bread, Politics and Political Economy*, 1:90–254, 2:409–50, 490–521; Shovlin, *Political Economy of Virtue*, 102–17; and Fox-Genovese, *Origins of Physiocracy*, 58–67.

107. On Turgot's relationship to the Physiocrats, see Vardi, *The Physiocrats*, 252–55; and Larrère, *L'invention de l'économie*, 214–18.

108. S. Kaplan, *Bread, Politics and Political Economy*, 2:611–70; Poirier, *Turgot*, 282–96; and Shepherd, *Turgot and the Six Edicts*.

109. Burson, *Rise and Fall*, 128–30.

110. Poirier, *Turgot*, 31–50 (quote from the archbishop of Tours cited on 31).

111. Turgot, *Discours sur les avantages que l'établissement de christianisme a procuré*, 194–214 (quotes on 195, 200, 206).

112. This interpretation departs from that of Sheehan and Wahrman in *Invisible Hands*, 252–57, where they identify Turgot with a decline in theological preoccupations among theorists of self-organization.

113. Archives nationales, Paris, Fonds Turgot, 745AP 40, Dossier 4 (Philosophie, métaphysique), "Project d'article (pour l'*Encyclopédie*) sur l'existence de Dieu." The dossier's title page lists 1755 as a possible date. Gustave Schelle, in his edition of Turgot's works, proposes 1753; see Schelle, "Turgot, sa vie et ses œuvres," 58.

114. Turgot, "Sur le mot amour," 358–64 (quotes on 359, 362, 364).

115. On the composition of Turgot's *Réflexions*, see Poirier, *Turgot*, 101–2.

116. Turgot, *Réflexions*, 536–41 (quotes on 538, 541).

117. Poirier, *Turgot*, 103.

118. Turgot, *Réflexions*, 550, 551.

119. Turgot, 554–70 (quotes on 554, 557, 560, 567).

120. Turgot, 575–79 (quotes on 575, 577, 578).

121. Turgot, 581–601 (quotes on 584, 588, 599, 600, 601).

122. Turgot, "Instruction lue à la assemblée," 205–19 (quotes on 205, 206, 207).

123. On the Physiocrats' complex relationship to secular liberalism, see Mastier, *Turgot, sa vie et sa doctrine*, 80; Fox-Genovese, *Origins of Physiocracy*, 304–5, 313–14; and Larrère, *L'invention de l'économie*, 5–6.

124. Réguis, *La voix du pasteur* (1773 ed.), 2:173–79 (quote on 179).

125. Butel-Dumont, *Théorie du luxe*, 1.iii–ix, 32–43 (quotes on 32, 41, 43).

126. Butel-Dumont, 1.46–48, 93–99 (quotes on 46, 95). On Butel-Dumont's appropriation of sensationalist psychology, see Kwass, "Ordering the World," 102–5.

127. Butel-Dumont, *Théorie du luxe*, 1.8–62, 107–24 (quote on 61).

128. Butel-Dumont, 1.98–99.

129. Butel-Dumont, 1.171–83, 2.66–127 (quotes on 1.171, 2.122–23).

130. Baudeau, "Théorie du luxe," 182, 186, 202 (emphasis in the original).

131. Turgot, *Valeurs et monnaies*, 88.

132. Rosenfeld, *A Revolution in Language*, 13–56.

133. Terjanian, *Commerce and Its Discontents*, 50–51.

134. Butel-Dumont, *Théorie du luxe*, 2.193–94.

135. On the *guerre des farines*, see S. Kaplan, *Bread, Politics and Political Economy*, 2:670, 693–98; and Bouton, *The Flour War*.

136. Poirier, *Turgot*, 334–47.

137. On the decision in the Angoulême case, see Orain, "The Second Jansenism," 483.

138. Prigent, *Observations sur le prêt*, 106, 116–23, 130–44 (quotes on 119–20, 134, 136).

139. Jennings, "The Debate about Luxury," 85–89.

140. Raynal, *Histoire*, 1:12, 14, 265, 461 (quote on 14).

141. On this point, see also Terjanian, *Commerce and Its Discontents*, 54–55.

142. Raynal, *Histoire*, 4:506.

143. Raynal, 3:91, 201.

144. Raynal, 4:595, 631.

145. On this theme, see Garraway, *The Libertine Colony*, esp. 20–34.

146. Genty, *Discours sur le luxe*, 3, 7–9, 16–17 (quotes on 3, 16, 17).

147. Genty, 33–42 (quotes on 33, 34, 39, 42). Cf. Marx and Engels, *The German Ideology*, 52.

148. Pluquet, *Traité philosophique et politique sur le luxe*, 1:1–41 (quotes on 18, 37).

149. Pluquet, 1:59, 60.

150. Pluquet, 1:60–65 (quotes on 64, 65).

151. Pluquet, 1:66–112 (quotes on 69, 76, 82, 90, 104 [italics in original]).

152. Pluquet, 1:104, 2:36–48 (quotes on 1:104, 2:36, 37, 38).

153. Pluquet, 2:49–51 (quotes on 49, 50).

154. Pluquet, 2:82–101, 129–65, 242–63 (quotes on 129, 130, 146, 152, 245).

Epilogue: Encounters with Economic Theology

1. De Brosses, *Du culte des dieux fétiches*, 10, 18, 52 (italics in original). On the etymology of the term, see also Pietz, "Problem of the Fetish II," 23–45; and Morris, "After de Brosses," 142–43.

2. De Brosses, *Du culte des dieux fétiches*, 63, 64.

3. De Brosses, 5–17, 110–17, 182–98 (quotes on 7, 182–83). On de Brosses's critique of both Christian and Enlightenment pretensions to intellectual superiority, see Leonard, "Introduction," 3–5, 10–15, 34–39.

4. De Brosses, *Du culte des dieux fétiches*, 275–82; Leonard, "Introduction," 13–14.

5. On the place of Christianity in the history of fetishism and the problematic nature of the Eucharist, see Pietz, "Problem of the Fetish I," 10–11; and Pietz, "Problem of the Fetish II," 25–30, 39–40.

6. On this point, see Mitchell, *Iconology*, 193; and Morris, "After de Brosses," 195.

7. Leonard, "Introduction," 36–37; Poirier, *Turgot*, 36, 38.

8. See, in particular, the extended treatment of this subject recently offered by Roland Boer in *Marxism and Theology*.

9. Marx, *Contribution to the Critique*, 175, 176 (emphasis in original).

10. Marx, *Capital*, 1:83 (emphasis in original).

11. See G. Jones, *Karl Marx*, 102–3; and Pietz, "Fetishism and Materialism," 134–35.

12. Marx, *Capital*, 1:46.

13. Marx, 54.

14. Marx, 58, 59, 72.

15. Marx, 77.

16. On Marx's familiarity with these debates through Hegel, see Cole, *The Birth of Theory*, 86–104. Cole concludes that Marx's understanding should be approached in terms of "consubstantiation of the sort most often associated with Luther" (97), a position that occludes the specifically Catholic economic-theological elements of his critique in *Capital*.

17. Marx, "Comments on James Mill," 212, 213 (emphasis in original).

18. Marx, *Capital*, 1:95, 96. On the allusion to Jerome, see Van Leeuwen, *Critique of Earth*, 210.

19. Marx, *Capital*, 1:111, 129.

20. Marx, 1:132–33, 152.

21. Marx, *Capital, Volume 3*, 587.

22. Marx, *Theories of Surplus Value*, 449, 450, 451 (emphasis in original).

23. Marx, 490, 494.

24. Benjamin, "Capitalism as Religion," 259, 260.

25. On this theme, see Markus, "Walter Benjamin."

26. Benjamin, "Paris, Capital of the Nineteenth Century," 17, 18, 19.

27. Yet, as Gyorgy Markus points out, the occlusion of labor in the commodity form also allows for "a weak remnant of the sacred" in a "world of re-enchantment." See Markus, "Walter Benjamin," 16.

28. Benjamin, "Paris, Capital of the Nineteenth Century," 19.

29. Benjamin, "Paris of the Second Empire, 85, 86.

30. On this theme, see Spencer, "Allegory in the World," 66–68.
31. Benjamin, *Central Park*, 146, 148–49.
32. Spencer, "Allegory in the World," 68. See also Benjamin, *Central Park*, 169.
33. Benjamin, *Central Park*, 155, 161.
34. Benjamin, "Capitalism as Religion," 259, 260.
35. Benjamin, "First Sketches," 862.
36. Benjamin, Convolute B, "Fashion," 68, 69. On the emancipatory potential of fashion in Benjamin, see Markus, "Walter Benjamin," 27–33.
37. On Benjamin's engagement with theology, see Boer, *Criticism of Heaven*, 70–86.
38. Benjamin, Convolute N, "On the Theory of Knowledge," 471.
39. On Marchand's life and career, see Barrovecchio, "Plaidoyer"; and Lilti, *The Invention of Celebrity*, 16.
40. [Marchand], *L'enthousiasme français*, 4, 9, 12, 43, 56, 80. On the authorship of the text, see Conlon, *Le siècle de lumières*, 14:475.
41. See Heyd, *Be Sober and Reasonable*; and Goldstein, "Enthusiasm or Imagination."
42. Todd, *Free Trade*, 5.
43. On the commercialization of pilgrimage at Lourdes, see Kaufman, *Consuming Visions*; and Harris, *Lourdes*.
44. Kaufman, *Consuming Visions*, 4–5, 9–10, 16–18, 45–48.
45. Marx, *Capital*, 1:58. On the fraught issue of religious debasement at Lourdes, see Kaufman, *Consuming Visions*, 4, 62–94.
46. Todd, *Free Trade*, 9–10; Crouzet, "The Historiography of French Economic Growth," 224, 232; M. Miller, *The Bon Marché*, 31–32; Horn, *The Path Not Taken*.
47. The account of the department store in this paragraph follows that of M. Miller, *The Bon Marché*, esp. 48–53.
48. On fantasy and the rise of mass consumption in nineteenth-century France, see R. Williams, *Dream Worlds*, 58–106; and M. Miller, *The Bon Marché*, 165–89.
49. Zola, *Au bonheur des dames*, 521–22.
50. Zola, 522. On Zola's fallacy of secularization, see also Kaufman, *Consuming Visions*, 63, 74–79.
51. See DeJean, *The Essence of Style*, 9–10.
52. DeJean, 267. On the "wish image," see Benjamin, "Paris," 4.
53. Metropolitan Museum of Art, "1,659,647 Visitors."
54. Tracy, "The Catholic Imagination," 13–15 (quote on 15).
55. Mann, "A Vision of Beauty," 107.
56. "Début of the Winter Mode," 60.
57. Chaney, *Coco Chanel*, 17–27, 306.
58. Benjamin, "Paris, Capital of the Nineteenth Century," 18.

Bibliography

Primary Sources/Manuscripts

Archives nationales de France, Paris
    Fonds Turgot, 745AP 40, Dossier 4 (Philosophie, métaphysique).
    Minutier central, Étude CV, liasse 796.
    Series G^8 111, IIIe Armoire, Chap. 9.
    Series G^8 112, IIIe Armoire, Chap. 9.
    Series G^8 796 *.
    Series K 884, no. 1/bis.
    Series K 910, nos. 19, 23.
    Series O^1 * 50, fol. 84 v°.
    Series O^1 * 70, fols. 67–69.

Bibliothèque nationale de France, Paris, Département des Manuscrits
Français 463. Robert Desgabets, *La philosophie eucharistique, contenant l'explication de la manière dont Notre-Seigneur est présent au Très-Saint Sacrement de l'autel, suivant l'opinion de St. Jean de Damas, par le P. Desgabets, religieux bénédictin de la congrégation de St.-Vannes.*
Français 20344, fol. 340. *Indulgences du chappelet de nostre seigneur.* Rome: l'Imprimeur de la Chambre Apostolique, 1658.
Français 20344, fol. 344. *Formulaire des indulgences extraordinaires, pour les fidelles de Jesus Christ, de l'un et l'autre sexe, qui auront en leur maison en particulier, quelque couronne, rosaire, croix, ou image beniste.* Rome: l'Imprimerie de la Chambre Apostolique, 1657.

Bibliothèque nationale de France, Paris, Département des Estampes et de la photographie
Collection Michel Hennin. Vol. 101, pièce 8727, Réserve QB-201 (101)-FOL, p. 20. Médaille (*Custos unitatis schismatis ultrix*) [1752].
Collection Michel Henin. Vol. 171, pièce 7688, Réserve QB-201 (171, 17)-FT 5. *Almanach pour l'année M.DCC XVII.*

Primary Sources/Printed

Abrégé de la dévotion du Saint Rosaire, qui renferme l'origine, l'exercise, l'excellence, l'utilité et les indulgences accordées à cette confrerie. Grenoble: André Faure, n.d. [1754].

Abrégé des fruits du Rosaire de la Sainte Vierge Marie mère de Dieu. Avec une instruction pour bien reciter le chapelet. Paris: André Cramoisy, 1696.

L'affaire du refus des sacremens à l'article de la mort fait par le curé de S. André des Arts à un de ses paroissiens, avoit d'abord fait beaucoup de bruit, et cependant paroissoit assoupie, lorsque le curé de S. Étienne du Mont, sous prétexte du défaut d'un billet de confession, fit le même refus le 22 mars dernier, à un prêtre mourant de sa paroisse. N.p., n.d.

Alembert, Jean Le Rond d'. *Éloge de Jean Terrasson*. In *Œuvres de d'Alembert*. Vol. 3.1:370–79. 1821–22. Reprint, Geneva: Slatkine, 1967.

Almanach pour l'année M.DCC XVII. Paris: F. G. Jollain, n.d. [1717].

Aquinas, Thomas. *The "Summa Theologica" of St. Thomas Aquinas*. Translated by the Fathers of the English Dominican Province. 22 vols. London: Burns, Oates and Washbourne, 1929.

Arnauld, Antoine. *De la fréquente communion, où les sentimens des Pères, des Papes, et des Conciles, touchant l'usage des sacremens de penitence et d'Eucharistie, sont fidèlement exposez*. Paris: Antoine Vitré, 1643.

———. *La perpétuité de la foy de l'Église catholique touchant l'Eucharistie, défendue contre les livres du Sieur Claude, ministre de Charenton*. New ed. 6 vols. Paris: la Veuve Charles Savreux, 1702-4.

Arnoulx, François. *Du paradis et de ses merveilles, où est amplement tracté de la félicité éternelle, et de ses joye*. Rouen: Jacques Loudet, 1676.

———. *Merveilles de l'autre monde, contenant les horribles tormens de l'enfer, les admirables joyes de paradis, avec le moyen d'éviter l'un et acquérir l'autre, divisé en trois livres, le tout recueilly des Écritures sainctes et docteurs de l'Église*. Rouen: J. Courant, 1676.

Arrest de la cour de parlement concernant le refus de sacrement fait à Me Lagarde, conseiller au présidial de Montpellier. N.p., n.d. [1756].

Arrest de la cour de parlement, qui condamne Jacques Boulleau, Claude Vidy, Nicolas Naudin et Jeanne Lepage, femme de Jacques Filion, au carcan et au bannissement pour 9 ans, pour usures. Paris: Pierre-Guillaume Simon, Imprimeur du Parlement, 1777.

Arrest de la cour de parlement, qui condamne un imprimé intitulé: Mandement de Monseigneur l'évêque de Troyes, du 23 juillet 1756, à être lacéré et brulé par l'exécuteur de la haute-justice. Paris: P. G. Simon, 1756.

Arrest du Conseil d'état du roy, du 21 septembre 1706, qui réunit la Communauté des maistres émailleurs, verriers-fayanciers, patenostriers-boutonniers en émail, verre et cristalin, de la ville et fauxbourgs de Paris, avec les marchands verriers-fayanciers, maistres couvreurs de flacons et bouteilles en osier, de ladite ville. In *Articles, statuts, ordonnances et règlemens,* 28–32.

Arrest du Conseil d'état du roy, qui révoque le privilege accordé pour l'impression du livre intitulé, "L'esprit de Jésus-Christ et de l'Église sur la fréquente communion, etc." Paris: l'Imprimerie royale, 1748.

Arrest du parlement, du 30 juin 1755, qui condamne Me Granet, curé de la paroisse Notre-Dame-des-Tables de Montpellier, à un bannissement perpétuel. Toulouse: Bernard Pijon, n.d. [1755].

Arrest du parlement qui condamne Me Aymé, curé de la paroisse Sainte-Anne de Montpellier à un bannissement perpétuel. Toulouse: Bernard Pijon, 1756.

Arrêt de la cour de parlement, confirmatif de la sentence de Monsieur le lieutenant criminel au Châtelet de Paris, qui condamne le nommé François Chevaucheur usurier public, à faire amende honorable au Parc civil du Châtelet, et au bannissement pour neuf ans. Paris: l'Imprimerie de P. J. Mariette, 1736.

Arrêt du parlement ordonnant lacération et destruction par le feu de l'écrit imprimé intitulé: "Consultation de plusieurs canonistes et avocats de Paris sur la compétence des juges séculiers par rapport au refus de sacremens." N.p., n.d. [1753].

Articles, statuts, ordonnances et règlemens de la communauté des gardes jurez, anciens bacheliers et marchands verriers, maistres couvreurs de flacons et bouteilles en ozier. Paris: M. Rebuffé, 1712.

Augustine of Hippo. *The City of God.* Translated by Henry Bettenson. London: Penguin, 2003.

Bansilion, Jean. *L'idolâtrie papistique, opposée en réponse à "L'idolâtrie huguenote" de Louis Richeome.* Geneva: Paul Marceau, 1608.

Barry, Paul de. *Le paradis ouvert à Philagie par cent dévotions à la mère de Dieu.* Lyon: Mathieu Liberal, 1681.

Baudeau, Nicolas. "Théorie du luxe." *Ephémérides du citoyen, ou Bibliothèque raisonnée des sciences morales et politiques* 9 (1770): 181–206.

Beaumont, Christophe de. *Lettre de Monseigneur l'archévêque de Paris, aux curés et aux confesseurs séculiers et réguliers de son diocèse; par laquelle il leur adresse la rétraction de l'auteur du livre intitulé, "L'esprit de Jésus-Christ et de l'Église sur la fréquente Communion."* Paris: Claude Simon and Claude-François Simon, 1748.

Belin, Jean-Albert. *Apologie du grand œuvre, ou Élixir des philosophes.* Paris: Pierre de Bresche, 1659.

———. *Les emblèmes eucharistiques.* Paris: Pierre de Bresche, 1647.

———. *Traité des talismans ou figures astrales: dans lequel est monstré que leurs effets, vertus admirables sont naturelles, enseigné la manière de les faire et de s'en servir avec un profit et advantage merveilleux.* 3rd ed. Paris: Pierre de Bresche et Jacques de Laize de Bresche, 1671.

Benedict XIV. *Lettre encyclique* (Rome: l'Imprimerie de la Chambre Apostolique, 1745). In Laforest, *Traité de l'usure,* 266–93.

———. *Ex omnibus christiani orbis.* Paris: Typographia Regia, 1756.

Benjamin, Walter. *The Arcades Project.* Translated by Howard Eiland and Kevin McLaughlin. Cambridge, MA: Belknap Press of Harvard University Press, 1999.

———. "Capitalism as Religion." In *Selected Writings, 1: 1913–1926,* edited by

Marcus P. Bullock and Michael W. Jennings, 259–62. Cambridge, MA: Belknap Press of Harvard University Press, 1996.

———. *Central Park*. In *The Writer of Modern Life*, 134–69.

———. "Convolute B: Fashion." In *The Arcades Project*, 62–81.

———. "First Sketches, Paris Arcades I." In *The Arcades Project*, 827–68.

———. "Convolute N: On the Theory of Knowledge, Theory of Progress." In *The Arcades Project*, 456–88.

———. "Paris, Capital of the Nineteenth Century (Exposé of 1939)." In *The Arcades Project*, 14–26.

———. "Paris of the Second Empire in Baudelaire." In *The Writer of Modern Life*, 46–133.

———. *The Writer of Modern Life: Essays on Charles Baudelaire*. Edited by Michael W. Jennings. Translated by Howard Eiland, Edmund Jephcott, Rodney Livingstone, and Harry Zohn. Cambridge, MA: Belknap Press of Harvard University Press, 2006.

Bernard, Jean-Frédéric, and Bernard Picart. *Cérémonies et coutumes religieuses des peuples idolâtres*. 2 vols. Amsterdam: J. F. Bernard, 1723–28.

———. *Cérémonies et coutumes religieuses de tous les peuples du monde*. 7 vols. Amsterdam: J. F. Bernard, 1723.

Bernard, Jean-Vincent. "Merveille d'une image du S. Rosaire de simple papier." In *Rosier mystique*, n.p.

———. *Rosier mystique, ou cent cinquante Roses mystiques, comprenant toute la vie intérieure*. In *Le triple Rosaire*, 3–220.

———. *Le triple Rosaire augmenté, sçavoir le grand Rosaire, le perpétuel et le quotidien*. 3rd ed. Toulouse: B. Bosc, 1676.

Berny, Louis. *Instruction pour les confrères du Rosaire, avec la manière de se bien préparer à la confession et à la communion*. Paris. L. Sevestre, 1740.

Blairye, Nicolas de. *Le thrésor des grandes richesses de l'Église et ce que doivent faire ceux qui les reçoivent et qui les distribuent*. Amiens: Jacques Hubault, 1618.

Blumenberg, Hans. *The Legitimacy of the Modern Age*. Translated by Robert M. Wallace. Cambridge, MA: MIT Press, 1985.

Bodin, Jean. "Discours de Jean Bodin sur le rehaussement et diminution tant d'or que d'argent." In René Herpin, *Apologie de René Herpin pour "La république" de J. Bodin*, 45–77. Lyon: Barthélemy Vincent, 1593.

———. *Six livres de la république*. Lyon: Barthélemy Vincent, 1593.

Boileau, Jacques. *De l'abus des nuditez de gorge*. Paris, 1680.

Boisguilbert, Pierre Le Pesant de. *Dissertation sur les richesses, l'argent et les tributs*. In Daire, *Collection des principaux économistes*. Vol. 1, *Économistes-financiers du 18ᵉ siècle*, 394–424.

———. *Factum de la France*. In Daire, *Collection des principaux économistes*. Vol. 1, *Économistes-financiers du 18ᵉ siècle*, 267–351.

———. *Traité de la nature, culture, commerce et intérêt des grains*. In Daire, *Collection des principaux économistes*. Vol. 1, *Économistes-financiers du 18ᵉ siècle*, 352–93.

Bossuet, Jacques Bénigne. "Abrégé d'un sermon de M. Bossuet, prêché à l'hôpital général." In Bossuet et al., *Les avocats des pauvres*, 1:553–84.

———. *Méditations sur la rémission des péchéz pour le temps du jubilé et des indulgences, tirées principalement du Concile de Trente*. Vienna: Jean Pierre van Ghelen, 1750.

———. *Œuvres de messire Jacques-Bénigne Bossuet*. New ed. 18 vols. Paris: Antoine Boudet, 1772–88.

———. *Politique tirée des propres paroles de l'Écriture sainte*. Edited by Jacques le Brun. Genève: Droz, 1967.

Bossuet, Jacques Bénigne, et al. *Les avocats des pauvres, ou sermons de Bossuet, Bourdaloue, Massillon, Fléchier, La Colombière, La Rue, Neuville, Le Chapelain, Élisée et de Beauvais, Évêque de Sénez. Sur les richesses, sur l'avarice et sur l'aumône*. 2 vols. Paris: Francart, 1814.

Bourdaloue, Louis. *Sermon du P. Bourdaloue sur le jubilé*. Paris: Gabriel Martin, 1751.

———. *Sermons du P. Bourdaloue, de la Compagnie de Jesus, sur les mystères*. 2nd ed. 2 vols. Paris: Rigaud, 1709.

Bourgeois, Jean. *Relation de M. Bourgeois, docteur de Sorbonne et deputé de vingt évêques de France vers le S. Siège pour la défense du livre "De la fréquente communion," composé par M. Arnaud*. N.p., n.d. [1695].

La bulle de N. S. Père le Pape Innocent XI qui confirme les indulgences du Très-Saint Rosaire. Nancy: Charles et Nicolas Les Charlots, 1686.

Bulteau, Louis. *Le faux dépôt, ou Réfutation de quelques erreurs populaires, touchant l'usure*. Rouen: La Veuve de Louis Behourt and Guillaume Behourt, 1698.

Butel-Dumont, Georges-Marie. *Théorie du luxe; ou Traité dans lequel on entreprend d'établir que le luxe est un ressort non–seulement utile, mais même indispensablement nécessaire à la prospérité des états*. 2 pts. N.p., 1771.

Calvin, John. *Institutes of the Christian Religion*. Translated by Elsie Anne McKee. Grand Rapids, MI: William B. Eerdmans, 2009.

Camus, Jean-Pierre. *La déffense du pur amour*. Paris: Robert Bertault, 1640.

———. *Théodoxe, ou de la gloire de Dieu, opuscule*. Rouen: François Vavlitier, 1639.

———. *L'usage de la pénitence et communion*. Paris: Robert Bertault, 1644.

Canons and Decrees of the Council of Trent. Translated by H. J. Schroederer. Rockford, IL: Tan Books, 1978.

Carpuac, Père. *Examen et réfutation du "Traité de l'usure et des intérêts," etc*. Montauban: Teulieres, 1780.

Carrel, Louis-Joseph. *De la pratique des billets, où les sentimens de l'Écriture, des Pères, des Conciles, des souverains pontifes, et des saints docteurs, sont fidèlement exposez pour servir d'adresse aux personnes qui veulent faire valoir l'argent par des voies légitimes, et aux pasteurs et confesseurs zélez pour le bien des âmes*. New ed. Brussels: Lambert Marchant, 1699.

Caussin, Nicolas. *La cour sainte*. 2 vols. Paris: Denis Bechet, 1653.

Chambon, Joseph. *Traité des métaux et des minéraux*. Paris: Claude Jombert, 1714.

[Chastain, Jean]. *Le moine secularisé, augmenté de nouveau de la vie des moines*. N.p., 1678.

Chrétien-Deschamps, François-Michel. *Lettres sur le Visa des dettes de l'état ordonné en 1721*. Edited by François R. Velde. Paris: Éditions Classiques Garnier, 2015.

Collet, Pierre. *Traité historique, dogmatique et pratique des indulgences et du jubilé*. 2 vols. Louvain: Jean-François Van Overbeke, 1775.

Colombière, Claude La. "Réflexions chrétiennes sur l'aumône." In Bossuet et al., *Les avocats des pauvres*, 2:264–75.
Colonia, André de. *Éclaircissement sur le légitime commerce des intérêts*. Lyon: Antoine Cellier, 1675.
Consultation de plusieurs canonistes et avocats de Paris, sur le compétence des juges séculiers, par rapport au refus des sacremens. N.p., n.d. [1753].
Consultation de quarante docteurs en droit canon de la Faculté de Paris, sur les refus de sacremens faits aux Jansénistes, Appellans et Quenellistes notoires d'une notoriété de fait. N.p., n.d. [1753].
Consultation sur les convulsions. Utrecht: Corneille Guillaume Le Febvre, 1735.
Cy commence ung devot et salutaire traicte intitule La marchandise spirituelle laquelle est tres utile et necessaire à tous marchands et marchandes. Paris: Jehan Sainct Denys, n.d. [1529].
Daire, Eugène, ed. *Collection des principaux économistes*. 15 vols. 1841–52. Reprint, Osnabrück: O. Zeller, 1966.
De Brosses, Charles. *Du culte des dieux fétiches, ou Parallèle de l'ancienne religion de l'Égypte avec la religion actuelle de Nigritie*. N.p., 1760.
Déclaration du roi. Donnée à Versailles le 10 décembre 1756. Paris: l'Imprimerie royale, 1756.
Déclaration du roi. Donnée à Versailles le 2 septembre 1754. Paris: P. G. Simon, 1754.
Déclaration du roy, concernant les justiciables de la chambre de justice et la procedure qui doit être observée en ladite chambre. Lyon: l'Imprimerie de Pierre Valfray, 1716.
Déclaration du roy, pour convertir la Banque générale en Banque royale. Paris: l'Imprimerie royale, 1718.
Délibération de l'Assemblée générale du clergé de France, du 11 juillet 1711, portant pouvoir d'emprunter huit millions de livres accordez au roy en l'Assemblée générale extraordinaire, tenu par permission du roy à Paris en 1711. Paris: Veuve François Muguet, 1711.
Descartes, René. *Discours de la méthode*. Introduced by Étienne Gilson. Paris: Librairie Philosophique J. Vrin, 1989.
———. *Meditations on First Philosophy*. In *Meditations, Objections, and Replies*, translated and edited by Roger Ariew and Donald Cress, 1–50. Indianapolis, IN: Hackett, 2006.
———. *Notae in programma quoddam*. In *Œuvres de Descartes*, 8:335–70.
———. *Œuvres de Descartes*. Edited by Charles Adam and Paul Tannery. 12 vols. Paris: L. Cerf, 1897–1913.
Desgabets, Robert. *Considérations sur l'estat présent de la controverse touchant le Très-Saint Sacrement de l'autel*. N.p., 1671.
———. *Le guide de la raison naturelle*. In *Œuvres philosophiques inédites*, 106–50.
———. *Œuvres philosophiques inédites*. Edited by J. Beaude, with an introduction by Genviève Rodis-Lewis. Amsterdam: Quadratures, 1983–85.
———. *Traité de l'indéfectibilité des créatures*. In *Œuvres philosophiques inédites*, 15–100.
Dictionnaire de l'Académie française. 4th ed. 1762. ARTFL Dictionary Project. https://artflsrv03.uchicago.edu/philologic4/publicdicos/.

Diderot, Denis. *Observations sur le Nakaz*. In *Œuvres politiques*, edited by Paul Vernière, 343–458. Paris: Garnier frères, 1963.

Diderot, Denis, and Jean Le Rond d'Alembert, eds. *Encyclopédie, ou Dictionnaire raisonné des sciences, des arts et des métiers, par une société de gens de lettres*. 35 vols. 1751–80. Reprint, Stuttgart: F. Frommann, 1966–88.

Dissertation, si la grandeur temporelle de l'Église n'est point contraire à la loi de Dieu et aux maximes des temps apostoliques. N.p., 1751.

Du Bosc, Jacques. *L'Eucharistie paisible, ou la paix des sçavans et le repos des simples, touchant l'usage de la communion et de la pénitence*. Paris: Jean Remy and Robert de Nain, 1647.

Dufresnoy, Nicolas Lenglet. *Histoire de la philosophie hermétique*. 3 vols. Paris: Coustelier, 1742.

Du Pradel, Jean. *Traité contre le luxe des hommes et des femmes, et contre le luxe avec lequel on élève les enfans de l'un et de l'autre sexe*. Paris: Michel Brunet, 1705.

Durand de Maillane, Pierre-Toussaint. *Dictionnaire de droit canonique et pratique bénéficiale*. 2nd ed. 4 vols. Lyon: Benoît Buplain, 1770.

Dutot, Nicolas. *Réflexions politiques sur les finances et le commerce, où l'on examine quelles ont été sur les revenus, les denrées, le change étranger, et conséquemment sur notre commerce, les influences des augmentations des valeurs numéraires des monnoies*. 2 vols. The Hague: Les Frères Vaillant et Nicolas Prevost, 1754.

Duvergier de Hauranne, Jean, abbé de Saint-Cyran. *Maximes saintes et chrétiennes*. New ed. Paris: Antonin Deshayes and Étienne Savoye, 1735.

Édit du roi, portant qu'à l'avenir le denier de l'intérêt de l'argent sera fixé au denier vingt-cinq. Grenoble: André Giroud, 1766.

Édit du roy, portant érection et création des articles, statuts et règlemens de la Communauté des maistres patenostriers-boutonniers d'émail, de la ville et fauxbourgs de Paris (May 23, 1583). In *Articles, statuts, ordonnances et règlemens*, 15–23.

Explication de la possibilité de la transsubstantiation. In Terrasson, *Traité de l'infini créé*, 157–172.

Extrait des registres de parlement. Du 14 mai 1755. Paris: P. G. Simon, 1755.

Extraits des assertions dangereuses et pernicieuses en tout genre, que les soi-disans Jésuites ont, dans tous les temps et persévéramment, soutenues, enseignées et publiées dans leurs livres. Paris: Pierre-Guillaume Simon, 1762.

Fabre, Pierre Jean. *L'alchimiste chrétien (Alchymista christianus): Traduction anonyme inédite du XVIIIe siècle avec le fac-similé de l'édition latine originale*. Edited by Frank Greiner. Paris: SÉHA, 2001.

Faiguet de Villeneuve, Joachim. *L'ami des pauvres, ou l'Économie politique*. Paris: Moreau, 1766.

———. *Légitimité de l'usure légale*. Amsterdam: Marc-Michel Rey, 1770.

Fénelon, François de. *Les aventures de Télémaque*. In *Œuvres complètes*, 6:388–566.

———. *La fréquente communion de l'homme du monde*. Paris: Beauchesne, 1913.

———. *Œuvres complètes de Fénelon*. Edited by Jean-Edme-Auguste Gosselin. 10 vols. 1848–52. Reprint, Geneva: Slatkine, 1971.

---. *Œuvres spirituelles de Messire François de Salignac de la Mothe-Fénelon.* 2 vols. Anvers: Henri de la Meule, 1718.

---. *Plans de gouvernement [Table de Chaulnes].* In *Œuvres complètes,* 7:182–94.

Fléchier, Esprit. "Sermon de M. Fléchier sur le précepte de l'aumône." In Bossuet et al., *Les avocats des pauvres,* 2:148–95.

Fondations faites à la confrairie du Très-Saint Sacrement, erigée en la paroisse de Saint Sulpice. Paris: l'Imprimerie de D. Jollet, 1706.

Fontigny, Varet de, trans. *Le catéchisme du Concile de Trente.* New translation. 2 vols. Lyon: Jean Baptiste De Ville, 1681.

Forestier, Pierre. *Histoire des indulgences et du jubilé.* Paris: Charles Robustel, 1702.

Formulaire des indulgences que N. S. Père le Pape Clément XI accordé aux chapelets, rosaires, images, croix et médailles bénites à l'occasion de la canonisation de Saint Pie cinquième Pape, Saint André d'Avelin, Saint Felix de Cantalice confesseurs, et de Sainte Catherine de Boulogne Vierge. Rennes: Gilles Le Barbier, 1713.

La fréquente communion du P. Pichon, convaincue d'impiété. Réflexions pour prévenir les fidèles contre la profanation de l'Eucharistie. N.p., 1747.

Genty, Abbé Louis. *Discours sur le luxe, qui a remporté le prix d'éloquence à l'Académie des sciences, belles-lettres et arts de Besançon, en 1783.* N.p., 1783.

Geoffroy, Étienne-François. "Des supercheries concernant la pierre philosophale." In *Histoire de l'Académie royale des sciences,* 61–70. Paris: l'Imprimerie royale, 1722.

Gerbais, Jean. *Lettre d'un docteur de Sorbonne à une dame de qualité touchant les dorures des habits des femmes.* Paris: F. Léonard, 1696.

Gerberon, Gabriel. *Le catéchisme des indulgences et du jubilé, à l'usage des confesseurs et des pénitens.* Paris: Louis Josse, 1722.

Gourdan, Pierre de. *Le chrestien heureux par la sainte messe prouvé par l'Écriture sainte et par les SS. Pères: Pour la conduite des vrais fidèles et des nouveaux Catholiques.* 2 vols. Lyon: François Comba, 1686.

Grangier, Père. *Examen théologique sur la société du prêt à rente: Dialogue entre Bail et Pontas, docteurs en théologie.* New ed. Nancy: Pierre Duranzo, 1762.

Héron, Nicolas. *De la modestie des postulantes contre l'abus des parures à leur pris d'habit.* Paris: Simon Benard, 1698.

Het Groote Tafereel der Dwaasheid Vertoonende de Opkomst, Voortgang en Ondergang der Actie, Bubbel en Windnegotie. 2 vols. Amsterdam, 1720.

Hume, David. *Treatise of Human Nature.* Edited by L. A. Selby-Bigge. Oxford: Clarendon Press, 1888.

Institution de la confrairie du Très-Saint Sacrement, en l'église paroissiale de la ville de Noyers. Paris: Antoine Lambin, 1693.

L'institution et les merveilles du Saint Scapulaire, avec un recueil des privilèges, indulgences et devoirs de la confrérie de Notre-Dame du Mont-Carmel. Paris: Gonichon, 1746.

Instruction pour ceux de l'archiconfrérie de la Ceinture de S. Augustin et de Sainte Monique, sous l'invocation de N. Dame de Consolation. Lyon: La Veuve de Louis Servant, n.d. [1643].

Instructions touchant l'adoration perpétuelle du Très-Saint Sacrement de l'autel, où l'on explique les fondemens de cette dévotion, avec les véritables moyens d'y satisfaire chrétiennement. New ed. Rouen: Jean-Baptiste Besongne, 1716.

Joly, Claude. *Doctrine des indulgences et du jubilé, pour servir d'instruction aux fidèles dans ce tems de l'année sainte.* Paris: Laurent d'Houry, 1701.

———. *Prônes de messire Claude Joly, évêque et comte d'Agen, pour tous les dimanches de l'année.* New ed. 4 vols. Paris: Louis Roulland, 1712.

Jubilé universel de notre S. Père Innocent par la providence divine, Pape XIII du nom, afin d'implorer le secours divin au commencement de son pontificat, pour le gouvernement salutaire de la Ste. Église catholique. Avec le mandement de Monseigneur l'Illustrissime et reverendissime évêque comte de Chaalons. Châlons: l'Imprimerie de Seneuse, 1722.

Jugement souverain rendu en la cour du Parlement de Bordeaux, qui condamne un grand nombre de voleurs d'église, sacrilèges et profanateurs des choses saintes, de la nouvelle bande du fameux scélérat Jean Louis Hongrest, dit La Botte. Bordeaux: Bernard, n.d. [1756].

La Chétardie, Joachim de. *Homélie VI. Pour le huitième dimanche d'après la Pentecôte, sur l'économe infidèle.* Paris: Raymon Mazières, 1706.

Laforest, Paul-Timoléon. *Traité de l'usure et des intérêts.* Cologne: Valat-la-Chapelle, 1769.

[La Haye, Jacques de]. *Remarques judicieuses sur le livre initulé "De la fréquente communion," par Monsieur Arnauld.* Paris: Sébastien Cramoisy, 1644.

Lambert, Joseph. *Décision théologique sur les actions de la Compagnie des Indes.* N.p., n.d.

La Porte, Barthélémi de. *Principes théologiques, canoniques et civils, sur l'usure, appliqués aux prêts de commerce entre les négocians, au trafic de toute espèce de papier signe des valeurs, et en général à tout intérêt de l'argent.* 3 vols. Paris: Delevaque, 1769.

Law, John. *Mémoire sur la Banque générale* (1717). In *Œuvres complètes*, 3:11–20.

———. *Mémoire sur le discrédit* (June 1720). In *Œuvres complètes*, 3:163–66.

———. *Money and Trade Considered: With a Proposal for Supplying the Nation with Money.* Glasgow: R. & A. Foulis, 1750.

———. *Œuvres complètes*, ed. Paul Harsin. 3 vols. Paris: Librairie du Recueil Sirey, 1934.

———. *Second mémoire sur les banques.* In Daire, *Collection des principaux économistes.* Vol. 1, *Économistes-financiers du 18e siècle*, 554–61.

[Le Correur, Jean.] *Traité de la pratique des billets entre les négociens.* 2nd ed. Mons: Gaspard Migeot, 1684.

Le Gros, Nicolas. *Lettres théologiques contre "Le traité de prêts de commerce."* N.p., n.d.

Le Semelier, Jean-Laurent. *Conférences ecclésiastiques de Paris, sur l'usure et la restitution, où l'on concile la discipline de l'Église, avec la jurisprudence du royaume de France.* New ed. 4 vols. Paris: La Veuve Estienne & Fils, 1748.

Lettre à M. L. G. P. au sujet du nouveau bref de Benoît XIV. N.p., n.d. [1756].

Lettre à Monsieur ***, Avocat au Parlement de Paris, ou Défense de la Consultation de plusieurs canonistes et avocats de Paris sur la compétence des juges séculiers, par rapport au refus des sacrements. N.p., n.d.

Lettre de Monseigneur l'évêque de Troyes, à Monsieur le procureur général du Parlement de Paris, à l'occasion de l'arrest rendu par ce tribunal le douze du mois d'avril dernier. N.p., n.d. [1756].

Lettre de M ***, docteur de Sorbonne, à Monseigneur l'évêque de ***, à Paris, le 21 juin 1747. N.p., n.d. [1747].

Lettre d'un saint prêtre en réponse à Madame la Comtesse de ***. N.p., n.d. [1756].

Lettres patentes du roy, contenant règlement pour la Banque générale, accordée au Sieur Law, et à sa Compagnie. Paris: La Veuve de François Muguet, Hubert Muguet et Louis Denis de la Tour, 1716.

Lettres patentes du roy, portant privilege au Sieur Law et sa Compagnie d'establir une Banque générale. Paris: La Veuve de François Muguet, Hubert Muguet et Louis Denis de la Tour, 1716.

L. M. D. M. *La vie de Philippe d'Orléans, petit-fils de France, Régent du royaume pendant la minorité de Louis XV.* 2nd ed. 2 vols. London: Aux Dépens de la Compagnie, 1737.

Loyseau, Charles. *Traité des ordres et simples dignitez.* Châteaudun: Abel l'Angelie, 1610.

Luther, Martin. "The Pagan Servitude [Babylonian Captivity] of the Church." In *Martin Luther: Selections from His Writings*, edited by John Dillenberger, 249–362. New York: Anchor, 1962.

Maignan, Emmanuel. *De l'usage licite de l'argent, dissertation théologique où est enseigné un moyen de le faire profiter sans usure, selon la doctrine de Saint Thomas.* Toulouse: Bernard Bosc, 1673.

———. *Philosophia sacra, sive entis tum supernaturalis, tum increati.* 2nd ed. Toulouse: Arnaldum Colemerium, 1664.

Malebranche, Nicholas. *Œuvres complètes.* Edited by André Robinet. 23 vols. Paris: Librairie philosophique J. Vrin, 1958–90.

Mandement de M. l'évesque de Troyes à Monsieur le Procureur général du Parlement de Paris. N.p., n.d. [1756].

Mandement de M. l'évesque de Troyes, pour ordonner des prières de Quarante Heures dans toute l'étendue de son diocèse. N.p., n.d. [1756].

Mandement et instruction pastorale de Monseigneur l'archévêque de Paris, touchant l'autorité de l'Église, l'enseignement de la foi, l'administration des sacremens, la soumission due à la Constitution Unigenitus, portant défense de lire plusieurs écrits, etc. Paris, 1756.

Mandeville, Bernard. *The Fable of the Bees: or, Private Vices, Publick Benefits.* 2 vols. Edited by F. B. Kaye. Indianapolis, IN: Liberty Fund, 1988.

[Marchand, Jean-Henri]. *L'enthousiasme français.* N.p., 1766.

Marmont Du Hautchamp, Barthélemy. *Histoire du système des finances sous la minorité de Louis XV.* 6 vols. The Hague: Pierre de Hondt, 1739.

Marx, Karl. *Capital: A Critique of Political Economy.* Edited by Frederick Engels. Translated by Samuel Moore and Edward Aveling. 3 vols. New York: International, 1967.

———. *Capital, Volume 3.* In Marx and Engels, *Collected Works,* 37:5–912.

———. "Comments on James Mill, *Élémens d'économie politique.*" In Marx and Engels, *Collected Works*, 3:211–28.
———. *Contribution to the Critique of Hegel's Philosophy of Law: Introduction.* 1843–44. In Marx and Engels, *Collected Works*, 3:175–87.
———. *Economic and Philosophical Manuscripts of 1844.* In Marx and Engels, *Collected Works*, 3:229–346.
———. *Theories of Surplus Value.* In Marx and Engels, *Collected Works*, 32:7–578.
Marx, Karl, and Frederick Engels. *Collected Works.* 50 vols. New York: International, 1975–2005.
———. *The German Ideology.* In Marx and Engels, *Collected Works*, 5:19–93.
Melon, Jean-François. *Essai politique sur le commerce.* N.p., 1734.
Mémoire pour les administrateurs de la confrérie du Très-Saint Sacrement, établie en l'église de Saint Étienne du Mont. Paris: P. G. Le Mercier, 1766.
Mémoire pour les prestres asssociez en la confrairie du Très-S. Sacrement de l'autel, établie en l'église paroissiale de S. Germain de la ville d'Argentan. N.p., n.d.
Mercier, Louis-Sébastien. *Tableau de Paris.* New ed. 12 vols. Amsterdam, 1782–88.
Mercure de France. 89 vols. Reprint, Geneva: Slatkine, 1968–70.
Mespolié, François. *Exercices spirituels ou les véritables pratiques de piété pour honorer Jésus-Christ et sa sainte Mère contenues dans le Rosaire.* Paris: Edme Couterot, 1703.
Mignot, Étienne. *Traité des prêts de commerce, ou De l'intérêt légitime et illégitime de l'argent.* New ed. 4 vols. Amsterdam: Vincent, 1759.
———. *Traité des prêts de commerce, où l'on compare la doctrine des Scholastiques sur ces prêts, avec celle de l'Écriture sainte et des saints pères.* Lille: Pierre Mathon, 1738.
Moncrif, François-Augustin Paradis de. *Lettre première à milady ***.* In *Observations pour servir à l'histoire des gens de lettres qui ont vécu dans ce siècle-ci*, 3–16. N.p., 1751.
Montchrétien, Antoyne de. *Traicté de l'œconomie politique.* Edited by Théophile Funck-Brentano. Paris: Librairie Plon, 1889.
Montesquieu, Charles Louis de Secondat, baron de. *De l'esprit des lois.* Edited by Jean Brethe de la Gressaye. 4 vols. Paris: Belles Lettres, 1950–61.
———. *Lettres persanes.* Edited by Paul Vernière. Paris: Garnier, 1975.
———. *Persian Letters.* Translated by C. J. Betts. London: Penguin, 1973.
Mouffle d'Angerville, Barthélemy-François-Joseph. *Vie privée de Louis XV.* 4 vols. London: John Peter Lyton, 1781.
Nicole, Pierre. *Essais de morale, contenus en divers traités sur plusieurs devoirs importants.* 4 vols. 1733–71. Reprint, Geneva: Slatkine, 1971.
Nouet, Jacques. *La vie mystique de Jésus dans le Très-Saint Sacrement.* Paris: François Muguet, 1683.
Le nouveau Mercure. Paris: Guillaume Cavelier, Pierre Ribou, and Grégoire, 1717–21.
Nouvelles ecclésiastiques, ou Mémoires pour servir à l'histoire de la Constitution Unigenitus. Paris: n.p., 1732–93.
Occupation intérieure pour les âmes associées à l'adoration perpétuelle du Très-Saint

Sacrement de l'autel, en esprit de réparation, avec des actes et des prières sur le même sujet. New ed. Paris: De Hansy, 1758.

Ordonnance contre le luxe (March 29, 1700). In *Recueil général des anciennes lois françaises, depuis l'an 420 jusqu'à la Révolution de 1789*. Vol. 20. Edited by François-André Isambert, Decrusy, and Athanase-Jean-Léger Jourdan, 355. Paris: Belin-Leprieur, 1830.

Ordonnance et instruction pastorale de Monseigneur l'évêque de Carcassonne, portant condamnation d'un Livre intitulé: "L'esprit de Jésus-Christ et de l'Église sur la fréquente communion," par le P. Jean Pichon, de la Compagnie de Jésus. Toulouse: N. Caranove, 1748.

Ordonnance et instruction pastorale de Monseigneur l'évêque de Soissons, portant condamnation d'un livre intitulé: "L'esprit de Jésus-Christ et de l'Église sur la fréquente communion." Soissons: La Veuve de Charles Courtois, 1748.

Pascal, Blaise. *Les provinciales, ou Lettres de Louis de Montalte*. 2 vols. Paris: Antoine Augustin Renouard, 1803.

Perrier, François, and Guillaume Raviot, eds. *Arrests notables du Parlement de Dijon*. 2 vols. Dijon: Arnauld-Jean-Baptiste Augé, 1735.

Philalèthe, Timothée. *De la modestie des femmes et des filles chrétiennes dans leurs habits et dans tout leur extérieur*. Lyon: Léon Plaignard, 1686.

Pichon, Jean. *L'esprit de Jésus-Christ et de l'Église sur la fréquente communion*. Paris: Hippolyte-Louis Guérin, 1745.

———. *L'esprit de Jésus-Christ et de l'Église sur la fréquente communion*. Liege: Charles Collette, 1747.

Piossens, Chevalier de. *Mémoires de la Régence de S. A. R. Mgr. le duc d'Orléans, durant la minorité de Louis XV, roi de France*. 3 vols. The Hague: Jean Van Duren, 1729.

Pipet, Jean. *Instructions chrétiennes sur plusieurs points de morale, tirées de l'Écriture sainte et des pères et particulièrement touchant le luxe et la vanité des femmes*. Paris: Gabriel Targa, 1678.

Pluquet, Abbé François-André-Adrien. *Traité philosophique et politique sur le luxe*. 2 vols. Paris: Barrois, 1786.

Pontas, Jean. *Examen général de conscience sur tous les pechez qu'on peut commettre dans les différens états de la vie*. Paris: Jacques Vincent, 1729.

Pousse, François. *Examen des principes des alchymistes sur la pierre philosophale*. Paris: Daniel Jollet and Barthélemy Girin, 1711.

Prigent, Abbé. *Observations sur le prêt à intérêt dans le commerce*. Paris: Charles-Pierre Berton, 1783.

Prost de Royer, Antoine-François. *Lettre à Monseigneur l'archévêque de Lyon, dans laquelle on traite du prêt à intérêt à Lyon, appellé dépôt de l'argent*. Avignon, 1763.

Quesnay, François. *Analyse du Tableau économique*. In Daire, *Collection des principaux économistes*. Vol. 2, *Physiocrates: Quesnay, Dupont de Nemours, Mercier de La Rivière, l'Abbé Baudeau, Le Trosne*, 57–79.

———. *Maximes générales du gouvernement économique d'un royaume agricole*. In

Daire, *Collection des principaux économistes*. Vol. 2, *Physiocrates: Quesnay, Dupont de Nemours, Mercier de La Rivière, l'Abbé Baudeau, Le Trosne*, 79–104.

———. "Observations sur l'intérêt de l'argent." *Journal de l'agriculture, du commerce et des finances* 4, no. 1 (Jan. 1766): 154–59.

Quesnay, François, Victor Riquetti Mirabeau, and Charles Richard de Butré. *La philosophie rurale, ou Économie générale et politique de l'agriculture*. Amsterdam: Les Libraries associés, 1763.

Quétel, Claude, ed. *La Bastille dévoilée par ses archives*. Paris: Omnibus, 2013.

Raynal, Guillaume-Thomas. *Histoire philosophique et politique des établissements et du commerce des européens dans les deux Indes*. 5 vols. Geneva: Jean-Léonard Pellet, 1780.

Recueil Clairambault-Maurepas: Chansonnier historique du XVIIIe siècle. 10 vols. Edited by Émile Raunié. Paris: A. Quantin, 1880–84.

Recueil de mandements et autres ouvrages publiés au sujet du livre du P. J. Pichon intitulé: "L'Esprit de Jésus-Christ et de l'Église sur la fréquente communion." N.p., n.d.

Receuil de pièces de tous les écrits qui ont été faits pour et contre le clergé au sujet de l'Assemblée tenue en l'année 1750 pour le vingtième. 9 vols. N.p., 1750.

Recueil de plusieurs indulgences que tout fidèle peut gagner, et de celles qui sont attachées aux chapelets ou rosaires, nommés brigittains, bénis par le souverain pontife. Falaise: Brée frères, 1809.

Règlements de la confrairie du S. Sacrement de l'église paroissiale de S. Barthélemy. N.p., n.d. [1708].

Règles et statuts de la confrérie du Très-Saint Sacrement, erigée dans l'église abbatiale de Faverney par N. S. P. le Pape Paul V. l'an 1609. Vesoul: P. F. Mareschal, [ca. 1630].

Réguis, François-Léon. *La voix du pasteur, discours familiers d'un curé à ses paroissiens, pour tous les dimanches de l'année*. 2 vols. Paris: C. Bluet, 1766.

———. *La voix du pasteur, discours familiers d'un curé à ses paroissiens, pour tous les dimanches de l'année*. 4 vols. Paris: Claude Bleuet, 1773.

Rémonstrances du Parlement de Paris au XVIIIe siècle. Edited by Jules Flammeront. Paris: Imprimerie nationale, 1898.

Réponse à la Consultation de plusieurs canonistes et avocats de Paris, sur la compétence des juges séculiers par rapport au refus de sacremens. N.p., n.d. [1753].

Réponse à la Consultation de quarante docteurs en droit canon, sur les refus de sacremens faits aux Jansénistes, Appellans et Quenellistes notoires d'une notoriété de fait. N.p., n.d.

Requeste présentée au roy par la Communauté des maistres patenôtriers-boutonniers d'émail, marchands verriers-fayanciers, concernant les trois articles y joints. In *Articles, statuts, ordonnances et règlemens*, 24–25.

Richeome, Louis. *Défence des pèlerinages contre le traducteur d'une lettre prétendue de S. Grégoire de Nisse sur les pèlerinages de Hierusalem, avec un discours des sainctes reliques, et un autre des richesses*. Arras: Guillaume de la Rivière, 1605.

———. *L'idolâtrie huguenote, figurée au patron de la vieille payenne*. Lyon: Pierre Rigaud, 1608.

———. *Tableaux sacrez des figures mystiques du très-auguste sacrifice et sacrement de l'Eucharistie*. Paris: Laurens Sonnius, 1601.

Rousseau, Jean-Jacques. *Correspondance complète de Jean-Jacques Rousseau*. Edited by R. A. Leigh. 52 vols. Geneva: Institut et Musée Voltaire, 1965–98.

———. *Discourse on the Origin and Foundations of Inequality among Men*. In *Basic Political Writings*. 2nd ed. Translated and edited by Donald A. Cress. Introduction and annotation by David Wootton, 27–120. Indianapolis, IN: Hackett, 2011.

———. *Discours sur l'économie politique*. In *Œuvres complètes*, 3:241–79.

———. *Discours sur les sciences et les arts*. In *Œuvres complètes*, 3:3–30.

———. *Discours sur l'origine et les fondemens de l'inégalité parmi les hommes*. In *Œuvres complètes*, 3:111–223.

———. *Du contrat social*. In *Œuvres complètes*, 3:349–470.

———. *Émile, ou de l'éducation*. In *Œuvres complètes*, 4:241–868.

———. *Julie, or the New Heloise: Letters of Two Lovers Who Live in a Small Town at the Foot of the Alps*. Translated by Philip Stewart and Jean Vaché. In *The Collected Writings of Rousseau*. Vol. 6. Edited by Roger D. Masters and Christopher Kelly. Hanover, NH: University Press of New England, 1997.

———. *Julie, ou La nouvelle Héloïse*. In *Œuvres complètes*, 2:5–794.

———. *Observations de J.-J. Rousseau, sur la réponse à son Discours*. In *Œuvres complètes*, 3:35–57.

———. *Œuvres complètes*. Edited by Bernard Gagnebin and Marcel Raymond. 5 vols. Bibliothèque de la Pléiade. Paris: Gallimard, 1959–95.

Saint-Albin, Charles de. *Quaestio theologica: Quis dominatur in virtute sua in aeternum?* N.p., n.d. [1718].

Saint-Simon, Louis de Rouvroy, duc de. *Mémoires*. Edited by Yves Coirault. 8 vols. Paris, 1983–88.

Sales, François de. *Introduction à la vie dévote*. New ed. Paris: Louis Genneau, 1735.

Savary, Jacques. *Le parfait négociant, ou Instruction générale pour ce qui regarde le commerce de toute sorte de marchandises, tant de France, que des pays étrangers*. 7th ed. 2 vols. Paris: Michel Guignard and Claude Robustel, 1713.

Sénac de Meilhan, Gabriel. *Considérations sur les richesses et le luxe*. Amsterdam: La Veuve Valade, 1787.

Sentence de police, du dix-sept janvier 1698, qui donne main-levée à Charles Favé, maître patenôtrier, de la saisie sur lui faite à la requête des jurés émailleurs. N.p., n.d. [1698].

Sirmond, Jacques. *La déffense de la vertu*. Paris: Sébastien Huvré, 1641.

Smith, Adam. *The Glasgow Edition of the Works and Correspondence of Adam Smith*. 6 vols. Oxford: Clarendon Press, 1976–83.

———. *The Theory of Moral Sentiments*. Edited by D. D. Raphael and A. L. Macfie. Indianapolis, IN: Liberty Fund, 1984.

———. *The Wealth of Nations*. Edited by Edwin Cannan. New York: Modern Library, 2000.

Statuts et règlements de la confrérie du Très-Saint Sacrement de l'autel. Érigée en l'honneur de cet auguste mystère dans l'église paroissiale de la ville de Menin. Tournay: Jacques Coulon, 1695.

Statuts, règlements, et prières de la confrairie de l'adoration perpétuelle de Jésus-Christ au Très-Saint Sacrement de l'autel, erigée en l'église paroissiale de S. Hilaire de Reims. Reims: Nicolas Pottier, 1722.

[Terrasson, Jean]. *Explications sur le mystère de l'Eucharistie suivant les principes de la philosophie de Descartes.* Edited by Antonella Del Prete. *La lettre clandestine* 10 (2001): 247–60.

Terrasson, Jean. "I. Lettre écrite à M*** sur le nouveau système des finances." In *Lettres sur le nouveau système des finances.*

———. "II. Lettre, où l'on traite du crédit et de son usage." In *Lettres sur le nouveau système des finances.*

———. "III. Lettre, où l'on traite encore des constitutions, et du crédit." In *Lettres sur le nouveau système des finances.*

———. *Lettres sur le nouveau système des finances.* N.p., 1720.

———. *Mémoire pour servir à justifier la Compagnie des Indes, contre la censure des casuistes qui la condamnent.* N.p., 1720.

———. *Traité de l'infini créé, avec L'explication de la possibilité de la transsubstantiation, traité de la confession, et de la communion.* Amsterdam: Marc Michel Rey, 1769.

Thiers, Jean-Baptiste. *De la plus solide, la plus nécessaire, et souvent la plus négligée de toutes dévotions.* 2 vols. Paris: Jean de Nully, 1702.

———. *Traité des superstitions, qui regard les sacremens selon l'Écriture sainte.* 4 vols. Paris: Jean de Nully, 1704 [1679].

Traité de la communion. In Terrasson, *Traité de l'infini créé*, 195–213.

Treuvé, Simon Michel. *Instruction sur les dispositions qu'on doit apporter aux sacremens de pénitence et d'Eucharistie, tirée de l'Écriture sainte, des SS. Pères et de quelques autres saints auteurs.* 2nd ed. Paris: Guillaume Desprez and Jean Desessartz, 1730.

Le triomphe de M. Arnaud. Copie de l'acte de dépôt fait par M. l'abbé de Pomponne, le 2 mars 1748. Contre le livre du P. Jean Pichon, "L'esprit de Jésus-Christ et de l'Église sur la fréquente communion." N.p., n.d. [1748].

Turgot, Anne Robert Jacques. *Le conciliateur, ou Lettres d'un ecclésiastique à un magistrat.* In *Œuvres de Turgot*, 1:391–411.

———. "Deuxième lettre à l'abbé de Cicé." In *Œuvres de Turgot*, 1:143–51.

———. *Discours sur les avantages que l'établissement de christianisme a procurés au genre humain.* In *Œuvres de Turgot*, 1:194–214.

———. "Instruction lue à la assemblée de charité de Limoges." In *Œuvres de Turgot*, 3:205–19.

———. *Mémoire sur les prêts d'argent.* In *Œuvres de Turgot*, 3:154–202.

———. *Œuvres de Turgot.* Edited by Gustave Schelle. 5 vols. Paris: F. Alcan, 1913–23.

———. *Réflexions sur la formation et la distribution des richesses.* In *Œuvres de Turgot*, 2:534–601.

———. "Sur le mot amour et sur l'amour de Dieu." In *Œuvres de Turgot*, 1:358–64.

———. *Valeurs et monnaies.* In *Œuvres de Turgot*, 3:79–98.

Varenne de Beost, Claude-Marc-Antoine. "Patenôtrier." In *Dictionnaire portatif des arts et métiers, contenant en abrégé l'histoire, la description et la police des arts et métiers, des fabriques et manufactures de France et des pays étrangers*, edited by Philippe Macquer, 2:326–38. Amsterdam: Arkstée & Merkus and M. M. Rey, 1767.

———. "Patenôtrier." In *Dictionnaire raisonné universel des arts et métiers, contenant l'histoire, la description, la police des fabriques et manufactures de France et des pays étrangers*, edited by Philippe Macquer and abbé Pierre Jaubert, new ed., 3:368–81. Paris: P. Fr. Didot Jeune, 1773.

Vassetz, Abbé de. *Traité contre le luxe des coiffures*. Paris: E. Couterot, 1694.

Vaubert, Luc. *La dévotion à Nostre Seigneur Jésus-Christ dans l'Eucharistie*. 2nd ed. 2 vols. Paris: Edme Couterot, 1706.

Voltaire [François-Marie Arouet]. *Candide*. In *Œuvres complètes de Voltaire*, 21:137–218.

———. *Dictionnaire philosophique*. In *Œuvres complètes de Voltaire*, 17.1–20.4.

———. *Le mondain*. In *Œuvres complètes de Voltaire*, 10:83–88.

———. *Observations sur MM. Jean Lass, Melon et Dutot; sur le commerce, le luxe, les monnaies et les impots*. In *Œuvres completes de Voltaire*, 22.1:359–70.

———. *Œuvres complètes de Voltaire*. Edited by Louis Moland. New ed. 52 vols. Paris: Garnier, 1877–85.

———. *Précis du siècle de Louis XIV*. In *Œuvres complètes de Voltaire*, 15.2:145–569.

Von Baldenstein, Josef Wilhelm. *Lettre de Son Altesse Monseigneur Joseph-Guillaume de Rinck de Baldenstein, Évêque de Basle, Prince du Saint Empire, à l'auteur du livre de "L'esprit de J.-C. et de l'Église sur la fréquente communion."* N.p., n.d. [1748].

Zola, Émile. *Au bonheur des dames*. Preface by Jeanne Gaillard. Edited by Henri Mitterand. Paris: Gallimard, 1980.

Secondary Sources

Adam, Michel. *L'eucharistie chez les penseurs français du dix-septième siècle*. Hildesheim: Georg Olms, 2000.

Aerts, Erik. "La religione nell'economia, l'economia nella religione: Europa, 1000–1800." In Ammannati, *Religione e istituzioni religiose*, 3–115.

Agamben, Giorgio. *The Kingdom and the Glory: For a Theological Genealogy of Economy and Government*. Translated by Lorenzo Chiesa and Matteo Mandarini. Stanford, CA: Stanford University Press, 2011.

———. *The Signature of All Things: On Method*. New York: Zone, 2009.

Alonso-Lasheras, Diego. *Louis de Molina's "De Iustita Et Iure": Justice as Virtue in Economic Context*. Leiden: Brill, 2011.

Althusser, Louis. *For Marx*. Translated by Ben Brewster. London: Verso, 2005.

———. *Philosophy of the Encounter: Later Writings, 1978–1987*. Edited by François Matheron and Oliver Corpet. Translated by G. M. Goshgarian. London: Verso, 2006.

Ammannati, Francesco, ed. *Religione e istituzioni religiose nell'economia europea, 1000–1800: Atti della "Quarantatreesima Settimana di Studi," 8–12 maggio 2011*. Florence: Firenze University Press, 2012.

Anidjar, Gil. *Blood: A Critique of Christianity*. New York: Columbia University Press, 2014.
Ariès, Philippe. *L'homme devant la mort*. Paris: Seuil, 1977.
Ariew, Roger. *Descartes among the Scholastics*. Leiden: Brill, 2011.
Armogathe, J.-R. *Theologia Cartesiana: L'explication physique de l'Eucharistie chez Descartes et Dom Desgabets*. The Hague: Martinus Nijhoff, 1977.
Austin, J. L. *How to Do Things with Words*. 2nd ed. Edited by J. O. Urmson and Marina Sbisà. Cambridge, MA: Harvard University Press, 1975.
Baker, Keith Michael. "Enlightenment and the Institution of Society: Notes for a Conceptual History." In *Main Trends in Cultural History: Ten Essays*, edited by Willem Melching and Wyger Velema, 95–120. Amsterdam: Rodopi, 1994.
Balzamo, Nicolas. "Une controverse sans débat: Jean-Baptiste Thiers, les chanoines de Chartres et la question du commerce sous les porches des églises (1677–1680)." In Lezowski and Tatarenko, "Façonner l'objet de dévotion chrétien," 51–71.
Bandelj, Nina, Frederick F. Wherry, and Viviana A. R. Zelizer. *Money Talks: Explaining How Money Really Works*. Princeton, NJ: Princeton University Press, 2017.
Barbier, Antoine-Alexandre. *Dictionnaire des ouvrages anonymes*. 3rd ed. Edited by Oliver Barbier, René Billard, and Paul Billard. 4 vols. Paris: Paul Daffis, 1872–79.
Barbier, Edmond-Jean-François. *Chronique de la Régence et du règne de Louis XV (1718–1763), ou Journal de Barbier*. Complete 1st ed. 8 vols. Paris: Charpentier, 1857.
Barrovecchio, Anne-Sophie. "Plaidoyer pour un avocat oublié." In *Voltairomanie: L'avocat Jean-Henri Marchand face à Voltaire*, edited by Anne-Sophie Barrovecchio, 7–20. Saint-Étienne: Publications de l'Université de Saint-Étienne, 2004.
Bataille, Georges. *The Accursed Share: An Essay on General Economy*. Translated by Robert Hurley. New York: Zone, 1991.
———. "The Notion of Expenditure." In *Visions of Excess: Selected Writings, 1927–1939*, edited by Allan Stoekl, translated by Allan Stoekl with Carl R. Lovitt and Donald M. Leslie Jr., 116–29. Minneapolis: University of Minnesota Press, 1985.
Bateman, Bradley W., and H. S. Banzhaf, eds. "Keeping Faith, Losing Faith: Religious Belief and Political Economy." Annual Supplement, *History of Political Economy* 40, no. 5 (2008).
Baudrillard, Jean. *The Consumer Society: Myths and Origins*. Thousand Oaks, CA: Sage, 1998.
Bell, David A. *The Cult of the Nation in France: Inventing Nationalism, 1680–1800*. Cambridge, MA: Harvard University Press, 2001.
Berg, Maxine. *Luxury and Pleasure in Eighteenth-Century Britain*. Oxford: Oxford University Press, 2005.
Berg, Maxine, and Elizabeth Eger, eds. *Luxury in the Eighteenth Century: Debates, Desires, and Delectable Goods*. New York: Palgrave Macmillan, 2003.
———. "The Rise and Fall of the Luxury Debates." In Berg and Eger, *Luxury in the Eighteenth Century*, 7–27.

Bergin, Joseph. *Church, Society, and Religious Change in France, 1580–1730*. New Haven, CT: Yale University Press, 2009.

———. *The Politics of Religion in Early Modern France*. New Haven, CT: Yale University Press, 2014.

Berman, Harold J. *Law and Revolution: The Formation of the Western Legal Tradition*. Cambridge, MA: Harvard University Press, 1983.

Berry, Christopher. *The Idea of Luxury: A Conceptual and Historical Investigation*. Cambridge: Cambridge University Press, 1994.

Bevilacqua, Alexander. *The Republic of Arabic Letters: Islam and the European Enlightenment*. Cambridge, MA: Belknap Press of Harvard University Press, 2018.

Binswanger, Hans Christoph. *Money and Magic: A Critique of the Modern Economy in Light of Goethe's "Faust."* Translated by J. E. Harrison. Chicago: University of Chicago Press, 1994.

Blanc, Jérôme. "La France de François Ier à Louis XVI: Souveraineté, richesse et falsifications monétaires." In *Les pensées monétaires dans l'histoire: L'Europe, 1517–1776*, edited by Jérôme Blanc et Ludovic Desmedt, 331–94. Paris: Classiques Garnier, 2014.

Blaufarb, Rafe. *The Great Demarcation: The French Revolution and the Invention of Modern Property*. Oxford: Oxford University Press, 2016.

Bloch, Marc. *The Royal Touch: Sacred Monarchy and Scrofula in England and France*. Translated by J. E. Anderson. London: Routledge and Kegan Paul, 1973.

Boer, Roland. *Criticism of Heaven: On Marxism and Theology*. Leiden: Brill, 2007.

Boer, Wietse de, Karl A. E. Enenkel, and Walter S. Melion, eds. *Jesuit Image Theory*. Leiden: Brill, 2016.

Bolton, Andrew, Barbara Drake Boehm, Marzia Cataldi Gallo, C. Griffith Mann, David Morgan, Gianfranco Cardinal Ravasi, and David Tracy. *Heavenly Bodies: Fashion and the Catholic Imagination*. 2 vols. New York: Metropolitan Museum of Art, 2018.

Bonzon, Anne. *L'esprit de clocher: Prêtres et paroisses dans le diocèse de Beauvais, 1535–1650*. Paris: Cerf, 1999.

Bouchot, Henri. *Histoire anecdotique des métiers avant 1789*. Paris: Lecène, Oudin, 1892.

Bouton, Cynthia A. *The Flour War: Gender, Class, and Community in Late Ancien Régime French Society*. University Park: Pennsylvania State University Press, 1993.

Brafman, David. "Picart, Bernard, Hermes, and Muhammad (Not Necessarily in That Order)." In Hunt, Jacob, and Mijnhardt, *Bernard Picart*, 139–64.

Braudel, Fernand. *The Mediterranean and the Mediterranean World in the Age of Philip II*. Vol. 1. Translated by Siân Reynolds. Berkeley: University of California Press, 1996.

Bremond, Henri. *Histoire littéraire du sentiment religieux*. 12 vols. Paris: Bloud et Gay, 1915–36.

Bremond, Henri. *La querelle du pur amour au temps de Louis XIII: Antoine Sirmond et Jean-Pierre Camus*. Paris: Bloud et Gay, 1932.

Brésard, Marc. *Les foires de Lyon aux XVe et XVIe siècles*. Paris: Picard, 1914.

Brewer, John, and Roy Porter, eds. *Consumption and the World of Goods*. London: Routledge, 1993.
Buckley, Susan L. *Teachings on Usury in Judaism, Christianity, and Islam*. Lewiston, NY: Edwin Mellen Press, 2000.
Burkardt, Albrecht. "Commerce et dévotions: Traditions historiographiques et recherches récentes." In Burkardt, *L'économie des dévotions*, 7–35.
Burkardt, Albrecht, ed. *L'économie des dévotions: Commerce, croyance et objets de piété à l'époque moderne*. Rennes: Presses universitaires de Rennes, 2016.
Burke, Peter. *The Fabrication of Louis XIV*. New Haven, CT: Yale University Press, 1992.
Burson, Jeffrey D. *The Rise and Fall of Theological Enlightenment: Jean-Martin de Prades and Ideological Polarization in Eighteenth-Century France*. Notre Dame, IN: University of Notre Dame Press, 2010.
Buvat, Jean. *Journal de la Régence (1715–1723)*. Edited by Émile Campardon. 2 vols. Paris: Henri Plon, 1865.
Bynum, Caroline Walker. *Christian Materiality: An Essay on Religion in Late Medieval Europe*. New York: Zone, 2011.
———. *Holy Feast and Holy Fast: The Significance of Food to Medieval Women*. Berkeley: University of California Press, 1987.
Cameron, Euan. *Enchanted Europe: Superstition, Reason, and Religion, 1250–1750*. Oxford: Oxford University Press, 2010.
———. *The European Reformation*. Oxford: Clarendon Press, 1991.
Cassirer, Ernst. *The Philosophy of the Enlightenment*. Translated by Fritz C. A. Koelln and James P. Pettegrove. Princeton, NJ: Princeton University Press, 1951.
———. *The Question of Jean-Jacques Rousseau*. 2nd ed. Translated and edited by Peter Gay. New Haven, CT: Yale University Press, 1989.
Certeau, Michel de. "The Formality of Practices: From Religious Systems to the Ethics of the Enlightenment (the Seventeenth and Eighteenth Centuries)." In *The Writing of History*, translated by Tom Conley, 147–205. New York: Columbia University Press 1988.
———. *The Mystic Fable*. Vol. 1, *The Sixteenth and Seventeenth Centuries*. Translated by Michael B. Smith. Chicago: University of Chicago Press, 1992.
Chalcraft, David J., and Austin Harrington, eds. *The Protestant Ethic Debate: Max Weber's Replies to His Critics, 1907–1910*. Translated by Austin Harrington and Mary Shields. Liverpool: Liverpool University Press, 2001.
Chaney, Lisa. *Coco Chanel: An Intimate Life*. London: Penguin, 2011.
Chartier, Roger. *The Cultural Origins of the French Revolution*. Translated by Lydia G. Cochrane. Durham, NC: Duke University Press, 1991.
Chaussinaud-Nogaret, Guy. *The French Nobility in the Eighteenth Century: From Feudalism to Enlightenment*. Translated by William Doyle. Cambridge: Cambridge University Press, 1985.
Cheney, Paul. *Cul de Sac: Patrimony, Capitalism, and Slavery in French Saint-Domingue*. Chicago: University of Chicago Press, 2017.

———. *Revolutionary Commerce: Globalization and the French Monarchy*. Cambridge, MA: Harvard University Press, 2010.

Chérel, Albert. *Fénelon au XVIIIe siècle en France (1715–1820)*. Reprint, Geneva: Slatkine, 1970.

Clark, Henry C. *Compass of Society: Commerce and Absolutism in Old-Regime France*. Lanham, MD: Lexington Books, 2006.

Clavero, Bartolomé. *La grâce du don: Anthropologie catholique de l'économie moderne*. Translated by Jean-Frédéric Schaub. Paris: Albin Michel, 1996.

Cognet, Louis. *Crépuscule des mystiques, Bossuet-Fénelon*. New ed. Preface by J. R. Armogathe. Paris: Desclée, 1991.

———. *Le jansénisme*. Paris: Presses universitaires de France, 1961.

Cole, Andrew. *The Birth of Theory*. Chicago: University of Chicago Press, 2014.

Coleman, Charly. "Resacralizing the World: The Fate of Secularization in Enlightenment Historiography." *Journal of Modern History* 82, no. 2 (June 2010): 368–95.

———. "The Vagaries of Disenchantment: God, Matter, and Mammon in the Eighteenth Century." *Modern Intellectual History* 14, no. 3 (Nov. 2017): 869–81.

———. *The Virtues of Abandon: An Anti-Individualist History of the French Enlightenment*. Stanford, CA: Stanford University Press, 2014.

Coleman, D. C. "Economic Problems and Policies." In *The New Cambridge Modern History*. Vol. 5, *The Ascendency of France, 1648–1688*, edited by F. L. Carsten, 19–46. Cambridge: Cambridge University Press, 1961.

Colodiet, François. "L'objet religieux dans le foyer parisien de la deuxième moitié du XVIIe siècle d'après les inventaires après-décès." Mémoire de Maîtrise, Université de Paris IV, 1982.

Conlon, Pierre M. *Le siècle des lumières: Bibliographie chronologique*. 32 vols. Geneva: Librairie Droz, 1983–.

Connolly, William E. *Capitalism and Christianity, American Style*. Durham, NC: Duke University Press, 2008.

Cooper, Julie E. *Secular Powers: Humility in Modern Political Thought*. Chicago: University of Chicago Press, 2013.

Coquery, Natacha. *Tenir boutique à Paris au XVIIIe siècle: Luxe et demi-luxe*. Preface by Daniel Roche. Paris: Éditions du Comité des travaux historiques et scientifiques, 2011.

Cornette, Joël. "La révolution des objets: Le Paris des inventaires après-décès (XVIIe–XVIIIe siècles)." *Revue d'histoire moderne et contemporaine* 36, no. 3 (July–Sept. 1989): 476–86.

Courdurié, Marcel. *La dette des collectivités publiques de Marseille au XVIIIe siècle: Du débat sur le prêt à intérêt au financement par l'emprunt*. Marseille: Institut historique de Provence, 1974.

Course, Didier. " 'La façon dequoi nos lois essayent à régler les folles et vaines dépenses': Rôles et limites des lois somptuaires au XVIIe siècle." *Littéraires classiques* 56 (2005): 107–17.

Courtwright, David T. *Forces of Habit: Drugs and the Making of the Modern World*. Cambridge, MA: Harvard University Press, 2002.
Cousin, Bernard. *Le miracle et le quotidien: Les ex-voto provençaux, images d'une société*. Preface by Michel Vovelle. Aix-en-Provence: Sociétés, mentalités, cultures, 1983.
Cranston, Maurice. *Jean-Jacques: The Early Life and Work of Jean-Jacques Rousseau*. London: Allen Lane, 1983.
Crocker, Lester. *Rousseau's Social Contract: An Interpretive Essay*. Cleveland, OH: Press of Case Western Reserve University, 1968.
Crouzet, François. *Britain Ascendant: Comparative Studies Franco-British Economic History*. Translated by Martin Thom. Cambridge: Cambridge University Press, 1990.
———. "The Historiography of French Economic Growth in the Nineteenth Century." *Economic History Review* 56, no. 2 (May 2003): 215–42.
Crow, Thomas E. *Painters and Public Life in Eighteenth-Century Paris*. New Haven, CT: Yale University Press, 1985.
Crowston, Clare Haru. *Credit, Fashion, Sex: Economies of Regard in Old Regime France*. Durham, NC: Duke University Press, 2013.
———. *Fabricating Women: The Seamstresses of Old Regime France, 1675–1791*. Durham, NC: Duke University Press, 2001.
Cullen, L. M. "History, Economic Crises, and Revolution: Understanding Eighteenth Century France." *Economic History Review* 46, no. 4 (Nov. 1993): 635–57.
Darnton, Robert. *Devil in the Holy Water, or the Art of Slander from Louis XIV to Napoleon*. Philadelphia: University of Pennsylvania Press, 2010.
De Bruyn, Frans. "*Het Groote Tafereel der Dwaasheid* and Its Readers, Then and Now." In Goetzmann et al., *The Great Mirror of Folly*, 21–34.
———. "Reading *Het Groote Tafereel der Dwaasheid*: An Emblem Book of the Folly of Speculation in the Bubble Year 1720." *Eighteenth-Century Life* 24, no. 2 (Spring 2000): 1–42.
"The Début of the Winter Mode." *Vogue*, October 1, 1926.
Decker, John R. *The Technology of Salvation and the Art of Geertgen tot Sint Jans*. New York: Routledge, 2009.
Decock, Wim. "The Catholic Spirit of Capitalism? Contrasting Views on Profit-Making through Capital Investment in the Age of Reformations." In *Law and Religion: The Legal Teachings of the Protestant and Catholic Reformations*, edited by Wim Decock, Jordan J. Ballor, Michael Germann, and Laurent Waelkens, 22–44. Göttingen and Bristol, CT: Vandenhoeck and Ruprecht, 2014.
DeJean, Joan. *The Essence of Style: How the French Invented High Fashion, Fine Food, Chic Cafés, Style, Sophistication, and Glamour*. New York: Free Press, 2005.
Dekoninck, Ralph. "The Jesuit *Ars* and *Scientia Symbolica*: From Richeome and Sandaeus to Masen and Ménestrier." In Boer, Enenkel, and Melion, *Jesuit Image Theory*, 74–88.
Del Prete, Antonella. Introduction to Jean Terrasson, *Traité de l'infini créé*, edited by Antonella Del Prete, 9–128. Paris: Honoré Champion, 2007.

Delumeau, Jean. *L'aveu et le pardon: Les difficultés de la confession, XIIIᵉ–XVIIIᵉ siècle.* Paris: Fayard, 1990.

———. *Catholicism between Luther and Voltaire: A New View of the Counter-Reformation.* Introduction by John Bossy. London: Burns and Oates, 1977.

———. *Rassurer et protéger: Le sentiment de sécurité dans l'Occident d'autrefois.* Paris: Fayard, 1989.

De Roover, Raymond. *L'évolution de la lettre de change, XIVᵉ–XVIIIᵉ siècle.* Paris: Armand Colin, 1953.

Desan, Christine. *Making Money: Coin, Currency, and the Coming of Capitalism.* Oxford: Oxford University Press, 2014.

Desmette, Pierre. "Les confréries religieuses dans le diocèse de Cambrai à l'époque moderne." In *Confréries et dévotions dans la catholicité moderne,* edited by Bernard Dompnier and Paola Vismara, 355–70. Rome: École française de Rome, 2008.

Dick, Steven J. *Plurality of Worlds: The Origins of the Extraterrestrial Life Debate from Democritus to Kant.* Cambridge: Cambridge University Press, 1982.

Dickey, Laurence. "Pride, Hypocrisy and Civility in Mandeville's Social and Historical Theory." *Critical Review* 4, no. 3 (Summer 1990): 387–431.

Dinet, Dominique. "Une déchristianisation provinciale au XVIIIᵉ siècle: Le diocèse d'Auxerre." *Histoire, économie et société* 10, no. 4 (1991): 467–89.

Dobbs, Betty Jo Teeter. "Alchemical Death and Resurrection: The Significance of Alchemy in the Age of Newton." In *Science, Pseudo-science, and Utopianism in Early Modern Thought,* edited by Stephen A. McKnight, 55–87. Columbia: University of Missouri Press, 1992.

Dompnier, Bernard. *La superstition à l'âge des Lumières.* Paris: H. Champion, 1998.

Dubois, Laurent. *Avengers of the New World: The Story of the Haitian Revolution.* Cambridge, MA: Belknap Press of Harvard University Press, 2004.

Duhamelle, Christophe. "Le pèlerinage dans le Saint-Empire au XVIIIᵉ siècle: Pratiques dévotionelles et identités collectives." *Francia* 33, no. 2 (2006): 69–96.

———. "Pèlerinage et économie dans l'Empire au XVIIIᵉ siècle." In Ammannati, *Religione e istituzioni religiose,* 713–27.

Duranton, Henri. "La ficelle de Law." In Magnot-Ogilvy, *Gagnons sans savoir comment,* 111–25.

Eagleton, Terry. *Why Marx Was Right.* New Haven, CT: Yale University Press, 2011.

Edelstein, Dan. *The Enlightenment: A Genealogy.* Chicago: University of Chicago Press, 2010.

———. "Introduction to the Super-Enlightenment." In *The Super-Enlightenment,* 1–33.

———. *On the Spirit of Rights.* Chicago: University of Chicago Press, 2019.

———, ed. *The Super-Enlightenment: Daring to Know Too Much.* Oxford: Voltaire Foundation, 2010.

———. *The Terror of Natural Right: Republicanism, the Cult of Nature, and the French Revolution.* Chicago: University of Chicago Press, 2010.

Eire, Carlos M. N. *War against the Idols: The Reformation of Worship from Erasmus to Calvin*. Cambridge: Cambridge University Press, 1986.
Ekberg, Carl J. *Colonial Ste. Geneviève: An Adventure on the Mississippi Frontier*. 2nd ed. Carbondale: Southern Illinois University Press, 1996.
Evennett, H. Outram. *The Spirit of the Counter-Reformation*. Edited by John Bossy. Notre Dame, IN: University of Notre Dame Press, 1968.
Faccarello, Gilbert. *The Foundations of Laissez-Faire: The Economics of Pierre de Boisguilbert*. London: Routledge, 1999.
Fairchilds, Cissie. "Marketing the Counter-Reformation: Religious Objects and Consumerism in Early Modern France." In *Visions and Revisions of Eighteenth-Century France*, edited by Christine Adams, Jack R. Censer, and Lisa Jane Graham, 31–52. University Park: Pennsylvania State University Press, 1977.
———. "The Production and Marketing of Populuxe Goods in Eighteenth-Century Paris." In Brewer and Porter, *Consumption and the World of Goods*, 228–48.
Farr, James R. *The Work of France: Labor and Culture in Early Modern Times, 1350–1800*. Lanham, MD: Rowman and Littlefield, 2008.
Faure, Edgar. *La banqueroute de Law: 17 juillet 1720*. Paris: Gallimard, 1977.
Feil, Ernst. *On the Concept of Religion*. Translated by Brian McNeil. Albany: State University of New York Press, 2000.
Feiner, Shmuel. *The Jewish Enlightenment*. Translated by Chaya Naor. Philadelphia: University of Pennsylvania Press, 2004.
Feller, François Xavier de. *Biographie universelle des hommes qui se sont fait un nom par leur génie, leurs talents, leurs vertus, leurs erreurs, ou leurs crimes*. Edited by Abbé François-Marie Simonin. 8 vols. Lyon: J. B. Pélagaud, 1867.
Firey, Abigail. *A New History of Penance*. Leiden: Brill, 2008.
Flandreau, Marc, Christophe Galimard, Clemens Jobst, and Pilar Nogués-Marco. "The Bell Jar: Commercial Interest Rates between Two Revolutions, 1688–1789." In *The Origins and Development of Financial Markets and Institutions: From the Seventeenth Century to the Present*, edited by Jeremy Atack and Larry Neal, 161–208. Cambridge: Cambridge University Press, 2009.
Fleming, John V. *The Dark Side of the Enlightenment: Wizards, Alchemists, and Spiritual Seekers in the Age of Reason*. New York: Norton, 2013.
Fontaine, Laurence. *The Moral Economy: Poverty, Credit, and Trust in Early Modern Europe*. Cambridge: Cambridge University Press, 2014.
Force, Pierre. *Self-Interest before Adam Smith: A Genealogy of Economic Science*. Cambridge: Cambridge University Press, 2003.
———. *Wealth and Disaster: Atlantic Migrations from a Pyrenean Town in the Eighteenth and Nineteenth Centuries*. Baltimore: Johns Hopkins University Press, 2016.
Foucault, Michel. *Discipline and Punish: The Birth of the Prison*. 2nd ed. Translated by Alan Sheridan. New York: Vintage, 1995.
———. *The History of Sexuality, Volume 1: An Introduction*. New York: Vintage, 1978.
———. *The Order of Things: An Archaeology of the Human Sciences*. New York: Vintage, 1994.

———. *Security, Territory, Population: Lectures at the Collège De France, 1977–78*. Edited by Michel Senellart. Translated by Graham Burchell. New York: Picador, 2009.

Fox-Genovese, Elizabeth. *The Origins of Physiocracy: Economic Revolution and Social Order in Eighteenth-Century France*. Ithaca, NY: Cornell University Press, 1976.

Friant, Emmanuelle. "Le catholicisme matériel: Les objets de la piété privée dans la France des XVIᵉ et XVIIᵉ siècles." Doctoral thesis, Université de Nancy II, 2009.

Friedland, Paul. *Political Actors: Representative Bodies and Theatricality in the Age of the French Revolution*. Ithaca, NY: Cornell University Press, 2002.

———. *Seeing Justice Done: The Age of Spectacular Capital Punishment in France*. Oxford: Oxford University Press, 2014.

Froeschlé-Chopard, Marie-Hélène. "La dévotion du Rosaire à travers quelques livres de piété." *Histoire, économie et société* 10, no. 3 (1991): 299–316.

———. *Dieu pour tous et Dieu pour soi: Histoire des confréries et de leurs images à l'époque moderne*. Paris: L'Harmattan, 2006.

Galliani, Renato. *Rousseau, le luxe et l'idéologie nobiliaire: Étude socio-historique*. Oxford: Voltaire Foundation, 1989.

Garraway, Doris. *The Libertine Colony: Creolization in the Early French Caribbean*. Durham, NC: Duke University Press, 2005.

Gauchet, Marcel. *The Disenchantment of the World: A Political History of Religion*. Translated by Oscar Burge. Forward by Charles Taylor. Princeton, NJ: Princeton University Press, 1997.

Gaukroger, Stephen. *Descartes: An Intellectual Biography*. Oxford: Oxford University Press, 1997.

Geppert, Anna. "The Sillon Lorrain (Nancy, Metz, Epinal, Thionville)." In *Soft Spaces in Europe: Re-negotiating Governance, Boundaries and Borders*, edited by Phil Allmendinger, Graham Haughton, Jörg Knieling, and Frank Othengrafen, 77–94. Abingdon: Routledge, 2015.

Girard, Marcel. *Histoire de la Louisiane française*. 4 vols. Paris: Presses universitaires de France, 1953–74.

Goetzmann, William N., Catherine Labio, K. Geert Rouwenhorst, and Timothy G. Young, eds. *The Great Mirror of Folly: Finance, Culture, and the Crash of 1720*. New Haven, CT: Yale University Press, 2013.

Goldie, Mark, and Robert Wokler, eds. *The Cambridge History of Eighteenth-Century Political Thought*. Cambridge: Cambridge University Press, 2006.

Goldsmith, James Lowth. *Lordship in France, 1500–1789*. New York: Peter Lang, 2005.

Goldstein, Jan. "Enthusiasm or Imagination? Eighteenth-Century Smear Words in Comparative National Context." In *Enthusiasm and Enlightenment in Europe, 1650–1850*, edited by Lawrence E. Klein and Anthony J. La Vopa, 28–49. San Marino, CA: Huntington Library Press, 1988.

Goodman, Dena. "Furnishing Discourses: Readings of a Writing Desk in

Eighteenth-Century France." In Berg and Eger, *Luxury in the Eighteenth Century*, 71–88.

Gorski, Philip S. "The Little Divergence: The Protestant Reformation and Economic Hegemony in Early Modern Europe." In Swatos and Kaelber, *The Protestant Ethic Turns 100*, 165–90.

Gottmann, Felicia. "Du Châtelet, Voltaire, and the Transformation of Mandeville's *Fable*." *History of European Ideas* 38, no. 2 (June 2012): 218–32.

———. "The Eighteenth-Century Luxury Debate: The Case of Voltaire." PhD diss., Somerville College, University of Oxford, 2010.

Gouhier, Henri. *La pensée religieuse de Descartes*. 2nd ed. Paris: Librairie philosophique J. Vrin, 1972.

Goux, Jean-Joseph. *Les monnayeurs du langage*. Paris: Galilée, 1984.

Gras, Maria-Carmen. "Les processions en l'honneur de Sainte Geneviève à Paris: Miroir d'une société (XVe–XVIIIe siècles)." *Histoire urbaine* 32 (2011): 5–30.

Greenblatt, Stephen. *Marvelous Possessions: The Wonder of the New World*. Chicago: University of Chicago Press, 1991.

Greengrass, Mark. *Governing Passions: Peace and Reform in the French Kingdom, 1576–1585*. Oxford: Oxford University Press, 2007.

Greiner, Frank, ed. *Aspects de la tradition alchimique au XVIIe siècle: Actes du colloque international de l'université de Reims-Champagne-Ardenne (Reims, 28 et 29 novembre 1996)*. Paris: SÉHA, 1998.

———. Introduction to Fabre, *L'alchimiste chrétien*, vii–ccvii.

Grenier, Jean-Yves. *L'économie d'Ancien Régime: Un monde de l'échange et de l'incertitude*. Paris: Albin Michel, 1996.

Grewal, David Singh. "The Political Theology of *Laissez-Faire*: From *Philia* to Self-Love in Commercial Society." *Political Theology* 17, no. 5 (Sept. 2016): 417–33.

Groethuysen, Bernhard. *The Bourgeois: Catholicism versus Capitalism in Eighteenth-Century France*. Introduction by Benjamin Nelson. Translated by Mary Ilford. New York: Barrie and Jenkins, 1968.

Grumett, David. *Material Eucharist*. Oxford: Oxford University Press, 2016.

Gutton, Anne-Marie. *Confréries et dévotion sous l'ancien régime: Lyonnais, Forez, Beaujolais*. Preface by René Taveneaux. Lyon: Éditions lyonnaises d'art et d'histoire, 1993.

Hamilton, Earl J. "Prices and Wages at Paris under John Law's System." *Quarterly Journal of Economics* 51 (Nov. 1936): 42–70.

Harris, Ruth. *Lourdes: Body and Spirit in a Secular Age*. New York: Viking, 1999.

Harsin, Paul. *Les doctrines monétaires et financières en France du XVIe au XVIIIe siècle*. Paris: Félix Alcan, 1928.

Hébrard, Pierre. *Histoire de Messire Claude Joly, évêque et comte d'Agen (1610–1678)*. Edited by P. Dubourg. Agen: F. Brousse, 1905.

Heron, Nicholas. *Liturgical Power: Between Economic and Political Theology*. New York: Fordham University Press, 2018.

Heyd, Michael. *Be Sober and Reasonable: The Critique of Enthusiasm in the Seventeenth and Early Eighteenth Centuries*. New York: E. J. Brill, 1995.

Higgs, Henry. *The Physiocrats: Six Lectures on the French Économistes of the 18th Century*. Hamden, CT: Archon, 1963.

Hilton, Boyd. *The Age of Atonement: The Influence of Evangelicalism on Social and Economic Thought, 1795–1865*. Oxford: Oxford University Press, 1988.

Hirschman, Albert O. *The Passions and the Interests: Political Arguments for Capitalism before Its Triumph*. Princeton, NJ: Princeton University Press, 1977.

Hochstrasser, T. J. "Physiocracy and the Politics of *Laissez-Faire*." In Goldie and Wokler, *Cambridge History of Eighteenth-Century Political Thought*, 419–42.

Hoffman, Philip T., Gilles Postel-Vinay, and Jean-Laurent Rosenthal. *Priceless Markets: The Political Economy of Credit in Paris, 1660–1870*. Chicago: University of Chicago Press, 2000.

Hogan, Edmund H. "Jansenism and Frequent Communion: A Consideration of the Bremond Thesis." *Irish Theological Quarterly* 53 (June 1987): 144–50.

Homer, Sidney, and Richard Sylla. *A History of Interest Rates*. 4th ed. Hoboken, NJ: John Wiley and Sons, 2005.

Hont, Istvan. "The Early Enlightenment Debate on Commerce and Luxury." In Goldie and Wokler, *Cambridge History of Eighteenth-Century Political Thought*, 379–418.

———. *Jealousy of Trade: International Competition and the Nation State in Historical Perspective*. Cambridge, MA: Belknap Press of Harvard University Press, 2005.

———. *Politics in Commercial Society: Jean-Jacques Rousseau and Adam Smith*. Cambridge, MA: Harvard University Press, 2015.

Horn, Jeff. *Economic Development in Early Modern France: The Privilege of Liberty, 1650–1820*. Cambridge: Cambridge University Press, 2017.

———. *The Path Not Taken: French Industrialization in the Age of Revolution, 1750–1830*. Cambridge, MA: MIT Press, 2006.

Hsia, R. Po-chia. *The World of Catholic Renewal, 1540–1770*. Cambridge: Cambridge University Press, 1998.

Hulliung, Mark. *The Autocritique of Enlightenment: Rousseau and the Philosophes*. Cambridge, MA: Harvard University Press, 1994.

Hundert, Edward J. "Bernard Mandeville and the Enlightenment's Maxims of Modernity." *Journal of the History of Ideas* 56, no. 4 (Oct. 1995): 577–93.

———. "Mandeville, Rousseau, and the Political Economy of Fantasy." In Berg and Eger, *Luxury in the Eighteenth Century*, 28–40.

Hunt, Lynn, Margaret C. Jacob, and W. W. Mijnhardt. *The Book That Changed Europe: Picart and Bernard's "Religious Ceremonies of the World."* Cambridge, MA: Belknap Press of Harvard University Press, 2010.

———, eds. *Bernard Picart and the First Global Vision of Religion*. Los Angeles: Getty Research Institute, 2010.

Iogna-Prat, Dominique. "Topographies of Penance in the Latin West (c. 800–c. 1200)." Translated by Graham Robert Edwards. In *A New History of Penance*, edited by Abigail Firey, 149–72. Leiden: Brill, 2008.

Jacob, Margaret C. *Strangers Nowhere in the World: The Rise of Cosmopolitanism in Early Modern Europe*. Philadelphia: University of Pennsylvania Press, 2016.
Jameson, Fredric. "The Vanishing Mediator: Narrative Structure in Max Weber." *New German Critique* 1 (Winter 1973): 52–89.
James-Sarazin, Ariane. *Hyacinthe Rigaud, 1659–1743*. 2 vols. Dijon: Faton, 2016.
Jaume, Lucien. *L'individu effacé, où le paradoxe du libéralisme français*. Paris: Fayard, 1997.
Jedin, Hubert. *A History of the Council of Trent*. Vol. 1, *The Struggle for the Council*. Translated by Ernest Graf. London: Thomas Nelson and Sons, 1957.
Jennings, Jeremy. "The Debate about Luxury in Eighteenth- and Nineteenth-Century French Political Thought." *Journal of the History of Ideas* 68, no. 1 (Jan. 2007): 79–105.
Jolley, Nicholas. "The Reception of Descartes' Philosophy." In *The Cambridge Companion to Descartes*, edited by John Cottingham, 397–407. Cambridge: Cambridge University Press, 1992.
Joly, Bernard. *Descartes et la chimie*. Paris: J. Vrin, 2011.
———. *Rationalité de l'alchimie au XVIIe siècle*. Paris: J. Vrin, 1992.
Jones, Colin. "The Great Chain of Buying: Medical Advertisement, the Bourgeois Public Sphere, and the Origins of the French Revolution." *American Historical Review* 101, no. 1 (Feb. 1996): 13–40.
Jones, Colin, and Rebecca Spang. "Sans-culottes, sans café, sans tabac: Shifting Realms of Necessity and Luxury in Eighteenth-Century France." In *Consumers and Luxury: Consumer Culture in Europe, 1650–1850*, edited by Maxine Berg and Helen Clifford, 37–62. Manchester, UK: Manchester University Press, 1999.
Jones, Gareth Stedman. *Karl Marx: Greatness and Illusion*. Cambridge, MA: Belknap Press of Harvard University Press, 2016.
Jones, Jennifer M. *Sexing La Mode: Gender, Fashion, and Commercial Culture in Old Regime France*. Oxford: Berg, 2004.
Julia, Dominique. "Les sources dans *Les Origines de l'esprit bourgeois*." *Les cahiers du Centre de Recherches Historiques* 32 (2003): 1–24.
Kaiser, Thomas E. "Money, Despotism, and Public Opinion in Early Eighteenth-Century France: John Law and the Debate on Royal Credit." *Journal of Modern History* 63, no. 1 (March 1991): 1–28.
———. "Public Credit: John Law's Scheme and the Question of *Confiance*." *Proceedings of the Western Society for French History* 16 (1989): 72–81.
Kantorowicz, Ernst H. *The King's Two Bodies: A Study in Mediaeval Political Theology*. Princeton, NJ: Princeton University Press, 1957.
Kaplan, Benjamin J. *Divided by Faith: Religious Conflict and the Practice of Toleration*. Cambridge, MA: Belknap Press of Harvard University Press, 2007.
Kaplan, Steven L. *The Bakers of Paris and the Bread Question, 1700–1775*. Durham, NC: Duke University Press, 1996.
———. *Bread, Politics and Political Economy in the Reign of Louis XV*. 2 vols. The Hague: Martinus Nijhoff, 1976.

Kates, Gary. "Fénelon's *Telemachus* and the Making of the Enlightenment." Unpublished manuscript.

Kaufman, Suzanne K. *Consuming Visions: Mass Culture and the Lourdes Shrine*. Ithaca, NY: Cornell University Press, 2005.

Kavanagh, Thomas M. *Enlightened Pleasures: Eighteenth-Century France and the New Epicureanism*. New Haven, CT: Yale University Press, 2010.

——. *Enlightenment and the Shadows of Chance: The Novel and the Culture of Gambling in Eighteenth-Century France*. Baltimore: Johns Hopkins University Press, 1993.

Kaye, Joel. *A History of Balance, 1250–1375: The Emergence of a New Model of Equilibrium and Its Impact on Thought*. Cambridge: Cambridge University Press, 2014.

Keefer, Michael H. "The Dreamer's Path: Descartes and the Sixteenth Century." *Renaissance Quarterly* 49, no. 1 (Spring 1996): 30–76.

Kerber, Peter Björn. "Vicar of Christ and Alter Christus: Benedict XIV's *Della S. Messa*." In *Benedict XIV and the Enlightenment: Art, Science, and Spirituality*, edited by Rebecca Messbarger, Christopher M. S. Johns, and Philip Gavitt, 297–312. Toronto: University of Toronto Press, 2016.

Kerschagl, Richard. *Die Jagd nach dem künstlichen Gold: Der Weg der Alchemie*. Berlin: Duncher, 1973.

Kessler, Amalia D. "Enforcing Virtue: Social Norms and Self-Interest in an Eighteenth-Century Merchant Court." *Law and History Review* 22, no. 1 (Spring 2004): 71–118.

——. *A Revolution in Commerce: The Parisian Merchant Court and the Rise of Commercial Society in Eighteenth-Century France*. New Haven, CT: Yale University Press, 2007.

Konings, Martijn. *The Emotional Logic of Capitalism: What Progressives Have Missed*. Stanford, CA: Stanford University Press, 2015.

Koyré, Alexandre. *From the Closed World to the Infinite Universe*. Baltimore: Johns Hopkins University Press, 1957.

Kreiser, B. Robert. *Miracles, Convulsions, and Ecclesiastical Politics in Early Eighteenth-Century Paris*. Princeton, NJ: Princeton University Press, 1978.

Kruckeberg, Robert D. "The Wheel of Fortune in Eighteenth-Century France: The Lottery, Consumption, and Politics." PhD diss., University of Michigan, 2009.

Kselman, Thomas. "Challenging Dechristianization: The Historiography of Religion in Modern France." *Church History* 75, no. 1 (2006): 130–39.

Kwass, Michael. "Between Words and Things: 'La Querelle du luxe' in the Eighteenth Century." *MLN* 130, no. 4 (Sept. 2015): 771–82.

——. "Big Hair: A Wig History of Consumption in Eighteenth-Century France." *American Historical Review* 111, no. 3 (June 2006): 631–59.

——. *Contraband: Louis Mandrin and the Making of a Global Underground*. Cambridge, MA: Harvard University Press, 2014.

——. "Ordering the World of Goods: Consumer Revolution and the Classification of Objects in Eighteenth-Century France." *Representations* 82, no. 1 (Spring 2003): 87–116.

———. *Privilege and the Politics of Taxation in Eighteenth-Century France: Liberté, Égalité, Fiscalité*. Cambridge: Cambridge University Press, 2000.

Labio, Catherine. "Staging Folly in the Dutch Republic, England, and France." In Goetzmann et al., *The Great Mirror of Folly*, 143–58.

Labrousse, Ernest, and Fernand Braudel, eds. *Histoire économique et sociale de la France*. Vol. 2, *Des derniers temps de l'âge industriel (1660–1789)*. Paris: Presses universitaires de France, 1970.

Landy, Joshua, and Michael T. Saler, eds. *The Re-enchantment of the World: Secular Magic in a Rational Age*. Stanford, CA: Stanford University Press, 2009.

Lange, Tyler. *Excommunication for Debt in Late Medieval France: The Business of Salvation*. Cambridge: Cambridge University Press, 2016.

Langholm, Odd. *The Aristotelian Analysis of Usury*. Bergen: Universitetsforlaget AS, 1984.

Larrère, Catherine. *L'invention de l'économie au XVIIIe siècle: Du droit naturel à la physiocratie*. Paris: Presses universitaires de France, 1992.

Laum, Bernhard. *Heiliges Geld: Eine historische Untersuchung über den sakralen Ursprung des Geldes*. Tübingen: Mohr, 1924.

Le Goff, Jacques. *Money and the Middle Ages: An Essay in Historical Anthropology*. Translated by Jean Birrell. Cambridge: Polity Press, 2012.

———. *La naissance du purgatoire*. Paris: Gallimard, 1981.

———. *Your Money or Your Life: Economy and Religion in the Middle Ages*. Translated by Patricia Ranum. New York: Zone, 1988.

Leonard, Daniel L. "Introduction: Fetishism, Figurism, and Myths of Enlightenment." In Morris and Leonard, *The Returns of Fetishism*, 1–39.

Lepoittevin, Anne. "*Picciolini, picolini* et *piccioli*: La fabrique romaine des *Agnus Dei* (1563–1700)." In Lezowski and Tatarenko, "Façonner l'objet de dévotion chrétien," 87–117.

Leridon-Segui, Thérèse. "Les objets de piété dans les inventaires après-décès de la première moitié du XVIIIe siècle." Mémoire de Maîtrise, Université de Paris IV, 1982.

Lériget, Marthe. *Des lois et impôts somptuaires*. Montpellier: Imprimerie L'Abeille, 1919.

Leshem, Dotan. *The Origins of Neoliberalism: Modeling the Economy from Jesus to Foucault*. New York: Columbia University Press, 2016.

Lezowski, Marie, and Laurent Tatarenko, eds. "Façonner l'objet de dévotion chrétien: Fabrication, commerce et circulations, XVIe–XIXe siècles." *Archives de sciences sociales des religions*, 183, no. 3 (July–Sept. 2018).

———. "Introduction: La matière et la manière." In Lezowski and Tatarenko, "Façonner l'objet de dévotion chrétien," 11–28.

Lilti, Antoine. *The Invention of Celebrity*. Translated by Lynn Jeffress. Malden, MA: Polity Press, 2017.

Maës, Bruno. "Artisans et commerçants des bourgs de pèlerinage." In Burkardt, *L'économie des dévotions*, 141–51.

———. "Les conditions de voyage des pèlerins sous l'ancien régime." *Annales de Bretagne et des Pays de l'Ouest* 121, no. 3 (Sept. 2014): 79–96.

———. "Légendaires de pèlerinages et construction de la nation France." In *Les généalogies imaginaires: Ancêtres, lignages et communautés idéales (XVIᵉ–XXᵉ siècles)*, edited by Pierre Ragon, 123–43. Rouen: Presses des universités de Rouen et du Havre, 2007.

———. "Le pèlerinage de Notre-Dame de Liesse de 1780 à la Révolution." In *Pratiques religieuses, mentalités et spiritualités dans l'Europe révolutionnaire (1770–1820)*, edited by Bernard Plongeron, 612–44. Paris: Brepols, 1988.

———. *Le roi, la Vierge et la nation: Pèlerinages et identité nationale en France entre guerre de Cent Ans et Révolution*. Paris: Publisud, 2002.

Magnot-Ogilvy, Florence, ed. *Gagnons sans savoir comment: Représentations du Système de Law du XVIIIᵉ siècle à nos jours*. Rennes: Presses universitaires de Rennes, 2017.

———. "Le Système au miroir de ses métaphores." In Magnot-Ogilvy, *Gagnons sans savoir comment*, 79–95.

Maillard, Jean-François. "Descartes et l'alchimie: Une tentation conjurée?" In Greiner, *Aspects de la tradition alchimique*, 95–109.

Maire, Catherine. *De la cause de Dieu à la cause de la Nation: Le jansénisme au XVIIIᵉ siècle*. Paris: Gallimard, 1998.

———. "Port-Royal: The Jansenist Schism." In *Realms of Memory: The Construction of the French Past*. Vol. 1, *Conflicts and Divisions*, edited by Pierre Nora and Lawrence D. Kritzman, translated by Arthur Goldhammer, 301–52. New York: Columbia University Press, 1996.

Mandrou, Robert. *De la culture populaire au 17ᵉ et 18ᵉ siècles: La Bibliothèque bleue de Troyes*. Preface by Philippe Joutard. Paris: Imago, 1985.

Mann, C. Griffith. "A Vision of Beauty: Fashioning Heaven on Earth." In Bolton et al., *Heavenly Bodies*, 2:106–8.

Marchal, Corinne, and Manuel Tramaux. *Le miracle de Faverney (1608): L'Eucharistie, environnement et temps de l'histoire*. Besançon: Presses universitaires de Besançon, 2008.

Marin, Louis. *La critique du discours: Sur la "Logique de Port-Royal" et les "Pensées" de Pascal*. Paris: Minuit, 1975.

———. *Le portrait du roi*. Paris: Minuit, 1981.

Markus, Gyorgy. "Walter Benjamin or the Commodity as Phantasmagoria." Special issue on Walter Benjamin, *New German Critique* 83 (Spring-Summer 2001): 3–42.

Martin, Philippe. "La boutique: Un lieu de dévotion dans la seconde moitié du XVIIᵉ siècle?" In Burkardt, *L'économie des dévotions*, 375–90.

Martin, Victor. *Le gallicanisme et la Réforme catholique: Essai historique sur l'introduction en France des décrets du concile de Trente (1563–1615)*. Reprint. Geneva: Slatkine, 1975.

Masson, Pierre-Maurice. *La religion de Jean-Jacques Rousseau*. 3 vols. Paris: Hachette, 1916.

Mastier, A. *Turgot, sa vie et sa doctrine*. Paris: Guillaumin, 1862.

Masuzawa, Tomoko. *The Invention of World Religions: Or, How European Universalism*

Was Preserved in the Language of Pluralism. Chicago: University of Chicago Press, 2005.

Matton, Sylvain. "Cartésianisme et alchimie: À propos d'un témoignage ignoré sur les travaux alchimiques de Descartes." In Greiner, *Aspects de la tradition alchimique*, 111–84.

Matytsin, Anton M. *The Specter of Skepticism in the Age of Enlightenment.* Baltimore: Johns Hopkins University Press, 2016.

Mauss, Marcel. *The Gift: The Form and Reason for Exchange in Archaic Societies.* Translated by W. D. Halls. Foreword by Mary Douglas. London: Routledge, 1990.

Mauzi, Robert. *L'idée du bonheur dans la littérature et la pensée françaises au XVIIIe siècle.* Geneva: Slatkine, 1979.

Maza, Sarah. *The Myth of the French Bourgeoisie: An Essay on the Social Imaginary, 1750–1850.* Cambridge, MA: Harvard University Press, 2003.

McCarraher, Eugene. *The Enchantments of Mammon: How Capitalism Became the Religion of Modernity.* Cambridge, MA: Belknap Press of Harvard University Press, 2019.

McCloskey, Deirdre N. *The Bourgeois Virtues: Ethics for an Age of Commerce.* Chicago: University of Chicago Press, 2006.

McCloy, Shelby T. "Government Assistance during the Plague of 1720–22 in Southeastern France." *Social Service Review* 12, no. 2 (June 1938): 298–318.

McGowan, Todd. *Capitalism and Desire: The Psychic Cost of Free Markets.* New York: Columbia University Press, 2016.

McMahon, Darrin M. "Happiness and *The Heavenly City of the Eighteenth-Century Philosophers*: Carl Becker Revisited." *American Behavioral Scientist* 49, no. 5 (Jan. 2006): 681–86.

McManners, John. *Church and Society in Eighteenth-Century France.* 2 vols. Oxford: Oxford University Press, 1998.

Melion, Walter S. "Introduction: The Jesuit Engagement with the Status and Functions of the Visual Image." In Boer, Enenkel, and Melion, *Jesuit Image Theory*, 1–49.

Merrick, Jeffrey. *The Desacralization of the French Monarchy in the Eighteenth Century.* Baton Rouge: Louisiana State University Press, 1990.

Messbarger, Rebecca, Christopher M. S. Johns, and Philip Gavitt, eds. *Benedict XIV and the Enlightenment: Art, Science, and Spirituality.* Toronto: University of Toronto Press, 2016.

Metropolitan Museum of Art. "1,659,647 Visitors to Costume Institute's *Heavenly Bodies* Show at Met Fifth Avenue and Met Cloisters Make It the Most Visited Exhibition in The Met's History." Metmuseum.org, Oct. 11, 2018. www.metmuseum.org/press/news/2018/heavenly-bodies-most-visited-exhibition#.

Meyssonnier, Simone. *La balance et l'horloge: La genèse de la pensée libérale en France au XVIIIe siècle.* Paris: Éditions de la Passion, 1989.

Michaud, Claude. *L'église et l'argent sous l'ancien régime: Les receveurs généraux du clergé de France aux XVIe et XVIIe siècles.* Paris: Fayard, 1991.

Michaud, Louis-Gabriel, ed. *Biographie universelle ancienne et moderne, ou Histoire par ordre alphabétique de la vie publique et privée de tous les hommes qui sont fait remarquer par leur écrits, leurs actions, leurs talents, leurs vertus ou leurs crimes*. New ed. 45 vols. Paris: A. Thoisnier Desplaces; Leipzig: F. A. Brokaus; Paris: Mme C. Desplaces, 1843–58.

Migne, Jacques-Paul, ed. *Dictionnaire des confréries et corporations d'arts et métiers*. Vol. 50 of *Nouvelle encyclopédie théologique*. Paris: J.-P. Migne, 1854.

———. *Encyclopédie théologique, ou séries de dictionnaires sur toutes les parties de la science religieuses*. 52 vols. Paris: Ateliers catholiques du Petit-Montrouge, 1851.

Miller, Michael. *The Bon Marché: Bourgeois Culture and the Department Store, 1869–1920*. Princeton, NJ: Princeton University Press, 1994.

Miller, Vincent J. *Consuming Religion: Christian Faith and Practice in a Consumer Culture*. New York: Continuum, 2004.

Mitchell, W. J. T. *Iconology: Image, Text, Ideology*. Chicago: University of Chicago Press, 1987.

Monod, Paul K. *Solomon's Secret Arts: The Occult in the Age of Enlightenment*. New Haven, CT: Yale University Press, 2013.

Montagnes, Bernard. "Les écrits dus à des Prêcheurs dans deux bibliothèques dominicaines." In *Les religieux et leur livres à l'époque moderne*, edited by Bernard Dompnier et Marie-Hélène Froeschlé-Chopard, 133–44. Clermont-Ferrand: Presses universitaires Blaise Pascal, 2000.

Moreton, Bethany. *To Serve God and Wal-Mart: The Making of Christian Free Enterprise*. Cambridge, MA: Harvard University Press, 2009.

Morris, Rosalind C. "After de Brosses: Fetishism, Translation, Comparativism, Critique." In Morris and Leonard, *The Returns of Fetishism*, 133–320.

Morris, Rosalind C., and Daniel H. Leonard. *The Returns of Fetishism: Charles de Brosses and the Afterlives of an Idea*. Chicago: University of Chicago Press, 2017.

Mousnier, Roland. "L'évolution des finances publiques en France et en Angleterre pendant les guerres de la Ligue d'Augsbourg et de la Succession d'Espagne." *Révue historique* 205, no. 1 (1951): 1–23.

———. *Les institutions de la France sous la monarchie absolue, 1598–1789*. Paris: Presses universitaires de France, 1974.

———. *The Institutions of France under the Absolute Monarchy*. Vol. 2, *The Organs of State and Society*, translated by Arthur Goldhammer. Chicago: University of Chicago Press, 1984.

———. *La stratification sociale à Paris aux XVIIe et XVIIIe siècles*. Paris: A. Pedone, 1976.

Moyer, Johanna B. "Sumptuary Law in Ancien Régime France, 1229–1806." PhD diss., Syracuse University, 1997.

Muceni, Elena. "Mandeville and France: The Reception of *The Fable of the Bees* in France and Its Influence on the French Enlightenment." *French Studies* 69, no. 4 (Oct. 2015): 449–61.

Murphy, Antoin E. *The Genesis of Macroeconomics: New Ideas from Sir William Petty to Henry Thornton*. Oxford: Oxford University Press, 2009.

———. *John Law: Economic Theorist and Policy-Maker*. Oxford: Oxford University Press, 1997.

Nadler, Steven M. *Arnauld and the Cartesian Philosophy of Ideas*. Manchester: Manchester University Press, 1989.

———. "Arnauld, Descartes, and Transubstantiation: Reconciling Cartesian Metaphysics and Real Presence." *Journal of the History of Ideas* 49, no. 2 (1988): 229–46.

———. *Occasionalism: Causation among the Cartesians*. New York: Oxford University Press, 2011.

Narbonne, Pierre. *Journal des règnes de Louis XIV et Louis XV*. Edited by J.-A. Le Roi. Paris: A. Durand et Pedone Lauriel, 1866.

Nelson, Benjamin N. *The Idea of Usury: From Tribal Brotherhood to Universal Otherhood*. Princeton, NJ: Princeton University Press, 1949.

Nelson, Robert H. *Economics as Religion: From Samuelson to Chicago and Beyond*. University Park: Pennsylvania State University Press, 2001.

Netz, Robert. "Grâce à une annotation de Jacob Constant de Rebecque, l'auteur du 'Moine secularisé' identifié." *Revue historique vaudoise* (1988): 121–29.

Newman, William R. "From Alchemy to 'Chymistry.'" In *The Cambridge History of Science*, edited by Katharine Park and Lorraine Daston, 497–517. Cambridge: Cambridge University Press, 2006.

———. *Promethean Ambitions: Alchemy and the Quest to Perfect Nature*. Chicago: University of Chicago Press, 2004.

Noonan, John Thomas. *The Scholastic Analysis of Usury*. Cambridge, MA: Harvard University Press, 1957.

Norberg, Kathryn. "The French Fiscal Crisis of 1788 and the Financial Origins of the Revolution of 1789." In *Fiscal Crises, Liberty, and Representative Government*, edited by Philip T. Hoffman and Kathryn Norberg, 253–99. Stanford, CA: Stanford University Press, 1994.

Nummedal, Tara. *Alchemy and Authority in the Holy Roman Empire*. Chicago: University of Chicago Press, 2007.

———. "Alchemy and Religion in Christian Europe." *Ambix* 60, no. 4 (Nov. 2013): 311–22.

O'Malley, John W. *Trent: What Happened at the Council*. Cambridge, MA: Belknap Press of Harvard University Press, 2013.

Orain, Arnaud. *La politique du merveilleux: Une autre histoire du Système de Law (1695–1795)*. Paris: Fayard, 2018.

———. "The Second Jansenism and the Rise of French Eighteenth-Century Political Economy." *History of Political Economy* 46, no. 3 (Fall 2014): 463–90.

Orain, Arnaud, and Maxime Menuet. "Liberal Jansenists and Interest-Bearing Loans in Eighteenth-Century France: A Reappraisal." *European Journal of the History of Economic Thought* 24, no. 4 (August 2017): 708–41.

Orain, Arnaud, and Laurent Thézé. "Publicité, contre-publicité, et représentations économiques du Système de Law: Le motif alchimique." In Magnot-Ogilvy, *Gagnons sans savoir comment*, 127–46.

Ossa-Richardson, Anthony. "Image and Idolatry: The Case of Louis Richeome." In *Method and Variation: Narrative in Early Modern French Thought*, edited by Emma Gilby and Paul White, 41–53. Oxford: Legenda, 2013.

Ozouf, Mona. *Festivals and the French Revolution*. Translated by Alan Sheridan. Cambridge, MA: Harvard University Press, 1988.

Palmer, R. R. *Catholics and Unbelievers in Eighteenth Century France*. New York: Cooper Square, 1961.

Pardailhé-Galabrun, Annik. *La naissance de l'intime: 3,000 foyers parisiens, XVIIe–XVIIIe siècles*. Paris: Presses universitaires de France, 1988.

Parkman, Francis. *France and England in North America*. Edited by David Levin. 2 vols. New York: Literary Classics of the United States, 1983.

Perrot, Jean-Claude. *Une histoire intellectuelle de l'économie politique: XVIIe–XVIIIe siècle*. Paris: Éditions de l'École des Hautes Études en Sciences Sociales, 1992.

Peterson, Erik. "Monotheism as a Political Problem." In *Theological Tractates*, edited and translated by Michael J. Hollerich, 68–105. Stanford, CA: Stanford University Press, 2011.

Pietz, William. "Fetishism and Materialism: The Limits of Theory in Marx." In *Fetishism as Cultural Discourse*, edited by Emily S. Apter and William Pietz, 119–51. Ithaca, NY: Cornell University Press, 1993.

———. "The Problem of the Fetish I." *RES: Anthropology and Aesthetics* 9 (Spring 1985): 5–17.

———. "The Problem of the Fetish II: The Origin of the Fetish." *RES: Anthropology and Aesthetics* 13 (Spring 1987): 23–45.

Piketty, Thomas. *Capital in the Twenty-First Century*. Translated by Arthur Goldhammer. Cambridge, MA: Belknap Press of Harvard University Press, 2014.

Poirier, Jean-Pierre. *Turgot: Laissez-faire et progrès social*. Paris: Perrin, 1999.

Polanyi, Karl. *The Great Transformation: The Political and Economic Origins of Our Time*. Boston: Beacon, 1944.

Préclin, Edmond. "Les conséquences sociales de jansénisme." *Revue d'histoire de l'Église de France* 21, no. 92 (1935): 355–91.

Principe, Lawrence M. "The End of Alchemy? The Repudiation and Persistence of Chrysopoeia at the Académie Royale des Sciences in the Eighteenth Century." *Osiris* 29, no. 1 (Jan. 2014): 96–116.

———. *The Secrets of Alchemy*. Chicago: University of Chicago Press, 2013.

Principe, Lawrence M., and William R. Newman. "Some Problems with the Historiography of Alchemy." In *Secrets of Nature: Astrology and Alchemy in Early Modern Europe*, edited by William R. Newman and Anthony Grafton, 385–431. Cambridge, MA: MIT Press, 2001.

Proust, Jacques. "Deux Encyclopédistes hors de l'*Encyclopédie*: Philippe Macquer et l'abbé Jaubert." *Revue d'histoire des sciences et de leur applications* 11, no. 4 (1958): 330–36.

Provost, Audrey. *Le luxe, les Lumières et la Révolution*. Paris: Champ Vallon, 2014.

Rétat, Pierre. "La jouissance physiocratique." In *Ordre, nature, propriété*, edited by Gérald Klotz, 179–211. Lyon: Presses universitaires de Lyon, 1985.

Rey, Jean-Michel. *Le temps du crédit*. Paris: Desclée de Brouwer, 2002.
Riley, Patrick. "Fénelon's 'Republican' Monarchism in *Telemachus*." In *Monarchisms in the Age of Enlightenment: Liberty, Patriotism, and the Common Good*, edited by Hans Blom, John Christian Laursen, and Luisa Simonuttim, 77–100. Toronto: University of Toronto Press, 2007.
———. *The General Will before Rousseau: The Transformation of the Divine into the Civic*. Princeton, NJ: Princeton University Press, 2014.
———. "Rousseau, Fénelon, and the Quarrel." In Riley, *Cambridge Companion to Rousseau*, 8–93.
———. "Rousseau's General Will." In Riley, *Cambridge Companion to Rousseau*, 124–53.
Riley, Patrick, ed. *The Cambridge Companion to Rousseau*. Cambridge: Cambridge University Press, 2001.
Riskin, Jessica. *The Restless Clock: A History of the Centuries-Long Argument over What Makes Living Things Tick*. Chicago: University of Chicago Press, 2016.
———. *Science in the Age of Sensibility: The Sentimental Empiricists of the French Enlightenment*. Chicago: University of Chicago Press, 2004.
Roberts, Hazel Van Dyke. *Boisguilbert: Economist of the Reign of Louis XIV*. New York: Columbia University Press, 1935.
Robertson, Hector Menteith. *Aspects of the Rise of Economic Individualism: A Criticism of Max Weber and His School*. Cambridge: Cambridge University Press, 1935.
Roche, Daniel. *La culture des apparences: Une histoire du vêtement (XVIIe–XVIIIe siècle)*. Paris: Fayard, 1989.
———. *The Culture of Clothing: Dress and Fashion in the Ancien Régime*. Translated by Jean Birrell. Cambridge: Cambridge University Press, 1994.
———. *Histoire des choses banales: Naissance de la consommation dans les sociétés traditionnelles (XVIIe–XIXe siècle)*. Paris: Fayard, 1997.
Rogister, John. *Louis XV and the Parlement of Paris, 1737–55*. Cambridge: Cambridge University Press, 1995.
Rosenblatt, Helena. *Rousseau and Geneva: From the "First Discourse" to the "Social Contract," 1749–1762*. Cambridge: Cambridge University Press, 1997.
Rosenfeld, Sophia A. *Common Sense: A Political History*. Cambridge, MA: Harvard University Press, 2011.
———. *A Revolution in Language: The Problem of Signs in Late Eighteenth-Century France*. Stanford, CA: Stanford University Press, 2001.
Rothbard, Murray N. "Time Preference." In *The New Palgrave: Utility and Probability*, edited by John Eatwell, Murray Milgate, and Peter Newman, 270–75. New York: Norton, 1990.
Rothkrug, Lionel. *Opposition to Louis XIV: The Political and Social Origins of the French Enlightenment*. Princeton, NJ: Princeton University Press, 1965.
Rothschild, Emma. "An Alarming Commercial Crisis in Eighteenth-Century Angoulême: Sentiments in Economic History." *Economic History Review* 51, no. 2 (May 1998): 268–93.

———. *Economic Sentiments: Adam Smith, Condorcet, and the Enlightenment*. Cambridge, MA: Harvard University Press, 2001.

Rowlands, Guy. *The Financial Decline of a Great Power: War, Influence, and Money in Louis XIV's France*. Oxford: Oxford University Press, 2012.

Rubin, Miri. *Corpus Christi: The Eucharist in Late Medieval Culture*. Cambridge: Cambridge University Press, 1991.

Russell, Daniel S. *The Emblem and Device in France*. Lexington, KY: French Forum, 1985.

Sabbagh, Gabriel. "The *Philosophie rurale* of Quesnay, Mirabeau, and Butré, after 250 Years." *Contributions to Political Economy* 34 (June 2015): 105–24.

Santner, Eric L. *The Royal Remains: The People's Two Bodies and the Endgames of Sovereignty*. Chicago: University of Chicago Press, 2011.

Santner, Eric L., with Bonnie Honig, Peter E. Gordon, and Hent de Vries. *The Weight of All Flesh: On the Subject-Matter of Political Economy*. Edited by Kevis Goodman. Oxford: Oxford University Press, 2016.

Schachter, Gustav. "François Quesnay: Interpreters and Critics Revisited." *American Journal of Economics and Sociology* 50, no. 3 (July 1991): 313–22.

Schelle, Gustave. "Turgot, sa vie et ses œuvres." In Turgot, *Œuvres de Turgot*, 1:1–76.

Schmaltz, Tad M. *Radical Cartesianism: The French Reception of Descartes*. Cambridge: Cambridge University Press, 2002.

Schmitt, Carl. *Political Theology: Four Chapters on the Concept of Sovereignty*. Translated by George Schwab. Chicago: University of Chicago Press, 2005.

Sepinwall, Alyssa G. *The Abbé Grégoire and the French Revolution: The Making of Modern Universalism*. Berkeley: University of California Press, 2005.

Sewell, William H., Jr. "Connecting Capitalism to the French Revolution: The Parisian Promenade and the Origins of Civic Equality in Eighteenth-Century France." *Critical Historical Studies* 1, no. 1 (Spring 2014): 5–46.

———. "The Empire of Fashion and the Rise of Capitalism in Eighteenth-Century France." *Past & Present* 206, no. 1 (Feb. 2010): 81–120.

———. *Logics of History: Social Theory and Social Transformation*. Chicago: University of Chicago Press, 2005.

Sheehan, Jonathan. *The Enlightenment Bible: Translation, Scholarship, Culture*. Princeton, NJ: Princeton University Press, 2007.

Sheehan, Jonathan, and Dror Wahrman. *Invisible Hands: Self-Organization and the Eighteenth Century*. Chicago: University of Chicago Press, 2015.

Shell, Marc. *Art and Money*. Chicago: University of Chicago Press, 1995.

———. *Money, Language, and Thought: Literary and Philosophical Economies from the Medieval to the Modern Era*. Berkeley: University of California Press, 1982.

Shepherd, Robert Perry. *Turgot and the Six Edicts*. Studies in History, Economics and Public Law, vol. 18, no. 2. New York: Columbia University Press, 1903.

Shovlin, John. "The Cultural Politics of Luxury in Eighteenth-Century France." *French Historical Studies* 23, no. 4 (Fall 2000): 577–606.

———. "Jealousy of Credit: John Law's 'System' and the Geopolitics of the Financial Revolution." *Journal of Modern History* 88, no. 2 (June 2016): 275–305.

———. *The Political Economy of Virtue: Luxury, Patriotism, and the Origins of the French Revolution*. Ithaca, NY: Cornell University Press, 2006.
Simmel, Georg. *The Philosophy of Money*. Edited by David Frisby. Translated by Tom Bottomore and David Frisby. London: Routledge, 1990.
Singh, Devin. *Divine Currency: The Theological Power of Money in the West*. Stanford, CA: Stanford University Press, 2018.
Slezkine, Yuri. *The Jewish Century*. Princeton, NJ: Princeton University Press, 2004.
Sluhovsky, Moshe. *Patroness of Paris: Rituals of Devotion in Early Modern France*. Leiden: Brill, 1998.
Smith, Pamela H. *The Business of Alchemy: Science and Culture in the Holy Roman Empire*. Princeton, NJ: Princeton University Press, 1994.
Soll, Jacob. *The Reckoning: Financial Accountability and the Rise and Fall of Nations*. New York: Basic Books, 2014.
Sombart, Werner. *The Jews and Modern Capitalism*. London: T. F. Unwin, 1913.
Sonenscher, Michael. *Before the Deluge: Public Debt, Inequality, and the Intellectual Origins of the French Revolution*. Princeton, NJ: Princeton University Press, 2007.
———. "The Empire of Fashion and the Rise of Capitalism." *Past and Present* 216 (Aug. 2012): 247–67.
———. *Sans-Culottes: An Eighteenth-Century Emblem in the French Revolution*. Princeton, NJ: Princeton University Press, 2008.
———. *Work and Wages: Natural Law, Politics, and the Eighteenth-Century French Trades*. Cambridge: Cambridge University Press, 1989.
Sorkin, David J. *The Religious Enlightenment: Protestants, Jews, and Catholics from London to Vienna*. Princeton, NJ: Princeton University Press, 2008.
Spahn, Heinz-Peter. *From Gold to Euro: On Monetary Theory and the History of Currency Systems*. Berlin: Springer, 2001.
Spang, Rebecca. *Stuff and Money in the Time of the French Revolution*. Cambridge, MA: Harvard University Press, 2015.
Spector, Céline. *Au prisme de Rousseau: Usages politiques contemporains*. Oxford: Voltaire Foundation, 2011.
———. *Rousseau et la critique de l'économie politique*. Persac: Presses universitaires de Bordeaux, 2017.
Spencer, Lloyd. "Allegory in the World of the Commodity: The Importance of *Central Park*." *New German Critique* 34 (Winter 1985): 59–77.
Spengler, Joseph J. "Boisguilbert's Economic Views vis-à-vis Those of Contemporary Réformateurs." *History of Political Economy* 16, no. 1 (Spring 1984): 69–88.
Spieth, Darius A. "The French Context of *Het Groote Tafereel der Dwaasheid*: John Law, Rococo Culture, and the Riches of the New World." In Goetzmann et al., *The Great Mirror of Folly*, 219–34.
Spinks, Bryan D. *Do This in Remembrance of Me: The Eucharist from the Early Church to the Present*. London: SCM Press, 2013.
Steiner, Philippe. *La "science nouvelle" de l'économie politique*. Paris: Presses universitaires de France, 1998.

Stockland, Étienne. "Insects, Anthropogenic Change and Rural Environments in the Global French Enlightenment." PhD diss., Columbia University, 2017.

Stone, Darwel. *A History of the Doctrine of the Holy Eucharist*. 2 vols. London: Longmans, Green, 1909.

Stroumsa, Guy G. *A New Science: The Discovery of Religion in the Age of Reason*. Cambridge, MA: Harvard University Press, 2010.

Subirade, Patricia. "Commerce et pèlerinage en Franche-Comté aux XVIIe et XVIIIe siècles: Besançon et Sainte-Claude." In Burkardt, *L'économie des dévotions*, 105–40.

Swatos, William H., Jr., and Lutz Kaelber, eds. *The Protestant Ethic Turns 100: Essays on the Centenary of the Weber Thesis*. Boulder, CO: Paradigm, 2005.

Tackett, Timothy. *Religion, Revolution, and Regional Culture in Eighteenth-Century France: The Ecclesiastical Oath of 1791*. Princeton, NJ: Princeton University Press, 2014.

Taeusch, Carl F. "The Concept of 'Usury': The History of an Idea." *Journal of the History of Ideas* 3, no. 3 (June 1942): 291–318.

Takeda, Junko Thérèse. *Between Crown and Commerce: Marseille and the Early Modern Mediterranean*. Baltimore: Johns Hopkins University Press, 2011.

Tallon, Alain. *La Compagnie du Saint-Sacrement (1629–1667): Spiritualité et société*. Preface by Marc Venard. Paris: Cerf, 1990.

———. *La France et le Concile de Trente (1518–1563)*. Rome: École français de Rome, Palais Farnèse, 1997.

Taveneaux, René. *Le catholicisme dans la France classique, 1610–1715*. 2 vols. Paris: Société d'édition d'enseignement supérieur, 1980.

———. *Jansénisme et prêt à intérêt: Introduction, choix de textes et commentaires*. Paris: J. Vrin, 1977.

Taylor, George V. "Types of Capitalism in Eighteenth-Century France." *English Historical Review* 79, no. 312 (July 1964): 478–97.

Terjanian, Anoush F. *Commerce and Its Discontents in Eighteenth-Century French Political Thought*. Cambridge: Cambridge University Press, 2013.

Thanh, Hélène Vu. "L'économie des objets de dévotion en terres de mission: L'exemple du Japon (1549–1614)." In Lezowski and Tatarenko, "Façonner l'objet de dévotion chrétien," 207–25.

Theological Dictionary of the Old Testament. Revised and edited by G. Johannes Botterweck and Helmer Ringgren. Translated by John T. Willis. 15 vols. Grand Rapids, MI: William B. Eerdmans, 1975.

Théré, Christine, and Loïc Charles. "The Writing Workshop of François Quesnay and the Making of Physiocracy." *History of Political Economy* 40, no. 1 (Spring 2008): 1–42.

Tierney, Brian. *The Idea of Natural Rights: Studies on Natural Rights, Natural Law, and Church Law, 1150–1625*. Grand Rapids, MI: William B. Eerdmans, 1997.

Timmerman, Achim. "A View of the Eucharist on the Eve of the Protestant Reformation." In *A Companion to the Eucharist in the Reformation*, edited by Lee Palmer Wandel, 365–98. Leiden: Brill, 2014.

Tingle, Elizabeth C. *Indulgences after Luther: Pardons in Counter-Reformation France, 1520–1720*. London: Pickering and Chatto, 2015.
Todd, David. *Free Trade and Its Enemies in France, 1814–1851*. Cambridge: Cambridge University Press, 2015.
Todeschini, Giacomo. *Franciscan Wealth: From Voluntary Poverty to Market Society*. Translated by Donatella Melucci. Saint Bonaventure, NY: Franciscan Institute, 2009.
———. *I Mercanti e il Tempio: La società cristiana e il circolo virtuoso della ricchezza fra Medioevo et Età Moderna*. Bologna: Il Mulino, 2002.
Tracy, David. "The Catholic Imagination: The Example of Michelangelo." In Bolton et al., *Heavenly Bodies*, 1:10–16.
Trentmann, Frank. *Empire of Things: How We Became a World of Consumers, from the Fifteenth Century to the Twenty-First*. New York: Harper Collins, 2016.
Trivellato, Francesca. "Between Usury and the 'Spirit of Commerce': Images of Jews and Credit from Montesquieu to the Debate on Emancipation in Eighteenth-Century France." *French Historical Studies* 39, no. 4 (Oct. 2016): 645–83.
———. *The Promise and Peril of Credit: What a Forgotten Legend about Jews and Finance Tells Us about the Making of European Commercial Society*. Princeton, NJ: Princeton University Press, 2019.
Troyon, O. "Les 'Agnus Dei': Leur bénédiction à Rome et leurs usages." *Rome* 99 (March 1912): 69–78.
Valeri, Mark R. *Heavenly Merchandize: How Religion Shaped Commerce in Puritan America*. Princeton, NJ: Princeton University Press, 2010.
Van Kley, Dale K. "Christianity as Casualty and Chrysalis of Modernity: The Problem of Dechristianization in the French Revolution." *American Historical Review* 108, no. 4 (Oct. 1, 2003): 1081–1104.
———. *The Jansenists and the Expulsion of the Jesuits from France, 1757–1765*. New Haven, CT: Yale University Press, 1975.
———. "Pierre Nicole, Jansenism, and the Morality of Enlightened Self-Interest." In *Anticipations of the Enlightenment in England, France, and Germany*, edited by Alan Charles Kors and Paul J. Korshin, 69–85. Philadelphia: University of Pennsylvania Press, 1987.
———. "The Religious Origins of the French Revolution." In *From Deficit to Deluge: The Origins of the French Revolution*, edited by Thomas E. Kaiser and Dale K. Van Kley, 104–38. Stanford, CA: Stanford University Press, 2011.
———. *The Religious Origins of the French Revolution: From Calvin to the Civil Constitution, 1560–1791*. New Haven, CT: Yale University Press, 1996.
Van Leeuwen, Arend Theodoor. *Critique of Earth*. Cambridge: James Clarke, 2002.
Vardi, Liana. *The Physiocrats and the World of the Enlightenment*. New York: Cambridge University Press, 2012.
Velde, François R. Introduction to Chrétien-Deschamps, *Lettres*, ix–lxiv.
Velde, François R., and David R. Weir. "The Financial Market and Government

Debt Policy in France, 1746–1793." *Journal of Economic History* 52, no. 1 (March 1992): 1–39.
Vidal, Daniel. *Miracles et convulsions jansénistes au XVIIIe siècle: Le mal et sa connaissance.* Paris: Presses universitaires de France, 1987.
Viguerie, Jean de. *Le catholicisme des français dans l'ancienne France.* Paris: Nouvelles Éditions Latines, 1989.
———. "La dévotion populaire à la messe en France aux XVIIe et XVIIIe siècles." In *Histoire de la messe, XVII–XIXe siècles,* 7–26. Angers: Université d'Angers, U.E.R. des Lettres et Sciences Humaines, Centre de Recherches d'Histoire Religieuse et d'Histoire des Idées, 1980.
Vilar, Pierre. *A History of Gold and Money, 1450–1920.* Translated by Judith White. London: NLB, 1976.
Viller, M., J. de Guibert, A. Rayez, A. Derville, and A. Solignac, eds. *Dictionnaire de spiritualité ascétique et mystique, doctrine et histoire.* 17 vols. Paris: Beauchesne, 1932–95.
Viner, Jacob. *Religious Thought and Economic Society: Four Chapters of an Unfinished Work.* Edited by Jacques Melitz and Donald Winch. Durham, NC: Duke University Press, 1978.
Vovelle, Michel. *Piété baroque et déchristianisation en Provence au XVIIIe siècle: Les attitudes devant la mort d'après les clauses de testaments.* Paris: C. T. H. S., 1997 [1978].
Vries, Jan de. *The Industrious Revolution: Consumer Behavior and the Household Economy, 1650 to the Present.* Cambridge: Cambridge University Press, 2008.
Waterman, Anthony Michael C. *Revolution, Economics, and Religion: Christian Political Economy, 1798–1833.* Cambridge: Cambridge University Press, 1991.
Watson, Richard A. "Transubstantiation among the Cartesians." In *Problems of Cartesianism,* edited by T. M. Lennon, John M. Nicholas, and John W. Davis, 127–48. Montreal: McGill-Queen's University Press, 1982.
Weber, Max. *From Max Weber: Essays in Sociology.* Translated by H. H. Gerth and C. Wright Mills. Oxford: Oxford University Press, 1958.
———. *The Protestant Ethic and the Spirit of Capitalism.* Translated by Talcott Parsons. London: Routledge, 2001.
Weir, David R. "Les crises économiques et les origines de la Révolution française." *Annales: Histoire, Sciences sociales* 46, no. 4 (July-August 1991): 917–47.
Wennerlind, Carl. *Casualties of Credit: The English Financial Revolution, 1620–1720.* Cambridge, MA: Harvard University Press, 2011.
———. "Credit-Money as the Philosopher's Stone: Alchemy and the Coinage Problem in Seventeenth-Century England," in "Œconomies in the Age of Newton," edited by Margaret Schabas and Neil De Marchi, Annual Supplement, *History of Political Economy* 35, no. 5 (2003): 234–61.
Weuleresse, Georges. *Le mouvement physiocratique en France (de 1756 à 1770).* 2 vols. Paris: Félix Alcan, 1910.
Whitmore, P. J. S. *The Order of Minims in Seventeenth-Century France.* The Hague: Martinus Nijhoff, 1967.

Williams, Hannah. "Saint Geneviève's Miracles: Art and Religion in Eighteenth-Century Paris." *French History* 30, no. 3 (Sept. 2016): 322–53.

Williams, Rosalind H. *Dream Worlds: Mass Consumption in Late Nineteenth-Century France*. Berkeley: University of California Press, 1991.

Wilson, W. J. "An Alchemical Manuscript by Arnaldus de Bruxella." *Osiris* 2 (1936): 220–405.

Worcester, Thomas. "Friends as Liabilities: Christophe de Beaumont's Defence of the Jesuits." In *The Jesuit Suppression in Global Context: Causes, Events, and Consequences*, edited by Jeffrey D. Burson and Jonathan Wright, 65–79. Cambridge: Cambridge University Press, 2015.

Wyss-Giacosa, Paola von. *Religionsbilder der Frühen Aufklärung: Bernard Picarts Tafeln für die "Cérémonies et Coutumes religieuses de tous les Peuples du Monde."* Wabern: Benteli, 2006.

Yuran, Noam. *What Money Wants: An Economy of Desire*. Stanford, CA: Stanford University Press, 2014.

Index

Page numbers in italic type indicate illustrations.

Abrégé de la dévotion du Saint Rosaire, 193–94, 198, 202
Abrégé des fruits du Rosaire de la Sainte Vierge, 199
absolutism, 21, 22, 73–74, 78, 99, 126, 232, 235
abundance: in the afterlife, 219; of agriculture, 223; alchemical, 108; capitalism as source of, 240; Christian conceptions of, 46, 61–62, 80, 81, 141, 149, 214; of Church's treasure, 190, 196; in commerce, 23, 153; economic characterization of, 27; Eucharist characterized by, 39, 42, 52, 57–58, 62, 255; of God, 118, 213; of Jesus Christ, 199; luxury linked to, 247, 268; rosary as means of obtaining, 190, 196, 202; usury and, 141, 149, 172. *See also* plenitude; treasure
Academy of Besançon, 246
accumulation: Catholic attitude toward, 13, 181; limitless, 10, 24; Protestant ethic as condition for, 13

Adam, 72, 75
adoration of the host, 15, 53–55, 57, 59, 63–64, 214
Agamben, Giorgio, 12
Agatha, Saint, 52
agriculture, 17, 26, 215–16, 222–23, 230–36, 244, 250
Albertus Magnus: *De Alchimia*, 108; *De Eucharistia*, 108
Albigensian heresy, 194
alchemy: Catholicism associated with, 105; Eucharist likened to, 24, 42, 104, 106–13, 136–37; financial speculation likened to, 22, 24, 101, 103–6, 108, 129–30, 135–36; Louis XIV and, 128–29; money compared to, 106–7, 137; skepticism and criticism directed at, 108–9, 128–29; ubiquity of, 17, 103; usury compared to, 165. *See also* philosopher's stone
Alembert, Jean Le Rond d', 117, 133
Alexander VIII, Pope, 195, 200
Althusser, Louis, 275n45, 278n90, 306n132

357

Ambrose, Saint, *Book of Tobit*, 145
amour-propre. See self-love
Anidjar, Gil, 275n43
Anne of Austria, 78
annuities, 6, 125, 147–48, 150–51, 159, 161. See also *rentes perpétuelles*; *rentes viagères*
Antonio of Florence, 59
Aquinas, Thomas, and Thomism: and alchemy, 108; and infinity, 118; on money, 163–64, 166; on penance, 43, 199; on substance, 32; *Summa Theologica*, 145; on transubstantiation, 23, 33, 115; and usury, 145, 147, 156, 161, 162, 166
Aristotle and Aristotelianism: influence of, on Scholastics, 108; on money, 156, 163; on substance, 32, 114; on utility of religion, 249
Arlequyn actionist (*Harlequin the Stockjobber*), 101, *102*, 135, 141, 287n1
Arnald of Brussels, 109
Arnald of Villanova, 109
Arnauld, Antoine, 24, 41–42, 73–83, 115, 255; *De la fréquente communion*, 71, 75–78, 88, 97, 99
Arnoulx, François, 4, 60; *Du paradis et de ses merveilles*, 60–61; *Merveilles de l'autre monde*, 60
Assembly of the Clergy, 6, 41, 48. See also General Assembly of the Clergy
Assumptionists, 266
Athanasius, 98
Augustine, Saint: and church authority, 73; on church-state relationship, 98; and communion, 40, 72; on countervailing passions, 19; on human nature, 75, 214; and usury, 157
Ave Maria, 190, 192, 194, 196–98

Baldenstein, Josef Wilhelm Rinck von, 87–88
banknotes. *See* money
Bank of England, 106, 142
Banque royale. *See* Royal Bank
Bansilion, Jean, 182, 206
baptism, 37, 48
Barry, Paul de, *Le paradis ouvert à Philagie*, 197–98
Bataille, Georges, 68, 276n49
Battle of Lepanto, 194
Baudeau, abbé, 242–43
Baudelaire, Charles, 263–66
Bazin de Bezons, Armand, 86, 89
Beaumont, Christophe de, 86, 88–90, 93, 97, 99
belief: credit as linguistic relative of, 9; financial speculation dependent on, 104, 133, 136, 144; as ground of economic order, 250–51, 262
Belin, Jean-Albert, 111–13; *Apologie du grand œuvre*, 111–12; *Les emblèmes eucharistiques*, 112–13; *Traité des talismans*, 112
Bell, David, 7
Belt of Saint Augustine, 175, 204
Benedict XIV, Pope, 25, 89, 143, 200; *Ex omnibus*, 98; *Vix Pervenit*, 160, 162–63, 172
Benjamin, Walter, 13, 257, 262–65, 268, 271; *Arcades Project*, 262–65; "Capitalism as Religion," 262, 264; *Central Park*, 264; "The Paris of the Second Empire in Baudelaire," 263
Berengar of Tours, 32
Bernard, Jean-Frédéric, and Bernard Picart: *Cérémonies et coutumes religieuses des peuples idolâtres*, 204, *205*, 206; *Cérémonies et coutumes religieuses de tous les peuples du monde*, 1–3, *2*, 10, 22, 25, 203–7, 254, 256, 263

Bernard, Jean-Vincent, *Le triple Rosaire augmenté*, 193, 195
Bernard, Saint, 153
Berny, Louis, *Instruction pour les confrères du Rosaire*, 202
Bertin, Henri Léonard Jean Baptiste, 236
Bertrand, Louis, 198
billets de confession, 89, 91, 93, 98
bills of exchange, 15, 158
Biron, duc de, 244
Blairye, Nicolas de, 37
Blumenberg, Hans, 11, 275n44
Bodin, Jean, *Six livres de la république*, 120
Bohemia, 40
Boidot, Philippe, *Traité des prêts de commerce*, 160
Boileau, Jacques, 218
Boisguilbert, Pierre Le Pesant de, 8, 121–22; *Dissertation sur les richesses*, 121
Bon Marché, Paris, 267
Bosc, Jacques du, 37
Bossuet, Jacques Bénigne, 22, 44, 82, 90, 172, 222
Bouettin (curé), 91
Boulanger, Nicolas-Antoine, 66
boundlessness: Cartesianism and, 116–18; of the Eucharist, 26–27, 31, 33, 34, 42; financial speculation and, 105; of God, 143; of guilt and mercy, 53; of Jesus Christ, 61; of merit accrued by the saints, 45; spiritual ideal of, 24, 27; of wealth, 24, 26–27, 202
Bourdaloue, Louis, 47, 63–64, 100
Bourgogne, Louis de France, duc de, 222–23, 231
Bridget of Sweden, Saint, 200, 204
Brosses, Charles de, 26, 256, 258, 260; *Du culte des dieux fétiches*, 253–54
Bulteau, Louis, 146

Butel-Dumont, Georges-Marie, 26, 216, 247, 249; *Théorie du luxe*, 241–44
Butré, Charles Richard de, *La philosophie rurale* (with François Quesnay and the marquis de Mirabeau), 233–35
Buvat, Jean, 130–32
Bynum, Caroline Walker, 32

Calvin, John, 42, 48, 143, 146, 206
Calvinism, 13, 20, 97, 111, 145, 228, 262
Camus, Jean-Pierre, 80–82; *L'usage de la pénitence et communion*, 80
canon law: authority concerning last rites in, 94; and church-state relationship, 90; civil law in relation to, 17; codification of, 31; on usury, 145
capitalism: Benjamin on religious character of, 13, 262–65; consumption's role in development of, 4, 8, 177–79; desire's role in, 10, 179, 187, 247, 265; as an economic and cultural system, 8–10, 208–9, 240, 247–48, 261–62; economic theology in relation to, 4–5, 11–15; the Enlightenment and, 134–37, 240–41; Marx on fetishistic character of, 26–27, 259–62; Protestantism and, 14, 257–58; religious foundations of, 13, 26–27. *See also* French capitalism
Carpuac, Père, 162
Carrel, Louis-Joseph, 145, 153–55, 165
Cartesianism: and the Eucharist, 113–20; and infinity, 24, 116–18, 127, 137; and mechanical view of political-economic realm, 121; and plurality of worlds, 47, 118; and transubstantiation/transmutation, 113, 114–16

360 Index

Cassirer, Ernst, 17
Catherine II, Empress of Russia, 224
Catherine of Bologna, Saint, 200
Catholic ethic: capitalism linked to, 27; consumption linked to, 12, 16, 25, 243–44; and debt/redemption, 144; economization of, 180, 203, 263; expenditure's role in, 20, 68, 143, 208; fashion and, 266–71; features of, 11; images' role in, 185; legacy of, 257; liberality of, 28, 34, 45, 66–67, 169–72; overview of, 11–18; Protestant ethic compared to, 13–14, 18, 20, 258
Catholicism: alchemy associated with, 24, 105; attitudes toward *jouissance* in, 25, 228, 231, 255; attitudes toward wealth in, 15, 163, 181; church as *corpus mysticum*, 31–32; critiques of, 2, 183, 203, 204, 206; economic theology of, 3–4, 42; economic thought in relation to, 13, 17, 19, 22, 34, 214, 215, 222–23; Enlightenment role of, 7, 18–19; fetishism and, 3, 4, 26–27, 254; and luxury, 10, 214; *philosophes* opposed by, 236; roots of Marx's critique of capitalism in, 26–27, 207–8, 257–62. *See also* Catholic ethic; Catholic Reformation; Gallican church
Catholic League, 44
Catholic Reformation: attitudes toward wealth in, 15; Eucharistic devotion and, 48–59; and indulgences, 44; role of, in consumption, 180; rosary popularity as result of, 188; and the sacraments, 33–40, 43–45, 255
Caussin, Nicolas, 220, 225; *La cour sainte*, 217
celestial treasure. *See* spiritual treasure
celestial wealth. *See* spiritual wealth
Certeau, Michel de, 31–32, 276n62

chamber of justice, 139
Chambon, Joseph, 103
Champion de Cicé, Jérôme Marie, 135
Chanel, Gabrielle "Coco," 268, *269*, 271
Chantal, Jeanne de, 75
charity: divine, 34, 44; imitation of God through, 53; reward for, 24, 66–67; role of, in God's system, 66; as spiritual disposition, 45
Charles V, Emperor, 35, 39
Charles VI, King, 50
Chastain, Jean, *Le moine secularisé*, 175, *176*, 177, 188, 204, 254
Chevaucheur (artisan), 149
Chevreuse, Charles Honoré d'Albert, duc de, 222
Chrysostom, John, 32, 62, 145, 164
Church of Saint-Eustache, 50
Church of Sainte-Geneviève, 181
church-state relationship, 71, 89–100
civil law, canon law in relation to, 17
Cleirac, Étienne, 15
Clement VIII, Pope, 197
Clement IX, Pope, 196
Clement X, Pope, 54, 197
Clement XI, Pope, 74, 192–93, 200; *Unigenitus* (1713), 74, 88–98, 146, 200
Clerselier, Claude, 114
clothing. *See* fashion
Coffin, Charles, 91
Colbert, Jean-Baptiste, 67, 121, 150, 184, 185, 223
Cole, Andrew, 312n16
Collet, Pierre, 195–96
Colombière, Claude de la, 67
Colonia, André de, *Éclaircissement sur le légitime commerce des intérêts*, 152
commerce: abundance in, 23, 153; church's acceptance of, 145–46; crown's intervention in, 184;

Index   361

fecundity of money and, 163–70; interest charged in, 149–50, 152–53; Jesus Christ and, 60, 61

commodity fetishism: Benjamin and, 262–65, 271; Marx's theory of, 4, 26–27, 257–62; theological precursors of, 4, 26, 63, 214–15, 250. *See also* fetishism

commodity form, 10, 258

communion: behaviors appropriate to, 40; categories of communicants, 76; Council of Trent and, 24, 76; frequency of, 24, 40, 48, 71–72, 75–86, 96–97; penance in relation to, 75–77, 80–81, 86; power of, 62, 77; requirement of, 43. *See also* Eucharist; host

Compagnie du Saint-Sacrement, 50, 54

Company of China, 124

Company of the East Indies, 124

Company of the Indies, 101, 124, 132, 135, 171

Company of the West, 123–25

confession, 43, 48

confirmation, 37

confraternities: activities of, 51–52; administration of, 51; criticisms of, 204; Dominicans' establishment of, 190, 193; in economic perspective, 58–59; establishment and growth of, 49, 50, 54; Eucharist-focused, 15, 23, 29, 34, 49–59, 64; financial matters of, 51–52; indulgences granted to, 15, 16, 23, 29, 34, 50, 53, 54, 179, 193, 200; Jesuit critique of, 217; members of, 50–51, 53, 193; rosary-focused, 25, 193–94, 202–3

confréries du métier, 50

consubstantiation, 33

Consultation de plusieurs canonistes et avocats de Paris, sur le compétence des juges séculiers, 94

consumer revolution, 8, 12, 19, 25, 178–81, 187, 207–8, 262

consumption, 175–209; Benjamin on allure of, 262–65; Catholic ethic linked to, 12, 16, 25, 243–44; desire and satisfaction as drivers of, 179; devotional objects' role in, 179; economic theology and, 266–68; of the host, 32, 39, 40; pilgrimages and, 184–85, 266–67; religious and theological underpinnings of, 100, 178, 180, 187; role of, in development of capitalism, 4, 8, 177; semiotics associated with, 243, 267; women's role in, 177, 178, 215, 221. *See also* consumer revolution; fashion; luxury; spiritual goods; wealth

contract of Poissy (1561), 41

contractum trinius. *See* triple contract

convulsionnaires (sect), 88–89

Cord of Saint Francis, 175, 204

corpus mysticum, 31–32

corpus verum, 31–32

correspondences, divine and human/physical, 107, 109–10

Costume Institute, Metropolitan Museum of Art, 268

Council of Elvira (305–6), 159

Council of Lavaur (1368), 96

Council of Trent (1545–63): catechism of, 21, 23, 35–40, 42, 110; and communion, 24, 76; Descartes and, 114; and devotional objects, 25; economic conceptions in, 21, 23, 33, 35–42; and the Eucharist, 33, 34, 36–38, 71, 87, 96, 114, 244; Gallican church and, 40–42; on images and relics, 182; and indulgences, 199; and penance, 43–44; political context for, 35, 41; Protestant Reformers as target for, 34–35, 48; and the sacraments, 21, 24, 35–42, 48, 60

credit, belief as linguistic relative of, 9
crown. *See* king
Crusaders, 203
Cum occasione (1653 papal bull), 79
Custos unitatis schismatis ultrix engraving, 69, *70*, *71*

Darnton, Robert, 133
debt: of Christ's sacrifice, 11, 56–57, 141; of the crown, 6–7, 25, 41, 141–42, 168; in everyday life, 143, 147; forgiveness of, 35; in French economic thought, 5, 8; held by Gallican church, 6, 41, 143; patience and forgiveness concerning, 143; public, 106; religious uses of concept of, 4, 11, 21, 34, 43, 55, 59, 81; sin as, 4, 21, 35, 42, 45, 48, 53, 58, 78, 144, 172, 255. *See also* usury
Declaration of December (1756), 98–99
DeJean, Joan, 268
Delisle (alchemist), 128
Desbrulins, F., and Nicolas Henri Tardieu, *Loüé soit le très saint sacrement de l'autel*, 29, *30*, *31* (detail)
Descartes, René, 103, 113–15, 117–19, 126, 155. *See also* Cartesianism
Desgabets, Robert, 24, 115–18, 120; *Considérations sur l'état présent de la controverse touchant le Très-Saint Sacrement de l'autel*, 115; *Le guide de la raison naturelle*, 117; *Traité de l'indéfectibilité des créatures*, 96
desire: in capitalism, 247, 265; in Catholic ethic, 28; common good resulting from egoistic, 19; consumption driven by, 179; devotional objects as target of, 4, 180–81; in economic theology, 10, 34, 129; idolatry as danger of, 26, 62–64; for spiritual goods, 68, 82–83, 195; for worldly goods and wealth, 124, 129, 136, 241–43
Desmartes, Nicolas, 128
devotional objects: associated with pilgrimages, 184–85, 266–67; criticisms of, 186; debates over, 175, 177, 187; economic theology and, 179–80, 267; indulgences linked to, 195–96, 200; market for, 25, 179, 187–90; popularity of, 186–87; production of, 188; role of, in consumer revolution, 179, 262; roles of desire and satisfaction in, 4, 180–81; scholarship on, 187; spiritual wealth available through, 4, 10, 25, 181, 187. *See also* rosaries
Dictionnaire de droit canonique, 147
Dictionnaire portatif des arts et métiers, 189
Diderot, Denis, 213–14, 215, 246; *Observations sur le Nakaz*, 224
disenchantment of the world, 14, 161, 185, 187, 263
divine-right monarchy, 21, 74, 99, 106, 123
Domat, Jean, 19
Dominic, Saint, 190, 194
Dominican Order, 190, 193, 196
doux commerce, 19
Dubois (deacon), 91
Duguet, Jacques-Joseph, 214
Dumarsais, César Chesneau, 274n25
Duns Scotus, John, 32, 115
Dupont de Nemours, Pierre-Samuel, 231, 236, 238
Du Pradel, Jean, 26; *Traité contre le luxe des hommes et des femmes*, 221–22, 225
Dutot, Nicolas, *Réflexions politiques sur les finances et le commerce*, 135
Duvergier de Hauranne, Jean. *See* Saint-Cyran, Jean Duvergier de Hauranne, abbé de

economic theology: Benjamin and, 257, 262–65; capitalism in relation to, 4–5; Catholic, 3–4, 42, 207; and consumer revolution, 180, 208; consumption and, 266–68; as contingent outcome of classical theology, 12, 14, 208, 256; criticisms of, 207; debt as topic of, 142; defined, 3; desire's role in, 10, 34, 129; devotional objects and, 179–80, 267; Gallican form of, 41, 262; as historical corpus, 3, 12; historical development of, 12, 255–57; and idolatry, 217; as interpretive framework, 3, 12; Marx and, 17, 257–65; on material vs. spiritual realms, 23, 215, 217; metamorphosis as basic process in, 259; of money, 105, 136; political economy in relation to, 3, 7, 34, 241; refusal of sacraments controversy and, 100; scholarly interpretations of the concept, 12–14; semiotics of, 27; and sources of value, 18; Turgot and, 20, 236–41; and usury, 144, 147, 155–63, 171–72

économistes, 231–36

economy: Catholic theology in relation to, 13, 17, 19, 22, 34, 214; competing conceptions of, 6; divine, 110, 203; economic theologians' legitimation of, 23; *Encyclopédie*'s references to, 66; etymology of, 227; fetishization of, 250–51; historical development of French, 266; libidinal aspect of, 243; as metaphor for ordered systems, 66–67; redemption through, 3; relationship of material and spiritual, 59–60, 180, 187, 202, 217; resacralization of, 16, 23, 256. *See also* consumption

Edelstein, Dan, 17, 19, 232

Edict of Fontainebleau, 206

Edict of Melun, 41

Edict of Nantes, 15, 73, 84

Encyclopédie: economy concept in, 66; on the Eucharist, 151; on faith, 232; on God's earthly role, 7; linguistic concerns of, 214, 243; on luxury, 17, 215, 224, 247; on political economy, 227; Turgot's drafts for, 237; on usury, 17, 169

Engels, Friedrich, 10; *The German Ideology* (with Karl Marx), 177, 247

Enlightenment: agronomy associated with, 236; Benedict XIV and, 200; church's role in, 7, 18–19; conception of nature in, 185; consumption linked to, 63, 178; economic thought in, 15, 18–19, 147; Epicurean Stoicism of, 217; Law's System and, 134–37; luxury during, 223–24; the miraculous in, 4–5; as new form of faith, 17; the occult in, 17; pleasure's role in, 208; political economy of, 214, 215, 245, 250; role of religion in, 187; scholarly approaches to, 18–19; semantics in, 243; Turgot as exemplar of, 236

Ephémérides du citoyen (journal), 238, 242

Epicurean Stoicism, 217

Eucharist: alchemy likened to, 24, 42, 104, 106–13, 136–37; boundlessness and inexhaustibility of, 26–27, 31, 33, 34, 42; Cartesian perspectives on, 113–20; confraternities devoted to, 15, 23, 29, 34, 49–59, 64; controversies over, 32–33, 59; Council of Trent and, 33, 34, 36–38, 71, 87, 96, 114, 244; Descartes and, 114–15; in economic perspective, 16, 23, 24, 26, 31–34, 38, 40, 42, 53, 59, 62–65, 67, 84; fecundity of, 21, 85;

Eucharist (*continued*)
  financial speculation and, 103, *104*, 108, 126–31, 136; Gallican church and, 34; images of, 182; as luxury, 85; as medium of exchange, 21–22, 23; miracles associated with, 33; money likened to, 21, 24, 38, 104–7, 126–27, 133, 136–37, 259; as nourishment, 32–33, 38–39, 63–64, 72, 75, 82, 111, 119; paradoxical attributes of, 55; power of, 38, 85, 128; as property, 95–96; as Protestant sacrament, 48; representational character of, 37–38, 71; scriptural grounds of, 33; semiotic nature of, 119–20; spiritual gains from, 39; stage of life corresponding to, 37; theology of, 15, 16, 23, 31–32; value/pricelessness of, 15, 38, 53, 59, 63, 96, 136, 219. *See also* communion; host
Eve, 72, 215, 217
excommunication, 98–99, 143
expenditure: in Catholic ethic, 20, 68, 143, 208; Christian conception of, 11, 34, 58, 62; Eucharist as, 65; *jouissance* as outcome of, 235
extreme unction (last rites): purgatory avoided by, 197; refusal of, 89–98; requirements for receiving, 89; soul's consummation in, 63; stage of life corresponding to, 37

Fabre, Pierre Jean, 109–11; *Alchymista christianus/L'alchimiste chrétien*, 109
Faiguet de Villeneuve, Joachim, 169–71; *Légitimité de l'usure légale*, 170
Fairchilds, Cissie, 300n15
fashion: blessings pursued by means of, 10; Catholic ethic and, 266–71; French enthusiasm for, 266–68; growth of, 6, 177; modern designer, 268, *269*, *270*, 271; women and, 218. *See also* consumption; luxury

Faverney, confraternity in, 52
Feast of Corpus Christi, 32, 51, 64
Feast of Saint Bridget, 200
fecundity: of church's treasure, 46, 67; of the Eucharist, 22, 85; of God, 117–18; of money, 145, 163–70, 240; of sacraments, 11; transformation as means of endowing with, 27, 107; of the universe, 111
Fénelon, François de, 82, 215, 221–23, 227, 228, 231, 245, 256; *Télémaque*, 17, 214, 223, 225, 246
fetishism: adoration of the host distinguished from, 63; Catholicism and, 3, 4, 26–27, 214–15, 250, 254; De Brosses's theory of, 253–54, 258; economy as object of, 250–51; idolatry as, 4, 63; as religion's essence, 254. *See also* commodity fetishism
Filles du Saint-Sacrement, 49
First Estate, 6
Fitz-James, François de, 86–87, 89
flâneur, 263, 266
Fléchier, Esprit, 23, 67, 68
Fleury, Andre-Hercule de, 89, 92
Flour War, 244
Fontaine, Laurence, 300n132
Fontenelle, Bernard Le Bovier de, 47, 118
Forestier, Pierre, 196
Forty Hours, 49, 93
Foucault, Michel, 12, 288n18
Fouchet, Jean-Baptiste, 149
Fourth Lateran Council, 43
Franciscan Crown, 197
Franciscans, 14
François de Pâris, 89
François I, King, 35
Freemasons, 17
French capitalism, 5–11
French Louisiana, 106, 124–25, 132
French Revolution, 7, 257
Friedland, Paul, 21

Froeschlé-Chopard, Marie-Hélène, 193
Fronde (1648–53), 74, 78
Fuggers (banking family), 150

Galiani, Ferdinando, 235, 243; *Dialogues sur le commerce des blés*, 236
Gallican church: Augustinianism and, 73; and Council of Trent, 40–42; debt held by, 6, 41, 143, 148; economic functions of, 4, 6, 17, 25; economic theology of, 41, 262; economic thought of, 20; Eucharist's significance in, 34; and interest, 146; rights of, 92; the sacraments in, 34–35; and wealth, 40, 178, 181–82
Garden of Eden, 215, 217
gender. *See* women
General Assembly of the Clergy, 148. *See also* Assembly of the Clergy
general will, 17, 227–31
Geneviève, Sainte, 181, 183
Genty, Louis, 246–47, 250, 256, 257
Geoffroy, Étienne-François, 129
Gerberon, Gabriel, 46–47
Gertrude of Helfta, 197
Giry, François, 201
Gobelins, 184
God: correspondences between the human/physical and, 107, 109–10; in economic perspective, 82; essence of, 203; existence of, 237; fecundity of, 117–18; humans in relation to, 58, 71–72, 79; and infinity, 117–19, 127; invisible hand of, in the economy, 19, 23–24; and law, 153–54; Physiocrats' conception of, 233–34
Le Goff, Jacques, 142
gold, 121
Gondi, Jean-François de, 74

Gourdan, Pierre de, 25–26, 62–63, 215, 219–20, 255; *Le chrestien heureux*, 62, 219
Gournay circle, 241
grace: Catholic-Protestant conflict over, 35; dispositions necessary for, 45, 46; economic conception of, 4, 21, 27, 33, 40, 41, 43, 44; in economic contexts, 41; Eucharist and, 36, 42; human nature in need of, 75; Jansenists on, 77; of Jesus Christ, 27, 38; Jubilee as vehicle for, 47; proliferation of, 21, 27, 40, 44; sacraments and, 4, 35; spiritual, 41
Granet, Me, 93
Grangier, Père, 148, 155
Gratian, *Decretum*, 145
Gregory VI, Pope, 53
Gregory VII, Pope, 31
Gregory XIII, Pope, 196
Gregory of Nyssa, 21, 32, 164
Grimm, Melchior, 224
Groethuysen, Bernard, 18
Guise, Charles de, 40–41

Habsburg Monarchy, 35
Harsin, Paul, 291n81
Hartlib, Samuel, 106
Heavenly Bodies: Fashion and the Catholic Imagination (exhibition), 268, 271
Hegel, G. W. F., 259
Helvétius, 247
Henri IV, King, 159, 259
hermetic arts, 24, 108–11, 113, 134. *See also* alchemy; occultism
Héron, Nicolas, 218
Het groote tafereel der dwaasheid (The Great Mirror of Folly), 101, *102*, *103* (detail), 105
Hirschman, Albert, 19
holy orders, 37
Hont, Istvan, 308n60
Horn, comte de, 132

host: adoration of, 15, 53–55, 57, 59, 63–64, 214; Catholic vs. Protestant conceptions of, 21; consumption of, 32, 39, 40; legal and customary practices concerning, 38; marvelous nature of, 55; material nature of, 39; metaphors applied to, 32; paradoxical attributes of, 55–56; properties of, 64; significance of, 16, 21. *See also* communion; Eucharist

House of Dior, 270, 271

Huguenots, 25, 73, 84, 194

Hugues de Saint-Cher, 159, 165

humans/human nature: God in relation to, 58, 71–72, 79; Jansenist view of, 75, 214, 216; Jesuit view of, 74–75; and luxury, 242, 247–48; Rousseau's view of, 225

Hume, David, 19, 106, 107, 247, 259, 261

Hungary, 40

Hunt, Lynn, 305n119, 305n126

iconoclasm, 21, 182–83, 186. *See also* images, veneration of

idolatry: astronomical vs. human, 206; economic theology and, 217; luxury as, 26, 62–64, 215, 218–21; of material objects, 4, 63; Protestant critique of, 183

images, veneration of, 182–85. *See also* iconoclasm

Incarnation, 13, 33, 38, 58, 64, 83, 111, 182, 203, 235, 243

indefectibility, 115, 118–19

Index, of prohibited books, 115, 160

indulgences (pardons): for confraternities, 15, 16, 23, 29, 34, 50, 53, 54, 179, 193, 200; Council of Trent and, 199; critiques of, 43–44, 46–47, 199–200, 203–4; debates over, 46–48, 81–82; defined, 43; for devotional object use, 195–96, 200; instruction guides for, 44; for Jubilee activities, 44–45, 172; liberality in granting, 195–203; market for, 175, 177; personal vs. real, 196; post-Tridentine increase in, 44; practices worthy of earning, 53, 179, 195–97, 199–200, 204; Protestant critique of, 43–44, 81; for rosary use, 25, 177, 197, 199–200, 202, 208; value of, 258

infinity, 116–19, 137. *See also* boundlessness

Innocent VIII, Pope, 177, 196–97

Innocent X, Pope, 79; *Cum occasione* (1653), 79

Innocent XI, Pope, 57, 196, 197

Innocent XII, Pope, 222

Innocent XIII, Pope, 44

interest: ambiguity regarding, 15, 25, 143, 146–47, 160, 172; commercial perspective on, 149–50, 152–53, 160; debates over, 144–73; legal, 133, 141, 148–49; Marx on, 261–62; papal encyclical on, 25, 143; Protestant views on, 146; rates of, 148, 168; religious prohibition on, 6; Turgot on, 20, 25, 168–71, 239. *See also* usury

invisible hand: of God in the economy, 19, 23–24, 68; of God's creation, 66; Smith's concept of, 66–67

Islam, 206, 254. *See also* Muslims

Jacob, Margaret C., 305n119, 305n126

Jameson, Fredric, 20

Jansen, Cornelius, 75; *Augustinus*, 73, 79

Jansenists: attitudes toward, 73–74; contingent factors in development of, 99; and *convulsionnaires*, 88–89; economic thought of, 18, 19, 187; on frequency of communion, 71–72, 75–84; and the Fronde, 74,

78; on grace, 77; on human-God relationship, 71; on human nature, 75, 214, 216; and interest, 146; Jesuits in conflict with, 72, 73, 79, 83, 87–99, 265–66; on penance, 75–77; refusal of sacraments to, 24, 69, 71–73, 89–99; and sacramental re-presentation, 42
Jaucourt, Louis de, 66
Jerome, Saint, 145
Jesuits: and consumption, 217; on frequency of communion, 71–72, 75, 80, 83–86; on human-God relationship, 71; and indulgences, 200; and interest, 147, 150; Jansenists in conflict with, 72, 73, 79, 83, 87–99, 265–66; and *jouissance*, 217; liberality ascribed to, 75, 76, 79–80; Port-Royal vs., 24; and sacramental re-presentation, 42; state opposition to, 88
Jesus Christ: alchemical conception of, 110; body of, 39, 42; boundlessness of, 61; and commerce, 60, 61; in economic perspective, 11, 21–22, 26, 27, 56–58, 61; as lamb, 1, 29; at Last Supper, 31; on lending, 153, 170; meanings of, 29; as measure of value, 21–22; merit acquired by, 10, 45; and miracle of loaves and fishes, 26, 65, 67, 85, 181; and miracle of water turned to wine, 33; sacrifice/crucifixion of, 11, 31, 34, 37–38, 46–47, 53, 56–57, 61, 62, 110, 127, 139, 141, 202, 237, 255. *See also* Eucharist; host; transubstantiation
Jews, 15, 147, 154, 158, 178, 203
Johann Theodor of Bavaria, 86
John XXII, Pope, 108
John of Damascus, 21
Joly, Claude, 45–48, 218–19; *Doctrine des indulgences et du jubilé*, 45
Josepha, Margaret, 213

jouissance (enjoyment of possession): in the afterlife, 47, 249; boundless, 34; Catholic attitudes toward, 25, 228, 231, 255; desire for, 195, 238, 241–44, 262; expenditures as basis of, 235; Jesuits on, 217; Physiocrats' view of, 231–35; wealth linked to, 243, 246–47; worldly/economic, 26, 28, 136, 216, 228, 231–32, 235, 238–39, 241–44, 246, 250, 256
Journal de Trévoux, 87
Jubilees, 44–45, 47, 169, 172, 203, 234

Kaufman, Suzanne, 267
Kavanagh, Thomas M., 307n22
king: authority of, 21, 74, 90–91, 99, 106, 123; debt incurred by, 6–7, 25, 41, 141–42, 147–48; and finances, 120–22; and luxury, 185; Parlement of Paris vs., 98; parlements vs., 73–74, 99–100; "real presence" of, 22, 130; and refusal of sacraments controversy, 90–93, 95, 98–99; representations of, 22; and usury, 141–42
Kwass, Michael, 187, 301n18

Laforest, Paul-Timoléon, *Traité de l'usure et des intérêts*, 162–63, 166
Lagarde, Me, 93
La Haye, Jacques de, *Remarques judicieuses*, 79–80, 284n30
laissez-faire doctrine, 100, 232, 235, 240, 266
Lambert, Joseph, 132–33, 137, 245
land, as source of wealth, 232–35, 238–41
Lanfranc of Bec, 32
La Porte, Barthélémi de, 146, 161–63, 167; *Principes théologiques sur l'usure*, 161–62
last rites. *See* extreme unction
Last Supper, 31, 33, 38, 63, 65, 84, 110

Laurence, Bertrand-Sévère, 266

law, forms of, 153–54. *See also* canon law; civil law

Law, John, and Law's System: alchemy likened to, 22, 106, 108, 129–30, 135–36; bank established by, 123–24; Bernard and, 206; collapse of, 132–34, 142, 147; as controller-general of finances, 101, 124, 130–31, 133; conversion to Catholicism of, 130–31; economic theories and practices of, 16, 17, 105, 106, 122–23, 134–37; Eucharistic associations of, 108, 126–31, 136; life of, 122, 134; *Mémoire sur le discrédit*, 124; *Money and Trade Considered*, 122; moral considerations concerning, 132–33, 135; and paper money, 27, 101, 104–6, 120–28, 135; political and religious context for, 120–23; social mobility arising from, 131; as subject of satire, 16, 22, 101, 129–31, 134–35; Terrasson's championing of, 17, 24, 105, 114, 117, 120, 125–28, 131, 133, 135–37, 256; transmutation likened to, 24, 105, 106

Le Correur, Jean, 156; *Traité de la pratique des billets entre les négociens*, 152–53

Le Gros, Nicolas, 164

Leo X, Pope, 157

Leon X, King, 158, 198

Lepage, Jeanne, 149

Le Semelier, Jean-Laurent, *Conférences ecclésiastiques*, 155–60, 163–64

Lessius, Leonardus, 150

Leszczyński, Stanisław, 83–84, 225

Lismore, Daniel O'Brien, Earl of, 213

little black dress by Chanel, 268, *269*, 271

loans. *See* interest; usury

Locke, John, 90, 248

Lorraine, 83–84

Loterie de l'École militaire, 158

Loterie royale, 158

lotteries, 158

Louis IX, King, 159, 201

Louis XIII, King, 90

Louis XIV, King ("Sun King"), 50, 63, 67, 73–74, 78, 121, 128–29, 157–59, 184, 185, 201, 221–23, 225, 268

Louis XV, King, 50, 83, 91–92, 98, 130, 183, 213, 225, 236

Louis XVI, King, 20, 213, 236, 244

Louisiana. *See* French Louisiana

Lourdes, 266–67

Loyseau, Charles, 90–91

Luther, Martin, 3, 27, 33, 35, 42, 43–44, 48, 143, 204, 206

Lutherans, 35, 39, 146

luxury, 211–51; Butel-Dumont's championing of, 241–44; Catholic attitudes toward, 10, 214; converted into necessity, 178; crown's display of, 185; debates over, 16, 25–26, 213–30, 241–50, 256; economic role of, 239–40, 242, 248–49; in the Enlightenment, 223–24; as essential human desire, 242; etymology of, 243; Eucharist as, 85; Gallican church and, 181–83; as idolatry, 26, 62–64, 215, 218–21; increase in, 177; laws concerning, 183–84; meanings of, 213–14; political arguments against, 222–24; regulation of, 183–84, 217, 221; spiritual, 175; wealth and, 216, 224, 226, 247, 255; women associated with, 26, 64, 215, 217, 219, 221, 271. *See also* consumption; fashion; wealth

Macquer, Philippe, 189

Maffei, Scipion, 162; *Dell'Impiego del danaro*, 160

Maignan, Emmanuel, 155, 156, 163–

64; *De usu licito pecuniae*, 150–52; *Philosophia sacra*, 151
Malebranche, Nicolas, 12, 17, 90, 119, 230, 233–35
Malthus, Thomas, 10
Mandeville, Bernard, 17, 18, 214, 216, 247; *The Fable of the Bees*, 216, 220, 226–27
Mandrin, Louis, 178
Mann, C. Griffith, 268
Marchand, Jean-Henri, *L'enthousiasme français*, 265
Marin, Louis, 36
Markus, Gyorgy, 312n27
Marmont Du Hautchamp, Barthélemy, 131
marriage, 37
Marsilius of Padua, 145
Martinique, 5
marvel(s): as characteristic of Christianity, 34; of the host, 55; redemption as, 45; transubstantiation as, 39
Marx, Karl, 3, 4, 10, 26–27, 179, 207–8, 215, 248, 257–64, 268; *Capital*, 207, 257–61, 263; *Contribution to the Critique of Hegel's Philosophy of Law*, 257; *The German Ideology* (with Friedrich Engels), 177, 247; *Theories of Surplus Value*, 261–62
Mary, Virgin, 10, 45–46, 55, 61, 194, 197, 201, 203, 263, 266–71
Mass attendance, 48–49
Masuzawa, Tomoko, 305n126
materialism, Christian, 23, 57, 64, 75–76
Maurepas, Jean-Frédéric Phélypeaux, comte de, 244
Mauss, Marcel, 276n49
Mazarin, Jules Raymond, 78
McCarraher, Eugene, 14
McManners, John, 49
Melon, Jean François, 247; *Essai politique sur le commerce*, 135

Menuet, Maxime, 146
mercantilism, 3, 18, 121, 184, 232, 291n81
La merchandise spirituelle, 59–60
merchant courts, 6, 9
Mercier, Louis-Sébastien, 6
Mesland, Denis, 114, 115
Mesmerism, 17
Mespolié, François, *Exercices spirituels*, 200–201
metamorphosis: effected by sacraments, 36–37; of matter by mysterious forces, 4; metaphoric significances of, 107; of money, 133
Metropolitan Museum of Art, New York, 268
Mignot, Étienne, 146, 163–67; *Traité des prêts de commerce*, 160–61, 164–65
Mijnhardt, W. W., 305n119, 305n126
Mill, James, 259
Mirabeau, Victor Riquetti, marquis de, 231–34; *L'Ami des hommes*, 231; *La philosophie rurale* (with François Quesnay and Charles Richard de Butré), 233–35
miracles: of loaves and fishes, 26, 65, 67, 85, 181; of water turned to wine, 33
Mississippi Bubble, 105, 107
modernity, 216
Molina, Luis de, 74, 79
monarch. *See* king
money: alchemy compared to, 106–7, 137; economic theology of, 105; essence of, 20, 156, 164; Eucharist likened to, 21, 25, 38, 104–7, 126–27, 133, 136–37, 259; fecundity of, 145, 163–70, 240; fetishism of, 261–62; Law's System and, 27, 101, 104–6, 120–28, 135; in Old Regime, 9; paper vs. minted, 127–28, 136; sterility of, 146, 153, 156,

money (*continued*)
158, 163–67, 170; transmutation of, 133, 166; Turgot on, 239; value of, 120, 136, 165
Monroy, Antoine de, 196
Montazet, Antoine de, 167
Montesquieu, Charles-Louis le Secondat, Baron de La Bréde et de, 19, 134–36, 147, 223, 239, 245, 247; *De l'esprit des lois*, 135, 167, 223–24, 237; *Lettres persanes*, 134–35, 220–21
monts de piété (pawnshops), 147, 157–58, 161, 166, 169
Mouffle d'Angerville, Barthélemy-François-Joseph, 69, 71
Muslims, 204. See also Islam
mystical mill, 103, *104*

Narbonne, Pierre, 128
natural law, 145, 150, 153–54, 164–66, 168, 230–31, 233–34
Necker, Jacques, 245
Newton, Isaac, 109
Nicole, Pierre, 18, 72, 214, 216–17
Noailles, Louis Antoine de, 155
nominalism, 146
Nouet, Jacques, 83, 284n30
Nouveau Mercure (newspaper), 106, 125, 127, 131, 136, 211
Nouvelles ecclésiastiques (newspaper), 88
Noyers, confraternity in, 51

occasionalism, 233–34
occultism, 17, 113. See also alchemy; hermetic arts
Old Regime: absolutism under, 99; debt and sin under, 144; economic engagement of the church in, 4; economic theology under, 256; political theology of, 36; rosary-makers under, 189; usury as crime under, 141
Olier, Pierre, 75

Olivi, Peter, 145
Opalińska, Catherine, 83
Orain, Arnaud, 106, 146, 292n110
Order of the Visitation, 75
Ordinance of Blois (1579), 41
Les ordres du roy exécutez par sa chambre de justice pour punir le vice, abolir l'usure et faire regner l'abondance et la paix dans ses états, 139, *140*, 141
original sin, 37, 71–72, 214

papal revolution, 31
Paracelsus (Theophrastus von Hohenheim), 103, 109
pardons. See indulgences
Paris Faculty of Theology, 41, 79, 89, 96, 116, 245
Parlement of Paris: and Council of Trent, 41; Jansenist influence in, 74, 88; the king vs., 98; and Law's System, 132; and refusal of sacraments controversy, 24, 69, 71, 72, 89–99
parlements (sovereign law courts): and doctrinal controversies, 16, 73, 91, 93; the king vs., 73–74, 99–100
Pascal, Blaise, 216; *Lettres provinciales*, 198
Paul, Saint, 43, 63
Paul, Vincent de, 87
Paul III, Pope, 35, 50, 54
pawnshops. See *monts de piété*
penance: accepted as a sacrament, 43; Catholic-Protestant differences over, 76; communion in relation to, 75–77, 80–81, 86; Council of Trent and, 43–44; in economic perspective, 43–48; Jansenists on, 75–77; as Protestant sacrament, 48; stage of life corresponding to, 37; usury in relation to, 142–44
permissiveness, theological, 25, 48, 71, 147, 155, 160, 199
Perrin, Florence, 211

Philippe d'Orléans, 16, 122, 211
philosopher's stone, 17, 24, 42, 104, 107–8, 110–13, 128, 135–36. *See also* alchemy
philosophes: ascendancy of, 99; Catholic opposition to, 236; on generative power of things, 10–11, 18; and miracles, 89; on wealth, consumption, and luxury, 23, 26, 208, 215, 223
Physiocrats: and agriculture, 17, 26, 215–16, 230–35; background on, 231–32; critics of, 235–36, 242; economic thought of, 26, 230–36; and *jouissance*, 231–35; on luxury and consumption, 23; and political economy, 231–32, 235; religious foundations of, 235, 256; Turgot and, 236, 238; on usury, 234
Picart, Bernard, and Jean-Frédéric Bernard, *Cérémonies et coutumes religieuses de tous les peuples du monde*, 1–3, 2, 10, 22, 25, 203–7, 205, 254, 256, 258, 263
Pichon, Jean, 24, 71, 84, 100, 255; *L'esprit de Jésus-Christ et de l'Église sur la fréquente communion*, 83–89, 97, 99
piety, 45; instruments of (*see* devotional objects)
pilgrimages, 183–85, 188, 266–67
Piossens, chevalier de, 131
Pipet, Jean, 25, 215, 217–18; *Instructions chrétiennes*, 217
Pius IV, Pope, 40
Pius V, Pope, 190, 197, 200
pleasure. See *jouissance*
plenitude: in the afterlife, 199; of capital, 261; of Christ, 44; Christian conceptions of, 34, 58, 120; of the Eucharist, 100; of God, 82, 94; of grace, 43; of the sacraments, 72. *See also* abundance; treasure; wealth
Pluquet, François-André-Adrien, 215, 256, 257; *Traité philosophique et politique sur le luxe*, 247–50
Polanyi, Karl, 100
political economy: capitalism in relation to, 27; classical, 7, 27, 34; economic theology in relation to, 3, 7, 34, 241; Enlightenment-era, 214, 215, 245, 250; Law's System and, 171; Physiocrats and, 231–32, 235; Quesnay and, 240; resacralization of, 224–30; Rousseau's contributions to, 231–32; scholarly approaches to, 8; significance of "economy" in concept of, 66; Smith's theory of, 12; Turgot and, 240; and usury, 169, 171
political theology, 11, 142
polygamy, 154
Pompadour, marquise de, 231
Poncet de la Rivière, Mathias, 92–93
Pontas, Jean, 144–45, 149
populuxe commodities, 10, 177, 190, 207, 223
Port-Royal-des-Champs, 18, 24, 74, 83, 97, 100, 146, 255
Pousse, François, 128–29
Prades, Jean-Martin de, 89
Prades affair, 236
prayer: emphasis on, 48, 49, 54; rosaries associated with, 1, 25, 190, 192–94; as spiritual preparation, 43
Prigent, abbé, 142, 162–63, 245
property, 17, 24, 73, 95–96, 100, 149–52, 159, 162, 164–65, 168, 227–29
Prost de Royer, Antoine-François, 167–68
Protestant ethic, 13–14, 18, 20, 68, 187
Protestant Reformation: Council of Trent as response to, 34–35, 48; in France, 15; iconoclasm of, 21, 182–83, 186; indulgences as target of, 43–44, 81, 203–4; sacraments as target of, 15, 35–36, 40, 48; and usury, 146

purgatory, 10, 43, 46, 142, 169, 197, 201–2, 208
Puritans, 13, 14, 18, 146

Quarrel of the Ancients and the Moderns, 117
Quesnay, François, 17, 231–36, 238, 240–41, 243, 256, 261; *Maximes générales du gouvernement économique d'un royaume agricole*, 235; *La philosophie rurale* (with the marquis de Mirabeau and Charles Richard de Butré), 233–35; *Tableau économique*, 232–34, 236, 238
Quesnel, Pasquier, *Réflexions morales sur le Nouveau Testament*, 74
Quietism, 1, 82, 223

Rachfahl, Felix, 13
Raviot, Guillaume, 164, 166
Raynal, Guillaume-Thomas, *Histoire des deux Indes*, 132, 245–46
real presence, of Christ in the host, 39, 55, 63, 67, 82, 104, 115
redemption: church's role in, 10, 42, 45; economic conception of, 11; economy as means of, 3; marvel of, 45
Réguis, François-Léon, 23, 65–67, 68, 100, 171, 179, 208, 241; *La voix du pasteur*, 65
Reims, confraternity in, 57–59
relics, 182–83, 186
rentes constituées, 148, 151, 158, 166
rentes perpétuelles (perpetual annuities), 147, 148, 153, 159, 233. *See also* annuities
rentes viagères (lifetime annuities), 6, 147. *See also* annuities
Renty, Gaston Jean Baptiste de, 54
Réponse à la Consultation de plusieurs canonistes et avocats de Paris, 94, 100
re-presentation: alchemical, 110–13; defined, 21, 27, 36; Eucharistic, 37–38, 42, 112–13; sacramental, 21, 34, 60, 144, 180
resacralization: of land, 241; of material economy, 16, 23, 256; of political economy, 224–30; of worldly endeavors, 68, 265
Ricardo, David, 10
Richelieu, Armand Jean du Plessis, duc de, 73, 78
Richeome, Louis, 264; *L'idolâtrie huguenote*, 185; *Tableaux sacrez*, 182–83
Rigaud, Hyacinthe, *Charles de Saint-Albin, Archbishop of Cambrai*, 211, *212*, 213
rigorism, theological, 48, 145, 155, 160, 166, 168
Riskin, Jessica, 185
Roche, Daniel, 177
Rohault, Jacques, 151, 155
rosaries, *191, 192*; confraternities devoted to, 25, 193–94, 202–3; debates over, 197–203; indulgences linked to, 25, 177, 197, 199–200, 202, 208; linked to non-Christian traditions, 204; manufacture of, 188–89; missionary promotion of, 178; popularity of, 25, 175, 188–90; power and functions of, 194–95, 197–98, 201–3; power of, 207; prayer associated with, 25, 190, 192–94; role of, in consumer revolution, 179; special events associated with, 192–93
Rouen, confraternity in, 53–55, 59
Rougrave, comte de, 86
Rousseau, Jean-Jacques, 14, 17, 26, 66, 208, 215, 221, 223–31, 241, 246–48, 250, 256, 276n58; *Discours sur l'économie politique*, 229; *Discours sur les sciences et les arts (First Discourse)*, 224–25; *Discours sur l'inégalité*

(*Second Discourse*), 217, 226, 228, 229, 247, 249; *Du contrat social*, 229, 250; *Émile*, 229–30; *Julie, ou La nouvelle Héloïse*, 228–29; *Third Discourse*, 227–28
Royal Bank (Banque royale), 27, 123–24, 128, 134
Royal Plate Glass Company, 184
Rue, Charles de la, 218

sacraments: Catholic-Protestant disputes over, 15, 35–36, 40, 48; Catholic Reformation and, 255; church vs. state authority concerning, 89–99; Council of Trent and, 21, 24, 35–42, 48, 60; in economic perspective, 59–67; etymology of, 37; generative power of, 11, 37, 111; hermetic arts associated with, 111; refusal of, to Jansenists, 42, 69, 71–73, 89–90; re-presentational function of, 21, 34, 60, 144, 180; stages of life corresponding to, 37; system of, 32
Saint-Aignan, Paul de Beauvillier, duc de, 222
Saint-Albin, Charles d'Orléans de, *212*, 213
Saint-Barthélemy confraternity, 51
Saint-Cyran, Jean Duvergier de Hauranne, abbé de, 72, 75–76
Saint-Domingue, 5
Saint John Lateran basilica, 44
Saint-Lambert, Jean-François, 224, 242
Saint Peter basilica, 44
Saint-Simon, Louis de Rouvroy, duc de, 128, 134
Sales, François de, 72, 75, 80, 87, 198
Santa Maria Maggiore basilica, 44
Santa Maria Sopra Minerva church, 50
Savary, Jacques, *Le parfait négociant*, 149

Scapular of the Carmelites, 204
scarcity: economic, 10, 120, 127, 177; as punishment for sin, 215; religious perspective on, 34, 43, 72–73, 81, 97, 110, 177
schism, 69, 72, 90–93
Schmitt, Carl, 11
Scholasticism: criticisms of, 225; on fecundity of goods, 151; and infinity, 118; on money, 146, 163, 168, 239; on penance, 43; and transubstantiation, 39, 108, 154–55; and usury, 153, 161–62, 166
Second Council of Nicaea (325), 183
self-interest, 18–19, 81–82, 169, 202, 214, 216, 224, 247
self-love [*amour-propre*], 48, 63, 72, 80, 219–20, 225, 247
semantics, 243
semiotics: alchemy and, 112; Catholic vs. Protestant conceptions of, 21–23, 36, 40; of desire and consumption, 243, 267; of economic theology, 27; of the Eucharist, 119–20; power of, 67; and power of images, 21; and religious objects and decoration, 180; talismans and, 112
Sénac de Meilhan, Gabriel, 214
Sens, bishop of, 87
sensationalist psychology, 224, 242
Seraphic Rosary, 197
Seven Years' War (1756–63), 99, 147, 168, 236
Sewell, William, 8, 10, 137
Sheehan, Jonathan, 19, 106, 310n112
Simmel, Georg, 120
sin: as debt, 4, 21, 35, 45, 48, 53, 58, 78, 144, 172, 255; original, 37, 71–72, 214; punishment for, 53
Sion, bishop of, 88
Sirmond, Jacques, 80
Sixtus IV, 196

slavery, 8, 9, 245–46
Slezkine, Yuri, 13
Smith, Adam, 3, 12, 19, 27, 66–67, 106, 226
social status and mobility, 131, 213. *See also* society of orders
Société des Trente-Trois, 160
Society of Jesus. *See* Jesuits
society of orders, 10, 142, 178, 214. *See also* social status and mobility
Society of Saint-Sulpice, 75
sodomy, 165
Sombart, Werner, 13
Sonnius, Claude, 49
Sorbonne, 79, 89, 90, 135, 199, 236–37
Soubirous, Bernadette, 266
Spang, Rebecca, 9
speculation, 101–37; alchemy likened to, 22, 24, 101, 103–6, 108, 129–30, 135–36; belief required for, 104, 133, 136, 144; Eucharistic associations of, 103, *104*, 108, 126–31, 136; inflation resulting from, 132, 135; Law's System and, 120–34; social mobility arising from, 131
spiritual goods, 68, 82–83, 90, 113, 193–94, 217. *See also* economy: relationship of material and spiritual
spiritual manuals, 16
spiritual treasure, 4, 16, 23, 25–26, 46, 56, 60, 82, 85, 179, 183, 201, 202, 220, 237
spiritual wealth, 4, 10, 25–26, 31, 34, 37–39, 47–48, 55, 59, 67–68, 71, 77, 112, 143, 177, 180, 181, 187, 193, 201, 208, 213, 218–19
Stair, John Dalrymple, Earl of, 130
state. *See* church-state relationship
sumptuary laws, 183–84, 217, 221
Super-Enlightenment, 17

superfluity: Butel-Dumont's religion of, 26, 216, 242–44, 249–50; in Christian perspective, 46, 58, 196; of commodities, 264; in economic systems, 187, 255; luxury and, 64, 213, 233, 247–49; positive vs. negative, 221, 223–24
Synod of Nimes (1284), 96

talents, 60, 153, 167
talismans, 27, 112, 130, 135, 172
Tallon, Alain, 42
Tardieu, Nicolas Henri, and F. Desbrulins, *Loüé soit le très saint sacrement de l'autel*, 29, *30*, *31* (detail)
Tencin, Pierre Guérin de, 130
Terjanian, Anoush, 243
Terrasson, Jean, 17, 24, 105, 114, 117–20, 125–28, 131, 133, 135–37, 151, 166, 255–56; *Traité de l'infini créé*, 117–19, 127–28
Terror, 189
Tertullian, 98
textiles. *See* fashion
Theodosius, Emperor, 161
Thézé, Laurent, 292n110
Thiers, Jean-Baptiste, *De la plus solide, de plus nécessaire, et souvent la plus négligée de toutes dévotions*, 199–200, 204, 254, 255
Thirty Years' War (1618–48), 74
time preference, 169, 245
Tocqueville, Alexis de, 235
Todd, David, 266
Todeschini, Giacomo, 13–14
Tracy, David, 268
transmutation: alchemical, 108–9, 112; Cartesianism and, 113; economic functions likened to, 16; financial, 101, 103–5; of the host, 32; Last Supper as, 111; Law's System as example of, 24, 105–7; of material

into spiritual goods, 207; metaphoric significances of, 16, 24, 103, 107, 111, 129; of money, 133, 166
transubstantiation: alchemy likened to, 109, 136; of bread into flesh, 38; Cartesianism and, 113; confraternities' promotion of belief in, 50; consubstantiation vs., 33; controversies over, 39; Council of Trent and, 39; Descartes and, 114–15; doctrine of, 23, 26, 32, 108; economic functions likened to, 16, 17; as means to spiritual wealth, 34; metamorphosis at root of, 4; metaphoric significances of, 24, 103, 107, 111, 129; paper money likened to, 133; productive power of, 64; semiotic significance of, 21; spiritual and material convergence in, 84–85; in visual images, 29
treasure: of the church, 43, 45, 46, 67, 81, 196, 198–99, 222; of the divine, 44, 113; of the Eucharist, 33, 40, 42, 62; of grace, 107; of Jesus Christ, 46–48, 62, 72, 83, 113; of the Jubilee, 47; relationship of material and spiritual, 59–61, 113, 201, 222; spiritual/celestial, 4, 16, 22–23, 25–26, 46, 56, 60, 82, 85, 179, 183, 201, 202, 220, 237. *See also* plenitude; wealth
Trentman, Frank, 178
Treuvé, Simon Michel, 46–47
Trinity, 12, 13, 110, 117, 203
triple contracts, 150–52, 161, 162, 163
triple painting, 182
Trivellato, Francesca, 15, 147
Troyes, 92–93
Turgot, Anne Robert Jacques, 17; *Le conciliateur*, 97–98; as controller-general of finances, 236, 240, 244–45, 257; *Discours sur les avantages que l'établissement du christianisme a procurés au genre humain*, 237; and economic theology, 20, 236–41; economic thought of, 25, 26, 135–36, 168–71, 230, 231, 243, 247, 256; as exemplar of Enlightenment, 236; on interest and usury, 20, 25, 168–71, 239, 245; and Law's System, 135–36; *Mémoire sur les prêts d'argent*, 168–70, 245; on money, 239; and the Physiocrats, 236, 238; and political economy, 240, 261; *Réflexions sur la formation et la distribution des richesses*, 238–40; religious thought of, 20, 97–98, 100, 168, 237–38, 255, 256; *Valeurs et monnaies*, 243

Unigenitus (1713 papal bull), 74, 88–98, 146, 200
Urban VIII, Pope, 29, 50, 74, 109
Ursulines, 83
usury, 25, 139–74; adjudication of, 139, *140*, 141; Catholic conception of, 143; criminal status of, 141; debates over, 139, 144–73, 256; economic theology and, 144, 147, 155–63, 171–72; Gallican church and, 146; the king and, 141–42; moral considerations concerning, 142–43, 151–54, 170–71; penance in relation to, 142–44; Physiocrats on, 234; Protestants and, 146; punishments for, 141, 149; treatises on, 16; Turgot on, 239, 245; types of, 145. *See also* debt; interest

Valibouze, chevalier de, 91
value: Christ as measure of, 21–22; of the Eucharist, 15, 38, 53, 59, 63, 96, 136, 219; of money, 120, 136, 165; sources of, 3, 4, 17, 18, 243; use vs. exchange, 258–59, 261–62
vanity, 64, 217, 264

Van Kley, Dale, 74
Varenne de Beost, Claude-Marc-Antoine, 189–90
Vatican, 268
Vauban, Luc, 42
Vaucanson, Jacques de, 185
Versace, 268
Visitandines, 83
Vogue (magazine), 268
Voltaire, 9, 17, 134, 136, 206, 223, 225, 254, 265; *Candide*, 9; *Dictionnaire philosophique*, 186; *Le mondain*, 186, 223
Vovelle, Michel, 187

Wahrman, Dror, 19, 106, 310n112
War of Austrian Succession (1740–48), 148
War of Polish Succession (1733–35), 83
War of Spanish Succession (1701–14), 148
Wars of Religion (1562–98), 15, 41, 44, 73
wealth: boundless, 24, 26–27, 202; Catholic attitudes toward, 15, 163, 181; church's possession of, 40, 96, 163, 178, 181–82, 186, 256; essence of, 3, 256; Eucharist as source of, 31, 34; Jesus Christ as source of, 26, 44, 63, 83, 202; *jouissance* linked to, 243, 246–47; land as source of, 232–35, 238–41; luxury and, 216, 224, 226, 247, 255; paper money and creation of, 120–36, 144, 164–66, 171, 233; *philosophes* and, 250; Physiocrats' theory of, 232–35; Puritan relationship to, 13; relationship of material and spiritual, 3, 20, 33, 59–60, 83, 107, 136, 163, 171, 179–80, 187, 196, 198, 208, 213, 219; spiritual/celestial, 4, 10, 25–26, 31, 34, 37–39, 47–48, 55, 59, 67–68, 71, 77, 112, 143, 177, 180, 181, 187, 193, 201, 218–19; usury and creation of, 164–66, 233; worldly, 26–28, 39, 59–60, 177, 211, 213, 218, 255. *See also* consumption; luxury; plenitude; treasure
Weber, Max, 18–20, 146, 187; *The Protestant Ethic and the Spirit of Capitalism*, 3, 13–14, 68, 229
wedding ensemble by House of Dior, 270, *271*
Wennerlind, Carl, 106, 288n16
William of Ockham, 146
women: in Benjamin's work, 263–65, *265*; and commodification, 265; and consumption, 177, 178, 215, 221; and fashion, 218; luxury associated with, 26, 64, 215, 217, 219, 221, 271; men's concern for weak and sinful nature of, 215, 218, 219, 256, 265; pilgrimages to Lourdes by, 267; role of, in economic theology, 271; rosaries and necklaces of, 189–90

Zacchaeus (biblical tax collector), 76
Zeitblom, Bartolomeus, workshop of, Panel representing a mystical mill, *104*
Zola, Émile, *Au bonheur des dames*, 267–68

CURRENCIES

New Thinking for Financial Times
STEFAN EICH AND MARTIJN KONINGS, SERIES EDITORS

Amin Samman, *History in Financial Times*

Thomas Biebricher, *The Political Theory of Neoliberalism*

Lisa Adkins, *The Time of Money*

Martijn Konings, *Capital and Time: For a New Critique of Neoliberal Reason*

The authorized representative in the EU for product safety and compliance is:
Mare Nostrum Group
B.V Doelen 72
4831 GR Breda
The Netherlands

www.ingramcontent.com/pod-product-compliance
Lightning Source LLC
Chambersburg PA
CBHW030603230426
43661CB00053B/1815